THINKING,
PROBLEM SOLVING,
COGNITION

A Series of Books in Psychology

Editors: Richard C. Atkinson
Gardner Lindzey
Richard F. Thompson

THINKING,
PROBLEM SOLVING,
COGNITION

RICHARD E. MAYER

**UNIVERSITY OF CALIFORNIA,
SANTA BARBARA**

W. H. FREEMAN AND COMPANY
NEW YORK   SAN FRANCISCO

Project Editors: Judith Wilson, Patricia Brewer
Copyeditor: Pat Tompkins
Designer: Nancy Benedict
Production Coordinator: Linda Jupiter
Illustration Coordinator: Richard Quiñones
Artist: J&R Art Services
Compositor: Typothetae
Printer and Binder: The Maple-Vail Book Manufacturing Group

Library of Congress Cataloging in Publication Data
Mayer, Richard E., 1947–
    Thinking, problem solving, cognition

    (A series of books in psychology)
    Bibliography: p.
    Includes index.
    1. Thought and thinking. 2. Problem solving.
3. Cognition. I. Title. II. Series.
BF455.M347   1983   153.4'2   83-1554
ISBN 0-7167-1440-X
ISBN 0-7167-1441-8 (pbk.)

1 2 3 4 5 6 7 8 9 0   MP   1 0 8 9 8 7 6 5 4 3

Dedicated to
Beverly
and Kenny, David, and Sarah

CONTENTS

PREFACE

When I wrote *Thinking and Problem Solving* in 1977, it represented something unique—a textbook that surveyed the cognition part of cognitive psychology, that was both up-to-date and historical in coverage, and that was written for the introductory student. The welcome reception it received confirmed the need for such a book.

It has been a pleasure to see *Thinking and Problem Solving* used in nearly 200 universities, colleges, and community colleges. The many communications that I have received from instructors and students are greatly appreciated—even when they raised points of disagreement. The book has also been translated into Japanese, German, Spanish, and Portuguese.

With such success, you might wonder why I wrote a new book. My reason is the virtual explosion of research and theory in the area of problem solving in recent years. In contrast to the slow movement of this field in the past, the study of human problem solving has enjoyed substantial growth since I sat down to prepare the first manuscript six years ago.

You can appreciate the growth of information in problem solving if you assume that we can break cognitive psychology into three rough groups: perception, memory, and cognition. The history of modern work on cognitive psychology has shown that the analytic tools of information-processing psychology have been applied to topics in the order just indicated. The first breakthroughs were in the cognitive analysis of perception, as shown by Neisser's *Cognitive Psychology* (1967). The next breakthroughs were in the cognitive analysis of human memory, as surveyed in Klatzky's *Human Memory* (1975, 1980). At last, the analytic power of cognitive psychology has been applied to the upper end of cognitive life— cognition. *Thinking, Problem Solving, Cognition* provides an updated survey of that work.

If you are familiar with *Thinking and Problem Solving,* this book will also seem familiar. *Thinking, Problem Solving, Cognition* retains the same goal: to introduce the current state of the cognition side of cognitive psychology. It retains the same style and assumes that the reader has no prior experience in cognitive psychology. The book's audience is the same: students in such courses as cognitive psychology, learning and memory, problem solving, educational psychology, as well as courses in mathematics and engineering that involve problem solving. Since it covers the cognition side, this book may also be used in conjunction with books that emphasize memory, such as Klatzky's *Human Memory* (1980).

Thinking, Problem Solving, Cognition is divided into four parts:

Historical Perspective (Chapters 1 to 4) introduces the classic theories of problem solving: associationism and Gestalt theory.

Basic Thinking Tasks (Chapters 5 and 6) discusses the research and theories concerning two specific types of problem solving: induction and deduction.

Information-Processing Analysis of Cognition (Chapters 7 to 10) presents techniques for analyzing problem-solving strategies, cognitive skills, and verbal knowledge.

Implications and Applications (Chapters 11 to 14) gives examples of the application of the techniques and findings of cognitive psychology to such real problems as human cognitive development, description of differences in intellectual ability, teaching of creative problem solving, and mathematical problem solving.

All the material from *Thinking and Problem Solving* has been rewritten, reorganized, and updated. Three new chapters in *Thinking, Problem Solving, Cognition* represent areas that have developed greatly during the past few years. "Intelligence" (Chapter 12) shows how cognitive psychology theories can be used to describe individual differences in mental ability. "Creativity Training" (Chapter 13) explores the nature of creativity and presents techniques for helping people become better problem solvers. "Mathematical Problem Solving" (Chapter 14) shows how cognitive psychology can be applied to the teaching of problem solving in mathematics courses.

Readers will need a fair tolerance for a lack of closure. Although the field of human cognition has received much attention lately, it remains in a state of change. No single approach can bring order to the entire field. Instead of trying to artificially organize the book around a theme that has not yet emerged, I have attempted to present an honest assessment of what we now know about human problem solving. Thus, I have written each chapter as a self-contained survey of a specific topic, and at the same time I have pointed out the interrelations among chapters.

In addition to the acknowledgments I offered in *Thinking and Problem Solving*, I would like to thank W. Hayward Rogers and the staff of W. H. Freeman and Company for their efforts. This book owes much to the editing skills of Judith Wilson, Pat Brewer, and Pat Tompkins, the typing skills of Nancy Fraser, and the graphic skills of Nancy Benedict. I also appreciate the advice of the anonymous reviewers of the manuscript. Although they cannot be held responsible for short-comings in the book, they clearly are responsible for many improvements. This book also profited from my recent sabbatical at the Learning Research and Development Center at the University of Pittsburgh. I appreciated opportunities to interact with Jim Greeno, Lauren Resnick, Bob Glaser, Jim Voss, Micki Chi, and others at the center, and with Jill Larkin at Carnegie-Mellon University. They helped me to learn that I still have a lot more to learn about human problem solving. Finally, the support of my family is greatly appreciated; the interest of my parents, James and Bernis Mayer, and of my brothers, Robert and Bernie Mayer, certainly spurred me on. The patience of Beverly, and of Kenny and David and Sarah, also made this book possible. Again, I dedicate this book to them, with love.

January 1983   Richard E. Mayer

THINKING,
PROBLEM SOLVING,
COGNITION

PART ONE

HISTORICAL
PERSPECTIVE

Chapters 1 through 4 provide a concise history of the early approaches to psychological research on problem solving. Chapter 1 takes you from the inception of scientific psychology in the late 1800s to the first major school of problem-solving research in the early 1900s, the Wurzburg school. The failure of the Wurzburg school to develop rigorous methods and useful theories led to two quite different reactions: associationism and Gestalt theories of thinking. Chapter 2 introduces you to the associationist theory of thinking, which reached its height of popularity between the 1920s and the 1950s. As you will see, associationist theory emphasizes the behaviors that are emitted by a problem solver and how one element in a problem-solving chain is associated with another. Chapters 3 and 4 acquaint you with the Gestalt theory of thinking, which was most popular between the 1920s and 1940s. Gestalt theory emphasizes the role of understanding and mental organization of elements into a whole structure.

The research strategy suggested in Chapters 1 through 4 is to take the theoretical perspective of some developed field in psychology such as perception and then to apply that approach to an undeveloped field such as problem solving. Since the study of learning had advanced greatly under an associationist approach, some psychologists borrowed the associationist approach for the study of problem solving. Similarly, since the study of perception had progressed with a Gestalt approach, some psychologists borrowed the Gestalt approach to study problem solving. The issues, tasks, methods, and explanations in each chapter are based on the particular theoretical approach of that chapter.

In Chapters 1 through 4 you will come to understand how associationist and Gestalt theories provided the first frameworks for describing the thinking process. Although these approaches are no longer alive in their "pure" forms, it would be a mistake for you to dismiss these chapters as of only historical interest. To understand what is happening in cognitive psychology today, you need to understand what happened yesterday. Current theories and issues are not divorced from older associationist and Gestalt traditions. Instead, if you scratch the veneer of a modern theory hard enough, you are likely to discover layers of its deeper associationist or Gestalt character. Thus, while associationist and Gestalt schools no longer dominate the field, their underlying themes and conceptions are still at the core of contemporary cognitive psychology.

CHAPTER 1

BEGINNINGS

Definition of Basic Terms

The Study of Thinking

Main Topics in the Psychology of Thinking

Historical Foundations of the Psychology of Thinking

Introspection Task

In a moment you will be given a word and a question about the word. Your job is to say the first answer that comes to your mind and then to describe all the details of the thought process that led to it.

Your test word is BITE, and your question is, What is the CAUSE? Now describe the thinking process that led you to whatever word you answered.

If the word "dog" came to your mind, your response corresponds to that obtained by the German psychologist Otto Selz in the early 1900s (Humphrey, 1963). Check the top of Box 1-1 to see how Selz's subject described his chain of thought. Note that an image of a wounded leg came first followed by the conscious words, "dogs bite." Did you also experience an image while you were thinking?

Now try the word—and question: POEM. In what LARGER CATEGORY does it belong? A typical response from Selz's experiment is "work of art," and the introspections of one subject about how the answer was derived are given in Box 1-1. Note that no images were involved in the subject's thinking about this problem. Did you experience an image?

Finally, try to describe your thought process for: PARSON. What is an EQUIVALENT OCCUPATION? The introspections of a typical subject appear in Box 1-1. The answer this subject made was "chaplain" (remember these introspections are translations from German) and again no imagery was involved.

These tasks are examples of the first type of experimental studies on human thought processes ever carried out. The method is called *introspection* because the thinker must inspect his or her own mental events and report them to the experimenter. Long before the birth of psychology, human beings undoubtedly introspected, perhaps trying to understand themselves, but it was not until the beginning of this century that the method of introspection was taken into the experimental laboratory and systematically applied to the study of human thought. We shall talk more about introspection later in this chapter.

DEFINITION OF BASIC TERMS

To study human cognitive processes effectively, it is useful to define the basic terms such as *problem* and *thinking*.

Problem

Although they express the terms differently, most psychologists agree that a problem has certain characteristics:

Givens—The problem begins in a certain state with certain conditions, objects, pieces of information, and so forth being present at the onset of work on the problem.

Goals—The desired or terminal state of the problem is the goal state, and thinking is required to transform the problem from the given to the goal state.

Obstacles—The thinker has at his or her disposal certain ways to change the given state or the goal state of the problem. The thinker, however, does not already know the correct answer; that is, the correct sequence of behaviors that will solve the problem is not immediately obvious.

BOX 1–1   Method of Introspection

Problem 1

Bite. Cause?

"As soon as I had read the [words] the search was on. I had also a picture of a leg with a wound on it and saw nothing else. Then 'dog' came to me in the form of an idea, with the consciousness: dogs bite" (1963, p. 138).

Problem 2

Poem. In what *larger category* does it belong?

"Once again, immediately a full understanding of the [question]. Then again an intensive glance, the symbolic fixation of that which is sought; then at once the flitting memory of art, poetry, and so on appeared. The word 'art,' I think, in auditory-motor terms. Then the thought that I cannot subsume poetry under art but only under artistic production. With this, I am certain, no words and images; then I said, 'work of art' " (p. 137).

Problem 3

Parson. What is an *equivalent occupation?*

"I read the words successively and with understanding. Immediately came the consciousness that something [equivalent] was very familiar. Then came the word 'chaplain,' internally spoken. It is certain that the consciousness of the familiarity of a solution preceded the, as yet, uneffected appearance of the word 'chaplain' " (p. 134).

From Humphrey (1963)

In short, any definition of "problem" should consist of the three ideas that (1) the problem is presently in some state, but (2) it is desired that it be in another state, and (3) there is no direct, obvious way to accomplish the change. This definition is broad enough to include problems ranging from geometry (Polya, 1957) and chess (Newell and Simon, 1972) to riddles (Reitman, 1965).

Reitman (1965) has further analyzed four categories of problems according to how well the given and goal states are specified.

Well-defined given state and well-defined goal state: "How can you turn a sow's ear into a silk purse?" Note, however, that although the given state (sow's ear) and the goal state (silk purse) are clearly specified in this problem, there is a serious lack of possible ways to solve it.

Well-defined given state and poorly defined goal state: "How can you redesign a Cadillac El Dorado to get better gas mileage?" The given state, the automobile, is clearly designated, but what does "better gas mileage" mean exactly?

Poorly defined given state and well-defined goal state: "Explain the mechanisms responsible for sun spots." The goal, "sun spots," is clear, but the initial state that causes this goal is not.

Poorly defined given state and poorly defined goal state: "What is red and goes put-put?" The answer is "an outboard apple," and you can blame Reitman for this one.

Greeno (1978) has suggested a three-part typology of problems:

1. *Problems of inducing structure*—Several instances are given, and the problem solver must discover the rule or pattern involved. Examples include series completion problems (as described in Chapter 5) or analogy problems (see Chapter 12).
2. *Problems of transformation*—An initial state is given, and the problem solver must find a sequence of operations that produces the goal state. Examples include water jug problems (in Chapter 3) or tower of Hanoi problems (described in Chapters 4 and 7).
3. *Problems of arrangement*—All of the elements are given, and the problem solver must arrange them in way that solves the problem. Examples include anagram problems (see Chapter 2) and cryptarithmetic problems (described in Chapters 3 and 7).

As Greeno points out, however, not all problems can be neatly classified into one of these three types. Instead, many of the most interesting problems include aspects of several types of problems.

Thinking and Problem Solving

There are many definitions of *thinking, problem solving,* and *cognition,* but this book will use these three terms interchangeably based on a single, general definition common to them all. Unfortunately, we begin with a serious lack of agreement among psychologists about whether thinking should be generally defined as an external, behavioral process or an internal, cognitive process. The behavioral argument is that the science of psychology must deal only with empirical, observable behaviors as its primary data; internal states or processes cannot be directly observed and therefore cannot be part of psychology. Behaviorists consider a view of thinking as an internal process with no relationship to behavior to be useless; for example, a famous critique of an early cognitive theory of rat maze learning was that the rat was "left buried in thought at the choice point"—there was no relationship between internal mechanisms and external observable events. In this view, psychological definitions must be tied firmly to behavior. The cognitive argument, on the other hand, is that behavior is merely the manifestation or result of thinking and therefore psychological definitions must be tied firmly to the mechanisms that underlie behavior.

A compromise that most, but not all, psychologists who study thinking might accept is that concepts such as internal, cognitive processes have a place in psychology if and only if they generate clearly testable predictions, that is, if they suggest observable predictions concerning human behavior. In short, a general definition of thinking includes three basic ideas:

1. Thinking is *cognitive,* but is inferred from behavior. It occurs internally, in the mind or cognitive system, and must be inferred indirectly.

2. Thinking is a *process* that involves some manipulation of or set of operations on knowledge in the cognitive system.

3. Thinking is *directed* and results in behavior that "solves" a problem or is directed toward solution.*

In other words, thinking is what happens when a person solves a problem, that is, produces behavior that moves the individual from the given state to the goal state—or at least tries to achieve this change. Thus, Johnson (1972) defined thinking as "problem solving" and similarly Polya (1968, p. ix) suggested that problem solving is based on cognitive processing that results in "finding a way out of a difficulty, a way around an obstacle, attaining an aim that was not immediately attainable." The remainder of this book aims at making the general definition of thinking more specific, although, as you will see, currently there is agreement neither on a definition of thinking nor on exactly what mechanisms underlie thinking.

Other terms used in the study of thinking such as *induction, deduction,* and *reasoning* have more restricted meanings than those we have discussed, and can be considered as subsets of thinking. Induction, which we shall examine in Chapter 5, refers to a situation in which a thinker is given a series of examples and must "leap" to the creation of a general rule; deduction refers to a situation in which a thinker is given a set of general rules and must draw a logical conclusion, as we shall see in Chapter 6. Induction and deduction are both types of reasoning.

THE STUDY OF THINKING

People are endowed with a number of basic cognitive processes which, although closely related, have been separated and studied individually by psychologists.

---

*Some types of thinking may not be directed, such as autistic thinking, daydreaming, or the fragmented thinking of schizophrenics; however, this book will deal mainly with normal, directed thinking.

These cognitive processes include: sensation and perception (reception and recognition of input stimuli), learning (encoding of input information), memory (retrieval of input information), and thinking (manipulation of perceived, learned, and remembered information). These topics form the core of what has been called *cognitive psychology,* and to the extent that each involves active manipulation of information, each involves thinking. Bruner (1973) emphasized the role of problem solving in perception by suggesting that perception involves ''going beyond the information given.'' Bartlett (1932) stressed the role of problem solving in memory and learning by suggesting that learning and recall require an ''effort after meaning.'' Thinking has also been investigated in many other contexts in psychology including social psychology (attitude formation and change), developmental psychology (cognitive development), personality (cognitive style), and testing and measurement (intelligence tests).

Thinking is thus a component of experimental psychology; while the main focus is on a complex cognitive process, thinking depends on and is part of simpler processes. Because thinking is so complex and because it may be based on lower cognitive processes, many psychologists have argued that we should understand the simpler or lower cognitive processes before trying to study the complex or higher processes. However, there have always been some psychologists who ignored these warnings and who were challenged by the prospect of studying one of the supreme achievements of the human species, the ability to think and deal with complex learning:

> . . .The topic has fascinated psychologists in and out of the laboratory. They have worried it as a dog worries a bone. It was always there, sometimes buried, sometimes dug up again and brought to a high sheen, never quite cracked or digested, and never forgotten. Even the Wundts and the Hulls promised themselves to get back to the problem sooner or later while they counseled patience and attention to simpler problems that seemed to contain the principles needed to unlock the complexities of human thought. But for every Wundt psychology had a Buhler, for every Hull a Wertheimer—psychologists impatient with the programmatic building-block approach, unwilling to wait for the solution of the simple, and eager to plunge into the complexities and wonders of full-blown human thought [Mandler and Mandler, 1964, p. 1].

MAIN TOPICS IN THE PSYCHOLOGY OF THINKING

The psychology of thinking and complex learning has held a regular, albeit modest, position in the mainstream of psychology ever since William James (1890) included a chapter on reasoning in his famous textbook. Yet the subject has never been completely unified or well understood, and the basic knowledge has remained hard to define. There are now, however, encouraging signs that some progress has been made since Humphrey's assessment (1963, p. 308) of the first fifty years of work by experimental psychologists on thinking: "Fifty years' experiments on the psychology of thinking or reasoning have not brought us very far, but they have at least shown the road which must be traversed."

New roads that have been traversed since Humphrey's critique include exciting developments in an information processing approach to cognition such as computer simulation of human thinking (Chapter 7), new theories of semantic memory representation (Chapter 10), and the fresh interest of American psychologists in cognitive development motivated largely by Piaget's work (Chapter 11). Older roads that have continued to stimulate further travel include the Gestalt approach to problem solving based on the idea that thinking involves "restructuring" a problem (Chapters 3 and 4), the study of concept learning, which suggests that the testing of "hypotheses" may be a part of thinking (Chapter 5), and the associationist approach to thinking, which is based on the principle of learning by reinforcement (Chapter 2).

This book, then, is organized into fourteen chapters, each covering a main road or side road of the study of thinking. The first four chapters provide an historical perspective by showing you the oldest paths.

- *Chapter 1 (Beginnings)* defines key terms and summarizes the early history of research on thinking.

- *Chapter 2 (Associationism)* investigates the idea that thinking is based on the principle of learning by reinforcement. It includes such classic research as Thorndike's work on cats in a puzzle box as well as more recent research, such as the analysis of anagram solving and the physiological correlates of thinking.

- *Chapter 3 (Gestalt)* investigates the idea that thinking involves restructuring the elements of the problem in a new way; the famous Gestalt experiments on insight and rigidity in problem solving and current work on the analysis of stages in problem solving are covered.

- *Chapter 4 (Meaning)* considers a refinement of the Gestalt approach that describes thinking as relating the new problem to ideas or experiences already familiar to the solver. The classic studies of meaningful learning of mathematics and solution of mathematical puzzles, as well as recent work on imagery in problem solving, are included.

Part Two provides two chapters on thinking tasks that have been heavily studied by psychologists.

- *Chapter 5 (Rule Induction)* examines the idea that thinking involves forming and testing hypotheses. It describes original research on concept learning by Hull and Heidbreder plus up-to-date work on strategies in concept learning, serial pattern learning, visual prototype formation, and errors in induction.

· *Chapter 6 (Deductive Reasoning)* investigates how people draw conclusions from premises. It presents the classic work on deduction and emphasizes ongoing work on models of deductive reasoning.

The chapters in Part Three explain the approach of information processing to the analysis of cognition processes and structures.

· *Chapter 7 (Computer Simulation)* presents an information-processing analysis of problem-solving strategies; the computer simulation of human thinking is highlighted.

· *Chapter 8 (Mental Chronometry)* analyzes cognitive skills; the use of process models such as flow charts is emphasized.

· *Chapter 9 (Schema Theory)* provides an analysis of verbal knowledge, focusing on how meaningful information is comprehended and stored in memory.

· *Chapter 10 (Question Answering)* explores the problem of how people search their existing semantic memory to answer questions. The topics covered include recent work on categorization of objects in memory and psycholinguistics.

The final section of the book covers recent implications and applications of research in problem solving, with special focus on practical issues.

· *Chapter 11 (Cognitive Development)* presents the currently popular theories of cognitive development based on Piaget's work. It includes relevant research on the development of adult logic, development of information-processing strategies, and whether cognitive development can be taught.

· *Chapter 12 (Intelligence)* investigates individual differences in intellectual ability and how they can best be described.

· *Chapter 13 (Creativity Training)* considers whether thinking can be taught just like any other skill.

· *Chapter 14 (Mathematical Problem Solving)* concerns the implications of problem-solving research for learning mathematics in the classroom.

HISTORICAL FOUNDATIONS OF THE PSYCHOLOGY OF THINKING

Associationist Philosophy

Before psychology began as an experimental science in the late nineteenth century, the issues of psychology were already well established within the domain of mental philosophy. The dominant philosophy of human mental processes then was *associ-*

ationism, the belief that mental life can be explained in terms of two basic components: ideas (or elements) and associations (or links) between them. Associationism is usually traced back to three laws of learning and memory expressed by the Greek philosopher Aristotle:

Doctrine of association by contiguity—Events or objects that occur in the same time or space are associated in memory, so that thinking of one will cause thinking of the other.

Doctrine of association by similarity—Events or objects that are similar tend to be associated in memory.

Doctrine of association by contrast—Events or objects that are opposites tend to be associated in memory.

In addition, Aristotle claimed that thinking involves moving from one element or idea to another via a chain of associations and that such thought was impossible without images: ''We cannot think without imagery'' (Humphrey, 1963, p. 31). Aristotle's dogma about imagery later became a key issue when the psychology of thinking was first subjected to empirical rather than philosophical study.

The British associationists, led by Hobbes and Locke in the seventeenth and eighteenth centuries, reformulated the concepts and principles of associationism, including the three laws of Aristotle. Their theory of mental life can be summarized as containing four main characteristics:

Atomism—The unit of thinking is the association between two specific ideas. All mental life can be analyzed into specific ideas and associations.

Mechanization—The process of thinking or of moving from one idea to another is automatic and based solely on strength of associations.

Empiricism—All knowledge, that is, all ideas and associations, come from sensory experience. The mind begins as a ''blank slate'' and is filled by reproducing the world exactly as it is received through the senses.

Imagery—Thus, thinking is merely the automatic movement from point to point along mental paths established through learning, and since each point is a sensory experience, thinking must involve imagery (or some other sensory experience).

Wundt: Founder of Psychology

By the late nineteenth century, people were increasingly applying the methods of empirical science to the study of the physical world all around them—to the planets and space (astronomy), to moving objects and weights (physics), to the makeup of earth, water, and fire (chemistry), to the world of plants and animals (biology), and even to their own bodies (physiology and medicine). One of the last areas to be subjected to scientific study was what Wilhelm Wundt called the "new domain of science": the human mind and behavior.

Wundt is often identified as the "father" of psychology, and his opening of a psychology laboratory at the University of Leipzig in 1879 is generally considered the beginning of psychology as a science. Wundt subjected some of the old issues of mental philosophy to the rigors of empirical science and experimental study and created the new science on the principle that "all observation implies . . . that the observed object is independent of the observer" (Mandler and Mandler, 1964, p. 132).

Wundt also influenced the study of thinking when he divided the subject matter of psychology into two classes. Simple psychical processes—such as physiological reflexes and sensation and perception that could be studied by direct experimental methods—is one class; the other is higher psychical processes, about which "nothing can be discovered in such experiments" (Wundt, 1973). Thus Wundt decreed that the higher level mental processes *could not* be studied in the scientific laboratory; instead they could be studied by looking at the mental products of an entire society such as its art, stories, and so on. Although Wundt had shown that science could be directed at ourselves, our own mental processes and behaviors, he drew the line at studying thinking and complex learning. The nineteenth century ended with no major experimental work having yet begun on the psychology of human thinking.*

The Wurzburg Group

Working against Wundt's dogma forbidding the study of thinking, a group of German psychologists in the city of Wurzburg did finally in the early part of this century attempt to study human cognitive processes experimentally. This Wurzburg group set out to refine the old associationist theory of the philosophers by using the new experimental method of introspection.

In a typical early experiment, the psychologists would present a word to a subject, ask the subject to give a free association to the word, and then ask the person to describe the thought process that led to the response, or they might ask a subject to describe the thought process of answering some question (see Mayer and Orth; Marbe; and Messer in Mandler and Mandler, 1964). A major finding of these studies was a sort of negative result—many of the subjects reported that they were not consciously aware of any images in their associations (see Box 1-1). This finding was called "imageless thought."

A second type of experiment used different questions for the same stimulus

---

*A notable exception was Ebbinghaus' (1885) exciting monograph *Memory,* which provided a solid study of learning and memory of verbal material.

words. For example, Watt ([1905] 1964) found a different pattern of response for a word if he presented flash cards that said "name a whole of" rather than "name an example of." In a more elaborate experiment, Ach ([1905] 1964) hypnotized subjects and while they were under hypnosis, instructed them to add, subtract, multiply, or divide numbers. Then he brought them out of the hypnotic state and gave them cards with number pairs such as 4,2 and asked the subjects to respond. Answers such as 2 or 8 came instantly, depending on the hypnotic suggestion, in this case to divide or to multiply. A major conclusion of this line of research was that thought is directed by some "determining tendency" that is relevant for a particular problem (Kulpe, [1912] 1964).

The work of the Wurzburg group has been justly criticized: their method of introspection was challenged as being based on subjective experience rather than observable data; their results were largely negative; they had no theory. However, they did show it was possible to study human thinking, and their work began to cast doubts on the foundations of the associationist philosophy as their results showed:

Antiatomism—Preliminary reports indicated that the elements of thought changed as they were combined.

Antimechanization—Evidence showed that thought is directed and guided by some human motive or purpose.

Antiempiricism—Evidence began to mount that experience is not reproduced or copied in the mind exactly as it occurs in the world.

Antiimagery—Images are particular, but the Wurzburgers found examples of general and abstract thought and also of "imageless thought."

Selz

Although the early research of the Wurzburg group began to challenge the philosophy of associationism, alternative theories did not develop until the work of Otto Selz ([1913] 1964). Selz used the method of introspection and examples like those shown in Box 1-1, but unlike his predecessors, he developed a theory independent of images and associations. The main concepts in Selz' theory were that the unit of thought is a structural complex of relations among thoughts rather than a string of particular responses and that the process of thinking is filling in or completing a gap in the structural complex rather than following a chain of associations.

For example, in Benjamin Franklin's problem of how to bring electricity from the lightning to the ground, Selz claimed the solution involved the development of a complex of ideas, in this case a kite as a means of producing contact between the earth and the storm clouds. The solution involved filling in the complex with "kite" to build an organized structure in which objects had certain relationships to each other. Thus, thinking is simply the tendency of a "complex toward completion."

BOX 1–2   Historical Events in the Psychology of Thinking

400 B.C.	Aristotle's doctrine of association by contiguity, similarity, and contrast.
1700 A.D.	British associationists reformulate associationism.
1800	1879. Wundt opens the first psychology laboratory, but thinking is not studied.
1900	The Wurzburg group brings thinking to the laboratory, discovers imageless thought and determining tendencies.
1910	1913. Selz proposes first nonassociationist theory of thinking.
1920	Rise of Gestalt psychology in Germany.
1930	Behaviorism stifles American research on thinking. Nazism destroys Gestalt psychology in Germany; some Gestaltists move to the United States.
1940	
1950	
1960	Rebirth of interest in cognitive psychology.
1970	
1980	

Selz's contributions can be summarized in three points: he confirmed that thinking can occur independently of images; he produced the first nonassociationist theory of thinking; and he developed the idea that thinking involves organized complexes or wholes.

Two events have heavily influenced the course of the study of thinking since Selz' time. The rise of Nazism in Germany put an end to the work of many Gestalt psychologists who were attempting to take Selz' theory one step further, although many did continue their work elsewhere, mostly in the United States. The rise of behaviorism in America, partly brought on as a reaction against the abuses of the introspection method, emphasized the study of observable stimuli and observable responses only; to some psychologists this meant that internal mental events such as thinking could not be observed and therefore should not be studied. This view helped stifle research on thinking until the current rebirth of cognitive psychology. These events are summarized in Box 1-2.

EVALUATION

One major criticism of the early work in thinking is methodological. The method of introspection is a very difficult one since the experimenter must rely on the subject's self-reports. It fits the requirements of science only if we assume that the data are the subjects' reports rather than the subjects' experiences: the reports are observable for all to see and hear, but the experiences are not. The real problem is that these reports may not have much to do with the actual mental processes involved; that is, subjects may not be able to report on their own cognitive experiences accurately. Since the days of the early twentieth century, many clever methods have been developed to study thinking. In addition, the method of introspection has been ingeniously used and refined in recent work on computer simulation in an attempt to program computers to behave the way humans do during problem solving.

A second criticism of the early work in thinking is theoretical. The associationist theory of the philosophers was inconsistent with some of the findings of the Wurzburg group, but the early psychologists proposed no real alternative and Selz' theory was vague. The clash between the associationist theory and the pre-Gestalt work of Selz is still far from resolved, although many current theories such as information processing may be seen as compromises.

Finally, we are left with the question of legitimacy. Although there is currently a renewed interest in cognitive psychology, some question of the place of thinking and complex learning in psychology remains. Ultimately, the question of whether we can find out how the human mind works will be answered in the laboratory.

Suggested Readings

Humphrey, G. *Thinking: An introduction to its experimental psychology.* New York: Wiley, 1963. An excellent introduction to the historical ideas and findings underlying modern cognitive psychology.

Mandler, J. M., and Mandler, G. *Thinking: From association to Gestalt.* New York: Wiley, 1964. A set of condensed readings from the early studies in the psychology of thinking.

CHAPTER 2

ASSOCIATIONISM: Thinking as Learning by Reinforcement

Anagram Task

Suppose someone gave you the following letters and asked you to rearrange them to form a word: GANRE. Get a piece of paper and work on this one.

There are two solutions to this anagram (that we know of). Most college students give the answer RANGE, and their median response time is about 8 seconds. A less frequent answer is ANGER, which takes about 114 seconds (median solution time). If you cheated on GANRE, here's another to try before you read on: TARIL.

This anagram also has two solutions, so try to find both. Don't read on until you have found both words or until you give up. The easiest answer seems to be TRAIL, which takes about 7 seconds, and the more difficult is TRIAL, which takes about 240 seconds.

For more anagrams and median solution times to amuse yourself and your friends, see Tresselt and Mayzner (1966). Anagrams like these have long been enjoyed as mental puzzles, but recently their solutions have been analyzed in psychological experiments. Since each five-letter anagram has 120 possible letter arrangements, solving anagrams may be viewed as trying arrangements until one works.*

Puzzle Box Task

Another favorite task that has been studied closely involves problem solving in a puzzle box—a closed box with an escape hatch like the one shown in Box 2–1—in which an animal must perform a certain response to solve the problem. In 1898, Edward Thorndike published his famous monograph, Animal Intelligence, in which he described the process of thinking and problem solving. Thorndike placed a cat into what he called a puzzle box; if the cat performed a certain response, such as clawing down a loop of string or pushing a lever, a trap door opened and allowed it to escape and eat food set out nearby. Thorndike supposed (correctly) that cats do not like being cooped up in a box and do like the chance to get out and have a snack.

From his observations of cats in the puzzle box, Thorndike developed a theory of thinking and problem solving that formed the basis for further ideas that we call in this book the *associationist* theories of thinking. One of Thorndike's most famous observations was that his cats solved the puzzle box problem by trial and error—that is, they responded in an almost random fashion without much evidence at all of any thinking. The cat might meow, or squeeze a bar, or claw at a loose object, or jump onto things in the box until it would hit accidentally upon the required solution to open the escape hatch. Thorndike observed that the next time the cat was put in the box, it still performed by *trial and error*—by trying various responses at random until one worked—but as practice increased the animal had a tendency to perform the responses that didn't work less often and to perform the responses that did work

---

*If you are baffled trying to figure out how there can be 120 possible arrangements for a five-letter anagram, then read this footnote: otherwise you can skip it. Suppose you have five letters, a, b, c, d, e, and five blank spaces to fit one letter each: — — — — —. Pick one letter and place it in any one of the five spaces; you have five choices as to where to put it. Let's say you pick the second blank: — a — — —. Now there are four spaces left for the next letter so you have only four choices. Let's say you decide to put b in space five: — a — — b. No matter where you put a, you have four places to put b; and no matter where you put b, you have three places to put the next letter. You may pick the following arrangement: $c\ a$ — — b; there are now two choices for the next letter. When you pick one, say $c\ a\ d$ — b, there is one blank left for the last letter: $c\ a\ d\ e\ b$. Therefore, there are always 5 first choices, 4 second choices, 3 third choices, 2 fourth choices, and 1 last choice; this yields $5 \times 4 \times 3 \times 2 \times 1$, or 120 ways to arrange five letters in five spaces. The number of ways to arrange X things in X spaces is called the number of permutations, and the general formula for calculating it is: Number of Permutations = X! The "!" is read "factorial" and simply means to multiply the number times one less than the number, times two less than the number, times three less, and so on down to one. In this example: $5! = 5 \times 4 \times 3 \times 2 \times 1 = 120$.

BOX 2–1   A Puzzle Box for Cats

"When put into the box the cat would show evident signs of discomfort and of impulse to escape from confinement. It tries to squeeze through any opening; it claws
and bites at the wire; it thrusts its paws out through any opening and claws at everything it reaches . . . It does not pay very much attention to the food outside but
seems simply to strive instinctively to escape from confinement . . . . The cat that is
clawing all over the box in her impulsive struggle will probably claw the string or
loop or button so as to open the door. And gradually all the other unsuccessful im-
pulses will be stamped out and the particular impulse leading to the successful act
will be stamped in by the resulting pleasure, until, after many trials, the cat will, when
put in the box, immediately claw the button or loop in a definite way."

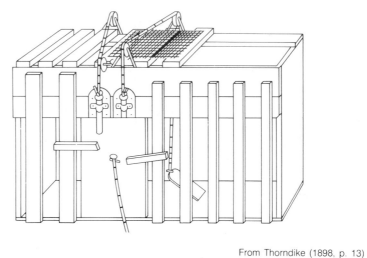

From Thorndike (1898, p. 13)

sooner. Eventually, after being placed in the box many times, the cat would go to
the string and pull it almost immediately. According to Thorndike, the cat was
learning "by trial, and error, and accidental success."

Both solving anagrams and the puzzle box task may require a subject to try many
responses until one solves the problem, and the thinking process may, among other
things, be conceived of as *response learning*.

ASSOCIATIONIST DEFINITION OF THINKING

Trial and Error Application of Habit Family Hierarchy

According to the associationist view, thinking can be described as the trial and error
application of the preexisting response tendencies we call "habits." This view is
called associationist because it assumes that for any problem situation, S, there are

BOX 2–2 Habit Family Hierarchy for Puzzle Box

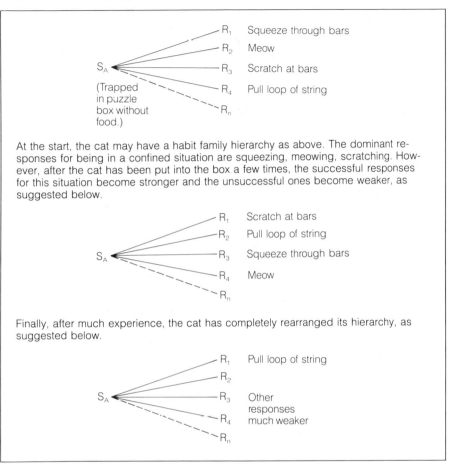

At the start, the cat may have a habit family hierarchy as above. The dominant responses for being in a confined situation are squeezing, meowing, scratching. However, after the cat has been put into the box a few times, the successful responses for this situation become stronger and the unsuccessful ones become weaker, as suggested below.

Finally, after much experience, the cat has completely rearranged its hierarchy, as suggested below.

associations or links to many possible responses, R_1, R_2, R_3 and so on. Thus the three elements in an associationist theory of thinking are: the stimulus (a particular problem-solving situation), the responses (particular problem-solving behaviors), and the associations between a particular stimulus and a particular response. The links are assumed to be in the problem solver's head, where they form a family of possible responses associated with any given problem situation. In addition, the responses may vary in strength with some associations being very strong and some being very weak. Thus the responses for any given situation may be put into a hierarchy in order of their strength.

A typical habit family hierarchy for Thorndike's puzzle box is shown in Box 2–2. A similar hierarchy could be constructed for behavior in the anagram problem since there are 120 possible responses for a five-letter anagram, some of which are initially stronger than others. In the problem-solving situation, the problem solver (either overtly or covertly) tries the most dominant response, R_1, in the habit family hierarchy for that situation and, if that fails, tries R_2 and so on until one works.

Laws of Exercise and Effect

Two laws of learning, which Thorndike termed the *law of exercise* and the *law of effect,* are required to describe the solution process.

> The law of exercise states that responses that have been previously practiced many times with a given situation are more likely to be performed when that situation is presented again, or, to state it another way, practice tends to increase the specific S-R link.

> The law of effect states that responses to a problem that do not help solve the problem lose strength and are demoted on the hierarchy while the responses that do solve the problem increase in strength and go up on the hierarchy until after many trials they reach the top.

Thus the associationists describe problem solving as the trial and error application of a thinker's existing habit family hierarchy. In a new situation such as the puzzle box or anagrams subjects try their most dominant response first (scratch head?), then their second strongest, and so on. Maltzman (1955) summarizes this view as follows: "thinking is not a response" but thinking results in a change in "a new combination of habit strengths" within a habit family hierarchy.

Covert and Overt Responding

Thorndike observed cats in his puzzle box and saw trial and error learning of solution responses. When the Gestalt psychologist Kohler (1925) presented similar problems to apes, he did not observe trial and error performance or activity at all but rather was sure that his animals solved by a flash of *insight*—that they thought about the problem and the solution suddenly fell into place. We shall talk more about the Gestalt interpretation of problem solving in Chapter 3, but it is puzzling that two psychologists observing a similar kind of problem-solving task in animals saw such different things and were inspired to develop such different theories.

Let's assume for a moment that both Thorndike and Kohler were correct, at least in their observations of trial and error and of insight. How would an associationist explain the phenomenon of apparent insight? That question was solved by the associationists in an ingenious way. Sometimes, especially with humans, trial and error may be *covert.* In other words, people tend to try out various solutions *in their minds* (or sometimes even in their muscles). According to this view, thinking is simply covert action: thinking involves trying all the likely responses mentally until the one that will work is found. Since this form of the trial and error process cannot be seen, the solution therefore appears to be achieved suddenly, as by a flash of insight.

THINKING AS COVERT BEHAVIOR

Mediation

The idea that thinking involves a chain of covert responses has led to changes in the traditional associationist idea that a stimulus (S) goes in, a response (R) comes out, and everything that goes on in between can be summarized by a hyphen (S-R). How then does the habit family hierarchy change? Or, to put it another way, what comes between or *mediates* between the overt problem-solving situation (S) and the solution response (R)? A mediational theory suggests that the S evokes a miniature internal response called *mediational response* or r_m; the r_m creates a new internal state or s_m, this new s_m may evoke another different r_m followed by a new s_m and so on until an s_m finally evokes an overt solution response, R. For example, Berlyne (1965) presents a comprehensive mediational theory based on the principle that thinking is a chain of symbolic responses; thus, the "train of thought" may be represented as a series of internal responses and stimuli mediating an S and R:

$$S - r_{m1} - s_{m1} - r_{m2} - s_{m2} - r_{m3} - s_{m3} - \ldots - r_{mn} - s_{mn} - R$$

The capital S is the overt problem situation, the capital R is the overt response, and the lowercase s's and r's represent internal covert responses and stimulus situations.

Mediational theories such as Berlyne's are generally extensions of Hull's (1943) claim that animals make tiny responses in anticipation of the goal as they learn to solve a maze; he called these responses "fractional goal responses." For example, rats made miniature licking movements as they ran down a maze toward a liquid reward. These fractional goal responses helped the animal mediate between being put in the maze and performing the needed solution behavior. More recently, Kendler and Kendler (1962) used the idea of mediating responses to describe developmental changes in discrimination learning; Osgood (1957, 1966) used "mediating reaction" to explain the human use of language meanings; and Underwood (1965) developed "implicit associative responses" to explain the course of human verbal learning. These theories are examples of mediational theory because they are based on the idea that tiny, covert responses mediate between a stimulus and a response.

Two Views of Covert Thinking

There are various ways to interpret how covert or mediational responses relate to the habit family hierarchy approach to thinking. A relatively liberal interpretation, such as that cited by Maltzman (1955), is that the habit family hierarchy represents a set of dispositions and that thinking can be conceived of as changes in the state of the hierarchy. According to this view, thinking is not a chain of responses, but "responses may be taken as a criterion or manifestation of thinking" (p. 282). In other words, covert responses may occur as a result of thinking, but they are not equivalent to thinking.

A more strict and literal interpretation that is probably less popular today than the one just given is that thinking *is* covert responding, especially covert verbal responding. This view received serious attention during the 1920s and 1930s because it was consistent with the behaviorist revolution in psychology—the idea that psychologists must study only what can be directly observed (behavior) and should not hypothesize about unseen phenomena (thoughts). One focus of this interest was to determine where in the human body the covert responses occur: the peripheralists tended to study muscle changes during thinking because they claimed that responses occurred in the muscles; the centralists tended to study electrical brain activity during thinking because they claimed that responses occurred in the brain.

Peripheral Theory: Muscle Activity

The behaviorist psychologist Watson (1930) claimed that since human problem solving involves language, silent thinking is subvocal speech. In other words, thinking is simply "talking to oneself," and the locus of thinking behavior should be in the muscles related to talking. For example, Jacobson (1932) measured electrical activity in the muscles of human subjects during various periods of intellectual activity. When the subjects were relaxed and not concentrating on anything, their muscles showed little electrical activity. However, when he asked them to *think* about picking up a heavy object with their left hands, changes occurred in readings for muscles in their left arms. Similarly, when Jacobson asked a subject to imagine a certain object, he noted increased electrical activity from the muscles around the eyes.

Max (1935, 1937) investigated the muscle activity of deaf mutes when they were thinking. Since his subjects normally used sign language to communicate, he thought that perhaps subvocal speech could be detected by changes in electrical activity in the arm muscles even if no overt signs were made. As Max expected, he did find increased electrical activity in the arm muscles of these deaf mute subjects when they were thinking about how to solve a problem or about a past conversation, and even when they were asleep and apparently dreaming.

Although the peripheral theory of thinking has not received much attention since Max's interesting study, McGuigan (1966, 1973) has done further work on the subject. For example, McGuigan, Keller, and Stanton (1964) measured the muscle activity of students while they read silently. As these researchers predicted, changes occurred in chin and lip muscle activity and in the breathing rates of the students during the reading period but not during rest. Unfortunately, a major problem with this study, as with earlier studies by the peripheralists, is that muscle changes may be due to the awareness of the subjects that they are being studied or to factors other than thinking. McGuigan (1966) has suggested that a more convincing test of the peripheralist theory might be to inject subjects with a chemical (curare) that numbs both the smooth and the skeletal muscles and then ask them to solve problems. If injected subjects were still able to solve problems, it would follow that something must be wrong with the theory that thinking occurs in the muscles.

The peripheral correlates of thinking are not limited to muscle movements in speech. Another behavior that seems related to thinking is *laterality of gaze* — the direction in which your eyes gaze when you answer a question. For example, suppose you are asked a question that required a moment's reflection before answering. As you think about the question, you might briefly gaze to one side. Kinsbourne (1972) has hypothesized that the direction of the gaze is related to which side of the brain is being most heavily used. A gaze to the right indicates that the problem solver is using the left side of the brain, an area that may be specialized for verbal and mathematical thinking; a gaze to the left indicates that the responder is using the right side of the brain, an area that may be specialized for spatial thinking.*

To test these ideas, Kinsbourne observed subjects' gazes as they answered difficult questions. Some questions were verbal, such as having to explain a proverb. These questions tended to elicit gazes to the right, suggesting that the left side of the brain was being used. Some questions were spatial, such as deciding which way the Indian faces on a nickel. These questions tended to elicit gazes to the left, suggesting that the right half of the brain was being used. Similiar results obtained by Kocel, Galin, Ornstein, and Merrin (1974) support Kinsbourne's theory.

However, before you try these experiments on your friends, you should know that the methodology and theory are still far from perfect. First, there are individual differences among subjects, with some people "preferring" to gaze right (or left) regardless of the type of question (Bakan, 1969). Second, results may be influenced if you emphasize that you are watching eye gazes, if you stand in front rather than behind the subject, or if you ask complex questions. These events seem to increase the anxiety of the subject, and when the subject is anxious you can destroy the

---

*In some subjects, such as most left-handed subjects, the brain functions are specialized in the reverse order, that is, left for spatial and right for verbal. For additional information about brain lateralization, see Wittrock's (1980) *The Brain and Psychology.*

usefulness of the very sensitive measure of laterality of gaze (Ehrlichman, Weiner, and Baker, 1974; Gur, Gur, and Harris, 1975). Although there have been attempts to relate work on brain lateralization to practical issues in learning and problem solving (for example, Wittrock, 1980), the underlying theory concerning laterality of gaze is still vague.

Centralist Theory: Brain Activity

Although there are now more sophisticated techniques for measuring physiological correlates of mental activity, including some that focus on the electrical activity of brain neurons (see Penfield, 1958, 1969; Delgado, 1969), little work has been done as yet to relate physiological changes in the body to thinking. In a typical study, Chapman (1973) implanted electrodes in the brains of human subjects and recorded general electrical activity while the subjects solved problems. The pattern of electrical activity showed sharp changes during critical phases of problem solving.

McGuigan (1966) has suggested that since the centralist theory predicts that electrical stimulation of specific brain neurons should cause spontaneous thinking, further research using these new techniques is needed. McGuigan concluded: ''If the peripheralist theory that thinking is a behavioral phenomena is confirmed, thinking can be studied directly by recording responses. . . . If the centralist theory is confirmed . . . brain events can often be indirectly studied by recording their consequent responses . . . In either case we should get on with the measurement of covert responses'' (pp. 294–295).

Several researchers (John and Schwartz, 1978; Wittrock, 1980; Donchin and Israel, 1980) have recently reviewed studies on event-related potentials (ERPs)—brief, small jumps in electrical brain activity due to stimulus events. To record this brain activity, electrodes are placed on the scalp of the human problem solver. These electrodes are able to record the general level of electrical activity, rather than activity in a specific cell. In many problem-solving tasks such as deciding if two stimuli are the same, the following sequence of ERP changes occurs:

1. *Contingent negative variation* refers to a slowly increasing negativity that occurs in expectation of the stimulus.

2. *N100* refers to a jump in negative potential that occurs about 100 milliseconds after the problem is presented and may reflect the initial arrival of the information in short-term memory.

3. *P300* refers to a jump in positive potential that occurs about 300 milliseconds after a problem is presented. This jump may reflect a sort of ''aha'' experience in which the subject understands the significance of the information.

BOX 2–3 Event-Related Potentials (ERPs)

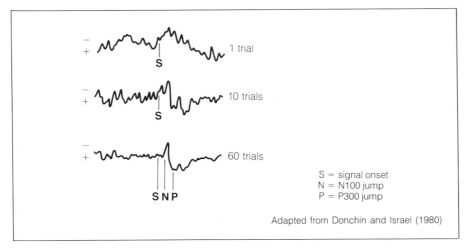

S = signal onset
N = N100 jump
P = P300 jump

Adapted from Donchin and Israel (1980)

Box 2–3 shows a typical ERP generated by averaging the presentation of a single stimulus over 1, 10, and 60 trials. The arrows show the point at which a stimulus was presented, followed by a negative jump and then a positive jump in brain-wave activity. As you can see, pattern is much clearer when ERPs are averaged over many single trials.

Donchin and Israel (1980), following earlier work (Sutton, Braren, Zubin, and John, 1965), point out that there are two basic kinds of ERP components. *Exogenous components* are obligatory responses to the stimulus based on activation of the sense organs. *Endogenous components* are not obligatory and are related to internal cortical processing imposed by the demands of the task. For example, the P300 component and other late positive components are influenced by the amount of information and instructions in the problem. In a typical study (Heffley, Wickens, and Donchin, 1978), subjects watched a screen with moving geometrical figures and counted the number of times one of those objects increased in brightness (that is, flashed). For example, a subject might be asked to count the number of times that a square flashed but to ignore a flashing triangle. As shown in Box 2–4, there is a strong P300 component for the target stimulus—when a square flashes—but almost no change in potential for the ignored stimulus—when a triangle flashes. Thus, the P300 component seems to be an endogenous component that is related to internal processing rather than an immediate sensory response. Several researchers (Shields, 1973; Preston, Guthrie, and Childs, 1974) have found that children with learning disabilities do not show the same endogenous brainwave patterns for attention that normal children display.

BOX 2–4 Event-Related Potentials for Target and Ignored Stimuli

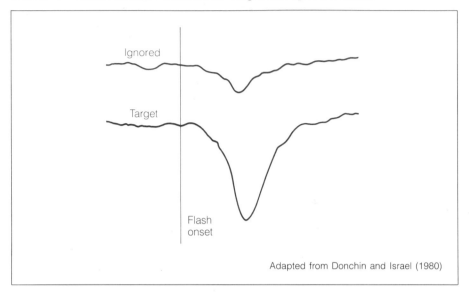

Ignored

Target

Flash
onset

Adapted from Donchin and Israel (1980)

You may be tempted to suppose that we will soon be able to describe thinking as a specific chain of electrical changes, clearly localized in the brain. However, John and Schwartz (1978) point out that it is "experimentally and logically untenable" to try to locate specific cells or brain areas that correspond directly to specific thoughts. Instead, the global or Gestalt aspects of the nervous system need to be taken into account. John and Schwartz conclude that "the neurophysiology of information processing and cognition is still in the early stages of infancy. . . Much work remains to be done, even at the level of defining questions that are to be asked and experimental techniques that are to be used" (1978, p. 25). Thus, it seems unlikely that an analysis of brain activity will provide a definitive theory of human thinking, although such work provides an increasingly important approach.

At this time, most psychologists are willing to concede that electrical and other physiological changes in the body are probably correlated with thinking, but very few people are willing to accept the extreme position that body muscle activity is thinking. In addition, the work on the psychophysiology of thinking has not yet stimulated useful theories of thinking nor has it been well integrated with other approaches. Thus, while we hope that some day we shall be able to describe thinking in physiological terms, the remainder of this chapter will focus on thinking defined as a change in the habit family hierarchy.

BOX 2–5   The Heart and Bow Problem

The heart and bow problem is a typical mechanical puzzle used to study trial and error problem-solving in humans. The problem is to disentangle the two pieces. Usually time to solution decreases for each successive trial since unsuccessful responses are weakened and the successful "twist" response becomes dominant.

Based on Ruger (1910)

HABIT FAMILY HIERARCHY: STEREOTYPED RESPONSES

As a follow-up to Thorndike's famous observations, a more thorough study was conducted by Guthrie and Horton (1946) half a century later. These researchers filmed cats in a puzzle box and analyzed the behaviors of a given cat on each successive trial. Each specific behavior was carefully defined in detail, and the order of behaviors was tallied for each trial. The results showed that the movements of a given cat were almost identical for a particular response from trial to trial; for example, it pulled the string in the same way. Since the behaviors were stereotyped, Guthrie and Horton concluded that the cats had specific response tendencies that changed in strength during problem solving rather than general plans.

The habit family hierarchy or trial and error description that Thorndike and Guthrie and Horton proposed for cats in the puzzle box has also been observed in human beings. For example, Ruger (1910) provided subjects with mechanical puzzles like the heart and bow problem shown in Box 2–5. At first the subjects tended to exhibit a series of apparently random behaviors, often not realizing what brought about the solution. Solution times fell from trial to trial, but the subjects in this experiment also tended to persist in using certain specific behaviors on several trials until finally only the successful twist response remained.

BOX 2–6   Median Solution Times in Seconds for Selected Anagrams

Familiar Words	Time	Unfamiliar Words	Time
beahc *to* beach	3.0	hroac *to* roach	9.5
odelm *to* model	4.5	ypeon *to* peony	12.0
ntrai *to* train	5.0	patoi *to* patio	22.0
chari *to* chair	10.0	tanog *to* tango	45.0
ugars *to* sugar	10.5	obrac *to* cobra	50.5

Low LTP Anagrams	Time	High LTP Anagrams	Time
rhtae *to* heart	28.5	ahter *to* heart	168.5
oeshr *to* shore	8.5	osher *to* shore	39.0
ietdr *to* tried	18.0	dteri *to* tried	71.0
aephs *to* phase	11.0	hesap *to* phase	115.5
aecrt *to* crate	18.0	atcer *to* crate	48.5

Familiar words occur 100 times per million or more and unfamiliar words occur 1 or less per million. Both familiar and unfamiliar word solutions require moving only 1 letter, yet familiar words are generally easier, presumably because they are higher on the habit family hierarchy. Solving anagrams made of pairs of letters that seldom occur together (low letter transition probability or low LTP) is generally easier than high LTP anagrams for the same solution words, presumably due to the difficulty in breaking up dominant letter pairs.

Based on Tresselt and Mayzner (1966)

HABIT FAMILY HIERARCHY: RESPONSE DOMINANCE

A few cats locked into puzzle boxes may not seem like much on which to build a theory of human problem solving. However, there is further evidence in support of the associationist theory, some of which has come from studying how people solve anagrams. One reason there has not been more research may be that the associationists have concentrated their efforts on the psychology of learning; you probably have sensed that Thorndike's theory is also the basis of a theory of learning and memory. On the other hand, the Gestaltists—the main competitors of the associationists—have focused on the psychology of thinking and perception; their chapter will be longer than this one.

Familiarity of Goal Word

One nice thing about the S-R association representation of thinking is that it makes precise predictions that can be tested. For example, suppose you presented a subject with one of the five-letter anagrams shown in Box 2–6. Each way of arranging the letters can be considered a response in the habit family hierarchy. Of course, for any given subject some potential responses should be stronger than others and thus higher on the hierarchy and more likely to be tried. The solution for an anagram should come faster if the solution is a common word.

To test this prediction, Mayzner and Tresselt (1958, 1966) constructed anagrams based on rearranging either common five-letter words or uncommon five-letter words in the same way. To measure how common a word was, they used the lists compiled by Thorndike and Lorge (1944) that contained a tally of how many times each of 30,000 words appeared in books, magazines, newspapers, and other randomly selected printed sources. Mayzner and Tresselt found that anagrams were generally solved more than twice as fast if the solution word occurred frequently in print—more than 100 times per million words—than if it occurred infrequently. Examples are given in Box 2–6. For example, TANGO, PEONY, or COBRA, which occurred less than once per million words, took much more time to solve than CHAIR, SUGAR, or TRAIN, which occurred more than 100 times per million. In addition, with anagrams that have two solutions, such as TABLE (more than 100 per million) and BLEAT (7 per million), the more common word was usually found first. These results are consistent with the idea of habit family hierarchy since the most dominant response—assuming past experience with word frequencies influences dominance—occurred before the weaker response in problem solving.

Letter Transition Probability of Goal Word

The associationist theory also predicts that past experience with the way one letter usually follows another letter should influence the response hierarchy. Certain letter pairs have high *transition probabilities* because the second letter often follows the first in normal English words, such as ch, th, es, and others. Since each five-letter word has four successive pairs of letters, word transition probabilities can be generated for them based on how common each of the four two-letter pairs are in ordinary English (Mayzner and Tresselt, 1959, 1962, 1966). For example, RANCH, TRAIN, and BEACH contain letters in a more common order (higher transition probability) than ENJOY, KNIFE, TRIBE. In general, solution words with high letter transition probabilities are solved faster than those with low. Again, these results are consistent with the idea that problem solving involves trial and error rearrangement of the letters based on 120 responses, but beginning with the most dominant responses first.

Number of Moves

The order of letters in anagrams influences problem solving (Mayzner and Tresselt, 1958, 1963). This finding is consistent with the finding that dominant responses are given first. In general, the fewer the number of letters that must be moved, the faster the solution. If two solution words are possible, such as TABLE and BLEAT, or ANGER and RANGE, the order in which the anagram letters are presented can influence which word is discovered. Again, subjects tend to make dominant responses such as moving just one or two letters first; if that doesn't work, they try weaker responses such as moving all five letters.

Letter Transition Probability of Presented Word

Finally, a fourth typical result with anagram problem solving is that if the anagram is already in the form of a word or if it has a high transition probability, it is more difficult to solve than if it is in the form of a nonsense syllable or if it has a low transition probability (Mayzner and Tresselt, 1959; Devnich, 1937; Beilin and Horn, 1962). Typical results are given in Box 2–6. For example, discovery of KANGAROO is generally easier if the subject is given OAG KRNOA than if given AGO KORAN. Beilin and Horn's subjects required about 17 seconds to solve word anagrams like CAUSE to SAUCE but only 9 seconds for nonsense anagrams matched for frequency and other variables such as ERTEN to ENTER. Mayzner and Tresselt (1966) also found that going from low transition probability words as anagrams (BOARD, TRIAL, ANGER, EARTH) to high transition probability solution words (BROAD, TRAIL, RANGE, HEART) was much easier than the reverse. However, Dominowski and Duncan (1964) found that anagrams with high transition probabilities (such as NILEN, GSEAT, HECAB) were more difficult than low transition probabilities (such as LNNIE, TSGAE, AEBHC) only when the solution words had high transition probabilities (LINEN, STAGE, BEACH). In general, these results seem to indicate that subjects have trouble breaking up letter combinations that occur frequently together. This kind of inflexibility can be compared to what the Gestaltists call rigidity of mental set. In the anagram experiments, subjects try the dominant response of re-arranging loose letters first before they begin on the more complex responses, which involve breaking up frequent letter combinations.

   In summary, the experiments with anagrams offer four different lines of support for the idea that problem solving involves trial and error application of a subject's habit family hierarchy. With many possible ways to arrange a five-letter anagram, it is clear that subjects do not try solutions at random but rather begin with the most dominant responses and go on to the weaker ones if those don't work. Thus, frequently used words, high transition probability solution words, words that require only minor re-arrangement, or words that do not require breaking up a combination of high transition probability letters are solved more quickly than others.

PROBLEM-SOLVING SET

In solving problems, not only is the general past experience of a subject important in determining the response hierarchy, but so are his or her experiences just prior to and during problem solving. These experiences form the subject's *problem-solving set*.

For example, Rees and Israel (1935) gave subjects ambiguous anagrams that could be solved by either one or two words. When the subjects were instructed to look for a certain type of word, such as "nature words," they found more words in this category than the subjects in a control group found. Subjects who found a high number of nature words in one block of anagrams were also more likely to find more nature words in the next block than were the controls. Maltzman and Morrisett (1952, 1953) also found that giving instructions to look for a certain class of words to subjects who had previous experience with anagrams soluble by that set strongly influenced the solutions of the ambiguous anagrams in the direction of the set.

Safren (1962) used two methods of dividing 36 anagrams into 6 sets of 6 anagrams each. In one grouping, solution words often associated with one another (like MILK, CREAM, SUGAR, COFFEE, SWEET, and DRINK) appeared on the same list. The other grouping of anagrams was in unorganized lists, with the associated words appearing on each of the 6 different lists. Overall, the median solution time for the organized lists was about 7 seconds compared with 12 seconds when the same anagrams were presented in separate lists.

In terms of the response hierarchy framework, these results indicate that several different habit family hierarchies (or response hierarchies) may exist for a given problem. According to Maltzman (1955, p. 281), problem solving "may involve the selection of habit family hierarchies as well as the selection of specific response sequences within a hierarchy." Thus the response hierarchy shown in Box 2–2 must now be changed into a "compound habit family hierarchy" to account for the effects of set. Thinking about nature words may lead to response hierarchy A, thinking about beverage words may lead to hierarchy B, thinking about no particular category of words may lead to hierarchy C, and so on.

EVALUATION

The associationist approach offers a means of representing thinking and problem solving that allows for clear predictions. Perhaps for this reason, associationist concepts are reappearing in some contemporary theories of human thinking, learning, and memory. For example, Anderson and Bower's (1973) book, *Human Associative Memory*, offers clearly testable "neoassociationist" theories of human memory; and Berlyne's (1965) *Structure and Direction in Thinking* offers an associationist theory of thinking.

However, the associationist approach may fail to capture the full-blown powers of human thought: is all thinking simply the trial and error application of past habits? Apparently, some kinds of thinking can be explained by the response hierarchy model, but there seems to be much more to human thinking than trial and error, and the following chapters will explore some other theories and possibilities.

Suggested Readings

Berlyne, D. E. *Structure and direction in thinking.* New York: Wiley, 1965. A modern extension of the associationist theory of thinking.

Donchin, E., and Israel, J. B. Event-related potentials: Approaches to cognitive psychology. In R. E. Snow, P. Federico, and W. E. Montague (eds.), *Aptitude, learning, and instruction. Vol. 2.* Hillsdale, N.J.: Erlbaum, 1980. Describes recent research on event-related potentials.

Duncan, C. P. (Ed.) *Thinking: Current experimental studies.* Philadelphia: Lippincott, 1967. Articles by Maltzman; Maltzman and Morrisett; and Mayzner and Tressett provide associationist theory and research in problem solving.

McGuigan, F. J., and Schoonover, R. A. *The psychophysiology of thinking.* New York: Academic Press, 1973. A book of readings on the psychophysiology of thinking. The papers by Jacobson, by McGuigan, and by Osgood and McGuigan are particularly interesting.

Thorndike, E. L. *Animal intelligence.* New York: Macmillan, 1911. Describes Thorndike's work with cats in the puzzle box.

GESTALT:
Thinking as
Restructuring Problems

Reorganization Tasks

Suppose you were given six identical matchsticks and asked to make four identical, equilateral triangles with them. Find six matchsticks (or toothpicks) and try it. What are you doing? According to the Gestalt psychologists, you are trying to *reorganize* the problem-solving elements—in this case, the six sticks—so they fit together in a new way.

An important contribution of the Gestaltists is the idea that people get stuck solving problems because they cannot change their *problem-solving set*—since they cannot look at the situation in a new way, they cannot see a new way to fit the elements together. For example, when trying to solve the six-stick problem, many people have trouble changing their problem solving set from two dimensions to three. Giving a hint like this (or as some Gestaltists have called it, giving *direction*) is important in problem solving because it helps people to break out of their old ways of organizing the situation. The new way of looking at this problem afforded by thinking in three dimensions is called *insight*—the "magical" flash that occurs when you suddenly see how to fit the sticks together. (Some Gestaltists have pointed out that the solution and flash of insight are often accompanied by the exclamation, "Aha!")

If you still have not solved the problem, leave it for a while and come back to it later. This process is called *incubation,* and although no one is sure why it helps, it often does. One reason may be that the time lapse allows confusing ideas to be forgotten. See if this helps you, but if you cannot solve it, then you may "cheat" by looking at Box 3–1.

Let's try another example. During World War I, Wolfgang Kohler, one of the founders of the Gestalt school of psychology, was stranded on the island of Tenerife in the Atlantic Ocean. Being a good scientist, Kohler was determined not to waste his time, and so he spent 7 years studying problem solving in the island's most willing subjects, some chimpanzees. Eventually he published a monograph on his research, *The Mentality of Apes* (1925). Here was a typical problem as he reported it: given that you are an ape in a cage, that there are some crates in your cage, and that there is a banana hanging from the ceiling out of reach, how do you get the banana?

What Kohler wanted was for the apes to place the crates on top of each other to form a stairway to the banana. This solution, like the solution to the six-stick problem, required that the problem elements be reorganized. Kohler reported that solutions were preceded by a period of intense thinking by the ape, followed by what appeared to be a flash of insight.

These two problems—the six-stick problem and Kohler's banana problem—are examples of the type of problem solving the Gestalt psychologists tried to understand. Their problems usually supply all the needed parts—either in the form of pieces of information or as concrete objects—and the solver's task is to arrange them in a certain way to solve the problem. The Gestaltists felt that these kinds of problems involved creative or novel solutions—although some later evidence has indicated that without appropriate past experience (in the case of the apes, for example, moving crates) such problems cannot be solved (Birch, 1945).

BOX 3–1   The Six-Stick Problem

The Problem

Given six sticks, arrange them to form four triangles that are equilateral and with each side one stick long.

The Solution

Some subjects take the six sticks,

and form a square with an X in it, such as,

However, this solution is not acceptable because the triangles are not equilateral— each has a 90 degree angle. In order to solve the problem, the solver must think in three dimensions, making a pyramid with a triangle base. For example, an overhead view is,

with the middle point raised from the triangle base.

GESTALT DEFINITION OF THINKING

What is problem solving? According to Gestalt psychologists, the process of problem solving is a search to relate one aspect of a problem situation to another, and it results in *structural understanding*—the ability to comprehend how all the parts of the problem fit together to satisfy the requirements of the goal. This involves *reorganizing* the elements of the problem situation in a new way so that they solve the problem.

Thus, although the Gestaltists limit themselves to one class of problems, and use certain imprecise terms such as ''insight'' and ''structural understanding,'' they are trying to comprehend and explain a very high level and creative type of mental process. Their emphasis on *organization*—on how elements fit together to form a *structure*—is consistent with the contributions of the Gestalt psychologists to the study of perception. The famous laws of perceptual organization, for example, were

BOX 3–2 Differences Between Gestalt and Associationist Theories

	Associationist	Gestalt
1. Type of Task	Reproductive	Productive
2. Mental activity	Try stimulus-response links	Reorganize elements
3. Unit of Thought	Stimulus-response links	Organizations
4. Detail of Theory	Precise	Vague

based on the Gestalt idea that perception involves the mind imposing an order or structure on incoming stimuli.

The differences between the Gestalt approach to thinking and the associationist approach are summarized in Box 3–2. These two approaches do not deal with the same kinds of problems—Gestaltists are concerned with creating novel solutions to new situations while the associationists are concerned with applying solution habits from past experience. Where the Gestalt theory views thinking as rearranging problem elements, the associationist view is that problem solving involves trying possible solutions until one works. In analyzing thinking into its component parts, the Gestaltists rely on mental structures or organizations as the unit of thought while the associationists describe thinking in terms of associations among stimuli and responses. And finally, although the Gestaltists deal with a more complicated kind of thinking than do the associationists, their theory is more vague and thus more difficult to test scientifically.

DISTINCTION BETWEEN TWO KINDS OF THINKING

One of the basic concepts in the Gestalt approach is that there are two kinds of thinking. One, based on creating a new solution to a problem, is called *productive* thinking because a new organization is produced; the other, based on applying past solutions to a problem, is called *reproductive* thinking because old habits or behaviors are simply reproduced. The distinction between productive and reproductive thinking (Wertheimer, 1959; Maier, 1945) has also been called a distinction between "insight" and "trial and error" (Kohler, 1925, 1929), "meaningful apprehension of relations" versus "senseless drill and arbitrary associations" (Katona, 1940), and "structural understanding" versus "rote memory" (Wertheimer, 1959). Unfortunately, however, the Gestaltists have never clarified their various distinctions, have often confused differences in instructional method with differences in a subsequent problem-solving approach, and have provided little or questionable empirical support for their claims.

The flavor of Gestalt distinction between productive and reproductive thinking can be found in an example by Wertheimer suggesting two methods of teaching students how to find the area of a parallelogram. One method emphasizes the geometrical or structural property—the triangle on one end of the figure could be placed on the other end of the figure thus forming a rectangle (see Box 3–3). The other method emphasizes a sort of recipe of steps to calculate the area by dropping the perpendicular and multiplying its height times the length of the base.

Although students taught by both methods should perform equally well on criterion tasks that involve finding the area of parallelograms like those they had learned about, Wertheimer reported that they differed in their ability to transfer what they had learned to new tasks. For example, the students who learned "by understanding" (the first method) were able to find the area of unusual parallelograms and shapes and to recognize uncalculable situations such as are shown in the figure, while the students who learned in a mechanical way (the second method) usually said something like, "We haven't had this yet."

In an example of memorizing digit strings, Katona (1940) claimed that learning by "understanding the structural relationships" not only improved subjects' ability to transfer but also improved their ability to retain information over time. He had one group learn the digit string 581215192226 by understanding the structural pattern of "add 3, add 4" as indicated by the organization 5-8-12-15-19-22-26, while another group learned by rote memorization of the string organized as 581-215-192-226. Although both groups performed equally well on immediate retention, Katona reported that the first group remembered the string longer.

Katona (1940) provided another set of problem-solving situations in the form of card tricks and matchstick problems. A typical card trick problem (trick 3 in the series) involved figuring out how to arrange eight cards in such a way that if the subject dealt the top card of the deck face up on the table, put the next card from the remaining seven in the pack at the bottom without determining what it was, placed the next card face up on the table, the one after that at the bottom and so on until all the cards were dealt; the cards put on the table would follow the sequence: red, black, red, black, red, black, red, black. The problem was to find the order of the red and black cards in the original deck.

The solution was taught by two methods: (a) *learning by memorizing,* in which the specific order of the cards required for solution (RRBRRBBB) was given in its entirety for the solver to memorize, and (b) *learning by understanding,* in which the solver was given a diagram to help him figure out the "structure" of the problem for himself. The diagram system involved writing down the required color for each card for each run through the deck as shown in Box 3–4.

BOX 3–3 Two Approaches to Wertheimer's Parallelogram Problem

Understanding Method

The understanding method encouraged students to see the structural relations in the parallelogram, for example, that the parallelogram could be rearranged into a rectangle by moving a triangle from one side to the other. Since the students knew how to find the area of a rectangle, finding the area of a parallelogram was easy once they discovered the appropriate structural relations.

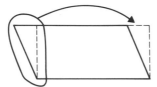

Rote Method

In the rote method, students were taught to drop a perpendicular and then apply the memorized solution formula.

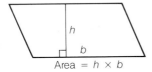

Area = $h \times b$

Transfer

Both groups performed well on typical problems asking for the area of parallelograms; however, only the understanding group could transfer to novel problems, such as finding the area of the three figures below

or distinguishing between solvable and unsolvable problems such as

The response of the "rote" group to novel problems was, "We haven't had that yet."

Based on Wertheimer (1945)

BOX 3–4   Two Approaches to Katona's Card Problem

The Problem

Deal out every other card onto the table, putting every skipped card on the bottom of the deck until all eight cards are on the table. The order of appearance on the table is RBRBRBRB. What was the order of the original deck?

Rote Method (Group Mem)

Subjects may be taught the solution by rote memorization: "The order of the original deck was RRBRRBBB."

Meaningful Method (Group Und)

Or they may learn by a more meaningful method involving a diagram:

1st run	R	?	B	?	R	?	B	?
2nd run		R		?		B		?
3rd run			R					?
4th run								B
Original	R	R	B	R	R	B	B	B

Results

Typical proportions correct on retention and transfer tests were as follows:

	Transfer Problems			Retention Problems		
Group	No. 1	No. 2	No. 3	No. 3	No. 4	No. 5
Mem	.23	.08	.42*	.32*	.36*	.18
Und	.44	.40	.44*	.48*	.62	.52
Control	.09	.03	.09	.09	.14	.09

*Subjects had practice on the problem prior to the test.

Adapted from Katona (1940)

In one experiment, subjects in the memorization group learned this card trick and card trick 4 (in which they produced a chain of spades from ace to eight by dealing out every other card) by memorizing the required order during four minutes. Subjects in the understanding group had the same time to learn, by means of the suggested diagram, how to arrange the deck for trick 3 only. A control group received no training. An immediate transfer task consisted of the previously learned task (trick 3), an easy variation of trick 3 (trick 1, output BRBRBR by dealing every

BOX 3–5 Two Approaches to Katona's Matchstick Problem

The Problem

Given matchsticks which form five squares, move three sticks to form four squares.

Rote Method (Group Mem)

The complete solution steps are presented to the subject in order, moving one stick at a time, and repeating six times. For the above problem, the required moves shown are:

Meaningful Method (Group Help)

The second method involves giving a series of hints to the subject accompanied by the comment, "Try to understand what I am doing."

Results

Typical proportion correct on retention and transfer tests were as follows:

	Test After 1 Week		Test After 3 Weeks	
Group	Practiced Tasks	New Tasks	Practiced Tasks	New Tasks
Mem	.67	.25	.53	.14
Help	.58	.55	.52	.55
Con	.12	.12	.12	.12

Note: The subjects who took the test after three weeks were a different group than those who took it after one week.

From Katona (1940)

other card), and a difficult variation (trick 2, output same as trick 3 by dealing every third card); a four-week retention transfer task consisted of tricks 3, 4, and 5 (same output as trick 1 but by dealing out every third card).

The results summarized in Box 3–4 show the proportion correct. As you can see, the memorization subjects (Group Mem) performed slightly better on immediate retention but much worse on transfer and long-term retention than understanding subjects (Group Und).

Katona also reported studies in which subjects learned to solve matchstick problems by several instructional methods. Two of these methods were: (1) Group Mem, in which the experimenter presented the complete series of solution steps in order, moving one stick at a time, and repeating the series six times and (2) Group Help, in which the experimenter presented a series of hints to help the subjects understand the structure of the problem, such as by shading in the squares that were essential and pointing to the sticks that had to be moved. For example, in the problem shown in Box 3–5, the subject was shown five squares made of matchsticks and was required to move three sticks to make four squares; no sticks could be removed and all squares had to be one stick wide and one stick long. The first method (memorization) involved showing the required moves to the subject repeatedly and the second method (understanding) encouraged the subject to discover the principle that some sticks served as the sides of one square and some bordered two squares by the experimenter giving a series of hints and saying, ''Try to understand what I am doing.''

In a typical experiment, all the subjects were given (1) a pretest to ensure their initial state of inexperience, (2) practice on two tasks by one of the two methods, and (3) delayed tests (some after one week and others after three weeks) on the learned problems as well as on the two new transfer tasks.

The results, in terms of percent correct, are given in Box 3–5. The Group Mem subjects performed quite well—better than the Group Help subjects—on retention of the solution for practiced tasks both after one week and after three weeks; however, Group Help subjects excelled (as did Group Und subjects with card tricks) on transfer tasks.

The experimental design, the lack of clear definitions, and, particularly, the lack of statistical analysis have all been criticized (Melton, 1941; Katona, 1942), and to the extent that these criticisms are justified, an interpretation of Katona's results is difficult. However, there is some evidence for the idea that giving solvers hints so they can discover the ''structure of the problem situation'' does aid in transfer— what the Gestaltists would call productive problem solving. For example, in a similar experiment performed under more controlled conditions, Hilgard, Irvine, and Whipple (1953) found that the understanding group took significantly longer than the memorizing group to solve the two practice problems, performed no differently from the memorizing subjects on a one-day retention test, and performed significantly better on a set of transfer problems.

A major practical question raised by this work is how to help learners ''understand'' so they will be productive thinkers who are able to transfer their experience to novel problems. For example, Hilgard, Irvine, and Whipple (1953) pointed out that many so-called understanding subjects did not really understand the diagraming device in the full sense. In another experiment, Hilgard, Ergren, and Irvine (1954) taught subjects by one of five variations of learning by understanding. Although there were no overall differences on a transfer task, the errors the subjects made were related to the type of method used, suggesting a mechanical or rote application of the various helps. Similarly, Corman (1957) found that giving subjects a statement of the "double function principle"—that a stick can be a part of one square or of two squares—did not aid in productive thinking on transfer although the diagram method did. Apparently, a supposedly meaningful principle such as the diagram or double function method can be learned in a mechanical way.

In more recent years, the distinction between these two kinds of learning to solve problems has taken the equally ambiguous form of a separation between "discovery" and "expository" methods of instruction (Shulman and Keisler, 1966). Bruner (1961, 1966, 1968) has been a major proponent of the discovery method. Although educators often describe discovery as an instructional method and as a desired outcome of learning and seldom empirically define either, they have produced several examples of Bruner's preferred method of instruction (see Shulman, 1968).

For example, Dienes' method of teaching children the concept of the quadratic equation involved allowing students to manipulate the shapes shown in Box 3–6 in such a way that they could see that the area of a square with sides of length x was x^2 and changed proportionately as other squares and rectangles were added to it—sides $(x + 2)^2$ had an area of $x^2 + 4x + 4$, for example (see Bruner and Kenney, 1966). The discovery method shares with the Gestalt learning by understanding method the promise of superior transfer and retention performance by the learner; in short, the road to productive thinking is paved with discovery of the structure of the problem. Although the idea of structural understanding is vague and hard to apply, psychologists and educators are still trying to clarify it and to determine if it does provide better transfer and retention of knowledge.

STAGES IN PROBLEM SOLVING

General Phases

There have been many attempts to break the thinking process down into several smaller stages. In his classic book, *The Art of Thought,* Wallas (1926) suggested four phases:

1. *Preparation*—the gathering of information and preliminary attempts at solution.
2. *Incubation*—putting the problem aside to work on other activities or sleep.
3. *Illumination*—the key to the solution appears (this is where the "flash of insight" and the "aha" occur).
4. *Verification*—checking out the solution to make sure it "works."

BOX 3–6   Discovery Learning of Quadratic Equation

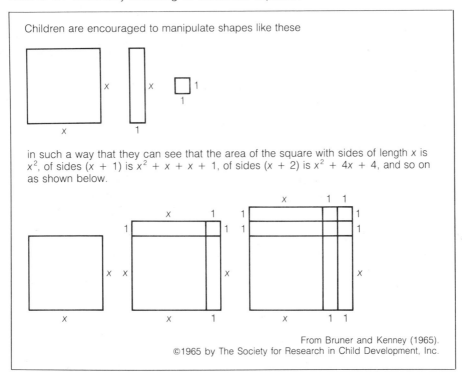

Children are encouraged to manipulate shapes like these

in such a way that they can see that the area of the square with sides of length x is x^2, of sides $(x + 1)$ is $x^2 + x + x + 1$, of sides $(x + 2)$ is $x^2 + 4x + 4$, and so on as shown below.

From Bruner and Kenney (1965).
©1965 by The Society for Research in Child Development, Inc.

Unfortunately, these four stages are based on introspections by Wallas and others about what they think they are doing when they solve problems, rather than on psychological experimentation. However, McKeachie and Doyle (1970) have shown how the analyses can be applied with partial success to reports of the thinking process such as the introspections of the mathematician Henri Poincaré (1913) shown in Box 3–7. The first 15 days of thinking are Poincaré's preparation period; preparation continues as ideas "collided until pairs interlocked," and is followed immediately by illumination and verification. In the second phase, preparation is followed by illumination and verification, apparently without a sudden burst of insight. The third part of the introspection completes Wallas' four stages, including an incubation period (during the geological excursion) and a sudden burst of insight in the illumination period.

More recently, Polya (1957, 1968) has introduced a series of steps in problem solving based on observations he has made as a teacher of mathematics. Polya's four steps—first described in *How To Solve It* (1957)—are:

BOX 3–7   Wallas' Phases of Problem Solving: An Example from Poincaré

"For fifteen days I strove to prove that there could not be any functions like those I have since called Fuchsian functions. I was then very ignorant; every day I seated myself at my work table, stayed an hour or two, tried a great number of combinations and reached no results. One evening, contrary to my custom, I drank black coffee and could not sleep. Ideas rose in crowds; I felt them collide until pairs interlocked, so to speak, making a stable combination. By the next morning I had established the existence of a class of Fuchsian functions, those which come from the hyper-geometric series; I had only to write out the results which took but a few hours.

"Then I wanted to represent these functions by the quotient of two series; this idea was perfectly conscious and deliberate, the analogy with elliptic functions guided me. I asked myself what properties these series must have if they existed, and I suc-ceeded without difficulty in forming the series I have called theta-Fuchsian.

"Just at this time time I left Caen, where I was then living, to go on a geologic excur-sion under the auspices of the school of mines. The changes of travel made me for-get my mathematical work. Having reached Countances, we entered an omnibus to go some place or other. At the moment when I put my foot on the step the idea came to me, without anything in my former thoughts seeming to have paved the way for it, that the transformations I had used to define the Fuchsian functions were identical with those of non-Euclidean geometry. I did not verify the idea; I should not have had time, as, upon taking my seat in the omnibus, I went on with a conversation already commenced, but I felt a perfect certainty. On my return to Caen, for conscience' sake I verified the result at my leisure."

From Poincaré (1913)

Understanding the problem — the solver gathers information about the problem and asks, "What do you want (or what is unknown)? What have you (or what are the data and conditions)?"

Devising a plan — the solver tries to use past experience to find a method of solution and asks, "Do I know a related problem? Can I restate the goal in a new way based on my past experience (working backwards) or can I restate the givens in a new way that relates to my past experience (working forward)?" (Here's where insight flashes.)

Carrying out the plan — the solver tries out the plan of solution, checking each step.

Looking back — the solver tries to check the result by using another method, or by seeing how it all fits together, and asks, "Can I use this result or method for other problems?"

Polya's steps are similar to Wallas' in general form. Polya's "understanding" step is similar to Wallas' preparation phase, his "devising a plan" step includes some of Wallas' preparation phase and both the incubation and illumination phases, and the "carrying out the plan" and "looking back" steps relate to Wallas' verification.

BOX 3-8 Stages in Solution of Polya's Frustum Problem

The Problem

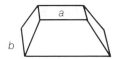

Find the volume F of the frustum of a right pyramid with square base given the altitude h of the frustum, the length a of a side of its upper base, and the length b of a side of its lower base.

The Solution Process

1. Understanding the problem. Solver asks: What do you want? Answer: The volume of frustum F. Solver asks: What have you? Answer: a, b, and h.

2. Devising a plan. If you cannot solve the proposed problem, look around for an appropriate related problem. Solver asks: What is a related problem that I can solve? Answer: The volume of a full pyramid. Solver asks: Can I restate the goal or the givens differently? Answer: Restate the goal as the volume of the full pyramid minus the volume of the smaller pyramid in the upper portion. Restate the givens to yield the height of the full pyramid and the height of the smaller pyramid in the upper portion.

3. Carrying out the plan. Use known formulas to find the height of the full pyramid, the height of the smaller pyramid, and the volumes of each.

4. Looking back. Solver asks: Can I use this method for other problems? Do I see the overall logic of this method?

Based on Polya (1965)

Box 3-8 gives an example of Polya's (1968) four phases of problem solving based on a mathematical problem. The "understanding the problem" phase requires that the solver ask what is given (a, b, and h are given) and what is unknown (F is unknown). The "devising a plan" phase requires the solver to "look around for an appropriate related problem." (Let's assume the solver already knows how to find the volume of a pyramid.) In addition, the solver must try to restate either the goal or the givens to fit the related problem. In the frustum problem, the solver may restate the goal to find the volume of the big pyramid minus the volume of the

BOX 3–9   Solution Tree for One Subject Working on Duncker's Tumor Problem

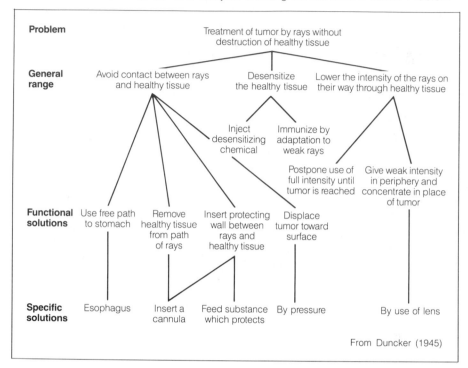

From Duncker (1945)

smaller pyramid and to then use the givens to produce the needed variables. The "carry out plan" phase requires the solver to make the calculations by using the formula for volume of a pyramid. The "looking back" phase requires the solver to see the logic of what he or she has done and to check to see if the method works on other problems.

As you can see, Polya's idea of restating the goal (working backward from the unknown to the givens) and restating the givens (working forward from the givens to the goal) are examples of the Gestalt idea of "restructuring." While Polya gives many excellent intuitions about how the restructuring event occurs and how to encourage it, the concept is still a vague one that has not been experimentally well studied.

Functional Solutions and Reformulations

Duncker (1945) attempted to study the stages in solving a problem empirically by giving a problem to a subject and asking him to report his thought process aloud as he was thinking. The problem Duncker used was the tumor problem shown in Box

3–9 and was stated as follows: "Given a human being with an inoperable stomach tumor, and rays which destroy organic tissue at sufficient intensity, by what procedure can one free him of the tumor by these rays and at the same time avoid destroying the healthy tissue which surrounds it?" The protocol of a typical subject led Duncker to conclude that problem solving proceeds by stages, going from general solutions to more specific ones, with the original problem being continually reformulated. An example of how problem solving moves from *general solutions* to *functional solutions* to *specific solutions* is shown in the solution tree for the tumor problem. For example, a general solution might be "avoid contact between rays and healthy tissue"; once solvers had thought of this they would generally hit upon several functional solutions such as "use free path to the stomach," or "insert protecting wall," or "remove healthy tissue from path" and ultimately reach specific solutions such as "use esophagus" or "insert a cannula." If that general plan or those functional solutions failed, solvers would think up new general and functional solutions such as "lower intensity of rays on their way through healthy tissue"; more specific ideas that followed from this general idea were "turn down ray when it gets near healthy tissue and turn it up when it gets to the tumor" (wrong), or "use focused lens" (right).

Like Polya and the other Gestalt psychologists, Duncker noted several basic phenomena in the process of problem solving.

Functional solution or *value* —elements of the problem must be seen in terms of their general or functional usefulness in the problem, and general or functional solutions precede specific solutions.

Reformulating or *recentering* —problem solving involves successive stages of reformulating (or restructuring) the problem with each new partial solution creating a new, more specific problem. In this example, the general solution of desensitizing healthy tissue is a reformulation of the original goal.

Suggestion from above —reformulating the goal to make it closer to the givens, for example, thinking of protecting the healthy tissue by somehow desensitizing it, similar to Polya's "working backward."

Suggestion from below —reformulating the givens so they more closely relate to the goal, for example, thinking of using the rays somehow in a weak form, similar to Polya's "working forward."

Another example comes from Duncker's (1945) 13 problem; "Why are all 6 place numbers of the form 276,276 or 591,591 or 112,112, and so on, divisible by 13?" The solution, according to Duncker, involves a suggestion from below to reformulate or recenter the originally given material from *abcabc* to *abc* $\times$ 1001. Once the solver restates the givens in this form it can be argued that any number divisible by 1001 is also divisible by 13. In his experiments, Duncker found that

BOX 3–10   Determining the Number of Stages in Problem Solving

---

Assumptions

1. Problem solving involves completing a sequence of stages. When one stage is completed, the solver goes on to work on the next.

2. Each stage is independent.

3. Each stage is equally difficult. Average time to move from any one stage to the next is constant.

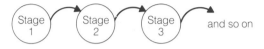

Stage 1   Stage 2   Stage 3   and so on

Based on Restle and Davis (1962)

---

when he told subjects "The numbers are divisible by 1001," over 59 percent of the subjects solved the problem, but when he gave the general rule or no help the solution rate was 15 percent or below. Thus, as Duncker noted, "the real difficulty of the 13 problem is overcome as soon as the common divisor 1001 emerges"—that is, as soon as the givens are reformulated.

Subgoals

More recently, there have been more sophisticated attempts to investigate how problems are reformulated into smaller problems or *subgoals* as Duncker suggested. One technique, developed by Restle and Davis (1962) is based on the idea that problem solving involves an individual's going through a number of independent and sequential stages and solving a subproblem at each stage that allows the solver to start work on the next stage (see Box 3–10). The number of stages, k, for any given problem can be roughly determined, according to the Restle and Davis argument, by the square of the average time to solution, t, divided by the square of the standard deviation of the time to solution, s. The theory is summarized in the formula, $k = t^2 \div s^2$.

Data from three different problems were used. The rope problem asks how it is possible for a prisoner to escape from a tower using a rope that is half as long as he needs by dividing the rope in half and tying the halves together. The answer—that he divides the rope lengthwise—takes an average of 131 seconds and a standard deviation of 115 seconds, yielding a value of $k = 1.3$. Thus the rope problem is a one-stage problem. A second problem was the word tangle: "If the puzzle you solved before you solved this one was harder than the puzzle you solved after you solved the puzzle you solved before you solved this one, was the puzzle you solved before you solved this one harder than this one?'' The answer—yes—took an average of 265 seconds with a standard deviation of 154 seconds so that k, the number of stages, is roughly three. Finally, the gold dust problem asks subjects to figure out how to get exactly 77 units of gold dust using containers of size 163, 14, 25, and 11. The answer—163 minus 25 minus 25 minus 14 minus 11 minus 11, or 163 minus 25 minus 25 minus 25 minus 11, and so on—took an average of 373 seconds with a standard deviation of 167, yielding approximately five stages. Although the Restle and Davis technique allows an empirical determination on the number of stages, it does not tell what those stages are; the model's assumption that all stages in the problem are equally difficult also does not seem to be correct.

A method for studying subgoals in problem solving that overcomes some of these problems was developed by Hayes (1965, 1966) in his study of spy problems (see Box 3–11). Subjects memorized a list of connections among spies and were then asked to tell out loud how to get a message from one spy to another. Hayes gave subgoals to some subjects such as, ''Get a message from JOE through APE and WATERFALL to CAT,'' while other subjects were not given subgoals but were told only, ''Get a message from JOE to CAT. The average times taken to make each of the nine required steps to solution for a typical problem are shown in Box 3–11. As the graph shows, the subgoals seemed to break the problem into three smaller chunks—from JOE to the third spy, APE, from the third spy to the sixth, WATERFALL, and from the sixth to the last, CAT. The subjects worked faster as they approached a subgoal and more slowly on the steps that followed subgoals. Apparently, after they reached one subgoal, there was a period in which the subjects thought about how to carry out the next subproblem, which was followed by their going rapidly through the steps to the next subgoal; they slowed again while figuring out how to solve the next subproblem, and so on. The subjects who were not given subgoals seem to have cut the problem into two main subproblems—their solution times fell moving from the given spy, JOE, to the fourth spy, there was a pause, and then the times speeded up moving from the fifth to the final spy, CAT. The fact that solution times tended to accelerate as a subject approached a subgoal and to slow on the steps following a subgoal suggests that the subjects restructured or chunked the problems into smaller ones and tried to solve the subproblems.

Thomas (1974) used a similar procedure to determine whether subjects imposed subgoals on a more difficult problem—the hobbits and orcs problem. The problem is to get three hobbits and three orcs across a river using a boat that can hold only one or two creatures at a time with at least one creature in the boat during each crossing. The other condition is that orcs must never outnumber hobbits on either bank of the river (Box 3–12A). An analysis of mean time to make each move and of errors on each move shows peaks at state 321 and 110 (Box 3–12B). The difficulties at these stages in the solution process are not completely determined by

BOX 3–11 Spy Problem

The Problem

Subjects memorized a list of connections for spies who can pass messages from one to the other, such as:

SHOWER to CLERK
DROUGHT to HILL
LARYNX to BETH
ADJECTIVE to SHOWER
HILL to HORSE
BEEF to LARYNX
ADJECTIVE to PARCHEESI
DROUGHT to KEVIN
SHOWER to BEEF
LARYNX to DROUGHT
BEEF to TAFT

The connections from the network (not shown to subjects):

ADJECTIVE → SHOWER → BEEF → LARYNX → DROUGHT → HILL
   ↓   ↓   ↓   ↓   ↓   ↓
PARCHEESI CLERK   TAFT   BETH   KEVIN   HORSE

Results

The average time for each move is shown below for subjects given subgoals (broken line) and subjects not given subgoals (solid line).

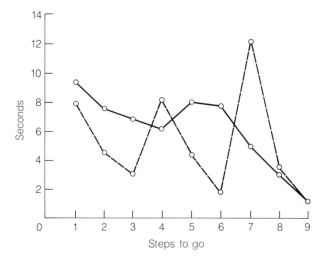

From Hayes (1966)

BOX 3–12 Steps in Solving the Hobbits and Orcs Problem

A. The Problem Space

Each state is specified by a three-digit code: (1) the number of hobbits on the starting side, (2) the number of orcs on the starting side, (3) the location of the boat—1 if it is on the starting side and 0 if it is on the opposite side.

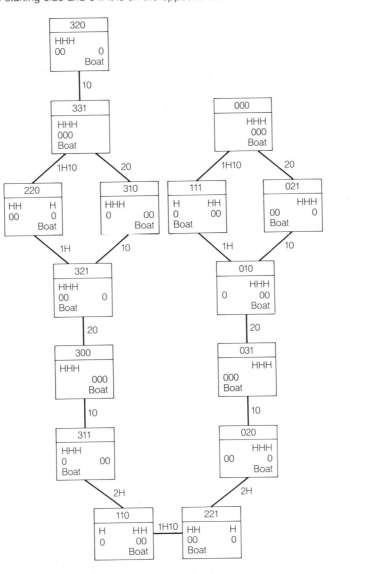

BOX 3–12, *continued*

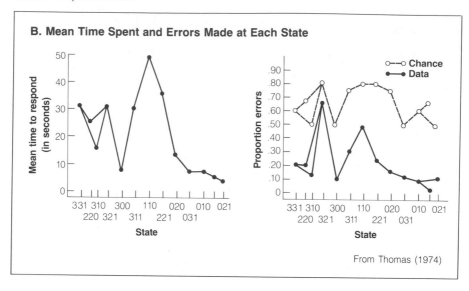

B. Mean Time Spent and Errors Made at Each State

From Thomas (1974)

the number of alternative responses, which seems to indicate that subjects cut the problem into three subproblems—from the start at 320 to state 310 or 220, from that point to 300 or 311, and from there to the goal, 000. As in Hayes' study, the subjects tended to divide problems into subproblems; their error rates and times seemed to fall as they neared a subgoal and to rise on the steps that directly followed subgoals.

RIGIDITY IN PROBLEM SOLVING

Problem-Solving Set

Another major contribution of the Gestalt psychologists is their finding that prior experience can have negative effects in certain new problem-solving situations. The idea that the reproductive application of past habits inhibits productive problem solving has been called *functional fixedness* (Duncker, 1945), *einstellung* (German for *attitude*) or *problem-solving set* (Luchins, 1942), and *negative transfer* (Bartlett, 1958).

The Luchins' work (Luchins, 1942; Luchins and Luchins, 1950) provides an often-cited example of how prior experience can limit an individual's ability to develop a solution rule of sufficient breadth and generality. Their water jar problem involved presenting subjects with the hypothetical situation of three jars of varying sizes and an unlimited water supply and asking them to figure out how to obtain a

BOX 3–13   A Water Jar Problem

| Problem | Given Jars of the Following Sizes | | | Obtain the Amount |
	A	B	C	
1.	29	3		20
2. Einstellung 1	21	127	3	100
3. Einstellung 2	14	163	25	99
4. Einstellung 3	18	43	10	5
5. Einstellung 4	9	42	6	21
6. Einstellung 5	20	59	4	31
7. Critical 1	23	49	3	20
8. Critical 2	15	39	3	18
9.	28	76	3	25
10. Critical 3	18	48	4	22
11. Critical 4	14	36	8	6

Possible Answers for Critical Problems (7, 8, 10, 11)

Problem	Einstellung Solution	Direct Solution
7	$49 - 23 - 3 - 3 = 20$	$23 - 3 = 20$
8	$39 - 15 - 3 - 3 = 18$	$15 + 3 = 18$
10	$48 - 18 - 4 - 4 = 22$	$18 + 4 = 22$
11	$36 - 14 - 8 - 8 = 6$	$14 - 8 = 6$

Performance of Typical Subjects on Critical Problems

Group	Einstellung Solution	Direct Solution	No Solution
Control (Children)	1%	89%	10%
Experimental (Children)	72%	24%	4%
Control (Adults)	0%	100%	0%
Experimental (Adults)	74%	26%	0%

Adapted from Luchins (1942)

required amount of water. The problems, in order of presentation (about two minutes allowed for each), are reproduced in Box 3–13.

Item 1 is an example-practice problem. The experimental group was given problems 2 through 11 in order, one at a time, to be solved by each subject without aid from the experimenter. The control group was given the same introduction and practice problem but began working on problems 7 through 11. Luchins called problems 2 through 6 *einstellung* problems because they all evoked the same problem-solving set of $b - a - 2c$ as a solution. Problems 7, 8, 10, and 11 were critical problems because they could be solved by either a shorter, more productive method ($a - c$ or $a + c$) or by the longer method used to solve 2 through 6. Problem 9 was inserted to help the subjects "recover" from their mechanized or einstellung response, since the $b - a - 2c$ formula would not work on this problem; the recovery, if any, could be noted by a greater tendency to use the shorter solution on 10 and 11 than on 7 and 8. Luchins performed this experiment on over 900 subjects ranging from elementary school students to students in his graduate seminars.

Typical results are shown in Box 3–13. The control group almost always discovered the short, direct solution whereas the experimental group frequently used the longer, *einstellung* solution even on problems 10 and 11. Luchins summarized the findings as follows (Luchins and Luchins, 1950): "This basic experiment and its variations have been administered by the author to over 900 subjects. Most of these subjects showed considerable einstellung effect. Recovery from mechanization was in general not large for adult groups and was negligible in most elementary school groups." Based on these findings, Luchins (1942, p. 15) noted the consequences of mechanized thought: "*Einstellung*—habituation—creates a mechanized state of mind, a blind attitude toward problems; one does not look at the problem on its own merits but is led by a mechanical application of a used method."

This monumental work provided the basis for the Gestalt claim that reproductive application of past habits could be a detriment to effective and productive problem solving in a new situation. There is, of course, another explanation that is often cited by associationist-oriented psychologists: that the experimental subjects who used the einstellung method to solve new problems were actually more efficient because they did not have to waste time trying to create a new method for each problem. However, the Luchins' results provide evidence that past experience can limit the type of solution a subject devises in a new situation.

Bartlett (1958) noted a similar effect, which he called *negative transfer,* when he observed how subjects solved the DONALD + GERALD = ROBERT problem shown in Box 3–14. The task was to substitute numbers for the letters, given that D = 5, that every number from 0 to 9 has its corresponding letter, and that each letter must be given a number different from any other letter. In observing his subjects, Bartlett (1958, p. 59) noted that much of the difficulty they had was due to their past habits or methods of solving addition and subtraction problems, such as working from right to left: "Several more students tried the problem, but couldn't do it. They substituted 5 for D and zero for T, but since no direct clue is provided for L and R, they said they couldn't get any farther. It seems that the habit of starting to make an addition sum from the right-hand column and continuing to the left with succeeding

BOX 3–14   Donald + Gerald = Robert Problem

```
   DONALD
 + GERALD
   ROBERT
```

"This is to be treated as an exercise in simple addition. All that is known is: (1) that D = 5; (2) that every number from 0–9 has a corresponding letter; (3) that each letter must be assigned a number different from that given for any other letter. The operation required is to find a number for each letter, stating the steps of the processes and their order."

From Bartlett (1958, p. 51)

columns was so deeply ingrained that they couldn't conceive of any other method of approach, and they soon tired of trying to find L and R by trial and error.''*

Functional Fixedness

Using a slightly more experimental approach, Duncker (1945) also investigated how past experience could limit problem-solving productivity. For example, he devised a diagram for his tumor problem with an arrow (representing the ray) going thru a black dot (representing the tumor) surrounded by a circle (representing the healthy tissue). When the diagram was shown with the problem, the solution rate was 9 percent compared to 37 percent when no diagram was given. This finding suggested to Duncker that the diagram helped to fix the function of the ray as a single line going through the body and thus blocked the ability of the subject to think of it as several rays focused on the tumor. Duncker called this phenomenon *functional fixedness* because the past experience of seeing the diagram limited the number of different functions a subject could devise for the ray.

Duncker thus defined functional fixedness as a mental block against using an object in a new way that is required to solve a problem. To investigate this phenomenon more carefully, he devised a series of problems that he thought might involve functional fixedness and presented them to subjects in his laboratory. For example, in the box problem (see Box 3–15), the subject was given three cardboard boxes, matches, thumb tacks, and candles. The goal was to mount a candle vertically on a nearby screen to serve as a lamp. Some subjects were given a box containing matches, a second box holding candles, and a third one containing tacks—

*The solution, by the way, is: T = 0, G = 1, O = 2, B = 3, A = 4, D = 5, N = 6, R = 7, L = 8, E = 9.

BOX 3–15   Materials in Duncker's Box Problem

Based on Duncker (1945)

preutilization of the boxes—while other subjects received the same supplies but with the matches, tacks, and candles outside the boxes—no preutilization. The solution—to mount a candle on the top of a box by melting wax onto the box and sticking the candle to it and then tacking the box to the screen—was much harder to discover when the boxes were given filled rather than empty. Duncker's explanation, like those of Luchins and Bartlett, was that the placement of objects inside a box helped to fix its function as a container, thus making it more difficult for subjects to reformulate the function of the box and think of it as a support.

In the paper-clip problem, the subject was given one large square, four small squares, several paper clips, and an eyelet screwed to an overhead beam. The task was to attach the small squares to the large one and hang it from the eyelet. The preutilization group had to use some of the paper clips to attach the small squares to the large one first, but for the group without preutilization the small squares were already stapled to it. The solution—bending one paper clip to form a hook from which to hang the large square—was much harder for the preutilization group to discover. Again, Duncker suggested that using the clip as an attacher made it more difficult for subjects to conceive of it in a different function, namely, as a hook. In all, half a dozen tasks of this sort were given; typical results were for the preutilization group to solve 58 percent and the group without preutilization to solve 97 percent.

Although these results are consistent with Luchins', they are suspect because there were only 14 subjects in Duncker's original study, the experiment was poorly specified, and no statistical analysis was performed. To overcome some of these problems, Adamson (1952) reran several of Duncker's experiments, including the box problem and the paper-clip problem. Fifty-seven subjects were divided into two groups—preutilization and no preutilization—and each subject received three different problems for a maximum of 20 minutes each. The results were similar to Duncker's original study. For example, with the box problem, 86 percent of the subjects solved the problem within 20 minutes when the boxes were presented empty, but only 41 percent solved the problem when the boxes were presented as containers. All subjects solved the paper-clip problem, but those in the preutilization group (the group that had to first use the paper clips to attach the squares together) took almost twice as much time.

Adamson's replication seemed to confirm Duncker's original idea—that subjects who utilize an object for a particular function will have more trouble in a problem-solving situation that requires a new and dissimilar function for the object. There is one drawback to the Duncker and Adamson experiments: since the same situation was used both for preutilization and for the new task, it was difficult to locate the source of the problems the preutilization subjects had; furthermore, there was no control for the experience the subjects had with the objects prior to the experiments. Birch and Rabinowitz (1951) conducted an experiment that attempted to overcome these two criticisms with a problem different from those used by Duncker. The two-cord problem, adapted from an experiment by Maier (1930, 1931), is shown in Box 3–16. In this experiment a subject was given a room with two cords hanging from the ceiling to the floor just out of reach of one another and two heavy objects, an electrical switch and an electrical relay, placed nearby. The goal was to tie the cords together. Some subjects, group S, were given a pretest task of completing an electrical circuit on a "breadboard" by using a switch; other subjects, Group R, were given the same pretest task, but were given a relay to use to complete the circuit; and a third group, the control Group C, was given no pretest experience. The solution required a subject to tie one of the cords to a heavy object, swing it as a pendulum and, while holding the other cord, catch the pendulum on the upswing. If the subjects had not solved the problem within nine minutes the experimenter gave a helpful hint by walking by one of the cords and "accidentally" setting it in motion. The results are shown in Box 3–16. All of the subjects solved the problem, but the Group R subjects tended to use the switch as a weight and the Group S subjects tended to use the relay as a weight. When asked why they used one heavy object instead of the other, subjects in both groups replied, "Anyone can see this one is better."

BOX 3–16 Functional Fixedness in the Two-Cord Problem

The Problem

Given two cords hanging from the ceiling and two heavy objects around the room, tie the cords together.

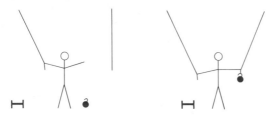

Frequency of Choice of Objects in Problem Solving

Group	N	Number Using Relay	Number Using Switch
Preutilization with Relay	10	0	10
Preutilization with Switch	9	7	2
No Preutilization	6	3	3

Based on data from Birch and Rabinowitz (1951)

These results seem to fit nicely with those of Duncker and with the idea of functional fixedness. Previous experience with the object as a relay made it much more difficult to think of it as a weight—previous experience had fixed the function of the object. The Gestalt psychologists would not, of course, claim that all previous experience is detrimental to problem solving. Broad, nonspecific, general experience and certain basic past learning "represents an essential repertoire of behavior which must be available for restructuring when the new situation demands"; however, "productive thinking is impossible if the individual is chained to the past," and in cases where a subject relies on very specific, limited habits, "past experience may become a hindrance" (Birch and Rabinowitz, 1951, p. 121).

There are the additional questions of how long the effects of functional fixedness last, and whether functional fixedness with respect to a certain object tends to affect similar objects. Adamson and Taylor (1954) investigated these questions with a variation of the two-cord problem just described. Before the subjects tackled this problem, they were given a task of working on an electrical circuit board with a pair of pliers. Then, when they tried to solve the two-cord problem, Adamson and Taylor found they were far less likely than control subjects to use those same pliers as a weight for the pendulum; in addition, they had more difficulty than control subjects in using another pair of pliers or even a pair of scissors as weights which, however, they preferred to using the original pliers. Apparently the effect of functional fixedness does spread to objects that are similar to the fixed object. However, the effect seems to fade with time, as Adamson and Taylor (1954) showed by giving the two-cord problem at varying intervals following the initial experience of their subjects with the pliers and the circuit board. They tested subjects immediately following the experience, one hour later, one day later, and one week later. The longer the time elapsed between the use of the pliers on the circuit board and the introduction of the two-cord problem, the larger the number of subjects who used the pliers as the weight.

A more recent series of experiments (Glucksberg and Danks, 1968; Glucksberg and Weisberg, 1966; Weisberg and Suls, 1973) has provided information concerning the role of labeling problem-solving elements. In the box problem, for example, subjects were more likely to generate the preferred answer of using the box as a platform if the instructions explicitly named the box as part of the given materials. Apparently, when only the tacks, matches, and candles were labeled in the instructions, the boxes that held them were not thought of as separate elements.

In another study, subjects were given elements for an electric circuit (such as a switch, bulb, battery, and wrench) and were asked to make a complete circuit. In contrast to the box experiment, when the wrench was explicitly named in the instructions, subjects were less likely to use it to conduct electricity and complete the circuit. Why does labeling an object help problem solving in the box problem but hinder problem solving in the circuit problem? Apparently, thinking of an object as a box is compatible with using it as a platform, but thinking of an object as a wrench is not compatible with using it as an electrical conductor. Thus, labels that might be associated with the desired use of an object in a problem are helpful in breaking functional fixedness, but labeling objects with names that are not associated with the desired use are likely to promote functional fixedness.

POSITIVE EFFECTS OF PAST EXPERIENCE

The work of Luchins, Duncker, and others has often been cited as evidence that reapplication of very specific, rigid, past habits can hinder productive problem solving. There is, of course, complementary evidence that in some cases specific past experience may aid problem solving. For example, Maier (1945) asked subjects to solve the string problem as shown in Box 3–17: given several wooden poles, clamps, and a string, subjects had to hang the string from the ceiling without damag-

BOX 3–17 Materials in Maier's String and Hatrack Problems

String Problem

Given several wooden poles, clamps, and string, hang the string from the ceiling to the floor without defacing the ceiling.

The solution is to tie the string around a pole and then brace the pole against the ceiling using poles clamped together.

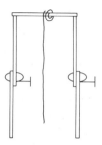

Hatrack Problem

Given poles and clamps, make a hatrack.

The solution is to clamp two poles together from floor to ceiling and use a clamp as a hook from which to hang a hat.

Based on Maier (1945)

ing it. The solution consisted of tying the string around one stick and bracing it horizontally against the ceiling at both ends with two long sticks made by clamping the wooden poles together. Another problem asked subjects to make a hatrack given objects similar to those in the preceding experiment. The solution to the hatrack problem consisted of clamping two sticks together to make a pole that reached from the floor to the ceiling and using the handle of the clamp to hang the hat. Of subjects with no prior experience with the string structure, only 24 percent solved the hatrack problem; of subjects who had solved the string problem, which had been removed from their sight, 48 percent solved the hatrack problem; and of subjects who had solved the string structure problem and could still see the solution, 72 percent solved the new problem.

Maier's results seem to conflict directly with those of Duncker and the others who found that past experience limited future problem-solving effectiveness. Instead of negative transfer, Maier found strong evidence for *positive transfer* —the fact that past experience with the string structure helped subjects in a new problem solving situation. In trying to reconcile the Maier experiment with those in the previous section, three facts are important: (1) the change from function one to function two is very small in Maier's experiment since the hatrack is part of the string structure, but the two functions of box as container and box as support are very different in the experiments by Duncker; (2) the change from the normal use to function one is great in Maier's experiment in that using a braced pole to hang a string is uncommon, but small in Duncker's experiments because boxes are often used as containers; (3) the first function facilitates the second function in Maier's experiment, but in the Duncker experiment the functions are mutually exclusive. Apparently, specific habits and experiences are useful in situations that require those specific ideas applied in much the same form, but are a hindrance in situations that require using objects in a new way.

One interpretation of the value of past experience is that in some cases it can make functions of objects available, especially if the past experience with a certain function of an object and the required function in a new situation are similar. Saugstad and Raaheim (1960; Raaheim, 1965) presented subjects with the following problem: given newspapers, string, pliers, rubber bands, and a nail, figure out a way to transfer a few steel balls from a glass jar on a wheeled platform to a bucket about 10 feet away from you without crossing a chalk line. (See Box 3–18.) The solution, believe it or not, is to bend the nail with the pliers to make a hook, attach the hook to the string, throw it out to catch the movable glass full of steel balls and pull it toward you, roll the newspapers into tubes that you hold in shape with the rubber bands, and drop the balls through the tubes into the bucket.

Suppose you gave the subjects, before starting the experiment, a bent nail and said, ''This object could be used to catch things with. Could you give some exam-

BOX 3–18   Materials in Saugstad and Raaheim's Transfer Problem

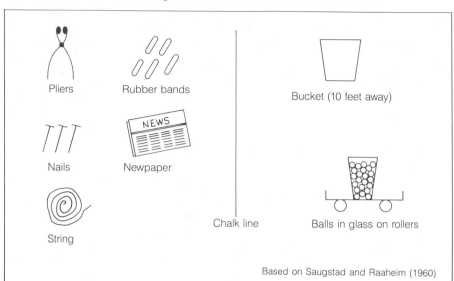

Pliers

Rubber bands

Bucket (10 feet away)

Nails

Newpaper

String

Chalk line

Balls in glass on rollers

Based on Saugstad and Raaheim (1960)

ples?'' and suppose you showed them the newspaper rolled into a tube and said, ''This object you may use to conduct something through. Can you give me some examples?'' Saugstad and Raaheim (1960, p. 97) called this ''making the functions of objects available''; Duncker would probably have called it giving the problem away. After 30 minutes on this problem, 95 percent of the subjects solved it if they had the experience described above, but only 22 percent of the subjects solved the problem if they had not been familiarized with the two new functions of the nail and the newspaper.

In a similar, slightly more subtle experiment, subjects were given the nail and the newspaper prior to the experiment and asked to think of all possible uses for them. They were then given the task of transporting the steel balls. Of the subjects who mentioned both the hook as possible function of the nail and the tube as a possible function of the newspaper during the pretest, 89 percent solved the problem; of subjects who mentioned either the hook or the tube function during the pretest but not both, 42 percent solved the problem; and of subjects who thought of neither function during the pretest, only 19 percent solved the problem. Again, Saugstad and Raaheim claimed that success in problem solving sometimes depends on appropriate functions being available to the solvers at the appropriate time.

''Making the functions available'' may result from general experience with the solution objects. For example, Birch (1945) examined the role of insight in apes—

over 20 years after Kohler—by placing some food out of reach outside the cage and giving them a hoe with which to rake it in. Only two out of four chimpanzees could solve this task, so Birch allowed them to play with short sticks for the next few days. The chimps invented many new uses for the sticks while playing with them, including prying, shoveling, and noise making. After a few days of such play, the apes were given the hoe problem again and this time they solved it quite easily. Apparently, insight is aided by and builds on useful past experiences.

Taken together, the work of Maier, of Saugstad and Raaheim, and of Birch seems to supplement the idea of functional fixedness described by Duncker: in situations where similar functions are required, past experience is an aid. Note, however, that the type of problem solving that Maier and Saugstad and Raaheim are discussing is very close to the definition of reproductive thinking. What these results indicate is that problems that seem to require productive solutions—reorganization of the problem elements—are more easily solved by a mind that is prepared with appropriate general past experiences. On the other hand, if those past experiences specifically tend to fix the function of objects in one way, creative problem solving can be hurt.

One way to resolve this problem, and one that most good teachers aim for, is to provide learners with certain basic, specific facts coupled with more general problem-solving techniques. Although Luchins successfully demonstrated that past experience in solving problems can limit problem-solving ability, there is also evidence that such practice can lead to a more general ability to deal with all sorts of problems. For example, Harlow (1949) gave monkeys problems (Box 3–19) in which they were given two (or three) objects on a tray and had to pick one up. If they picked up the "correct" object, they received a piece of banana. (When three objects were presented, the correct object was the odd object.) The monkeys were given the same problem over and over again, with the position of the objects randomly arranged on each trial. Then a new problem was presented with variations for hundreds of repetitions (monkeys are more patient than human subjects). Harlow found that the monkeys performed better on new problems as the experiment progressed; although it took them many trials to respond consistently to the early problems, they never made a mistake after the second trial on the problems presented toward the end of the experiment. Specific aspects of problems at the end were different or even opposite from those at the beginning, but the monkeys had apparently picked up a *general* strategy for responding. They seemed to follow a rule that we can express as, "If you get food for picking that object keep picking it, and if you do not, then pick the other object." Harlow called this use of general past experience, "learning set" or "learning to think." His work shows that general experience as well as specific can be an aid in problem solving if the problem situation resembles prior problems.

BOX 3–19   Materials Used in a Study of Learning Sets

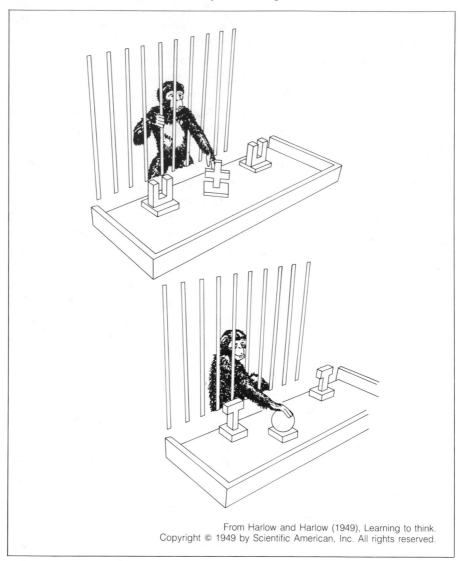

DIRECTION

The experiments by Maier, by Saugstad and Raaheim, and by Harlow indicate that part of solving a problem is finding out how it relates to past experience. Polya cited ''finding a related problem'' as a main factor in devising a solution plan, and Birch and Rabinowitz talked about using "an essential repertoire" of past behaviors and experiences in solving Duncker's problems. How does a problem solver find the relationship between past experience and the needed reformulation of the problem? According to Maier (1930; 1931; 1933), the leap to solution requires *direction*.

Since past experience alone is not enough for an original solution, a subject needs some organizing principle, some new way of looking at the problem situation, in short, some direction. Maier provided an example of the crucial importance of direction in his two-cord problem. In one experiment, he waited some time as the subject tried to solve the problem and then provided the first hint: he walked by the string, thus setting it in gentle motion. He waited a little more time, and if there was still no solution, gave a second hint: he handed the subject a pair of pliers and said, "This is all you need."

He waited again and if no solution occurred, repeated hint one. Of 61 college student subjects, 39 percent solved the problem before any hints were given and 38 percent solved it with hints. Those in the group who solved it with hints generally did so almost immediately after the hints were given—an average of 42 seconds from the last hint to solution. The solution appeared suddenly and in complete form and many subjects were not consciously aware of hint one. From this experiment, Maier concluded that direction is needed in problem solving—that subjects need some clue, which may be either externally or internally generated, about how to reformulate the problem. Putting the string in motion helped the subjects to reformulate the function of the string as a swing on a pendulum. Apparently, direction can be very subtle, and in some cases the problem solver does not realize it has occurred: "When an idea suddenly appears, what sets it off may be lost to consciousness" (Maier, 1933, p. 192).

In a more subtle use of direction, Cofer (1951) used the same two-cord situation but had his subjects memorize lists of words before they were given the problem. Subjects who had memorized lists with words such as rope, swing, and pendulum produced more solutions than subjects who had memorized neutral words.

In another variation of the same problem, Battersby, Teuber, and Bender (1953) provided direction by restricting the number of potential solution objects among three groups of subjects. The restricted group could only use objects the experimenter put on the table; the objects were added to the table every two minutes for a total of five objects with any one capable of serving as a weight for the pendulum. The less restricted group could use any object in the room including the five objects the experimenter was adding at the same rate. Finally, the unrestricted group could use any object in the room including the five objects that were already placed upon the table with no attention drawn to them. The average solution times were much faster for the restricted group (2.4 minutes) than for the less restricted (7.5 minutes) or the unrestricted group (15.2).

EVALUATION

The Gestaltists attempted to understand some highly complex mental processes—
what they called "productive thinking." They enriched the study of thinking by
introducing several provocative ideas: the distinction between productive and reproductive thinking, the idea that thinking occurs in stages, and the demonstration of
rigidity of problem-solving set. Their main tool for understanding such processes
was the idea that problem solving involves reorganizing or restructuring the problem. Most critics point out, however, that the theory is much too vague to be tested
directly in experiments. More recently, cognitive psychologists have been partially
successful in clarifying some of the ideas of the Gestaltists, and their work will be
discussed in Part III on information processing.

Suggested Readings

Johnson, D. M. *A systematic introduction to the psychology of thinking.* New York: Harper &
Row, 1972. Chapters 4, 5, and 7 survey the Gestalt approach.
Katona, G. *Organizing and memorizing.* New York: Columbia University Press, 1940. This
monograph describes Katona's experiments on learning to solve matchstick and card
problems.
Kohler, W. *The mentality of apes.* New York: Harcourt, 1925. A famous study of problem solving
and insight in apes.
Luchins, A. S., and Luchins, E. H. *Rigidity of behavior: A variational approach to Einstellung.*
Eugene, Oreg.: University of Oregon Press, 1959. Discusses rigidity in problem solving.
Polya, G. *How to solve it.* Garden City, N.Y.: Doubleday, 1957. A mathematician explains "how
to" solve problems.
Wason, P. C., and Johnson-Laird, P. N. *Thinking and reasoning.* Baltimore: Penguin, 1968.
Articles by Duncker, by Maier, by Luchins and Luchins, and by Adamson provide an excellent
collection of basic Gestalt research and theory in problem solving.
Wertheimer, M. *Productive thinking.* New York: Harper & Row, 1959. A Gestalt view of problem
solving and how to teach it.

CHAPTER 4

MEANING:
Thinking as
Representing Problems

Meaning Theory Definition of Thinking

Two Kinds of Cognitive Structure

Concretizing

Activity

Imagery

Problem Representation

Suppose you were solving "oddity problems" in which your job was to circle the word that does not belong. Try this problem:

SKYSCRAPER   CATHEDRAL   TEMPLE   PRAYER

If you circled PRAYER, your response is consistent with the results that have generally been obtained in experiments with this kind of problem (Judson & Cofer, 1956). Now try the following problem:

CATHEDRAL   PRAYER   TEMPLE   SKYSCRAPER

If you circled SKYSCRAPER, your response is also consistent with Judson & Cofer's (1956) results.

In fact, these researchers found that in many ambiguous oddity problems like these, the order of presentation of the words was very important. The first problem, for example, evoked the concept of building while the second evoked the idea of religion. One explanation of this shift is that problem solving requires assimilation of the problem into the past experience of the subject; that is, the subject must find what part of his or her past experience will help in the interpretation of the problem.

This chapter will focus on the issue of how we interpret and relate a problem situation to a particular aspect of our individual past experience.

MEANING THEORY DEFINITION OF THINKING

You will remember from Chapter 3 that the Gestalt psychologists view thinking as restructuring or relating the elements of a problem in a new way. According to Duncker, this process often involves what he called finding the *function* of problem-solving elements and what Maier reported as the importance of *direction* in restructuring. Many of these Gestalt ideas are closely tied to a slightly different view of thinking which we call here *meaning theory*. The Gestalt view of thinking involves finding how problem elements relate to one another, that is, internal relations among elements. The meaning view of thinking involves finding how the present problem relates to those concepts and ideas that already exist in a problem solver's memory, that is, external relations between elements and schemata. The problem must be assimilated or incorporated into the thinker's own experience and must be translated into familiar terms. According to this view, thinking is mainly a process of figuring out which schema or set of past experiences the new problem should be related to and then interpreting and restructuring the new situation in accord with the particular schema that is selected. When a problem situation is assimilated to schemata that are not useful, the result is what the Gestalt psychologists call "functional fixedness."

Obviously, the meaning theory adds a new element to the Gestalt interpretation—the idea, albeit vague, of schemata and of assimilation. Bartlett (1932, p. 201) popularized the concept of the schema and attempted to define it as follows: "Schema refers to an active organization of past reactions which must always be supposed to be operating in any well-adapted organic response." He expressed the idea of assimilation as a search for the appropriate "setting" or "schema" in past experience: "Whenever such settings are found, facts of 'meaning' emerge . . . all the cognitive processes, from perceiving to thinking, are ways in which some fundamental 'effort after meaning' seeks expression. Speaking very broadly, such effort is simply the attempt to connect something that is given with something other than itself'' (p. 227).

TWO KINDS OF COGNITIVE STRUCTURE

More recently, the concept of assimilation to schema has been expressed as ''assimilation to cognitive structure'' (Ausubel, 1968). Although there are various ways to define *schema* and *cognitive structure,* a lack of precise operational definitions for any of them suggests that it is not useful to detail the differences at this time. A major contribution of the meaning theory, however, is a distinction between two types of cognitive structure—two types of knowledge in a problem solver's memory:

> *Meaningful* (Ausubel, 1968), or *propositional* (Greeno, 1973) knowledge, which is made up of concepts from general experience such as, ''Collies are dogs.''
>
> *Rote* (Ausubel, 1968) or *algorithmic* (Greeno, 1973) knowledge, which is made up of mechanical formulas or rules for how to operate on concepts, such as $a + b - 2c$.

Problem-solving information may be assimilated to different types of schemata and thus result in different types of problem-solving performances. For example, Bransford and Johnson (1972) found that giving their subjects the title *before* reading a story greatly increased performance on a comprehension test, but giving the title *after* reading had little effect. Knowing the title in advance apparently told the subjects how to assimilate the material and hence allowed an encoding that was useful for later problem solving.

In a study on solving binomial probability problems, Mayer and Greeno (1972) varied the sequencing of instruction in the following manner: group 1, the concepts group, began by learning about general concepts such as ''trial,'' ''success,'' and ''probability of success'' in terms of their past experience with batting averages or the probability of rain, and gradually learned to put the concepts together into a formula, while group 2, the formula group, began with the formula and gradually learned how the component concepts figured in calculating with it. Although both groups received the same general information—albeit in different ordering and emphasis—and the same examples, they showed completely different patterns of performance on a subsequent problem-solving test. The formula group performed best on solving problems that were very much like those in the instruction booklet (near transfer), but very poorly on questions about the formula and on problems they should have recognized as impossible to solve (far transfer); the concepts group showed the reverse pattern. These results were taken as evidence that the two instructional methods produced "structurally different learning outcomes"—one, the formula group, which supported near transfer and the other, the concepts group, which improved far transfer. Mayer and Greeno (1972, p. 166) discussed these findings using the idea that the two groups had assimilated the problem-solving concepts to different schemata: "New learning involves development of cognitive structure that results from relating new ideas and accommodating existing structures. According to this idea about learning, different instructional procedures could activate different aspects of existing cognitive structure. And since the outcome of learning is jointly determined by the new material and the structure to which it is assimilated, the use of different procedures could lead to the development of markedly different structures during the learning of the same new concept." Apparently, the formula group assimilated the new information to a narrow range of past experience with computation and formulas (algorithmic) while the concepts group connected the new information to more general experience with probability situations.

In a related study, Mayer (1975) taught a simple computer programming language to subjects using a standard 10-page text. Some of the subjects were introduced to a concrete model of the computer expressed in familiar terms prior to learning and were allowed to use this model during learning; other subjects were introduced to the same model after they had received the instruction. For the model, the memory was a scoreboard, the program was a shopping list with an arrow, input was a ticket window, and output was a telephone message pad. On a subsequent transfer test, the after group was better at writing simple programs like those taught in the booklet, but the before group was better at tasks that had not been specifically taught, such as interpreting what a program would do or writing complex looping programs. Apparently, the model served as a useful cognitive structure that allowed the subjects to relate new information to other knowledge they already had in memory; this broader learning outcome produced better transfer performance.

CONCRETIZING

As the previous studies suggest, another contribution of the meaning theory is the idea that representing the problem in a concrete way may result in a different method of solution than when it is expressed in abstract words. For example, Box 3–6 gave an example of a method used by Dienes to make the quadratic formula concrete. The supposed advantage of concretizing a difficult abstract problem is that it enables the problem solver to represent it quickly in familiar terms.

Brownell and Moser (1949) investigated the effects of making arithmetic problems "meaningful" to third-grade children. One group of several hundred children was taught a procedure for subtraction by using concrete objects like bundles of

BOX 4–1   How To Make Arithmetic Meaningful

Standard Method (Mechanical)

65	I can't take 8 from 5 so I think of 5 as 15.
− 28	8 from 15 is 7, and I write 7.
	Since I thought of 5 as 15, I must think of 6 as 5.
	2 from 5 is 3, and I write 3.

Meaningful Method

65	I can't take 8 from 5, so I borrow a ten from the 6 tens.
− 28	I cross out the 6 and write a little "5" to show that I borrowed a ten.
	I write a little "1" in front of the 5 to show that I now have 15 instead of 5.
	Then I subtract.

Weaver and Suydam (1972) point out that in the meaningful instruction for this sub-traction problem the teachers led pupils to understand the procedures by: using actual objects (for example, bundles of sticks) and drawings if necessary, writing the example in expanded notation, writing the "crutch" digit, and delaying learning of the verbal pattern until they understood it.

Adapted from Brownell and Moser (1949)

---

sticks with the subtraction rules of borrowing and grouping by tens shown in terms of rearranging the sticks. Another group was taught in "purely mechanical rote fashion" by being given the rules verbally at the outset of learning with no further explanation. Although both groups were taught to perform equally well, the children who had learned with the stick bundles performed much better on later tests with different problems (Box 4–1).

Using results obtained from similar earlier research, Brownell (1935) developed what he called a "meaning theory" of arithmetic learning based on the idea that students must understand how problem-solving rules relate to their past experiences and not simply memorize responses for quick computations. "If one is to be successful in quantitative thinking, one needs a fund of meanings, not a myriad of automatic responses" (p. 10). "Drill is recommended when ideas and processes already understood are to be practiced to increase proficiency" (p. 19). Brownell's view of problem solving was based on "full recognition of the value of children's experiences'' and aimed at making ''arithmetic less a challenge to the pupil's memory and more a challenge to his intelligence'' (p. 31). Unfortunately, an understanding of what is ''meaningful'' problem solving and how to produce it are still not well known, and most mathematics teachers probably must rely on a set of intuitions about quantitative thinking that involves both the importance of meaning—however defined—and computation.

Another attempt to foster better problem-solving performance by concretizing a problem was reported by Luchins and Luchins (1950). They made the water jar problems discussed in Chapter 3 concrete by supplying their subjects with cups and water. When sixth-graders were given these problems, all but two of them calculated the solution with paper and pencil first before they used the cups, and 68 percent gave einstellung solutions on the first two critical problems. Of the two who did not choose to use paper and pencil, a much lower einstellung effect was found, thus suggesting some aid from making the task concrete. However, when the sixth-graders were not allowed to use paper and pencil, many were not able to solve the problems using only the concrete objects. When college students were given the same problem with concrete objects, 60 percent showed the einstellung effect on the first two critical problems if they were allowed to use paper and pencil, and 55 percent showed the same effect if they were not. Apparently, concretizing the situation slightly reduced but did not eliminate the einstellung effect or mechanization of thought, in this case. One reason for the difficulty in eliminating the einstellung effect, according to Luchins and Luchins, was that the students carried over school-learned attitudes toward problem solving that counteracted the experimental manipulations.

ACTIVITY

There has been much interest in the idea that when students discover for themselves how to solve a problem, they learn something different than when they are simply given the solution. One explanation for this supposed difference is that when people actively work at solving problems they are trying to fit them into their knowledge, but when they are given the solution rules they relate them to a much narrower set of past experiences with rote-learned cognitive structures. Although active discovery learning is generally believed to result in better transfer and retention, there has been little experimental research to confirm it. As Wittrock (1966, p. 33) points out, ''Many strong claims for learning by discovery are made in educational psychology. But almost none of these claims has been empirically substantiated or even clearly tested in an experiment.''

Gagné and Smith (1962) investigated the role of active participation on the part of the problem solver in solving the disk problem (Ewert and Lambert, 1932) or what

BOX 4–2   The Disk Problem

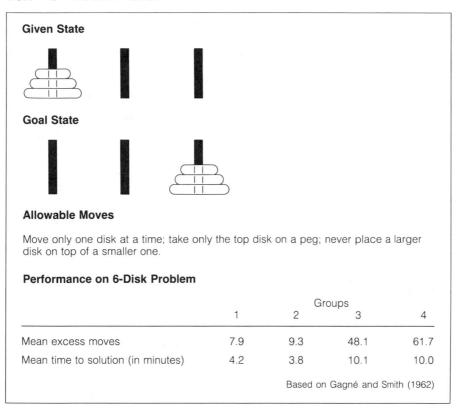

Given State

Goal State

Allowable Moves

Move only one disk at a time; take only the top disk on a peg; never place a larger disk on top of a smaller one.

Performance on 6-Disk Problem

	Groups			
	1	2	3	4
Mean excess moves	7.9	9.3	48.1	61.7
Mean time to solution (in minutes)	4.2	3.8	10.1	10.0

Based on Gagné and Smith (1962)

Ernst and Newell (1969) called the tower of Hanoi problem. This problem, shown in Box 4–2, is as follows: given three pegs with a number of disks on peg 1 arranged in order of size with the smallest on top, move the disks from peg 1 to peg 3 in the least number of moves, moving them one at a time and never putting a larger disk on top of a smaller one.

In four groups, the subjects solved this problem using 2, 3, 4, and 5 disks in order under the following conditions: group 1 (the verbalize and think group), in which the subjects were instructed to state the reason for each move and to think of a general principle involved, group 2 (the verbalize group), which received only the instruction to verbalize, group 3 (the think group), which was told only to think of a general principle, and group 4 (the control group), which received none of these instructions. All the subjects eventually found the solutions to all four problems with group 3 and group 4 taking less time but making more moves. However, on a transfer problem using six disks in which no verbalizations were required, the subjects who had verbalized during the previous four problems performed significantly better than the nonverbalization subjects. The effect of the instruction to think of a general principle was not significant. (See Box 4–2.) Apparently, the active verbalizations given for each move provoked subjects to think more about the basic rule involved in the problem, so that they were better able to transfer to a new situation.

In another study, Gagné and Brown (1961) allowed subjects to solve series sum problems such as, "What is the sum and formula for the sum of $1 + 3 + 5 + 7 + 9 . . . ?$" Some of the subjects (guided discovery group) were allowed to solve a set of problems with the help of some hints while others were given the same examples but were provided with the rules and answers. Although the guided discovery group took longer to learn, they performed much faster and made many fewer errors on subsequent transfer tasks that involved similar but different series sum problems.

Similar results were obtained by Roughead and Scandura (1968) who gave some subjects, the rule discovery group, three series sum examples *with* rules, followed by three examples to be solved using the same rule. Other subjects, the discovery rule group, received the same problems but in reversed order; that is, this group had to make up their own rules for the first three problems and were then given the rule with the second three problems. Although the discovery rule group had more trouble with the original problems, it outperformed the rule discovery group on a transfer task. The results obtained by Gagné and Brown and by Roughead and Scandura seem to show that some activity on the part of the problem solver results in a broader learning. However, it should be noted that activity per se does not guarantee this productive problem solving; for example, a learner who fails to solve a problem by discovery will have nothing to add to memory no matter how actively he or she has been thinking.

IMAGERY

Another way a person can relate a problem to past experience is to form an image. DeSoto, London, and Handel (1965), for example, have suggested that subjects solve linear ordering syllogisms by imagery. A subject who is told that "A is better than B" forms an image of A above B, and if he or she is then told "A is worse than C," puts C above A on the image. When asked, "Is B better than C?" the subject can refer to this image, and respond "No." Further refinements (Huttenlocher, 1968) and objections (Clark, 1969) to this "spacial paralogic" theory of syllogistic reasoning are discussed in a later chapter.

Paige and Simon (1966) investigated whether the kind of visual representations used to solve mathematical problems influenced performance. They gave a group of tenth-graders a series of algebra story problems that included several contradictions

BOX 4-3 Algebra Story Problems

The Problem

A board was sawed into two pieces. One piece was two-thirds as long as the whole board and was exceeded in length by the second piece by 4 feet. How long was the board before it was cut?

The Diagrams

Subjects who failed to recognize the contradictions tended to draw unintegrated diagrams such as

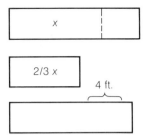

Subjects who recognized the contradictions tended to draw integrated diagrams such as

From Paige and Simon (1966)

and ambiguities like the one in Box 4-3. In addition, they asked the subjects to draw diagrams representing the information in the problem. The students who solved the problem correctly (or recognized the contradictions) were more likely to produce integrated diagrams. Nonsolvers tended to produce a series of diagrams, each representing a translation of a sentence in the story problem, or to change the information in the story into a diagram that made sense but differed from what was presented.

Another example, attributed to the Gestalt psychologist Duncker, concerns the following monk problem:

A monk began to climb a mountain at sunrise. He reached the temple at the top as the sun was setting and meditated all night. At sunrise of the next day, he came down the mountain, following the same path, but moving at a faster rate, of course. When he reached the bottom he proclaimed: "There is one spot along this path that I passed at

BOX 4–4 The Monk Problem

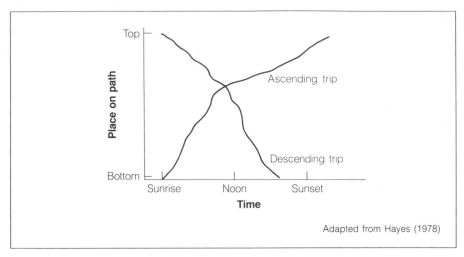

Adapted from Hayes (1978)

exactly the same time of day on my way up the mountain as on my way down.'' Can you prove that the monk is correct?

If you try to represent this problem algebraically or even in words, you will have a difficult time. However, if you visualize the problem as in Box 4–4, you will see that there must be a point at which the time of day is the same for the ascending and descending trips. Another way to state the problem is to say there are two monks, one at the bottom going up and one at the top going down, and to ask whether they will meet, or be at the same place at the same time. The problem is solved when you can think of the ascending and descending trips occurring simultaneously on the same day.

These results suggest that translation of problem information to a visual representation may involve a sort of assimilation and that integrated visual diagrams may be useful tools in certain types of problem solving.

PROBLEM REPRESENTATION

The meaning theory suggests that subtle differences in the way a problem is presented could have vastly different effects on how a subject assimilates the problem and thus on problem-solving performance. For example, consider the problem shown in Box 4–5 based on a similar example by Kohler (1969). The problem is to determine the length of line *l* in the circle. The figure on the left half of the box generally encourages subjects to work on manipulating the triangle and often makes

BOX 4–5   The Circle Problem

The Problem

Determine the length of the line *l*, if you know the radius of the circle is 5 inches.

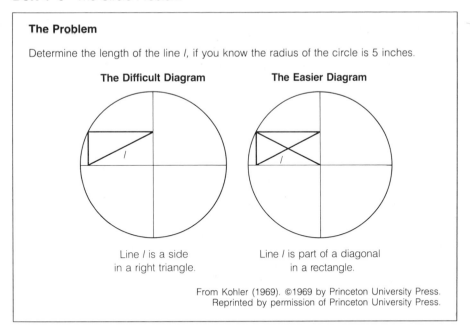

| The Difficult Diagram | The Easier Diagram |

Line *l* is a side
in a right triangle.

Line *l* is part of a diagonal
in a rectangle.

From Kohler (1969). ©1969 by Princeton University Press.
Reprinted by permission of Princeton University Press.

the problem quite hard to solve. However, if the problem is represented as trying to find an equivalent for line *l*, as in the figure on the right of Box 4–5 it becomes much easier. In the latter case the subjects work on manipulating the rectangle, which includes a radius. Kohler's example suggests that apparently minor differences in representation can influence how a problem is assimilated, in this case, as a problem about a triangle or as a problem about a rectangle.

Consider another example, this time an algebra story problem: "Two train stations are fifty miles apart. At 2 P.M. one Saturday afternoon, two trains start toward each other, one from each station. Just as the trains pull out of the stations, a bird springs into the air in front of the first train and flies ahead to the front of the second train. When the bird reaches the second train it turns back and flies toward the first train. The bird continues to do this until the trains meet. If both trains travel at the rate of 25 miles per hour and the bird flies at 100 miles per hour, how many miles will the bird have flown before the trains meet?" As Posner (1973, pp. 150–151) points out, if subjects interpret this problem in terms of the bird's flight pattern, the computations to determine the distance on each hop between the trains can become very difficult. However, if the problem asks instead, "how many hours will have elapsed, and how many miles will the bird have flown before the trains meet?" then the problem will more likely be interpreted as determining the elapsed

BOX 4–6   The Horse Problem

Representation 1

A man bought a horse for $60 and sold it for $70. Then he bought it back again for $80 and sold it for $90. How much did he make in the horse business?

a. lost $10
b. broke even
c. made $10
d. made $20
e. made $30

Representation 2

A man bought a white horse for $60 and sold it for $70. Then he bought a black horse for $80 and sold it for $90. How much money did he make in the horse business?

a. lost $10
b. broke even
c. made $10
d. made $20
e. made $30

Adapted from Maier and Burke (1967)

time; since the bird travels at 100 miles per hour, it can easily be determined that the bird flew 100 miles. Again, a minor change in representation can influence whether subjects assimilate the problem to the bird's path or to elapsed time.

Maier and Burke (1967) investigated different ways of representing story problems and found that minor changes in wording had important effects. As an example, look at the horse problem in Box 4–6. Subjects in Maier and Burke's experiment performed quite poorly on this problem when they were given the first representation, getting the correct answer ($20) less than 40 percent of the time. However, when the problem was changed as shown in the bottom half of Box 4–6 and given to a new group of subjects, the solution rate was 100 percent. Apparently, the first representation encouraged the subjects to think about *one* horse, whereas the second representation encouraged them to interpret the problem as two separate and independent transactions.

Adams (1974) has devoted a book, *Conceptual Blockbusting*, to techniques for breaking conceptual blocks, which he defines as "mental walls which block the problem solver from correctly perceiving a problem or conceiving its solution" (p. 11). As an example, consider the nine-dot problem shown in Box 4–7; it requires that four straight lines be drawn without lifting the pencil from the paper so that each

BOX 4–7   Conceptual Blocks in the Nine-Dot Problem

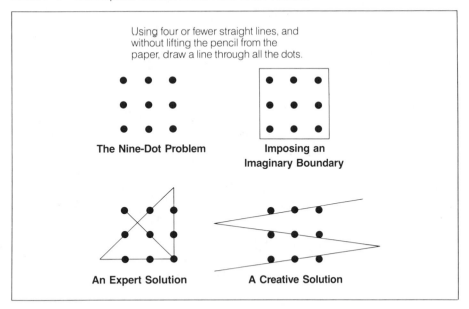

Using four or fewer straight lines, and without lifting the pencil from the paper, draw a line through all the dots.

The Nine-Dot Problem

Imposing an Imaginary Boundary

An Expert Solution

A Creative Solution

dot is crossed by one of the lines. According to Adams, most subjects "delimit the problem too closely"; for example, a subject might assume that the lines must be drawn within an imaginary boundary, as shown in the second panel of Box 4–7. One possible solution that is preferred by "experts" is given in the third panel of the box. The problem solver must go outside the self-imposed square boundary. Adams also suggests another creative solution that uses lines that do not go through the center of the dots, as shown in the fourth panel of the box. This solution involves overcoming another self-imposed limit on the problem—namely, realizing that it was not necessary to draw the lines through the center of each dot. Thus, Adams concludes that one major kind of conceptual block is the tendency to impose too many constraints on the problem, that is, to represent the problem in a way that limits the potential kinds of solutions. Overcoming conceptual blocks is similar to overcoming functional fixedness or einstellung, as discussed in the previous chapter; in these cases, look for alternative ways of representing the problem. Such blocks could also be reduced if the problem instructions included statements such as, "The lines may extend beyond the dots," or "The lines need not go through the exact center of each dot." (Chapter 13 deals more closely with techniques for stimulating creative problem solving.)

These examples suggest that seemingly minor factors influence how a subject represents a problem and thus affect problem solving.

EVALUATION

The meaning theory is closely related to Gestalt theory and is often not explicitly separated from it. While Gestalt theory emphasizes internal structure—how problem solving elements relate to one another—meaning theory contends that this restructuring process is guided by an additional process—finding external relations between the present problem-solving elements and other concepts in the thinker's memory. Unfortunately, the meaning theory suffers from several of the main defects of Gestalt theory, including lack of clarity and lack of experimental testability. Developments in the field of human verbal learning have some promise of spilling over into this area; for example, Ausubel's concept of "advance organizer" suggests that presenting learners with outlines or previews before learning will guide and aid them in the assimilation process. However, the task facing supporters of the meaning theory of thinking at present is to distinguish it clearly from Gestalt theory and express it in ways that invite testability.

Suggested Readings

Ausubel, D. P. *Educational psychology: A cognitive view.* New York: Holt, Rinehart & Winston, 1968. Chapters 2, 3, 14, 15, and 16 provide a statement of the assimilation-to-schema idea and its relationship to problem solving.
Bartlett, F. C. *Remembering.* London: Cambridge University Press, 1932. Bartlett's experiments and the theory of assimilation to schema.

BASIC THINKING TASKS

Chapters 5 and 6 discuss the basic tasks that have been associated with the study of thinking. Chapter 5 introduces you to inductive tasks such as concept learning. In these tasks, the problem solver is given a series of instances and must induce a rule that will predict future instances. Chapter 6 introduces you to deductive tasks such as syllogistic reasoning. In deduction, you are given premises and must logically deduce a conclusion, using the rules of logic. Both induction and deduction have long interested philosophers, and both received intensive study when scientific psychology turned its attention to human cognition. Induction and deduction represent the two most widely studied types of task in cognitive psychology.

The research strategy suggested in Chapters 5 and 6 takes a particular kind of task and then tries to study in detail how humans solve that task. Unlike the historical chapters (Chapters 1 through 4), which relied on one general theoretical perspective, Chapters 5 and 6 allow the study of problem solving to be driven by the particular type of task under consideration. These chapters describe human problem solving for specific prototypical tasks.

Chapters 5 and 6 present the basic research and explanations of how people solve inductive and deductive problems. Although there are many other problem-solving tasks, you should not regard these chapters as narrowly focused on simple tasks. Instead, induction and deduction were selected for intensive study by experimental psychologists (and by philosophers before them) because they represent cognitive processes that are the building blocks of all human cognition. Indeed, induction and deduction were chosen because they are prototypical tasks that are at the core of human intellectual life. Thus, if you are able to learn about how people solve inductive and deductive problems, what you have learned may be applicable to a wider variety of problems.

CHAPTER 5

RULE INDUCTION:
Thinking as Hypothesis Testing

Concept Formation Task

Suppose you have in front of you a pile of cards with pictures of different colors, shapes, sizes, and number of objects. The colors are RED or GREEN, the shapes are CIRCLE or SQUARE, the sizes are SMALL or LARGE, and the number of objects is ONE or

TWO. The experimenter picks out one card and places it in one of two boxes—Box Yes or Box No. Each time the experimenter picks out a card you must "guess" which box it belongs in. The cards and their group, Yes or No, are shown in Box 5–1. Cover the column marked Correct Group with a piece of paper and try to guess the group membership for each card, then check the correct answer and go on. See how long it takes you to predict group membership without error.

In another example of this kind of task, an experimenter enters the room, points down to the metal legs of a table, and says, "Oogle." Then he goes to a wooden chair, lifts it for all to see, points up to it and says, "Aagle." Having accomplished these two "scientific" tasks, he moves toward a door, points down to the metal doorknob and again utters, "Oogle." Next he points up to the top half of the wooden door and says, "Aagle." Suppose you were in a classroom experiencing all this; by now you might be sitting a little higher in your seat with your eyes brightening up a bit. When the experimenter points to the spout of a water fountain, what response do you suppose fills the room?

A chorus of "Oogle" you say? To this the experimenter smiles and replies, "No, it's an aagle." This process of pointing to things and telling to which category they belong continues until the people in the room are getting long runs of correct anticipations. The rule, the subjects later report, is based on which way the experimenter's finger points: if it points up, the object is an "oogle," if it points down, the object is an "aagle."

Consider another example. Young Billy is looking out the window and sees a poodle. His mother points to the poodle and says, "Dog." Then a German shepherd walks by and again mom points and says, "Dog." Next, a terrier wanders down the street and again mom points and says, "Dog." By now Billy is beginning to catch on, so when a new creature strolls into view he jumps up and down wildly, pointing to the little animal and shouting, "Dog!" However, this time his mom says, "No, Billy, that's a cat."

All these tasks are examples of *concept learning* because the subject must learn a rule for classifying objects into mutually exclusive categories. In general, each particular presentation of a to-be-classified stimulus is called a *trial* or *instance* (for example, one-red-large-circle is the first instance of a No category), each instance may have several *dimensions* (number, color, size, and so on), and each dimension may have several possible *values* or *features* (red or green color, large or small size, and so on).

These examples illustrate two main types of concept-learning tasks. When all the basic stimulus dimensions are described in advance to the subject who must then identify the relevant rule, this type of concept learning is called *concept identification;* in the first example, for instance, you were told all the dimensions such as red versus green color, large versus small shape, and so on. When the subject does not know the basic set of potentially important stimulus dimensions and must develop or produce it in addition to identifying the relevant rule, the task is called *concept*

BOX 5–1 A Concept-Learning Task

You will be given a series of stimuli, individually, with each item varying in shape (circle or square), size (large or small), color (red or green), and number (one or two). Cover the column labeled "Correct Group" with a folded piece of paper. For each item listed on the left, guess its group (either Group Yes or Group No), then slide the folded paper down one notch to check the correct answer, and so on.

Instance	Your Prediction	Correct Group
1 red large square	_____	No
1 green large square	_____	No
2 red small squares	_____	Yes
2 red large circles	_____	No
1 green large circle	_____	No
1 red small circle	_____	Yes
1 green small square	_____	Yes
1 red small square	_____	Yes
2 green large squares	_____	No
1 red large circle	_____	No
2 green small circles	_____	Yes
2 red small circles	_____	Yes
2 green large circles	_____	No
2 green small squares	_____	Yes
2 red large squares	_____	No
1 green small circle	_____	Yes

formation; the oogle-aagle problem, in which you were not told that the dimensions included wood versus metal, up versus down finger, and so on, is an example of that kind of concept learning. Note that when people try to solve problems like any of these, they sometimes begin by forming rules or hypotheses that are based on the wrong or too few dimensions—for example, small = yes; metal = oogle; animal = dog—but as more experience is acquired, correct performance increases. The remainder of this chapter will investigate the thinking process that underlies this improvement.

RULE LEARNING: DEFINITION OF THINKING

The concept-learning example provides a basis for a theory of thinking that can go beyond the simple response hierarchy model. The thinking process required in concept learning has been characterized in a number of ways, including two basic classes of theories:

> The *continuity theory* views concept learning as a direct extension of the S-R associationist model. Each feature of an instance serves as a stimulus, and the particular response is strengthened for all presented features on each trial; thus, after many instances are presented, only the relevant features will have consistent (and therefore strong) responses associated with them. Thinking is simply building response hierarchies.

> The *noncontinuity theory* views concept learning as *inducing rules* (or hypotheses) and *testing* them. If the rule can predict class membership for any instance, it is retained, but if it cannot predict class membership, a new hypothesis is generated. Thinking is hypothesis testing.

The continuity or S-R associationist view and the noncontinuity or hypothesis testing view yield different predictions about subject behavior, which the next two sections of this chapter will investigate in more detail.

CONTINUITY THEORY

The most obvious and straightforward theory of thinking is that the concept-learning task is a simple extension of the response (or habit) hierarchy model described in Chapter 2. During concept learning, the subject forms a response hierarchy for each attribute in the problem by tallying the number of times each category response has been or has not been associated with a given attribute. When a new example is given, the subject simply adds the response strengths for all the attributes present in the new example.

For example, consider the situation in Box 5–1 in which subjects are shown cards with drawings that are either red or green in color, large or small in size, round or square in shape, and one or two in number. The continuity theory assumes that each type of color, size, number, and shape builds its own response hierarchy (with the associated responses either Yes or No) based on past experience, as shown in Box 5–2. For example, suppose that the subject has just been shown the first six objects described in Box 5–1 and now must determine whether one green small square is a Yes or a No. In Box 5–2, the response hierarchy for green favors a No response since it has been associated with No many times and few times with Yes; similarly the hierarchy for one favors No; the hierarchy for small is strongly Yes, and there is equal preference for Yes and No for square. The individual tendencies for one, green, small, and square add (or subtract) to yield a weak Yes response as shown in Box 5–2. If one green small square turns out to be a Yes, the response strength for yes for each attribute would be modified and so on. As practice con-

BOX 5–2 Continuity Theory of Concept Learning

Using the example given in Box 5–1, the continuity theory suggests that subjects keep a tally of the number of times each attribute (for example, red, circle, and so on) has been associated or not associated with a Yes or a No. For the first few instances the tally could be as follows.*

Instance	Group	Number 1	Number 2	Color R	Color G	Size L	Size S	Shape C	Shape S
1 red large square	No	−	+	−	+	−	+	+	−
1 green large square	No	−	+	+	−	−	+	+	−
2 red small squares	Yes	−	+	+	−	−	+	−	+
2 red large circles	No	+	−	−	+	−	+	−	+
1 green large circle	No	−	+	+	−	−	+	−	+
1 red small circle	Yes	+	−	+	−	−	+	+	−

*Minus means the attribute was part of an object put into Group No or not part of an object put into Group Yes; plus means that the attribute was part of an object put into Group Yes or not part of an object put into Group No.

To determine the response hierarchy for each new instance, the tendency to say Yes or No for each attribute must be added up for all previous instances. For example, after the first three instances, the response tendencies for the fourth instance are:

Two—3 Yes and 0 No
Red—2 Yes and 1 No
Large—0 Yes and 3 No
Circle—2 Yes and 1 No

To determine the response for 2 red large circles, the total is 7 Yes and 5 No, so there may be a weak tendency to say Yes, the wrong answer. However, after more experience the irrelevant dimensions become neutral. If the seventh instance is 1 green small square, the tallies are:

One—2 Yes and 4 No
Green—2 Yes and 4 No
Small—6 Yes and 0 No
Square—3 Yes and 3 No

The totals are 13 Yes and 11 No, so the response may be a mild Yes.

tinues, the difference between Yes and No response strengths will become closer to zero for all nonsize attributes and the differences for large versus small size will continue to grow.

Hull (1920) was the first to investigate this abstraction process in concept learning experimentally. Subjects learned to give 1 of 12 responses to 12 Chinese characters like those in Box 5–3. First the character was shown, the subject made

BOX 5–3   Hull's Concept-Learning Experiment

Six of the Chinese radicals that Hull used are shown here. First, the subject was shown a Chinese character and guessed its "name" (for example, oo), then the experimenter gave the correct name, and so on. Characters with the same radicals always were given the same name so that after going through several packs of characters, the subjects improved their performances and were eventually able to correctly name characters they had never seen before.

Name	Concept	Pack I	Pack II	Pack III	Pack IV	Pack V	Pack VI
oo							
yer							
li							
ta							
deg							
ling							

From Hull (1920)

a response such as "oo," "li," "ta," and the correct response was then given to the subject. Once a subject had correctly responded to all 12 characters, a second pack of 12 was shown but the same 12 responses were associated with each character as with the first group. This process continued with several different packs. Chinese characters contain certain basic features called "radicals," and in the experiment the same radical was always associated with the same response. Subjects showed much improvement with later packs of characters and were often able to guess the correct response for characters they had never seen before. Hull concluded that they had abstracted the basic radicals and had developed strong tendencies to respond to them as described by the continuity theory. The relevant attributes, in this case the radicals, strongly evoked different responses while the irrelevant features around the radicals tended to become neutral. The abstraction process could be speeded up by coloring the radicals red, thus drawing the subject's attention to the relevant dimension. This speeding up is an example of "cue salience" discussed later in this chapter.

NONCONTINUITY THEORY

Can concept learning be explained by this straightforward view of the thinker as passively and gradually tallying past experience into multiple response hierarchies? An alternative view is that concept learning is not a process of gradually strengthening associations at all, but rather a noncontinuous or discontinuous process of constructing and testing hypotheses until one works. According to the hypotheses testing view, individuals actively try to formulate rules and they stick with their rule until it fails to work. This has been called the "win stay, lose switch" strategy.

For example, in the task shown in Box 5–1, a subject who is first told that one red large circle is No might hypothesize that "Red is No, Green is Yes," and when shown one green large square, will guess Yes. Since that is a wrong guess, the subject will make up a new hypothesis such as "One is No, Two is Yes" which works for two red small squares, but when this fails on two red large circles may change the hypothesis to "Small is Yes, Large is No" and from then on make no more errors. In this noncontinuity view, thinking involves making a hypothesis and keeping it until it is disconfirmed rather than being a gradual learning of associations. Finding the correct solution is an "all or none" process.

The Kendlers (Kendler and D'Amato, 1955; Kendler and Kendler, 1959, 1962, 1975) attempted to investigate the two theories of concept learning in a series of experiments involving shifts in the rules. Stimuli were presented in pairs, the subject picked one, and the experimenter then gave the correct answer. For example, suppose a subject learns the set of responses given in Box 5–4: Yes for black-large and white-large and No for black-small and white-small. The rule can then be switched in two ways: a *reversal shift,* in which the two larges become No and the two smalls become Yes, or a *nonreversal shift,* in which a new dimension is used such as labeling black as Yes and white as No. If concept learning involves strengthening single S-R associations (continuity theory) then the reversal shift should be more difficult to learn since it requires changing four associations while the nonreversal shift requires changing only two links. However, if concept learning involves forming a rule that *mediates* between the stimulus and the response (noncontinuity theory), then in a reversal shift the same dimension mediates and only new labels need be added while in the nonreversal shift a new dimension and new labels must be found. A long series of studies showed that the reversal shift was easier to learn than the nonreversal shift for college students and verbal children

BOX 5–4   Reversal and Nonreversal Shifts

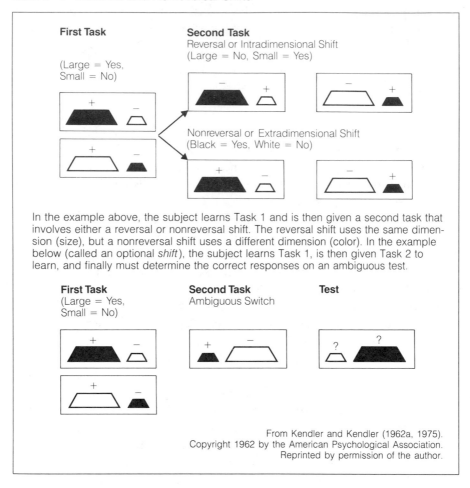

In the example above, the subject learns Task 1 and is then given a second task that involves either a reversal or nonreversal shift. The reversal shift uses the same dimension (size), but a nonreversal shift uses a different dimension (color). In the example below (called an optional *shift*), the subject learns Task 1, is then given Task 2 to learn, and finally must determine the correct responses on an ambiguous test.

From Kendler and Kendler (1962a, 1975).
Copyright 1962 by the American Psychological Association.
Reprinted by permission of the author.

(children over five years), but that the nonreversal shift was easier for preverbal children (children under five years) and for laboratory animals.

In another set of experiments, subjects were taught that the appropriate responses for figures such as black-large and white-large were Yes and for black-small and white-small were No. Then there was an ambiguous switch—for example, subjects learned black-small was now Yes and white-large was now No. What was black-large or white-small? If the subject responded that black-large was Yes and white-small was No, that was a nonreversal shift—two of the original associations were retained and the classification rule was based on a new dimension, color. If the subject said Yes for the black-large or white-small object, that was a reversal shift—all four of the original associations were changed but the original dimension, size, was retained. Since a nonreversal shift required changing fewer new associations, it could be predicted by the continuity view; the noncontinuity theory would predict that since thinking is based on rules instead of individual associations, a reversal shift was more likely. Younger children typically preferred nonreversal, but older children and adults tended to prefer reversal shifts. This is illustrated by the percentages of reversal shifts: 37 percent for three-year-olds, 50 percent for five-year-olds, and 62 percent for ten-year-olds. Kendler and Kendler concluded that as age increases thinking in the concept-learning situation is more likely to be mediated by a general rule rather than by individual associations.

Another test of the continuity-noncontinuity argument was conducted by Bower and Trabasso (1963; Trabasso and Bower, 1964, 1968). They gave college student subjects a concept-learning task similar to the one shown in Box 5–1 made up of six dimensions each with two attributes: color (red or blue), size (large or small), shape (square or hexagonal), number (three or four), position (right or left) shaded area (upper right and lower left or upper left and lower right). The stimuli were presented one at a time, with the subject asked to anticipate which of two classes each stimulus belonged to, the experimenter then giving the correct answer, and so on. In observing the performance of their subjects, Bower and Trabasso noted that the pattern of performance remained at chance level for a long time, then jumped suddenly to 100 percent correct. This observation seemed consistent with the noncontinuity theory, but to test the theory more closely, Bower and Trabasso performed a further experiment in which the solution rule was changed while the subjects were still responding at chance level, that is, before they had learned the original Red = 1, Blue = 2. The continuity theory predicts that such a switch would seriously hurt learning since associative strengths have been slowly getting stronger for the relevant cues; the noncontinuity theory predicts that the switch will not make any difference since the problem solver has not yet induced the classification rule. The results clearly supported the noncontinuity view: changing the solution rule prior to learning did not slow learning in a group of subjects compared with another group that retained the same rule throughout the experiment. Apparently these subjects formed a hypothesis, tested it on new stimuli, and changed it on the basis of negative feedback without the need to tally past experiences with particular attributes. The Bower and Trabasso results indicate that when these subjects picked a new hypothesis they did not benefit at all from a long chain of past experience; each new selection of a hypothesis may have been made independently of previous hypotheses. Mathematical models based on this idea were discussed by Restle and Greeno (1970).

On the basis of these findings, the noncontinuity theory seems to be the better description of the thinking of college students and some verbal children. Osler and Fivel (1961) investigated the pattern of performance before solution on a concept identification task with high school students. They observed that the students with IQs over 110 showed the same sudden learning noted by Bower and Trabasso—a period of chance performance, presumably while incorrect hypotheses were being selected, followed by 100 percent performance when the correct hypothesis was finally chosen. However, students of average and below average intelligence displayed a pattern in which the rate of correct response for each individual rose gradually. One interpretation of these findings is that the bright students made successive hypotheses while the strategy of the other students was learning by association.

DOMINANCE OF CUES

Dominance Hierarchy

When people form hypotheses for rule classification, they may not be choosing the features they notice entirely at random; certain elements of the stimuli may attract their attention more readily than others. In a classic series of concept-learning experiments, Heidbreder (1946, 1947) investigated this question. These experiments were like Hull's in that Heidbreder showed her subjects a series of pictures like those in Box 5–5 one at a time and asked them to guess the nonsense word associated with each picture. She then gave the correct response. After going through one set of pictures, Heidbreder repeated this procedure with a second set, and so on. The subjects did not see the same picture-name pair more than once but the response words were always associated with a certain kind of picture: for example, *leth* for building, *fard* for circle, *relk* for face, *mulp* for tree, *ling* for two, and *dilt* for five. The subjects could only guess on the first trial, of course, but as they continued through more trials they began to identify the names of the pictures correctly. Thus, like Hull's subjects, the subjects in Heidbreder's studies were able to abstract the appropriate feature of the picture and base their responses on it. Heidbreder was particularly interested in the finding that certain pictures were easier to learn than others. Pictures with concrete characteristics, like the buildings, faces, and trees were generally easier to identify than were shapes like circles or crosses, and pictures of abstract concepts, like the numbers two and five, were the hardest of all to identify.

Although other researchers have observed different patterns in their subjects (Dattman and Israel 1951; Baum, 1954), such work as Heidbreder's seems to indicate that subjects may enter the experimental situation with a set of preferences for which features of the situation they will attend to. Heidbreder referred to these preferences as a "hierarchy of dominance"; that is, subjects may have a tendency

BOX 5–5   Heidbreder's Concept-Learning Experiment

Subjects were shown drawings like these, one at a time, and asked to name them. Then the correct name was given. After Set 1, the drawings in Set 2 were given but the same name was given to the same kind of picture. After several trials, the subjects began to "guess" the names of new objects correctly.

Trial 1	Trial 2	Trial 3	Trial 4
Ling	Relk	Leth	(tree)
Fard	Dilt	Ling	(face)
Relk	Mulp	Fard	(house)
Leth	Ling	Dilt	(clock)
Dilt	Fard	Mulp	(boots)
Mulp	Leth	Relk	(snowflakes)

Adapted from Heidbreder (1947)

to attend to concrete objects first, and when these have been learned, to shapes, and then to abstract concepts like numbers. Dattman and Israel, as well as Baum, found that a factor influencing this hierarchy of attention was the number of interfering, similar concepts in the problem. For example, subjects often made errors with the number concepts by giving the word that stood for sixness when the picture called for the word for twoness; if only a single number concept was used it was learned much faster. In other words, when several number concepts were used, they may have been first interpreted as "number," and only later classified as particular numbers two or six, and so on, whereas trees, faces, and buildings were initially classified as such by the subjects.

Dominance Level

Underwood and Richardson (1956) developed the concept of *dominance level* to indicate the probability that a certain stimulus will elicit a certain sense impression as a response. For example, the concept of *white* has a high dominance level for words like *milk, chalk,* and *snow,* because people generally identify them as white, but a low dominance level for words like *baseball, fang,* and *sugar* because they rarely elicit the idea of white as a first response. In concept-learning experiments like Heidbreder's words that shared the same high dominance level for a sense impression were much easier to learn than words that shared low dominance level. Thus, modifying Heidbreder's idea that certain attributes are attended to before others, the dominance level theory supposes that when a stimulus is presented it elicits a response based on one of its characteristics. That characteristic is attended to unless it fails to help predict the concept, in which case the second most dominant feature of the stimulus is attended to, and so on.

Cue Salience

Trabasso (1963) investigated concept learning using flower designs that varied in the number and shape of the leaves, angles of the branches, colors, and so on. Trabasso found that certain cues were more meaningful or *salient* than others. For example, in one experiment in which the classification rule was based on color (angle fixed), the errors averaged 4, but when the relevant dimension was angle (color fixed), errors averaged 19.5. Using these results, Bower was able to assign salience weights to the factors in his flower designs that indicated the tendency of subjects to base their hypotheses on each cue. One interesting finding was that the weightings of cue saliences were cumulative; for example, if angle was the relevant dimension but color was always correlated with angle size, learning was much faster than when angle was relevant but the color varied.

These studies seem to indicate that in a given concept-learning situation, hypotheses are likely to be formed on the basis of certain "dominant" or "salient" dimensions; only if those hypotheses fail is the subject likely to develop new hypotheses on the basis of less salient dimensions. These ideas are closely related to the idea of "habit family hierarchy" discussed in Chapter 2.

BOX 5–6   Stimuli Used in Concept-Learning Experiments

Subjects either selected or were given one card at a time. Then they "guessed" whether it was a positive or negative instance and were told the correct answer. The cards varied in shape, color, number of borders, and number of objects.

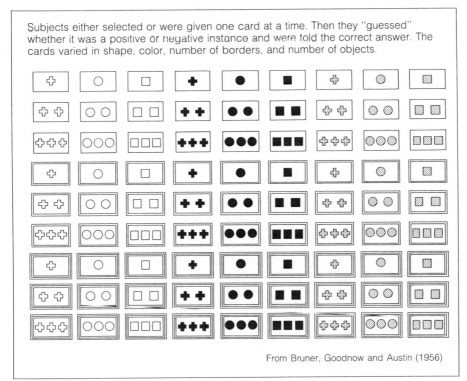

From Bruner, Goodnow and Austin (1956)

STRATEGIES

Probably the best known and most often cited concept-learning experiment was conducted by Bruner, Goodnow, and Austin (1956) and published in their classic monograph, *A Study of Thinking*. They used a set of 81 stimuli, shown in Box 5–6, which consisted of four *dimensions* with three *values* (or attributes) per dimension: *shape*—circle, square, cross; *color*—red, green, black; *number of borders*—1, 2, or 3; and *number of objects*—1, 2, or 3.

Classification rules could be made in several ways but the three main classes of rules used by Bruner, Goodnow, and Austin were: (1) *single-value concepts,* in which the concept was defined as having one particular value on one particular dimension, ignoring all other dimensions (for example, red); (2) *conjunctive concepts,* in which the concept was defined as having one value on one dimension *and* another value on another dimension (red crosses, for example); and (3) *disjunctive concepts,* in which the concept was defined as having one value on one dimension *or* a different value on another dimension (red or cross).

Once a classification rule had been selected, a method was needed for presenting the desired positive *instances* (or exemplars) of the concept and the negative instances (or nonexemplars) to the subject. The two most important methods used were: (1) the *reception method,* in which the experimenter picked the stimulus cards one at a time, the subject said whether she thought each card was a negative or positive instance, and the experimenter told her whether or not she was correct; and (2) the *selection method,* in which the subject looked at the entire board of 81 stimuli, picked the cards one at a time and said for each whether she thought it was a positive or negative instance of the rule, and the experimenter indicated whether or not the answer was correct.

In observing the solution process of concept-learning problems under these conditions, Bruner, Goodnow, and Austin noted that their subjects seemed to use certain strategies. With the reception method, for example, two distinct *reception strategies* were noted:

Wholist strategy—with this the subject had to remember all the attributes common to those instances where the response was correct and ignore everything else, thus eliminating attributes that were not part of a positive instance.

Partist strategy—here the subject focused on one hypothesis at a time (for example, color green = Yes), kept the hypothesis if it correctly predicted the membership of a stimulus card, and formed a new one based on all past experience if it did not.

These strategies are specified in Box 5–7.

In general, Bruner and his associates found that wholist strategy resulted in better learning performance, especially when the subjects were under time pressure. The partist strategy requires the subject to retain all prior information and select a hypothesis consistent with this information while wholist strategy incorporates a record of all past instances within the current hypothesis. The subject using a wholist strategy remembers all the values of the first correct response or positive instance and gradually eliminates those that fail to reappear on subsequent positive instances. Although negative instances have not been an important part of our discussion of Bruner's theory, other researchers have found that subjects can learn equally well with negative instances as with positive (Freibergs and Tulving, 1961).

With the selection method of presentation, Bruner, Goodnow, and Austin noted several similar selection strategies:

Simultaneous scanning, in which the subject began with all possible hypotheses and eliminated the untenable ones after each instance.

Successive scanning, in which the subject began with one hypothesis, kept it if it correctly predicted class membership, and changed it to another based on all past experience if it did not.

BOX 5–7 Strategies in Concept Learning

When subjects are presented with a series of instances selected from those shown in Box 5–6 and told whether each is a positive or negative instance, they may adopt one of the following strategies or a mixed combination.

Wholist Strategy

Take the first positive instance and retain all the positive attributes as the initial hypothesis. Then, as more instances are presented, eliminate any attribute in this set which does not occur with a positive instance:

	Positive Instance	Negative Instance
Confirming	Maintain the hypothesis now in force	Maintain the hypothesis now in force
Infirming	Take as the next hypothesis what the old hypothesis and the present instance have in common	Impossible unless one has mis-reckoned. If one has mis-reckoned, correct from memory of past instances and present hypothesis

Partist Strategy

Begin with part of the first positive instance as an hypothesis (for example, choose just one attribute). Then retain or change it in the following way:

	Positive Instance	Negative Instance
Confirming	Maintain hypothesis now in force	Maintain hypothesis now in force
Infirming	Change hypothesis to make it consistent with past instances: that is, choose an hypothesis not previously infirmed	Change hypothesis to make it consistent with past instances: that is, choose hypothesis not previously infirmed

From Bruner, Goodnow, and Austin (1956)

Conservative focusing, in which the subject picked one positive instance and selected subsequent cards that changed one attribute value at a time.

Focus gambling, in which the subject picked one positive instance and selected subsequent cards that changed several attribute values at a time.

The scanning strategies are similar to the partist strategies and the focusing strategies are similar to the wholist. Again, focusing is usually far more efficient because it does not require as much memorization.

BOX 5–8   Hypothesis Sampling Models

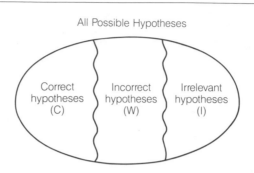

All Possible Hypotheses

Correct hypotheses (C)   Incorrect hypotheses (W)   Irrelevant hypotheses (I)

On the first instance, a subject selects one hypothesis (or a set) from the pool of all possible hypotheses. If the selection is in C, the subject makes a correct response and retains the hypothesis; if it is in W, the response is incorrect and the hypothesis is returned to the pool to be resampled on the next trial; if it is in I, then it may lead to either a correct response (retain the hypothesis) or an incorrect response (replace the hypothesis and resample). If "red" is the defining characteristic of positive instances, then the hypothesis "red" would be in C, "green" would be in W, and "large" would be in I, and so on.

Adapted from Restle and Greeno (1970)

MODELS OF HYPOTHESIS TESTING

The strategies by Bruner, Goodnow, and Austin suggest that subjects create and test hypotheses based on all relevant past instances. However, Restle (1962) and Bower and Trabasso (1964; Trabasso and Bower, 1968) have proposed a basic model to account for hypothesis testing. Represented in Box 5–8, this model has two ideas: (1) the *sampling idea* that the subject samples one hypothesis (or a set of hypotheses) from a pool of all possible hypotheses that may be correct, incorrect, or irrelevant and (2) the *no-memory idea* that if the hypothesis results in correct classification of an instance it is retained, otherwise it is replaced in the pool and a new hypothesis (or set of hypotheses) is selected.

To test this kind of model, Levine (1966) used a new approach to determine what strategy a subject was using in concept learning. In Levine's experiments subjects had to choose between two letters on a stimulus card like those shown in Box 5–9. The letters differed in color (black or white), position (left or right), size (large or small), and form (X or T). The subjects were told that they could choose from only eight possible hypotheses—right, left, large, small, black, white, T, or X—and were given four trials without being told if they were correct, followed by a fifth trial

BOX 5–9 Levine's Blank Trial Procedure

	Answer for Each Hypothesis							
Stimuli Pairs	Black	X	Left	Large	Small	Right	T	White
X ⊤	**X**	**X**	**X**	**X**	⊤	⊤	⊤	⊤
✕ **T**	**T**	✕	✕	**T**	✕	**T**	**T**	✕
T ✕	**T**	✕	**T**	✕	**T**	✕	**T**	✕
⊤ **x**	**x**	**x**	⊤	⊤	**x**	**x**	⊤	⊤

Adapted from Levine (1966)

in which the experimenter randomly said either "Correct" or "Wrong." Levine noted it was clear that the subjects used hypotheses since their responses on any set of four nonfeedback trials were consistent with one of the eight hypotheses over 92 percent of the time. Based on the prior four responses, their choices on the fifth trial could be correctly predicted 97 percent of the time. Furthermore, the subjects tended to retain the same hypothesis if they were given positive feedback (95 percent of the time) and to change to another hypothesis if given negative feedback on the fifth trial (98 percent of the time). Levine's experiment is consistent with the idea that subjects use strategies, that they sample hypotheses one at a time, and that they use the win-stay, lose-switch policy, but it does not support the no-memory assumption of the model. For example, if the subjects sampled with replacement, they had a 12.5 percent chance (one in eight) of picking the same hypothesis after an "error"; yet the retention rate was only 2 percent. Levine's results indicate that subjects used some of their past experience, but certainly not all of it.

In a further experiment, Wickens and Millward (1971) gave their subjects large amounts of practice on a concept-learning task and tried to describe performance in terms of a hypothesis sampling model. The results were consistent with the idea that subjects tend to consider a small number of dimensions simultaneously, that a dimension paired inconsistently with the correct response is eliminated, and that when all the dimensions in a set are eliminated the subject samples a new set. These subjects apparently retained some information about previous dimensions that had been tested, but there were large individual differences in how many prior hypotheses could be remembered. It was always more than zero—indicating some memory load—but it was definitely limited.

FACTORS THAT INFLUENCE DIFFICULTY

There have been many studies investigating what factors make concept problems more or less difficult. One question concerns the role of positive and negative instances. In general, a subject who has developed a hypothesis tends to pick test cards that confirm it—that is, subjects tend to rely on positive instances to test their hypotheses and may be less able to use the information from a negative instance they have correctly predicted. In a typical experiment, Freibergs and Tulving (1961) gave 20 different concept learning problems to a group of subjects. With each problem the subjects were given either all positive or all negative instances of the concept to be learned. For the first few problems, the subjects solved much faster with all positive instances (the median solution times were 50 to 140 seconds) than with all negative (no solutions within 210 seconds). However, after about 15 problems there was no difference between the groups. Apparently these subjects had a preference for using information in positive instances but could learn, in a relatively short time, to effectively use the information in negative instances as well.

Another important factor that influences the difficulty of concept-learning problems is the complexity of the concept rule that must be induced. For example, several experiments have shown that increasing the number of relevant dimensions tends to decrease solution time since a subject can use any dimension to solve the problem; increasing the number of irrelevant dimensions makes the problem more difficult because it allows the subject more chances to pick a useless hypothesis (Bourne, 1966; Bourne, Ekstrand, and Dominowski, 1971; Walker and Bourne, 1961). In addition, solution performance was made more difficult under some conditions by increasing the number of values per dimension (Battig and Bourne, 1961) and by using disjunctive rather than conjunctive classification rules (Haygood and Stevenson, 1967).*

Hunt, Marin, and Stone (1966) have represented classification rules as sequential decision trees such as the one shown in Box 5–10. Since decisions about new instances are based on a series of tests going down the tree, more complex trees should be harder to learn. Evidence to support this idea came from a study by Trabasso, Rollins, and Shaughnessy (1971) in which the subjects read statements like, ''large triangle and red circle'' and were shown a triangle and circle on a slide. The task was to verify the statement by responding Yes or No to the slide. Reading times were longer for complex trees than for simple ones, and decision times were also longer. Apparently, the classification can be represented as a sequential decision tree, and as more decisions are needed the problem becomes more difficult.

Bourne (1970) obtained similar results in a concept-learning task in which

---

*Haygood, Harbert, and Omlor (1970) have defined the limited conditions under which increasing the number of values per dimension increases problem difficulty.

BOX 5–10 A Sequential Decision Tree

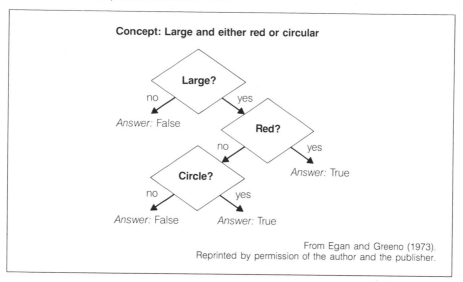

Concept: Large and either red or circular

Large?
no — Answer: False
yes

Red?
no
yes — Answer: True

Circle?
no — Answer: False
yes — Answer: True

From Egan and Greeno (1973).
Reprinted by permission of the author and the publisher.

subjects were presented with objects that varied in size (square, circle, triangle) and color (red, green, blue) and were asked to classify them as Yes or No. The experimenter provided feedback based on either very complex or on short rules that were not stated to the subject. For example, a complex rule that defined red triangle and red circle as No and all others as Yes took an average of 45 trials to learn: "If an object is red and is also a square, answer yes; if an object is red and is not a square, answer no; if an object is not red, answer yes." A simpler rule that defined red triangle as Yes and all others as No took an average of 18 trials to learn: "If an object is red and is also a triangle, answer yes; otherwise answer no." Bourne (1970) suggested that concept learning may require learning a hierarchy of rules and subrules with complex problems incorporating several lower-level rules.

ABSTRACTION OF VISUAL PROTOTYPES

An alternative, or refinement, to the hypothesis testing models of concept learning comes from a series of studies on learning to classify visual patterns. In previous sections, concept learning was broken down into two phases—learning to attend to the relevant attributes and learning the rule that should be applied to the attributes. However, another way of characterizing this initial process involves averaging all the instances of each category into a schematic or prototypical instance. For exam-

BOX 5–11   Prototype Pattern of Dots and Various Degrees of Distortion

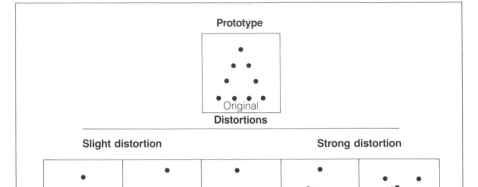

Note: Higher numbers indicate higher amount of distortion.

From Posner and Keele (1968, 1970)

ple, consider how someone learns to classify cars into categories such as Chevrolet, Ford, or Dodge, regardless of year or model, or how we learn to sort pocket change into pennies, nickels, dimes, and so on, regardless of mint year or amount of wear. There are several alternative theories to explain this, one of which is the *abstraction of prototype*. In the automobile example, an individual might have a mental image of a typical Chevy or Ford and compare any car against this ideal image. Another classification theory is *feature differentiation*. Here the subject learns to attend to particularly distinguishing cues, such as, say, the square headlights of Chevrolets versus the round headlights of Fords. Although the feature-differentiation view, which is an aspect of discrimination learning, is an implicit part of several models of concept learning, some subjects may use the prototype strategy in certain types of concept-learning tasks. Eventually, these two approaches must be reconciled to a theory of concept learning.

In a set of studies, Posner and Keele (1968, 1970) presented dot patterns like those shown in Box 5–11. Each pattern was constructed by distorting a nine-dot prototype; for example, to create a distortion, several of the dots, randomly selected, would be moved on the prototype either to the right or left or up or down. In a typical experiment, subjects were shown four different distortions of three separate prototypes and asked to classify each of these 12-dot patterns into one of three categories. Although the subjects never saw the actual prototypes, they were able to learn to classify their exemplars. More importantly, once the subjects had learned to classify the initial set of distorted patterns, they were given a test that consisted of classifying "new" distorted patterns made in the same way as the original ones, "old" distorted patterns, which were identical to those already learned, and the actual prototypes, which had never been presented. The results were that the old patterns were classified quite well (about 87 percent correct) and the new patterns were a bit more difficult (about 75 percent correct); however, the most striking finding was that the prototypes were classified correctly just as well as the old patterns, that is, the subjects behaved as if the prototypes were old patterns even though they had never been presented before. These results are consistent with the conclusion that the subjects *abstracted* the general prototype of the categories by averaging the characteristics of the distortions they saw and that they created the prototypes in their own memories.

Additional support for the "prototype abstraction" idea comes from a similar study by Posner (1969) in which the subjects looked at a set of dot patterns that were distortions of a prototype. On a subsequent recognition test, they showed strong tendencies to classify the prototype as having been in the initial set although it had not been presented before. Apparently, the prototype abstraction process occurs automatically even when deliberate concept learning is not called for.

Franks and Bransford (1971) obtained complementary results in a study using geometric figures like those shown in Box 5–12. Their subjects saw a series of figures that involved transformations of basic prototypes and were then given a recognition test. They were no better at recognizing "old" patterns from "new" distortions of the same prototypes; in addition, the subjects were most confident about having seen prototypes that had not previously been presented. They were also more confident about having seen patterns that differed from the prototype by only one transformation than by more than one, regardless of whether or not they had in fact seen the patterns. These results extend Posner's finding that what the subjects learned about the initial set of stimuli was an abstraction, that is, the prototype.

Reed (1972) obtained similar results using a different kind of visual pattern. College students learned to classify drawings of faces like those shown in Box 5–13 into two categories and were asked to report what strategy they used. The predominant strategy used by the students was to abstract a prototype and to compare the "distance" between the prototype and each new face pattern. This strategy is summarized as follows: "I formed an abstract image of what a face in category two should look like. Then I compared the projected face with the two abstract images and chose the category which gave the closest match" (p. 393). Other subjects, however, attended to certain distinguishing cues: "I looked at each feature on the projected face and compared how many times it exactly matched a feature in each of the two categories. I then chose the category which gave the highest number of matches" (p. 393).

BOX 5–12   Prototype and Transformations for Some Geometric Figures

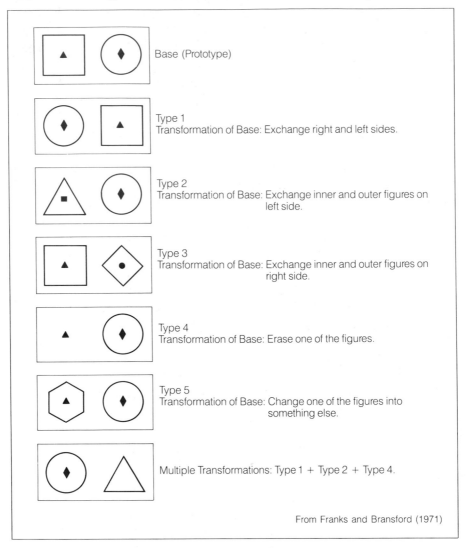

Base (Prototype)

Type 1
Transformation of Base: Exchange right and left sides.

Type 2
Transformation of Base: Exchange inner and outer figures on left side.

Type 3
Transformation of Base: Exchange inner and outer figures on right side.

Type 4
Transformation of Base: Erase one of the figures.

Type 5
Transformation of Base: Change one of the figures into something else.

Multiple Transformations: Type 1 + Type 2 + Type 4.

From Franks and Bransford (1971)

Both types of strategies—prototype abstraction and feature differentiation—were also found in a study by Hyman and Frost (1974). Dot patterns were distorted by stretching them vertically (tall category) or horizontally (wide category). Hyman and Frost reasoned that if the subjects abstracted schematic prototypes, then the *averages* of the tall and the wide groups would be most easily classified; however,

BOX 5–13 Two Categories of Faces

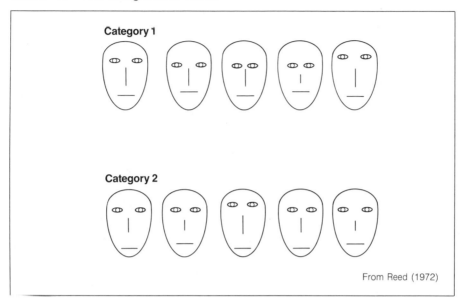

From Reed (1972)

if they attended to features, then the *tallest* of the tall category and the *widest* of the wide category should be easiest to classify. They measured the speed and accuracy with which the subjects classified the various patterns and, like Reed, obtained mixed results: some subjects tended to rely on prototypes and some tended to rely on distinctive features.

More recently, Neumann (1977) has provided some examples of situations in which subjects use different strategies for forming rules about visual stimuli. For example, in one study subjects were presented with eight faces (see Box 5–14). Each face was generated from the "identikit" used by police artists, and each varied along three dimensions. First, the age of the face was manipulated by adding wrinkles, ranging from level 1 (no wrinkles) to level 5 (many wrinkles). Second, the length of the face was manipulated by moving the hairline and chin, ranging from level 1 (short) to level 5 (long). Third, the length of the nose was manipulated from level 1 (short) to level 5 (long). Thus, it was possible to generate $5 \times 5 \times 5$ or 125 different faces. Eight faces were selected for the experiment so that for each dimension, there were three instances of level 1, three instances of level 5, one instance of level 2, one instance of level 4, and no instances of level 3. The faces therefore emphasized extremes—very long or very short faces, very long or very short noses, very young or very old faces.

On a subsequent recognition test, subjects were shown faces and asked to rate whether the faces had been previously presented. The test included faces that were at level 1 for all dimensions (called 1-1-1 faces), level 2 for all dimensions (called 2-2-2), and so on. Suppose that the subjects focused on individual features. Then, they would be expected to recognize the extreme faces—1-1-1 and 5-5-5—most readily since level 1 and level 5 were most frequently presented. However, suppose the subjects form visual prototypes. Then, the subject would average the extremes for each dimension; since there are equal numbers of level 1 and level 5 for each dimension, subjects should be most confident in recognizing the 3-3-3 face. The results shown in Box 5–14 indicate that the subjects were most confident about recognizing the prototypical face, 3-3-3. However, this pattern could be reversed by making the extreme features very obvious during learning. For example, if the eight presented faces consist only of level 1 and level 5 features, then subjects would be more confident about recognizing 1-1-1 and 5-5-5 faces on the test. Or, if subjects are explicitly told what the dimensions are, they tend to recognize the extreme levels better on the test.

In another experiment, Neumann (1977) used rectangular figures rather than faces. Each figure consisted of an overall rectangle that was 100 millimeters wide and varied along three dimensions. First, the overall rectangle varied in height from 200 to 300 millimeters, in five levels (for example, level 1 is 200 millimeters high and level 5 is 300 millimeters high). Each rectangle was bisected by a horizontal line. Above the center horizontal line was a rectangle divided into 2, 3, 4, 5, or 6 layers. Below the line was another smaller rectangle that varied in height at 5 levels from 37.5 (level 1) to 87.5 (level 5) millimeters. Examples of some of these figures are given in Box 5–14. The figures are labeled such that the first number refers to the overall height, the second number refers to the number of layers in the rectangle above the line, and the third number indicates the height of the rectangle below the center line. As in the face experiment, eight figures were presented to each subject, with extreme levels for each dimension (level 1 or 5) occurring three times each, and intermediate levels (2 and 4) occurring once each.

On a subsequent recognition test, subjects were most certain about seeing extreme figures—1-1-1 or 5-5-5. Unlike the faces experiment, there was no evidence that subjects averaged over the extremes to form a prototype. Instead, subjects appeared to focus on the fact that level 1 and level 5 were most frequently presented for each dimension. However, an alternative explanation is that subjects formed two prototypes, remembering that the rectangle could be very long or very short, for example.

Neumann's experiments are interesting because they show that people may use different rule induction strategies for different situations. Apparently, situational factors can influence whether we average the features into a prototype or whether we focus on distinctive features.

BOX 5–14   Inducing Rules About Faces and Figures

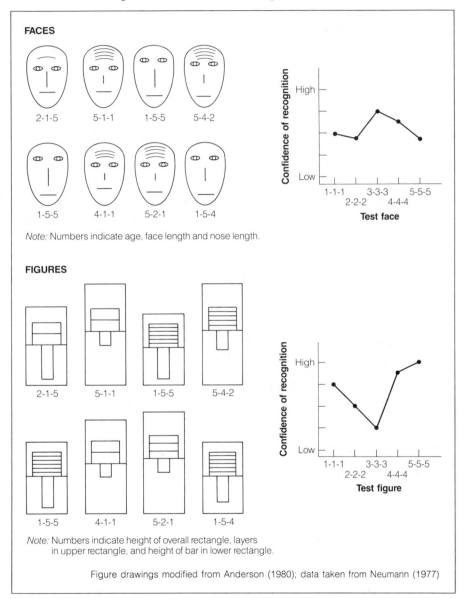

FACES

2-1-5   5-1-1   1-5-5   5-4-2

1-5-5   4-1-1   5-2-1   1-5-4

Note: Numbers indicate age, face length and nose length.

FIGURES

2-1-5   5-1-1   1-5-5   5-4-2

1-5-5   4-1-1   5-2-1   1-5-4

Note: Numbers indicate height of overall rectangle, layers in upper rectangle, and height of bar in lower rectangle.

Figure drawings modified from Anderson (1980); data taken from Neumann (1977)

SERIAL PATTERN LEARNING

Consider the problems shown in Box 5–15. Here the subject is given a series of letters and must figure out by induction what the next letter should be. Simon and Kotovsky (1963) found that the rule the subject must learn consists of four main ingredients:

> *Cycle*—the subject must determine how many letters make up one cycle; for example, in each of the problems cited the cycle is three: (atb/ata/atb/at-) (aaa/bbb/ccc/dd-) (wxa/xyb/yzc/zad/ab-) (urt/ust/ utt/u-).

> *Initialization*—the subject must note each of the letters in the first cycle; for example, in the first problem, letter 1 is a, 2 is t, and 3 is b.

> *Alphabet*—the subject must determine what are the possible letters that could occur for each letter space in the cycle; for example, in the first problem the first two spaces of each cycle are fixed and the third is either a or b; however, in the fourth problem the first and third positions are fixed but the second position can be any letter in the alphabet.

> *Sequence interaction*—the subject must determine what operation is performed on each letter when a new cycle occurs; for example, in the first problem, letter 1 is the same, letter 2 is the same, and letter 3 is changed to the next letter in the alphabet (only a and b appear in the cycles so this sequence goes from a to b to a, and so on).

The rules for each sequence can be represented as a program of things to do. For example, the sequence can be listed for the fourth problem as:

Write the letter L1.

Write the letter L2.

Add one letter to L2.

Write L3.

Go back to first step.

All the subject needs to know is that the system begins with L1 = u, L2 = r, L3 = t.

Simon and Kotovsky found that rules requiring long descriptions (such as long computer programs) were more difficult both for humans and computers and rules placing large demands on immediate memory, like the one in the third problem, were especially difficult. More recently, Kotovsky and Simon (1973) have revised the model based on analysis of the specific strategies used by individual subjects. Thus, the models can now be used to describe the performance of individuals.

BOX 5–15   Letter Series Completion Task

1. albataatbat ____

2. aaabbbcccdd ____

3. wxaxybyzczadab ____

4. urtustuttu ____

From Simon and Kotovsky (1963). Copyright 1963 by the American Psychological Association.
Reprinted by permission of the author.

How do subjects select rules to try in such complex situations? There is some evidence that when people are confronted with a serial pattern problem, they tend to rely on the most obvious or simplest rule based on their past experience and will not change that rule to a more complex one unless it fails. For example, Pollio and Reinhart (1970) presented number cards one at a time and asked their subjects to anticipate what numbers would be on each card. The cards were ordered by base 2, base 3, or base 4 such as 0, 1, 10, 11, 100, 101, 111, 1000, and so on (base 2.)* The results indicated that the subjects had the hardest time with base 2 (301 errors to learning), then with base 3 (143 errors to learning), and the least with base 4 (91 errors). Most errors occurred at the point of shift to a higher base unit (for example, with base 2, the subject would say 3 instead of 10, or 12 instead of 100). At first, there was generally a long pause *after* each base change (for example, 1 to 10, 11 to 100, 111 to 1000), but following a little practice there was a long pause *before* the change, suggesting that the subject was aware that something different happened at base changes. Pollio and Reinhart concluded that these subjects initially assumed that base 10 was being used (based on their successful past experience), but after they had made several errors discovered the correct solution rule. That the subjects learned a *rule* rather than a set of independent responses was suggested by the fact that they could add and subtract in base 2, base 3, and base 4 and could learn new base systems with relative ease.

When subjects are given a series of symbols—such as a sequence of numbers— more than one simple rule may be involved. Bjork (1968) constructed numerical sequences based on three separate rules, as shown in Box 5–16. The sequence given here, 042153264375, was based on the subrules "add 4," "subtract 2," and "subtract 1" for each set of three numbers. The subjects saw the numbers in order, one at a time, and were asked to anticipate the next number. The same sequence was

_____

*The first few numbers for base 3 were 0, 1, 2, 10, 11, 12, 20, 21, 22, 100, and for base 4 were 0, 1, 2, 3, 10, 11, 12, 13, 20, 21, 22, 23, 30, and so on.

BOX 5–16   Complex Rules for Serial Pattern Learning

Position	1	2	3	4	5	6	7	8	9	10	11	12
Subrule 1	+4			+4			+4			+4		
Subrule 2		−2			−2			−2			−2	
Subrule 3			−1			−1			−1			−1
Sequence	4	2	1	5	3	2	6	4	3	7	5	...

Based on Bjork (1968)

continued until they correctly anticipated the numbers 5 times in a row up to a maximum total of 25 trials. The overall results were that the proportion of correctly anticipated numbers gradually increased with more trials; however, Bjork found that if he focused on one subrule at a time (as in trials 1, 4, 7, 10, 13, and so on), the learning was not gradual but rather jumped in all-or-none fashion from a very low level on one trial to a very high level on the next and remained high. Thus although the overall learning of sequence appeared to be very complex, a more careful analysis by subrule indicated an orderly process of all or none.

Restle (1970) has further investigated how a complex set of rules is induced by subjects solving serial pattern problems made up of numbers from 1 to 6. Restle designed serial patterns based on *structural trees,* like the diagram in Box 5–17. Structrual trees represent a hierarchy of rules such as:

Mirror (M)—subtract each of the numbers in the preceding string of digits from 7 (change 1234 to 6543).

Transpose (T)—increment numbers in the preceding chunk by 1 (change 1234 to 2345).

Repeat (R)—reproduce the numbers in the preceding chunk (1234 becomes 1234).

Restle's subjects were seated in front of a set of six lights with a response button under each light. When a light would go on, the subject had to predict which one would go on next by pushing a button, then the next light would appear, and so on. Although sequences were based on a hierarchy of rules like that in Box 5–17, the subjects were not told of the rules and saw only a sequence of stimuli. In investigating the pattern of errors for the first 20 repetitions of the sequence, Restle found that subjects tended to learn the rules in order, starting with the lowest level and working up to the most complex. For example, the sequence 121223231211222323656554546-5644545 is made up of the hierarchy of rules shown in Box 5–17. The highest level

BOX 5–17   Structural Trees for Serial Pattern Learning

M means subtract number from 7, R means repeat number, T means add 1 to number. To read: begin at first (left) position in sequence (1), go to lowest applicable rule (T) and apply (2 for position 2); then use next lowest rule (R) to get 12 for positions 3 and 4; continue, always using lowest applicable rule.

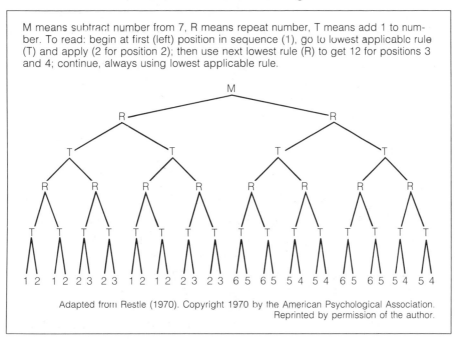

Adapted from Restle (1970). Copyright 1970 by the American Psychological Association.
Reprinted by permission of the author.

rule was M—with the most errors for the first six at the seventeenth position in the sequence—and the easiest rule was the lowest T—with subjects making fewest errors on the even numbered positions. Analysis of the errors for the first 20 repetitions of the sequence revealed an average of 50 percent correct for the highest rule, 55 percent for the second highest, 65 percent for the third highest, 80 percent for the fourth highest, and 85 percent for the lowest. Other patterns based on a five-level hierarchy of rules produced similar results. Apparently, when many rules must be induced, subjects work on the lowest, most obvious level first and build up to more complex ones.

You may have noticed that series completion tasks, like the ones discussed in this section, are often found on intelligence tests. Analogy problems are another kind of task on intelligence tests that require inducing a rule. For example, you might find an analogy like the following:

AUTOMOBILE:OIL: :TREE: (1) FLOWER,   (2) WATER,   (3) ELM.

Human performance on both verbal and pictorial analogies has been subjected to extensive study (Rumelhart and Abrahamson, 1973; Sternberg, 1977; Evans, 1968), which is presented in Chapter 12.

JUDGING FREQUENCY AND PROBABILITY

In everyday life you often must make judgments based on your past experience. How likely is it that the bus will be late? How many times will you have to visit a doctor during the next year? What are your chances of dying in a plane crash? When we answer questions like these, we must base our answers on previous experience with probabilities of certain events occurring.

Frequency

Tversky and Kahneman (1974) have provided many examples of the mistakes that people make when they try to make predictions based on past experience. For example, suppose I asked you to think of all the words you have ever read or heard spoken. Based on your experience, answer the following question: Consider the letter *r*. Is *r* more likely to appear in the first position of a word or in the third position? When Tversky and Kahneman posed this question to a large number of subjects, the great majority of people said that letters such as *r* (or *k* or *d*) occurred more frequently as the first letter of a word. However, an actual count of real words shows that these letters are more likely to occur in the third position.

How did people come up with the wrong generalization? According to Tversky and Kahneman (1973, 1974; Kahneman and Tversky, 1973), words that begin with *r* are easier to think of than words that have *r* as the third letter. In short, words that begin with *r* are more *available*. Apparently, people make generalizations about frequency based on the *availability* of the instances in memory rather than by an accurate count of actual past experience.

To test this idea in a controlled experiment, Tversky and Kahneman (1973) asked subjects to read a list of 39 names of well-known people. Some of the lists contained 19 female and 20 male names, but the women on the list were more famous than the men. Other lists contained 19 male and 20 female names, but the men on the list were more well known. Later, when subjects were asked whether there were more men or women on the list they read, frequency estimates were heavily influenced by the fame of the names. Subjects overwhelmingly decided that there were more female names on the list that contained famous women and over-whelmingly decided that there were more males on the list that contained famous men. Again, as with the previous study, people's generalizations about frequency of events seemed to be influenced by the *availability* of the items; since the famous names were easier to remember, there seemed to be more of them.

As a final example of how availability influences judgments about frequency, consider what Tversky and Kahneman (1974) call "illusory correlation"—the generalization that two events occur together more often than they really do in actual life. For example, Chapman and Chapman (1967, 1969) asked subjects to read diagnoses of mentally ill patients; the subjects were shown a picture of each patient. Later, subjects were asked to estimate how often certain diagnoses went with certain characteristics of the pictures. Subjects tended to overestimate related occurrences of salient associates, such as suspiciousness with peculiar eyes. Even when they were presented with contradictory evidence, subjects were reluctant to revise their judgments. Apparently, the expectation of a correlation between two attributes was so strong that people greatly overestimated how often the two occurred together in a given situation. Again, the association was highly *available* and thus influenced the subjects' judgments of frequency of co-occurrence.

Probability

Tversky and Kahneman (1974; Kahneman and Tversky, 1973) have also summarized errors people make concerning the prediction of probabilities. For example, can you be more sure of your inference if you base it on many instances than if you base it only on a small number of instances? Consider the following problem:

> A certain town is served by two hospitals. In the larger hospital about 45 babies are born each day, and in the smaller hospital about 15 babies are born each day. As you know, about 50 percent of all babies are boys. However, the exact percentage varies from day to day. Sometimes it may be higher than 50 percent, sometimes lower. For a period of one year, each hospital recorded the days on which more than 60 percent of the babies born were boys. Which hospital do you think recorded more such days: (1) the larger hospital, (2) the smaller hospital, or (3) about the same (that is, within 5 percent of each other)?

When college students were asked to answer this question, 22 percent selected the first answer, 22 percent selected the second answer, and 56 percent selected the third answer. They seemed to make no compensation for large versus small sample size. They thought that an extreme event—for example, boys being 60 percent of the births—was just as likely in a large hospital as in a small hospital. However, in fact, it is actually far more likely for an extreme event to occur in a small sample, since there are fewer cases to average. Apparently, people often fail to take sample size into account when they make an inference.

As another example, consider the urn problem:

> Imagine an urn filled with balls, of which two-thirds are of one color and one-third are of another. One person has drawn 5 balls from the urn, and found that 4 were red and 1 was white. Another individual has drawn 20 balls and found that 12 were red and 8 were white. Which person should feel more confident that the urn contains twice as many red balls as white balls rather than the opposite? What odds should each individual give?

Most of Tversky and Kahneman's subjects felt that getting 4 out of 5 red balls was much stronger evidence than getting 12 out of 20 red balls. However, the odds favor the latter as better evidence. These results suggest that people have trouble taking sample size into account when they make an inference. People ignore the fact that you can be surer of your generalization if it is based on a larger pool of past experience.

As a final example of errors in predicting probabilities, let's consider what can be called the "gambler's fallacy"—the idea that a past string of events is likely to be reversed. For example, say that you flipped a coin and it came up with heads five times in a row. What do you think the next outcome will be? Most people feel that tails is due to occur. Actually, of course, the probability of obtaining heads or tails is always the same 50 percent on each flip, regardless of previous results. However, Tversky and Kahneman (1974) reported that subjects think that some sequences, such as H T H T H T, are far more likely to occur than others, such as H H H H H T. Why do people think that a long string is unlikely? One explanation is what Tversky and Kahneman call *similarity*—the idea that patterns like H T H T H T are similar to typical patterns that subjects are familiar with, while long runs do not resemble many previous experiences.

The work of Tversky and Kahneman (1973, 1974; Kahneman and Tversky, 1973) shows that people do not form generalizations in ways that statistics or logic suggests. When we make inferences about events in the real world, based on our experience, we do not behave like statisticians. Rather we seem to be heavily influenced by salient features that stick out in our memory, and we are swayed by extreme events even when the sample size is small. Recently, Cohen (1979, 1980; Kahneman and Tversky, 1979) has reinterpreted many of the findings of Tversky and Kahneman. For example, Cohen argues that although subjects may not behave in correspondence to some mathematical theories, their behavior is consistent with other theories of logic. In any case, the work of Tversky and Kahneman has helped extend work on inductive reasoning to real-world problems.

EVALUATION

The concept-learning and rule-induction task has been a major paradigm (or method) in the study of human thinking. One advantage of concentrating on an agreed-upon task and method is that researchers have been able to amass an impressive amount of detailed and thorough information about human thinking with respect to concept learning. A disadvantage, however, is that the concept-learning task is just one kind of problem-solving situation. It is not clear how far one can generalize from laboratory studies on concept learning to the full range of human thought. A second problem concerns the finding that subjects tend to use rules and strategies in problem solving; in the concept-learning task, the rules and structure are built into the task by the experimenter (for example, defining red as positive, or making a structural tree), and therefore it is not entirely surprising that the subjects display some effects of the experimenter's rules and structure. In problem-solving tasks that are less structured, an entirely different set of strategies may be observed. Finally, there is the problem of individual differences in which different people may show different reasoning processes in the concept-learning task. The Kendlers have demonstrated that preverbal children do not share the strategies of adult college students, but further research is needed to determine whether the performance of college students (who have typically been the subjects in concept-learning experiments) is representative of all adult subjects.

Work on concept induction has passed through three distinct stages. Early work prior to 1950 was concerned largely with how animals learned in discrimination tasks (see Levine, 1975). Then, during the 1950s and 1960s, the concept learning paradigms designed for animals were adapted for humans. Results indicated that the continuity theory that was adequate for describing animal learning was not adequate for describing how humans induced rules. More recently, attention has shifted to formation of rules and concepts in commonplace situations—such as visual categories and judgments of probability. This line of research including the structure of "natural categories," is continued in Chapter 10.

Suggested Readings

Bourne, L. E., Jr. *Human conceptual behavior.* Boston: Allyn & Bacon, 1966. Describes research on concept learning.

Bourne, L. E., Jr., Ekstrand, B. R., and Dominowski, R. L. *The psychology of thinking.* Englewood Cliffs, N.J.: Prentice-Hall, 1971. Chapters 9, 10, 11, and 12 provide an excellent review of current research and theory in concept learning.

Bruner, J. S., Goodnow, J. J., and Austin, G. A. *A study of thinking.* New York: Wiley, 1956. Describes a classic set of experiments on concept learning.

Duncan, C. P. *Thinking: Current experimental studies.* Philadelphia: Lippincott, 1967. Papers by Bower and Trabasso, by Levine, by Laughlin, and by Hovland and Weiss provide a good survey of theories and research in concept learning.

Johnson, D. M. *A systematic introduction to the psychology of thinking.* New York: Harper & Row, 1972. Chapters 2 and 3 provide a detailed survey of recent experimental work.

Tversky, A., and Kahneman, D. Judgment under uncertainty: heuristics and biases. *Science,* 1974, *125,* 1124–1131. Reviews research on errors in forming hypotheses.

CHAPTER 6

DEDUCTIVE REASONING: Thinking as Logically Drawing Conclusions

Syllogisms

Consider the three problems in Box 6-1 and then pick the conclusion that logically follows each one.

If you think like most people—or at least like most people who participate in psychology experiments—problem 1 was probably the easiest for you (Answer: A). However, problems 2 and 3 generate much higher error rates—75 percent errors for problem 2, with most errors due to subjects picking C instead of E, and 90 percent errors in problem 3, mainly due to subjects picking D instead of E.

Although these results (based on data from Stratton, 1967, and reported by Johnson, 1972) do not suggest that people are stupid, they do indicate that formal logic and individual mental or psycho-logic are not necessarily the same.

BOX 6–1   Sample Syllogisms

Pick the conclusion you can be sure of.

1. All S are M
   All M are P
   Therefore,
   A. All S are P
   B. All S are not P
   C. Some S are P
   D. Some S are not P
   E. None of these conclusions is valid

2. As technology advances and natural petroleum resources are depleted, the securing of petroleum from unconventional sources becomes more imperative. One such source is the Athabasca tar sands of northern Alberta, Canada. Since some tar sands are sources of refinable hydrocarbons, these deposits are worthy of commercial investigation. Some kerogen deposits are also sources of refinable hydrocarbons. Therefore:
   A. All kerogen deposits are tar sands.
   B. No kerogen deposits are tar sands.
   C. Some kerogen deposits are tar sands.
   D. Some kerogen deposits are not tar sands.
   E. None of the above.

3. The delicate Glorias of Argentina, which open only in cool weather, are all Sassoids. Some of the equally delicate Fragilas, found only in damp areas, are not Glorias. What can you infer from these statements?
   A. All Fragilas are Sassoids.
   B. No Fragilas are Sassoids.
   C. Some Fragilas are Sassoids.
   D. Some Fragilas are not Sassoids.
   E. None of the above.

Adapted from Stratton (1967)

Now try the syllogisms in Box 6-2, and indicate for each one whether or not the conclusion logically follows.

If you are like most of Lefford's (1946) subjects, you had much more difficulty answering Yes to problem 1 than to problem 3 and more difficulty answering No to Problem 2 than to problem 4. Although problems 1 and 3 have the same formal characteristics and length (all A are B, all B are C, therefore all A are C), and 2 and 4 have the same formal characteristics and length (all A are B, all C are B, therefore all C are A), problems 1 and 2 are far more difficult. Apparently, human reasoning or psycho-logic is influenced not only by the form of the argument but also by the desirability or amount of agreement with the conclusion.

Syllogisms like the ones just given require deductive thinking—deducing or deriving a conclusion from given premises. This contrasts with inductive thinking, discussed in Chapter 5, which involves inducing or formulating or extrapolating a rule

BOX 6–2   Questionable Conclusions

Does the conclusion logically follow from the premise?

1. War times are prosperous times, and prosperity is highly desriable; therefore, wars are much to be desired.

2. All communists have radical ideas, and all labor union leaders have radical ideas; therefore, all labor union leaders are agents for communism.

3. Philosophers are all human, and all human beings are fallible; therefore, philosophers are fallible, too.

4. All whales live in water, and all fish live in water, too; therefore, all fish must be whales.

Adapted from Lefford (1946)

based on limited information. In deductive thinking, the propositions or rules are given and the thinker uses this given information to derive a conclusion that can be proven correct. Mathematical proofs, for example, are deductive. Inductive thinking, however, such as concept learning, can never result in a provable rule because new information may come along that violates the induced rule; since induced rules are based on a limited set of information, they require the thinker to go beyond that information, to generalize. Since human beings and many other kinds of animals are capable of solving both induction and deduction tasks, such tasks have received much research attention in psychology. Although induction and deduction are tasks rather than theories of thinking, each has an implied view of human thinking. In Chapter 5 we investigated the idea—fostered by examining induction—that thinking involves a constant searching (sampling) for a rule. In this chapter, we shall focus on an approach—suggested by work in deduction—that thinking involves combining information by using a set of psychological and mathematical operations.

DEDUCTIVE REASONING DEFINITION OF THINKING

Although deductive reasoning is not a theoretical approach in the same sense that associationism and Gestalt are, deduction implies that thinking involves the combining of existing information by following specific mental operations as in addition or subtraction. This approach—consistent with the information processing approach—interprets thinking as the processing of premises by using specifiable operators—similar but not identical to formal logical operators.

    William James (1890) devoted nearly an entire chapter of his classic textbook on psychology to describing the two main processes involved in deductive reasoning:

analysis and abstraction. Analysis refers to the process of breaking down an object into its parts and then substituting a part for the object, whereas abstraction refers to subsuming a specific property under a broader, more general rule. As an example of analysis, to process the proposition "Socrates is a man," a thinker must think of Socrates only in terms of one property. James argued that analysis requires a "mode of conceiving"—a way of referring to Socrates (as a man). As an example of abstraction, the thinker, to process the proposition "All men are mortal," must subsume Socrates as a man under the general heading of "mortality." Although James' conception of the analysis and abstraction processes may not necessarily be the best or the most precise (this is really an empirical question to be answered by sound experimental research), it does suggest that deduction may be viewed as a series of specific processes or operations performed on information.

The main focus of this approach is the *syllogism,* which consists of two premises and a conclusion. Three types of syllogisms will be discussed in this chapter: (1) *categorical syllogisms* such as, "All A are B, All B are C, Therefore, All A are C"; (2) *linear syllogisms* such as, "A is greater than B, B is greater than C, Therefore A is greater than C"; and (3) *conditional syllogisms* such as "If p, then q; p is true; Therefore, q is true." In each case, you are given some premises that you must accept as true, then you draw a logical conclusion. Aristotle claimed that syllogistic reasoning represented the highest achievement in human rational thought. Thus, many psychologists have focused on human performance in syllogistic tasks, with hopes of providing information about a task that may be fundamental to human rationality.

CATEGORICAL REASONING

Definitions

There are four types of propositions that describe the relationship between two sets (or categories) of things:

Universal affirmative (UA) such as "All A are B."

Universal negative (UN) such as "No A are B."

Particular affirmative (PA) such as "Some A are B."

Particular negative (PN) such as "Some A are not B."

Venn diagrams of each of these four basic categorical propositions are given in Box 6-3. Note that most of the propositions are ambiguous—you are able to generate more than one possible Venn diagram. For example, the universal affirmative proposition may result if set A and set B are identical or if set A is a subset of set B. Thus, "All A are B" does not necessarily imply "All B are A" but it does not

BOX 6–3 Possible Venn Diagrams for Four Types of Propositions

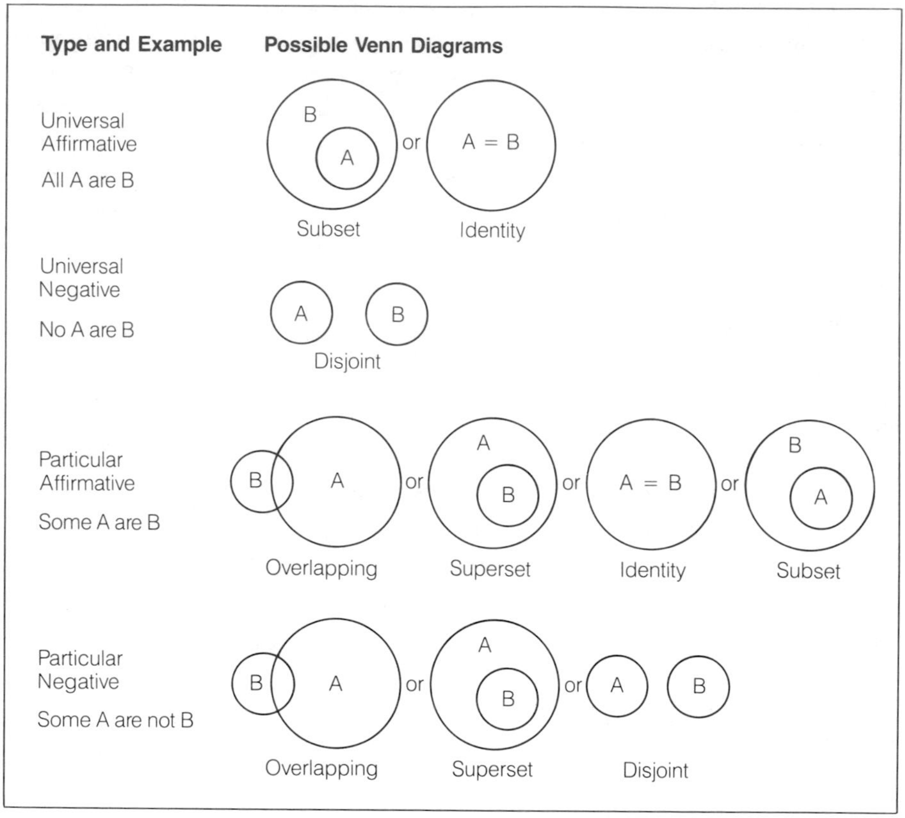

Type and Example	Possible Venn Diagrams

Universal Affirmative

All A are B

Subset   or   A = B Identity

Universal Negative

No A are B

Disjoint

Particular Affirmative

Some A are B

Overlapping or Superset or Identity (A = B) or Subset

Particular Negative

Some A are not B

Overlapping or Superset or Disjoint

rule it out either. Note also that "some" means "at least one and possibly all." Thus, the particular negative proposition may result from either set A and set B overlapping, from set A and set B being disjoint, or from set B being a subset of set A. "Some A are not B" does not necessarily imply "Some B are not A," although it does not rule it out either.

A categorical syllogism consists of two premises and a conclusion with each being any one of the four types of categorical propositions. For example, the syllogism

All magnificent things are preposterous
All syllogisms are magnificent
Therefore, all syllogisms are preposterous

consists of two universal affirmative premises and a universal affirmative conclusion. The subject of the conclusion ("syllogism") is the S term, the predicate of the

BOX 6-4 Form and Examples of Four Figures

Figure 1

M–P	All humans are mortals
S–M	All psychologists are humans
S–P	All psychologists are mortals

Figure 2

P–M	All mortals are humans
S–M	All psychologists are humans
S–P	All psychologists are mortals*

Figure 3

M–P	All humans are mortals
M–S	All humans are psychologists
S–P	All psychologists are mortals*

Figure 4

P–M	All mortals are humans
M–S	All humans are psychologists
S–P	All psychologists are mortals*

*Conclusion is not valid.

---

conclusion (''preposterous'') is the P term, and the middle term, which is in both premises but not in the conclusion (''magnificent''), is the M term. The *major premise* gives the relationship between the predicate (P) and middle (M) term; the *minor premise* gives the relation between the subject (S) and the middle (M) term. There are 4 ways of organizing the major and minor premises, called *figures*, as shown in Box 6-4. In addition, since any of the 4 types of premises may be the major premise and any of the 4 types of premises may be the minor premise, there are 16 possible combinations called *moods*. Each of the 16 moods may appear in any of the four figures. Consequently there are 64 possible pairs of premises; however, if you try to solve them you will find that only 19 of them are valid, that is, only 19 lead to an unambiguous conclusion. For each of the 64 premise pairs, there are 4 possible conclusions, yielding a total of 256 possible syllogisms.

Johnson-Laird and Steedman (1978) have recently argued that the conclusion for a pair of premises can concern the S-P relation—such as All S are P, Some S are P, Some S are not P, or No S are P—as in traditional logic summarized in Box 6-4. They also suggest that the conclusion for a pair of premises can concern the P-S relation—such as All P are S, Some P are S, Some P are not S, No P are S. Using this approach, there are 512 possible syllogisms: 64 premise pairs with 4 possible S-P conclusions and 4 possible P-S solutions for each. If we assume that each of the 64 premise pairs has 8 possible conclusions, then Johnson-Laird and Steedman are able to locate 27 valid syllogisms.

Logical Errors

Box 6-5 gives the form of three types of categorical syllogisms and an example of each. Syllogism 1 is a reasonably simple one with the conclusion following from the premises; however, using premises or conclusions that violate a subject's beliefs, attitudes, or expectancies makes accurate deduction more difficult for this and all syllogistic forms. Syllogisms 2 and 3 are presented in more difficult forms, with the conclusions not necessarily following from the premises. Each of these syllogisms is particularly susceptible to one of three predictable types of errors of logic:

Content errors, in which (as in the first syllogism) the truth or desirability of the premises or conclusion influence the subject's deductions regardless of the logic involved.

Undistributed middle-term errors, in which (as in the second syllogism) the subjects may overgeneralize the breadth of the middle term.

Particular premises errors, in which (as in the third syllogism) subjects may overgeneralize the breadth of "some" to mean "all."

Errors due to form—the latter two types—and to content may be confounded in any one situation, thus increasing the tendency to error. Since these types of errors are quite common, they have enjoyed a practical value for propagandists and others who wish to affect public opinion. However, they are also of theoretical interest because they suggest that formal logic and human logic are not the same, and thus these errors have received much research attention.

Content Errors

To study content errors, Janis and Frick (1943) presented syllogisms as short paragraphs and asked subjects to rate whether they agreed or disagreed with the conclusion and whether or not the conclusion was valid based on the premises. As expected, a high number of errors were obtained, showing a strong tendency for subjects to judge the conclusions they agreed with as valid and the conclusions they disagreed with as invalid. One explanation for these content effects is that deductive syllogisms do not occur in a vacuum, but rather they are assimilated or fitted into the general cognitive structure of the problem solver. *Cognitive consistency*—the tendency for information in a person's memory to be internally consistent—may play a role in deduction.

BOX 6-5   Three Types of Logical Errors

Content Errors

Any form of recreation that constitutes a serious health menace will be outlawed by the City Health Authority. The increasing water pollution in this area will make swimming at local beaches a serious health menace. Swimming at local beaches will be outlawed by the City Health Authority.

Content: undesirable conclusion.

From McGuire (1960)

Undistributed Middle Errors

Wallonians dance the polka. My worthy opponent dances the polka. Therefore, it is obvious that my worthy opponent is a Wallonian.

Form: All A are B, All C are B, therefore All C are A.

Particular Premises Errors

Some Republicans have inherited oil wells. Some Wallonians are Republicans. Hence we know that some Wallonians have inherited oil wells.

Form: Some A are B, Some C are A, therefore Some C are B.

From Wilkins (1928)

The four syllogisms used by Lefford (1946) produced similar results with more errors for conclusions with high emotional content than for less important ones, even though the logical form was identical. Using a different approach, Parrott (1969, cited in Johnson, 1972) presented three types of syllogisms that were identical in logical form but were constructed differently. One type used the symbols X, Y, and Z in the premises, the second contained premises that were true (consistent with the subject's past experience), and the third had premises that were false (not consistent with the subject's past experience). Although the instructions made it clear that the subject was to judge the validity of the conclusion assuming the premises were true, there were large differences in performance. The time to reason, in seconds, was: 21.9 for symbols, 24.2 for true-premise, and 29.4 for false-premise. Apparently, the content-free syllogisms allowed the subjects to reason logically on an independent syllogism and to be less influenced by the need for consistency with other information in their memories.

In an experiment on content effects, McGuire (1960) asked a group of subjects to rate a list of propositions for probability of occurrence and for desirability. Nested within the list were the components of several syllogisms with premises and conclusions separated by other propositions. If the subjects were entirely rational (thinking logically), the probability of a conclusion should be equal to the probability of premise 1 times the probability of premise 2. If the subjects were entirely irrational (indulging in wishful thinking), there should be a high correlation between desirability and probability—the subjects should rate highly desirable conclusions as highly probable regardless of the premises. As might be expected, McGuire found evidence for both logical and wishful thinking with a correlation of .48 between the judged probabilities of the conclusions and the products of the probabilities of the premises, and a correlation of .40 between the rated desirabilities of events and the rated probabilities of occurrence.* These results seem to indicate that deductive reasoning involves more than the three propositions in the syllogism, and that subjects try to fit the propositions within their existing cognitive structure or knowledge. Inconsistent or undesirable premises or conclusions must be dealt with in a way that may violate the rules of logic for a particular syllogism in exchange for preserving the cognitive consistency of the great mass of existing knowledge and beliefs.

Form Errors

The two main errors due to logical form—the fallacy of the undistributed middle and the fallacy due to particular premises—have also been explained in terms of underlying psychological mechanisms. Woodworth and Sells (1935) and Sells (1936) suggested that these errors resulted from an *atmosphere effect* in which the form of the two premises set an atmosphere favorable to accepting conclusions of certain forms. For example, two universal affirmative premises create an atmosphere for the acceptance of a universal affirmative conclusion or two particular negative premises lead to a particular negative conclusion. In addition, any one negative premise creates a negative atmosphere and any one particular premise creates a particular atmosphere. Predictions based on the atmosphere effect theory have been fairly accurate (Sells, 1936; Morgan and Morton, 1944).

Begg and Denny (1969, p. 351) restated the atmosphere theory as two principles: ''Whenever the quality of at least one premise is negative, the quality of the most frequently accepted conclusion will be negative; when neither premise is negative, the conclusion will be affirmative. Whenever the quantity of at least one premise is particular, the quantity of the most frequently accepted conclusion will be particular; when neither premise is particular the conclusion will be universal.'' Based on an

---

*Correlations such as .40 and .48 indicate a moderately strong positive relationship between variables.

analysis of errors in syllogistic reasoning, they concluded that the atmosphere theory was the best predictor of results.

The information-processing approach has encouraged the reformulation of old theories and the development of new ones based on the operation of specific models of the reasoning processes for various tasks. These models may be represented as computer programs, as mathematical equations, or as flow charts. For example, Box 6-6 shows a flow diagram of the processes involved in syllogistic reasoning based on a reformulation of the idea of atmosphere effect (Revlis, 1975).

In the first stage of the model, the subject extracts two pieces of information from each premise—whether the premises is *universal* (All A are B) or *particular* (Some A are B), and whether the premise is *affirmative* (are) or *negative* (are not). In stage 2, the subject determines the same two characteristics of the composite of the two premises based on two rules: (1) if both premises are universal, the composite is universal; if one or both are particular, then the composite is particular; (2) if both premises are affirmative, the composite is affirmative; if one or both are negative, the composite is negative. The subject then extracts the two characteristics of the conclusion (stage 3). Finally, in stage 4, the subject compares the two characteristics of the conclusion with the two characteristics of the composite and answers Yes if they match and No if they do not.

The advantage of specifying the atmosphere effect as a precise model of information-processing stages and rules is that it provides specific predictions that can be tested; as Revlis notes, "The model is sufficiently detailed to make predictions concerning solutions to every syllogism." For example, the model predicts that subjects would never respond that no valid conclusion could be drawn even though many premises were invalid, for example, All P are M, Some M are S. Further, of the syllogisms that have valid conclusions, errors are predicted for the following forms: All M are P, All M are S; All P are M, All M are S; No M are P, No M are S; and No P are M, No M are S. Thus, the model can make predictions about error rates in syllogistic reasoning; such predictions are easily tested. In this way, information-processing models help in creating testable theories—one of the main conditions for the advance of science (Popper, 1959).

A related psychological explanation of logical errors is *invalid conversion* —the tendency to assume that if "All A are B" then "All B are A" or if "Some A are not B" then "Some B are not A." Note that the conversion of the universal affirmative and particular negative propositions is not valid while conversion of the universal negative and particular affirmative propositions is valid. Chapman and Chapman (1959) gave two premises, in letter form, and asked their subjects to choose the correct conclusion:

Some L's are K's.

Some K's are M's.

BOX 6–6 An Information-Processing Model of Syllogistic Reasoning

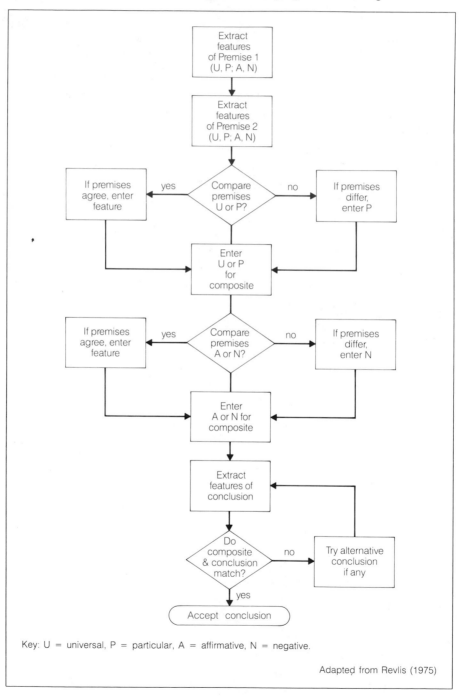

Key: U = universal, P = particular, A = affirmative, N = negative.

Adapted from Revlis (1975)

BOX 6-7 Subjects' Conclusions for Six Syllogisms

Which conclusions can you be sure of?

| | Proportion of Subjects' Conclusions | | | | |
Premises	All S are P.	Some S are P.	No S are P.	Some S are not P.	None of these.
All P are M, All S are M.	.81	.04	.05	.01	.09
All M are P, No S are M.	.02	.03	.82	.05	.08
All P are M, Some M are S.	.06	.77	.02	.06	.07
Some M are P, No S are M.	.01	.06	.62	.13	.18
Some M are not P, No M are S.	.03	.07	.41	.19	.30
No M are P, Some S are not M,	.03	.10	.24	.32	.32

Based on data from Chapman and Chapman (1959)

Therefore,

1. All M's are L's.

2. Some M's are L's.

3. No M's are L's.

4. Some M's are not L's.

5. None of these.

Although the correct answer was always "none of these" for each of 42 experimental syllogisms, the subjects chose other conclusions over 80 percent of the time. Some typical responses are shown in Box 6-7. As you can see, many of the responses, like the first three in the box, seemed to fit both the atmosphere effect explanation and the invalid conversion explanation; however, the atmosphere effect would predict that the main error for the latter three syllogisms should be "Some S are not P" while the more preferred response was often "No S are P," a response that could be derived if subjects made invalid conversions. Thus, the results indicated that invalid conversion could account for a large proportion of errors, including some that could not be accounted for by atmosphere effect.

You may note that the problems taken from Stratton in Box 6-1 result in errors that can be described as atmosphere effect (syllogism 2 has particular affirmative premises that encourage the particular affirmative conclusion, C), and invalid conversion (syllogism 3's statements that "All Glorias are Sassoids" may be converted to "All Sassoids are Glorias," thus encouraging conclusion D). Apparently, some errors may be explained by atmosphere and some by conversion, but while the former is a superficial attempt on the part of the thinker to be consistent, the latter reflects an attempt to be logical that simply is not quite right. Although conversions may be formally illogical, Chapman and Chapman (1959, p. 224) point out that they may be based on consistency with practical past experience since invalid conversions "although logically invalid often correspond to our experience of reality, and being guided by experience are usually regarded as justifiable procedures. One may realistically accept the converse of many, perhaps most particular negative propositions about qualities of objects; for example, some plants are not green and some greens are not plants. The acceptance of the converse of universal affirmative propositions is also often appropriate, for example, all right angles are 90 degrees and also all 90 degree angles are right angles." More detailed models based on the conversion hypothesis are presented in the next sections.

THEORIES OF CATEGORICAL REASONING

Having defined key terms in categorical syllogisms and provided examples of well-known form and content errors, we will now present three current theories of categorical reasoning: Erickson's set theoretic model, Revlin's conversion model, and Johnson-Laird's analogical model. As you will see, each theory emphasizes the importance of how premises are encoded as a major source of errors.

Erickson's Set Theoretic Model

Let's suppose that categorical reasoning involves two phases: (1) translating the premises into internally represented information and (2) combining these representations to generate a conclusion. Erickson (1974, 1978) has proposed that errors in reasoning may occur because subjects are limited in how they accomplish the translation phase and the combining phase.

During translation of premises, subjects may focus on just one interpretation of each premise, although several interpretations may be possible. For example, consider the premise, "All A are B." To deal correctly with this premise, you must be able to simultaneously interpret this premise to mean "A and B are identical" (called *set identity*) and "A is a subset of B" (called *set inclusion*). In order to study how subjects interpret premises, Erickson asked subjects to draw Venn diagrams to represent various premises. For a statement such as "All A are B," 60 percent opted for set identity diagrams and 40 percent preferred set inclusion diagrams, as shown in Box 6-8. Furthermore, subjects were very consistent, almost always drawing the same kind of representation for the same kind of premise. For example, if subjects are given pairs of premises like the ones in Box 6-8, they represent them either as two set identities or as two set inclusions. Apparently, subjects are able to choose one possible interpretation and ignore the others.

When combining the premises, subjects may focus on just one logical conclusion, although there may be several possible logical conclusions. For example, the premises

All C are B
All A are B

can generate five different conclusions. To study how subjects combine premises, Erickson and his colleagues gave two Venn diagrams to subjects and then asked them to draw the conclusion. Examples are given in Box 6-8. As you can see, two identity diagrams always lead to an identity conclusion. However, set inclusion diagrams lead to a variety of conclusions. For example, "C as a subset of B" and "A as a subset of B" lead to an identity conclusion for 20 percent of the subjects, to a disjoint diagram as a conclusion for 10 percent, to an overlap for 20 percent, and to none for 50 percent. Thus, subjects seem to reduce information. When there are many possible interpretations for how to combine premises or for how to interpret a premise, they tend to choose just one.

An interesting aspect of Erickson's theory is its ability to predict performance on categorical reasoning tasks. Box 6-9 shows the percentage of subjects who opted for various interpretations of how to translate and combine premises. For example, for the premises

All B are C
All A are B

60 percent of the subjects interpret the premises as two identity sets; to combine two identity sets, subjects opt for the identity conclusion, all A are C. However, 40 percent of the subjects opt for set inclusion interpretations of the premises; of these, 90 percent choose a set inclusion conclusion (All A are C) and 10 percent choose an overlap (Some A are B) conclusion. Thus, 60 percent plus 36 percent (90 percent of 40 percent) or 96 percent of the subjects should answer "All A are C," 4 percent (10 percent of 40 percent) should answer "Some A are C." Similar predictions were generated for each of the four syllogisms given in Box 6-9, based on the norms established in the experiments just described. The predictions are based on the idea that subjects will use just one interpretation for how to translate and combine premises, and the probabilities of which interpretations will be used can be based on the norms in the previous experiments. Erickson next looked at actual solutions

BOX 6-8 Subjects' Interpretations of Premise Pairs

Premises	Possible Interpretation of Premises		(AC)	(A) C	(C) A	(A)(C)	(A)(C)	None
All B are C (60%) / All A are B (40%)	BC AB		100%	0	0	0	0	0
	B–C A–B		0	90%	0	10%	0	0
All C are B (60%) / All A are B (40%)	BC AB		100%	0	0	0	0	0
	C–B A–B		20%	0	0	20%	10%	50%
All B are C (60%) / All B are A (40%)	BC AB		100%	0	0	0	0	0
	B–C B–A		20%	5%	5%	70%	0%	0%
All C are B (60%) / All B are A (40%)	BC AB		100%	0	0	0	0	0
	C–B B–A		5%	0	85%	10%	0%	0%

Based on Erickson (1974)

BOX 6–9 Predicted and Obtained Reasoning Performance

Premises	Possible Conclusions	Predicted	Obtained
All B are C	All A are C	96%	90%
All A are B	No A are C	0%	2%
	Some A are C	4%	4%
	Some A are not C	0%	1%
	None	0%	4%
All C are B	All A are C	68%	66%
All A are B	No A are C	4%	2%
	Some A are C	8%	12%
	Some A are not C	0%	1%
	None	20%	20%
All B are C	All A are C	70%	63%
All B are A	No A are C	0%	1%
	Some A are C	30%	30%
	Some A are not C	0%	1%
	None	0%	6%
All C are B	All A are C	62%	70%
All B are A	No A are C	0%	2%
	Some A are C	38%	23%
	Some A are not C	0%	2%
	None	0%	3%

Based on Erickson (1974)

given to syllogisms by subjects in several different studies (Erickson, 1974, 1975, Chapman and Chapman, 1959; Ceraso and Provitera, 1971) and developed a mean to indicate the obtained answers. Box 6-9 shows that the predicted and obtained answers for four syllogisms were amazingly close.

These results indicate that Erickson was able to account for much of the performance of subjects by assuming that subjects tend to ignore possible interpretations of how to translate and combine premises. However, Erickson's job is incomplete, since the analysis has not been extended to all syllogisms. Another problem is that other researchers have obtained quite different data concerning how subjects interpret premises as Venn diagrams (Neimark and Chapman, 1975). In addition, there may be other theories that account for more of the data. In any case, Erickson's theory proposes an account of human reasoning in which people are logical but overly restrictive in how they handle ambiguous information.

Revlin's Conversion Model

Revlin and his colleagues (Revlis, 1975; Revlin and Leirer, 1978) have provided an extension of Chapman and Chapman's conversion theory. Revlin's model is an

BOX 6-10 The Meaning Stack for "All A Are B"

Level	Description	Example
1	Converted Premise	All B are A
2	Unconverted Premise	All A are B
3	Atmosphere Relations	Universal, Affirmative
4	•	•
•	•	•
•	•	•

Adapted from Revlis (1975)

advance over Chapman and Chapman's theory because Revlin's model is far more detailed and able to make precise performance predictions. Actually, Revlin's model assumes that people are capable of using a conversion approach under some circumstances, a nonconversion (that is, correct) approach under some circumstances, an atmosphere approach under other circumstances, and even guess under yet other circumstances.

Revlin's theory has two main parts: (1) a *meaning stack*—a theory of how premises and conclusions are stored in memory—and (2) a *reasoning model*—a precise theory of how a conclusion is drawn from the encoded premises. Box 6-10 provides an example of the meaning stack for a premise such as "All A are B." The meaning stack assumes that the premise (or conclusion) is encoded as a stack of meanings, with the converted premise on top, the unconverted premise under it, followed by the atmosphere features (such as universal versus particular and negative versus positive) lower in the stack. For example, as Box 6-10 shows, the premise "All A are B" would be stored as "All B are A" for level 1, "All A are B" for level 2, "universal, positive" for level 3, and so on.

Box 6-11 gives a general overview of the model of reasoning. As you can see, there are four stages:

1. *Premise encoding*—The reasoner translates each premise into a stack of meanings with the converted version of the premise on top, and so on.

2. *Composite*—The reasoner puts the two premises together to generate a conclusion. A stack of possible conclusions is generated; at the top is the conclusion based on the converted versions of the premises, on the second level is the conclusion based on the unconverted version of the premises, on the next level is the atmosphere conclusion, and so on.

BOX 6–11   Revlin's Conversion Model

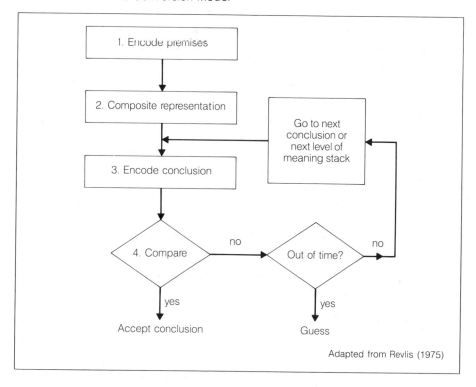

Adapted from Revlis (1975)

3. *Conclusion encoding*—The conclusion given in the problem is encoded with conversion as in stage 1. If there are five possible conclusions given in the problem, each one is processed in turn.

4. *Comparison*—The reasoner compares whether the conclusion encoded at stage 3 matches the top composite generated at stage 2. If so, the reasoner accepts the conclusion as valid. If there is no match, the procedure is carried out for each of the five possible conclusions until a match is found. If no match is found on any of the conclusions, then the reasoner moves on to the second level of meaning for the composite based on the unconverted premises. If this fails to yield at least one match, then the reasoner may move on to the third level of meaning for the composite based on atmosphere. If the reasoner runs out of time or motivation, a guess is made. Thus, the comparison process assumes that the reasoner prefers not to opt for ''none of the above'' as an answer.

In order to test this theory, Revlis (1975) asked subjects to solve a series of abstract syllogisms under some time constraint—a limit of 15 to 30 seconds, for example. First, Revlis examined performance on invalid syllogisms, those in which the correct answer is "none of the above." For some of these (called *differents*), the conversion model generates a conclusion other than "none"; thus, the conversion model predicts none correct for these invalid differents. For some of the invalid syllogisms (called *sames*), the conversion model and logic both generate the same conclusion; the conversion model predicts that a subject will guess when no answer can be found so there should be 20 percent correct. Subjects' performances approached the levels predicted by the conversion model: 6 percent on the invalid differents and 15 percent on the invalid sames.

Similarly, let's examine the predictions for valid syllogisms, those in which there is a correct answer. For some valid syllogisms, the conversion model and logic predict different answers; according to the conversion model, these syllogisms should yield a rate of none correct. For other valid syllogisms, the conversion model and logic generate the same answer; thus, on these there should be a 100 percent correct performance according to the conversion model. Results are consistent with these predictions with 13 percent on the valid differents and 73 percent correct on the valid sames. Thus, the conversion model is able to predict when answers are likely to be different from logic. More recently, Revlin and Leirer (1978) have shown that conversion can be blocked when certain kinds of concrete premises are used; in other words, subjects do not seem to convert premises when they can tell that such conversion is contrary to experience. For example, "All hammers are tools" is not converted to "All tools are hammers." In addition, Revlin and Leirer (1980) have provided evidence that categorical sentences are often converted even when they are not involved in reasoning.

What can be done to prevent erroneous conversions? Ceraso and Provitera (1971) were able to reduce conversions if they stated premises in a more explicit, less ambiguous form. For example, the premise, "All A are B" is ambiguous and can lead to such conversions as, "All B are A." However, the premise "All A are B, but some B are not A" defines an unambiguous relationship and is less likely to lead to conversion.

Johnson-Laird's Analogical Model

Johnson-Laird and his colleagues (Johnson-Laird and Steedman, 1978) have claimed that research on syllogistic reasoning should conform to four methodological requirements: (1) the subject should be asked to produce the conclusion rather than just tell whether a given conclusion is valid in a multiple choice test, (2) experiments should use a large selection of 512 possible forms of syllogisms, (3) syllogisms should be stated in neutral English rather than with abstract letters, and

BOX 6–12 Number of Subjects Producing A–C and C–A Conclusions

A–B, B–C Figure

Premise Pairs	Conclusions	Number of Subjects
All A are B	All A are C	(14)
All B are C	All C are A	(2)
Some A are B	Some A are C	(15)
All B are C	Some C are A	(2)
All A are B	No A are C	(13)
No B are C	No C are A	(2)
	Some A are C	(2)
Some A are B	Some A are not C	(10)
No B are C	Some A are C	(4)

B–A, C–B Figure

All B are A	All C are A	(12)
All C are B	All A are C	(4)
All B are A	Some C are A	(16)
Some C are B	Some A are C	(1)
All B are A	Some A are not C	(6)
No C are B	No A are C	(5)
	No C are A	(3)
Some B are A	Some A are not C	(9)
No C are B	No C are A	(2)
	Some C are A	(2)
	Some A are C	(2)

Adapted from Johnson-Laird and Steedman (1978)

(4) analysis should be performed for each syllogism rather than averaging over many different forms. Johnson-Laird and his colleagues claim that their studies are the first to adequately meet these requirements.

In a typical experiment (Johnson-Laird and Steedman, 1978), subjects were given pairs of premises, such as

None of the musicians are inventors.
All of the inventors are professors.

Subjects were asked to assume that the people mentioned in the syllogism are all in one room and to draw the conclusion that best fits the premises. Examples of the form of the syllogisms used in one study are given in Box 6-12. Some of the subjects' conclusions are also given in the box, with the number of subjects who gave each conclusion indicated in parentheses. Thus, in this study subjects were asked to form a concrete analogical representation of the premises—that is, musicians, inventors, and professors are all in one room—and to actually generate a conclusion.

One of the main findings was that the figure of the syllogism influenced the form of the conclusion that subjects produced. For the figure

$$A - B$$
$$B - C$$

such as All A are B, Some B are C, subjects tended to give a conclusion of the form $A - C$ such as All A are C. For the figure

$$B - A$$
$$C - B$$

such as All B are A, Some C are B, subjects tended to give a conclusion of the form $C - A$ such as All C are A. For the other figures

$$B - A \qquad\qquad A - B$$
$$B - C \qquad\qquad C - B$$

there were only mild biases for one form of the conclusion over the other. This figure effect was a new contribution that could only be observed when subjects were asked to generate conclusions.

To account for their new results, Johnson-Laird and Steedman proposed an "analogical theory" consisting of four stages.

1. *Translating into analogical representation.* The premises are translated into an analogical representation such as that shown in the top of Box 6-13. For example, the premise "All artists are beekeepers," means there are some artists (represented by letter a's) and each one is also (represented by an arrow) a beekeeper (represented by letter b's). In addition, some b's may not be a's.

2. *Heuristic combining of the premises.* Once the premises are represented analogically, they can be combined as shown in Box 6-13. For example, the middle terms (b's) can be connected by arrows or "not signs" (indicating no relationship) to both a's and c's.

3. *Drawing conclusions.* The next step is to draw all possible conclusions. The plus (+) indicates a possible conclusion while the question mark (?) indicates that it is not possible to draw a conclusion, as shown in Box 6-12. As you can see, when the format of the syllogism goes in the direction A to B to C, then a conclusion based on A to C is favored; however, when the direction is B to A and B to C, then the conclusion can be based on either A to C or C to A.

BOX 6–13 An Analogical Representation of Premises and Conclusions

---

1. Translating into Analogical Representation

All artists are beekeepers	a a a ↓ ↓ ↓ b b b (b) (b)	
Some artists are beekeepers.	a (a) ↓ b (b)	
No artists are beekeepers.	a a ⊥ ⊥ b b	
Some artists are not beekeepers.	a (a) ⊥ ↓ b b	

2. Heuristic Combining of Premises

All artists are beekeepers.
  (All A are B)

Some of the beekeepers are chemists.
  (Some B are C)

```
a   a
↓   ↓
b   b   (b)
↓
c       (c)
```

3. Drawing Conclusions

Some artists are beekeepers.
All beekeepers are chemists.
  ∴ Some A are C (16)
  ∴ Some C are A (3)

```
+   ?
a  (a)
↓
b  (b)          Optimal direction: A to C
↓   ↓
c   c  (c)
+   ?
```

All beekeepers are artists.
Some beekeepers are chemists.
  ∴ Some A are C (11)
  ∴ Some C are A (9)

```
+   ?
a   a
↑   ↑  (a)      No optimal direction
b  (b)
↓
c  (c)
+   ?
```

4. Logical Testing

All artists are beekeepers.
  (All A are B)

Some beekeepers are chemists.
  (Some B are C)
  ∴ No valid conclusion

```
?   ?
a   a
↓   ↓
b   b  (b)
        ↓
c      (c)
?       ?
```

Adapted from Johnson-Laird and Steedman (1978)

4. *Logical testing*. The last step is to try to reduce the number of possible conclusions, by accepting only those that are consistent with all interpretations of the premises. For example, Box 6-13 shows that the syllogism, all A are B, some B are C, suggests several conclusions based on heuristic combining, but they all can be eliminated under logical testing.

Errors may occur when the subject does not have time or resources to perform the final stage of logical testing. Based on this model, Johnson-Laird and Steedman were able to account for much of the performances of their subjects. Their theory assumes that errors occur because of incomplete processing of the information.

CONDITIONAL REASONING

Conditional syllogisms consist of two premises and a conclusion. The first premise is an implicative sentence of the form, *if p, then q,* where *p* is some antecedent condition and *q* is some consequent condition. The second premise is either an affirmation or denial of either the antecedent—"p is true" or "p is not true"—or consequent condition—"q is true" or "q is not true." For example, consider the conditional syllogism:

If there is a solar eclipse, then the streets will be dark.
There is a solar eclipse.
Are the streets dark?

In this example, the first premise is of the form, "if p, then q," with "solar eclipse" as the antecedent condition, and "the streets will be dark" as the consequent condition. The second premise affirms the antecedent condition, and the conclusion affirms the consequent condition.

Now that we have our terms straight, let's consider some of the basic research findings and theories concerning conditional reasoning. Staudenmayer and his colleagues (Staudenmayer, 1975, 1978; Taplin and Staudenmayer, 1973) have found that many errors in conditional reasoning can be attributed to subjects' misinterpretations of the first premise. For example, many subjects interpret the conditional statement, "if p, then q," as a *biconditional* relation; thus, subjects also assume "if q, then p." Actually, in formal logic you should assume only that "if p, then q" involves a *conditional* relation; thus, whether "if q then p" is true or not is unknown.

Box 6-14 provides examples of eight major conditional syllogisms. The column labeled "Conditional Interpretation" gives an evaluation of the conclusion assuming the first premise is interpreted as a conditional relation. The "Biconditional Interpretation" column gives an evaluation of the conclusion assuming that the first premise is interpreted as a biconditional relation. As you can see, both inter-

BOX 6–14   Answers for Eight Conditional Syllogisms Based on Conditional and Biconditional Interpretations

Example	Form	Answer for Conditional Interpretation	Answer for Biconditional Interpretation
1. If the switch is turned on, then the light will go on. The switch is turned on. ∴ The light goes on.	If p, then q p is true ∴ q is true	True	True
2. If the switch is turned on, then the light will go on. The switch is turned on. ∴ The light does not go on.	If p, then q p is true ∴ not q is not true	False	False
3. If the switch is turned on, then the light will go on. The switch is not turned on. ∴ The light goes on.	If p, then q not p is not true ∴ q is true	Sometimes	False
4. If the switch is turned on, then the light will go on. The switch is not turned on. ∴ The light does not go on.	If p, then q not p is not true ∴ not q is not true	Sometimes	True
5. If the switch is turned on, then the light will go on. The light goes on. ∴ The switch is turned on.	If p, then q q is true ∴ p is true	Sometimes	True
6. If the switch is turned on, then the light will go on. The light goes on. ∴ The switch is not turned on.	If p, then q q is true ∴ not p is not true	Sometimes	False
7. If the switch is turned on, then the light will go on. The light does not go on. ∴ The switch is turned on.	If p, then q q is not true ∴ p is true	False	False
8. If the switch is turned on, then the light will go on. The light does not go on. ∴ The switch is not turned on.	If p, then q not q is not true ∴ not p is not true	True	True

Adapted from Staudenmayer (1975)

pretations yield the same answers for syllogisms, 1, 2, 7, and 8, but they differ on problems 3, 4, 5, and 6. For example, in problem 5, a biconditional interpretation adds a second way of stating the first premise, "If the light goes on, then the switch is turned on."

In a series of experiments by Staudenmayer (1975, 1978), subjects were given

BOX 6–15 Performance on Eight Conditional Syllogisms

Example	Form	True (Always)	Sometimes	False (Never)
1. If the card has an A on the left, it has a 7 on the right. The card has an A on the left. The card has a 7 on the right.	If p, then q p is true ∴ q is true	100%	0%	0%
2. If the card has an A on the left, it has a 7 on the right. The card has an A on the left. The card does not have a 7 on the right	If p, then q p is true ∴ q is not true	0%	0%	100%
3. If the card has an A on the left, it has a 7 on the right. The card does not have an A on the left. The card has a 7 on the right.	If p, then q p is not true ∴ q is true	5%	79%	100%
4. If the card has an A on the left, it has a 7 on the right. The card does not have an A on the left. The card does not have a 7 on the right.	If p, then q p is not true ∴ q is not true	21%	77%	2%
5. If the card has an A on the left, it has a 7 on the right. The card has a 7 on the right. The card has an A on the left.	If p, then q q is true ∴ p is true	23%	77%	0%
6. If the card has an A on the left, it has a 7 on the right. The card has a 7 on the right. The card does not have an A on the left.	If p, then q q is true ∴ p is not true	4%	82%	14%
7. If the card has an A on the left, it has a 7 on the right. The card does not have a 7 on the right. The card has an A on the left.	If p, then q q is not true ∴ p is true	0%	23%	77%
8. If the card has an A on the left, it has a 7 on the right. The card does not have a 7 on the right. The card does not have an A on the left.	If p, then q q is not true ∴ q is not true	57%	39%	4%

Adapted from Rips and Marcus (1977)

BOX 6-16 Card Turning Problem

If a card has a vowel on one side, then it has an even number on the other side.

| A | D | 4 | 7 |

Select those cards that you definitely need to turn over to find out whether or not they violate the rule.

Adapted from Wason (1966)

conditional syllogisms such as those in Box 6-14 and were asked to evaluate whether the conclusion was "true", "false," or "sometimes true." Most of the subjects behaved as if they consistently used either a conditional interpretation on all syllogisms or a biconditional interpretation exclusively. For example, when the premise was in the form "if p, then q," 59 percent of the consistent subjects behaved as if they used a biconditional interpretation; for premises of the form "p causes q," 77 percent of the consistent subjects behaved as if they used a biconditional interpretation. Similarly, for abstract material (such as single letters) more people used biconditional interpretations than they did for concrete material (such as sentences). Staudenmayer concluded that errors in conditional reasoning answers can be attributed to the subjects' interpretations of the premises rather than to a faulty reasoning process.

Rips and Marcus (1977) asked subjects to judge conditional syllogisms such as those given in Box 6-15. The results indicated perfect performance on syllogisms 1 and 2, but many errors on the others. Rips and Marcus were able to develop a model that accounts for the error patterns in the box by assuming that: (1) some subjects use a biconditional interpretation of the premises, (2) negatives in a premise or conclusion tend to increase the probability of misinterpreting the information, and (3) many comparisons among premises and conclusions increase the probability of error. Thus, Rips and Marcus extended earlier work by assuming that biconditional interpretations are one factor that influences performance.

Additional evidence concerning subjects' interpretation of conditional statements is provided by Wason (1966, 1968; Johnson-Laird and Wason, 1970; Wason and Johnson-Laird, 1972). For example, Box 6-16 shows a problem in which subjects are given a conditional statement such as, "If a card has a vowel on one side, then it has an even number on the other side." In addition, subjects are given four cards corresponding to an affirmed antecedent (A), a denied antecedent (D), an affirmed consequent (4), and a denied consequent (7). The subject's job is to determine which cards should be flipped over to test the truth of the statement.

Let's assume that you use a biconditional interpretation of the statement and, as Anderson (1980) suggests, that you cannot use denied conditions. Then, you would assume both the given statement and its reversed interpretation, "If a card has an even number on one side, then it has a vowel on the other." To test the given statement, you would want to flip over the A card; if it lacked an even number you would know that the statement was not true. To test the reversed version of the statement, you would want to flip over the 4 card to make sure it had a vowel on the other side. This is the most popular strategy among Wason's subjects: 46 percent asked to flip over A and 4. However, let's assume that you use only a conditional interpretation of the premise and that you will not rule out the use of denied conditions. In this case, you would select A because you know that the premise says there must be an even number on the other side. In addition, you would choose the 7 card; if it had a vowel on the other side, you would know that the statement cannot be true. Only 4 percent of the subjects selected A and 7, although it is the logically correct answer. Note that flipping over the 4 card does not test the statement, since either a vowel or a consonant would be consistent with the statement. Wason's subjects opted for biconditional interpretations of conditional statements and were unable to use negative (that is, denied) conditions.

Is there any way to combat these misinterpretations of conditional statements? In one study (Johnson-Laird, Legrenzi, and Legrenzi, 1972; Johnson-Laird and Wason, 1977), subjects were given a concrete version of the previous task. For example, the conditional statement might be, "If an envelope is sealed, then it has a 50 lira stamp on it." The five instances were a sealed envelope (affirmed antecedent), an unsealed envelope (denied antecedent), envelope with a 50 lira stamp (affirmed consequent), an envelope with a 40 lira stamp (denied consequent), and an envelope with no stamp (denied consequent). The subject's job was to pretend that she was sorting mail in a post office and to determine which envelopes should be flipped over to test the statement. The task is summarized in Box 6-17. Unlike the abstract version of this task, the majority of the subjects in the envelope experiment said that the sealed envelope and the 40 lira envelope should be turned over. Thus, most subjects behaved logically, using a conditional interpretation and negative conditions. This study suggests that when a real context is used, the tendency to make incorrect interpretations is decreased.

The results of work on conditional reasoning suggest that errors occur when subjects misinterpret a conditional statement as biconditional and when they fail to deal adequately with information about denied conditions. Current research suggests that many errors on conditional reasoning tasks are due to people's failure to understand what "if" and "not" mean, rather than failures to reason logically.

BOX 6–17   Envelope Problem

If a letter is sealed, then it has a 50 lira stamp on it.

Select those envelopes that you definitely need to turn over to find out whether or not they violate the rule.

Adapted from Johnson-Laird and Wason (1977)

LINEAR REASONING

Another type of logic problem that has been carefully investigated involves linear reasoning tasks, such as A is better than B; B is better than C; Is A better than C? For example, DeSoto, London, and Handel (1965) allowed their subjects 10 seconds to respond Yes or No to conclusions based on premises like those shown in Box 6-18. According to the traditional view of logical reasoning, problems 1 and 4 ought to be easiest since they proceed from one extreme to the middle to the other extreme in presenting the three terms; however, problem 4 is one of the most difficult, and problems 5 and 6, which should be difficult, are among the easiest. The authors concluded that formal logic is not necessarily the system human beings use to reason. "Clearly, an altogether different paralogic is required to account for the findings. We would like to propose two paralogical principles . . . that people learn orderings better in one direction than the other . . . [and] that people end-anchor orderings." The first principle is demonstrated by the fact that the subjects performed better on an evaluative ordering when the terms were presented better-to-worse (as in problem 1) than on a mixed order (as in problems 2 and 3), and worst when presented worse-to-better (as in problem 4). The second principle—end-anchor orderings—is indicated by the fact that the subjects performed better with propositions that gave an extreme term first (that is, the best or worst) followed by a middle term than with propositions that stated the middle term first followed by an end term; for example, problems 5 and 6 have two propositions that go from ends to middle and are much easier than problems 7 and 8, which have two propositions that each go from middle to ends.

DeSoto, London, and Handel described the reasoning process as involving *spatial paralogic* in which an up-down or right-left series of spaces is imagined and the terms of the ordering (A, B, C) are placed in the spaces. Similar results were

BOX 6–18   Proportion Correct Response for Eight Deduction Problems

Premises	Proportion Correct Response	Form of Premises	
		Within Premises	Between Premises
1. A is better than B B is better than C	.61	better-to-worse	better-to-worse
2. B is better than C A is better than B	.53	better-to-worse	worse-to-better
3. B is worse than A C is worse than B	.50	worse-to-better	better-to-worse
4. C is worse than B B is worse than A	.43	worse-to-better	worse-to-better
5. A is better than B C is worse than B	.62	ends-to-middle	better-to-worse
6. C is worse than B A is better than C	.57	ends-to-middle	worse-to-better
7. B is worse than A B is better than C	.41	middle-to-ends	better-to-worse
8. B is better than C B is worse than A	.38	middle-to-ends	worse-to-better

The question for the subjects was stated in each of four ways:
Is A better than C? Is C better than A? Is A worse than C?
Is C worse than A?

obtained using "better-worse," "above-below," "lighter-darker," and "left-right" although performance was generally poorer for left-right possibly because it is more difficult to imagine horizontal than vertical ordering. Performance was poorer with "worse" than "better," with "below" than "above," and with "right of" than "left of," which suggested that the direction of filling the spatial ordering was important.

Huttenlocher (1968) has summarized a series of experiments that replicated the DeSoto findings but used orderings of the form, "Tom is shorter than Sam. Sam is shorter than Pete. Who is tallest?" Huttenlocher noted that the first premise set up a relationship between two terms (X is taller than Y or X is shorter than Y) and the second premise told the subject where to place the third term, either above or below the other two terms. If the subject of the second premise was the third term, such as Tom is taller than John, Sam is shorter than John, then the error rates and response

BOX 6–19   A Block Problem

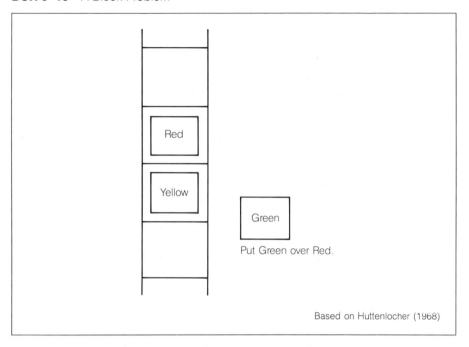

Put Green over Red.

Based on Huttenlocher (1968)

times to answer "Who is tallest?" were lower than if the third term (Sam) was the object of the second premise, such as Tom is taller than John; John is taller than Sam. Even when the premises were given in the passive voice, reasoning was better when the third (or mobile) term was the logical subject and grammatical object of the second premise. For example, Tom is leading John, Tom is led by Sam was easier than Tom is leading John, Sam is led by John. Apparently the ability to process the second proposition depends on how it fits into the fixed relation established by the first premise.

Huttenlocher's emphasis on the subject-object grammar of the mobile third term in the second premise added a new type of approach to DeSoto's principle of end anchoring. In experiments with children, Huttenlocher found that it was easier for the children to place a block in a concrete ladder or array, as shown in Box 6-19, if the subject of the instruction sentence was the block to be placed. If the ladder had a red block above a yellow block, the children could more easily place the third block (green) in the ladder when they were given sentences in which the green block was the subject, as in "put green over red," or "put green under yellow," than when the mobile block was the object of the sentence, as in "put red under green," or "put yellow over green." The deductive reasoning process of adults may involve

BOX 6–20   Mean Solution Time in Seconds for 16 Deduction Problems

Premises	Who is Best?	Who is Worst?	Mean
1a. A better than B; B better than C	5.4	6.1	5.8
1b. B better than C; A better than B	5.0	5.5	5.2
2a. C worse than B; B worse than A	6.3	6.5	6.4
2b. B worse than A; C worse than B	5.9	5.0	5.5
3a. A better than B; C worse than B	5.4	5.3	5.3
3b. C worse than B; A better than B	4.8	5.8	5.3
4a. B worse than A; B better than C	5.0	6.0	5.5
4b. B better than C; B worse than A	6.1	5.4	5.8
1'a. A not as bad as B; B not as bad as C	6.8	6.0	6.3
1'b. B not as bad as C; A not as bad as B	7.2	6.6	6.8
2'a. C not as good as B; B not as good as A	5.6	6.6	6.1
2'b. B not as good as A; C not as good as B	6.1	6.6	6.4
3'a. A not as bad as B; C not as good as B	6.3	6.7	6.5
3'b. C not as good as B; A not as bad as B	6.7	6.3	6.5
4'a. B not as good as A; B not as bad as C	6.1	6.2	6.1
4'b. B not as bad as C; B not as good as A	5.5	7.1	6.2

From Clark (1969). Copyright 1969 by The American Psychological Association. Reprinted by permission of the author.

this same sort of placing objects into an imaginary array, with the first proposition setting the fixed relation between two terms and the second proposition telling the thinker where in the array to place the third term. Answering questions about who is the tallest or shortest involves referring to the constructed spatial array. Thus, while Huttenlocher retained the idea that thinkers construct a spatial linear ordering, she considered that the difficulty in placing items in the imaginary array was influenced by the grammar of the second premise or what DeSoto called "ends-to-middle" end anchoring.

While DeSoto and Huttenlocher described the deductive reasoning process as constructing a spatial image, using such principles as end anchoring, Clark (1969) attempted to show that reasoning can better be described in terms of nonspatial linguistic processes. Clark asked subjects to respond to problems such as: If John isn't as good as Pete, and Dick isn't as good as John, then who is the best? The overall average response times for eight problem types are given in Box 6-20. The performance on the first eight problems seems to fit nicely with the results of DeSoto and Huttenlocher: performance was better on problems where the propositions went from better-to-worse, such as 1a and 1b, rather than worse-to-better, such as 2a and 2b; and performance was better when the third term was the subject of the second proposition (that is, was end anchored) as in 1b, 2b, and 3a and b rather than the object, as in 1a, 2a, and 4a and b. However, based on the new information provided by the eight negative examples, Clark proposed three principles to describe reasoning in terms of linguistic processes:

1. *The primacy of functional relations* —the idea that it is the logical (or functional) relations in a sentence that are stored rather than the grammatical relations of voice and negatives; for example, "A is led by B" may be translated as "B leads A," or "A is not as good as B" may be translated as "B is better than A."

2. *Lexical markings* —adjectives that imply both a scale name and a position on the scale (marked adjectives) such as "bad" or "short" require more effort to encode than adjectives that imply only the scale name but no position on the scale (unmarked adjectives) such as "tall" or "good." (To test whether an adjective is marked, you could ask whether there is a difference between "How tall is X?" versus "How short is X?" or "How good was dinner?" versus "How bad was dinner?" The marked adjectives imply that X is short or that dinner was bad.) Simpler lexicon such as "X is better than Y" is easier to store and process than "Y is worse than X."

3. *The principle of congruence* —thinkers compare the question with the functional information in memory and reformulate the question if necessary to make it congruent with this information.

The principle of functional relations correctly predicts that the eight problems with negatives will take longer to solve than the eight sentences without negatives, presumably due to an extra translation step. Similarly, the principle of lexical marking predicts that problems with "bad" or "worse," such as 2 and 1', should be more difficult than those with good or better such as 1 and 2'. The principle of congruence predicts that if the propositions are given in terms of "worse than," then the question "Who is worst?" will be easier, but if the propositions are given in terms of "better than" then "Who is best?" will be easier. This finding is generally upheld. In addition, the principles of congruence and functional relation suggest that problems 3 and 4' (with functionally identical sentences) should be easier than problems 4 and 3' (also with functionally identical sentences), since in the former if A is worse than B then A is worst, and if A is better than B then A is best, but not in the latter. Most of Clark's results are consistent with those of Huttenlocher and with DeSoto, and his linguistic interpretation provides a different—albeit not necessarily contradictory—analysis of the reasoning process primarily in terms of how individual propositions are encoded and processed. The differences between the a-form and b-form of the eight problems, however, are not well explained by Clark and seem to be best interpreted by the principle of the end anchoring of functional

BOX 6–21   Mean Response Time in Seconds for 12 Deduction Problems

Typical Passage

In a small forest just south of nowhere, a deer, a bear, a wolf and a hawk were battling for dominion over the land. It boiled down to a battle of wits, so intelligence was the crucial factor. The bear was smarter than the hawk, the hawk was smarter than the wolf, and the wolf was smarter than the deer . . . .   In the end, each of the battles was decided in its own way and tranquility returned to the area.

Typical Results

Question Form	Mean Response Time in Seconds
A > B?	1.1
B > C?	2.1
C > D?	2.0
A > C?	1.1
B > D?	1.8
A > D?	1.0
B > A?	1.8
C > B?	2.2
D > C?	1.7
C > A?	1.8
D > B?	1.7
D > A?	1.3

From Potts (1972, 1974)

propositions. For example, problem 2b presents items in the order B, A, C, so that the end term, C, is anchored into the A > B relations; while problem 2a presents items in the order C, B, B, so that first the B > C relation is established but the end term, A, is not mentioned next. As predicted by end anchoring, 2a takes more time to solve than does 2b.

Potts (1972) has focused on the cognitive processes a thinker goes through to answer a question about a linear ordering. Potts had subjects read a paragraph about a linear ordering in the form A > B, B > C, C > D as shown in Box 6-21. One interesting finding was that the subjects were more accurate in answering questions about the remote pairs such as A > C, B > D, and A > D than they were about the adjacent pairs A > B, B > C, and C > D, even though the former were not presented and had to be deduced from the adjacents. This "distance effect" result indicated that subjects did not simply copy the list of three presented propositions (that is, three separate sentences) in their memories, but rather may have formed a sort of ordering list such as a spatial list. When the subjects were presented with a question about the ordering of certain animals—bear > hawk > wolf > deer, like

"Is the hawk smarter than the deer?"—they used a sort of end-anchoring strategy, according to Potts. First they checked to see if either term in the question was an end term in the ordering. For example, is hawk the first or last term in the ordering, and is deer the first or last term in the ordering? If not, then they had to process more deeply by checking, for example, to see if the first term in the question was the second to last term in the ordering. Potts' results are given in Box 6-21. As predicted by the model, for example, questions of the form "Is B > C?" and "Is C > B?" took the longest time to answer since they required deeper processing in the model while questions beginning with the A term ("Is A > C?") took the least time to answer. Potts' work provides a good example of how cognitive models of the reasoning process may be established and, in this case, also provides a more detailed description of the end-anchoring effect.

In addition, Potts (1972) provided a process model to describe the steps that might be involved in solving deductions about a four-term linear ordering. The subject's reasoning process is represented as a flow chart as in Box 6-22. When the subject has learned an ordering such as A > B > C > D and is given a question—Is A > C?, for example—the model suggests the following stages: The first item in the test question is checked to see whether it is the first item in the ordering (if so, answer True) or the last item in the ordering (answer False). Otherwise, the second item in the test question is checked to see whether it is the first item in the ordering (if so, answer False) or the last item in the ordering (answer True). If none of these tests produces a response, the subject checks to see if the second item in the question pair is the second to last item in the ordering; if so, the subject answers True and if not, the answer is False. The model provides specific predictions that can be tested, for example, test questions with A or D as the first item should be answered most quickly, test questions with B or C as the first item but A or D as the second should be a little slower, and test questions with B or C as first and second items should be longest. Potts' model is partially a reformulation of the idea of end anchoring and provides a new and testable way of presenting the idea.

Potts' research (1972, 1978; Scholz and Potts, 1974) suggests that subjects form an integrated representation at the time of encoding. However, an alternative encoding strategy might be to memorize each premise as presented and then combine them to make inferences at the time of questioning. To test the idea that subjects may use either strategy, Mayer (1979) presented all adjacent and remote pairs of a five-term linear ordering to subjects. For some subjects, the information was in an artificial, or abstract, form such as "B > D." For other subjects the information was in a more familiar form, such as "Bill is taller than Dave." The artificial group performed as if they memorized each premise separately, making equivalent errors in learning both adjacent and remote pairs. The familiar group performed as if they formed a linear ordering, performing as in Potts' experiments: less errors on remote than adjacent pairs.

BOX 6–22   An Information-Processing Model of Reasoning with Four-Term
Linear Orderings

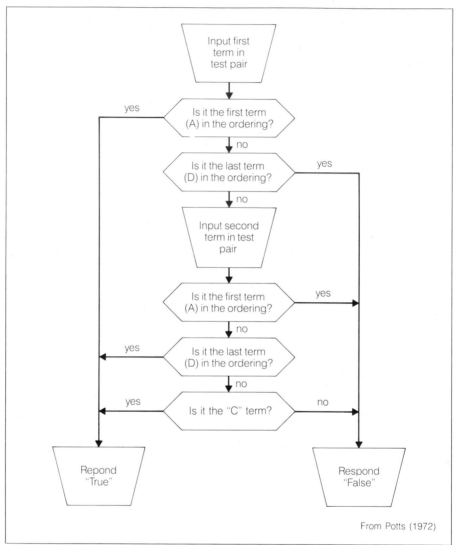

From Potts (1972)

In another study, Moeser and Tarrant (1977) asked subjects to learn a network of comparisons such as those shown in Box 6-23. The adjacent pairs were presented as ''Bill is older than John.'' Performance on a subsequent test revealed that subjects took almost twice as long to answer questions about remote pairs than about adjacent pairs. Apparently, the complex network structure prevented subjects from forming

BOX 6–23   A Network of Pairwise Relations

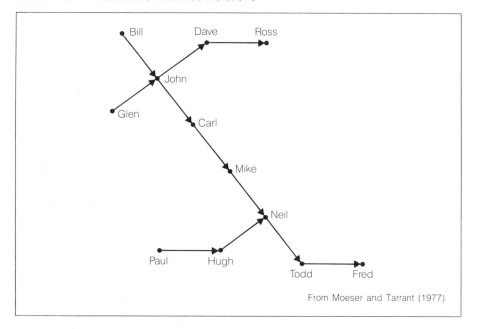

From Moeser and Tarrant (1977)

an integrated representation and encouraged them to memorize each premise separately. However, when Moeser and Tarrant presented the premises within a meaningful context, such as "Bill, who is ninety years old is older than John, who is sixty years old," performance on the test was just as fast for remote as for adjacent pairs. These results suggest that subjects tend to form integrated representations under certain circumstances such as when an obvious framework is available, but tend to memorize each separate premise under other circumstances.

EVALUATION

The syllogistic-reasoning task, like the concept-induction task discussed in Chapter 5, has been a major vehicle for studying human thinking. Like the concept-learning paradigm, the syllogistic-reasoning task has the advantage of providing an agreed-upon and well-known method and the disadvantage of being a specific type of reasoning that may have nongeneralizable characteristics.

The common thread running through this chapter has been that errors seem to be attributable to faulty or incomplete encoding of premises rather than to faulty logical processes in humans. The point of focus for much research on syllogistic reasoning seems to be on how people represent the premises. In addition, some of the misinterpretations seem to be blocked when actual premises are used. This rationalist view is not universally accepted. Several theorists hold that human reasoning is, indeed, faulty in the sense that it does not correspond to the rules of formal logic (Evans, 1980). Additionally, numerous other models describe categorical, conditional, and linear reasoning (Sternberg, 1980).

The fact that human logic and formal logic do not always coincide has been the source of many interesting insights into human thought processes. However, more efforts are needed to connect this work with other theories of human problem solving and memory processes. As you will see in Chapters 9 and 10, there is now an increasing literature on memory retrieval processes for set-subset information (Collins and Quillian, 1969; Rips, Shoben, and Smith, 1973) and on memory storage of propositions (Kintsch, 1972). These new developments should be integrated with conceptualizations of deductive reasoning.

Suggested Readings

Falmagne, R. (Ed.) *Reasoning: Representation and process.* Hillsdale, N.J.: Erlbaum, 1975. Good selection of readings on current topics in the psychology of deductive reasoning.

Johnson, D. M. *A systematic introduction to the psychology of thinking.* New York: Harper & Row, 1972. Chapter 6 surveys the basic literature in deductive reasoning.

Johnson-Laird, P. N., and Wason, P. C. *Thinking: Readings in Cognitive Science.* Cambridge: Cambridge University Press, 1978. Section on deduction includes an overview and several classic papers.

Revlin, R., and Mayer. R. E. *Human reasoning.* New York: Wiley/Winston, 1978. A collection of current research projects on deductive reasoning, including a general introduction to syllogisms.

Wason, P. C., and Johnson-Laird, P. N. *Thinking and reasoning.* Baltimore, Md.: Penguin, 1968. Classic papers by Chapman and Chapman, by Henle, and by DeSoto, London, and Handel.

Wason, P. C., and Johnson-Laird, P. N. *Psychology of reasoning: Structure and content.* London: Batsford, 1972. Basic research and theory in syllogistic reasoning.

PART THREE

INFORMATION-PROCESSING ANALYSIS OF COGNITION

The following four chapters introduce you to the information-processing approach to cognition. Although the information-processing approach is not a general theory in the way that associationism or Gestalt is, it does provide techniques for analyzing cognitive processes and structures into parts.

In these chapters you will see how the information-processing approach analyzes problem-solving strategies (Chapter 7), cognitive skills (Chapter 8), and verbal knowledge (Chapters 9 and 10). The information-processing approach provides techniques that incorporate aspects of associationism—for example, the atomistic approach—and Gestalt—the role of organization. Yet the information-processing approach to cognition is more like a set of tools for analyzing cognition than it is like a general theory of cognition.

Chapters 7 through 10 each start with a particular analytic tool—such as problem-space analysis or process models or schema theories of knowledge—and then show how these can be applied to cognitive tasks. In these chapters the study of problem solving is driven by the available techniques of analysis. The approach is to describe how the problem-solving process can be analyzed into parts. Note that these techniques are also described in Chapters 5 and 6 on induction and deduction, as well as later in Part Four.

Part Three covers several basic analytic tools in some detail, including models of strategy, process, schema, and semantic memory. Although these are techniques for describing cognitive processes and structures, they do not constitute a general theory of problem solving. At present, the information-processing approach is the closest thing yet to a unified theory of cognition. Yet you will see that the techniques are mainly a collection of tools, without any overall general integrating theme. In Chapters 7 through 10 you will see how far we have come in developing theories of problem solving and how far we must still go.

CHAPTER 7

COMPUTER SIMULATION: Thinking as a Search for a Solution Path

Natural Language Tasks

Box 7-1 is the protocol or transcript of part of a therapy session between a doctor (MD) and a patient (P). As you read the transcript, try to judge whether the MD is a human therapist or a computer. What is your verdict?

You may be surprised to learn that this discussion took place at a computer keyboard, with the patient typing in statements and the computer responding by teletype or videoscope. Therapist programs like this one, as well as programs that simulate neurotic symptoms, were developed to determine whether it is possible to describe a therapy technique or a mental syndrome with enough precision to express it as a computer program (Weizenbaum, 1968; Colby, 1965; Colby, Watt, and Gilbert, 1966). The programmers, of course, did not intend their Rogerian program to replace Carl Rogers (1961) and his disciples, but their program does demonstrate a basic advance in theories of human cognitive processing. A theory of what a therapist does while giving therapy, or what a chess player does while playing chess, or what a problem solver does while solving a problem may be specified in very exact terms as a list of things to do—in short, as a computer program. Theories of human cognitive processes may thus be generated and expressed as computer programs and *tested* by seeing if they work—that is, if they do give therapy, play chess, or solve problems the way a person does. Programs that "understand" natural language as in Box 7-1 aid in the development of theories of memory and psycholinguistics; however, programs that solve problems are more specifically important for theories of human thinking.

MOVE Tasks

Computers can solve induction and deduction problems as described in Chapters 5 and 6. However, the computer simulation work covered in this chapter focuses on MOVE problems. MOVE problems have a well-defined initial state, a well-defined goal state, and a well-defined set of allowable operators, or moves. MOVE problems include aspects of Greeno's (1978) transformation problems and arrangement problems, as discussed in Chapter 1. Simon (1978) has pointed out that computer simulation of problem-solving strategies has been particularly successful for well-defined problems—like our MOVE problems—rather than for poorly defined problems that occur in everyday life.

Examples of MOVE problems that have been exposed to computer simulation include the disk problem as shown in Box 4-3 of Chapter 4 (Ernst and Newell, 1969) and river-crossing problems such as the Hobbits and Orcs problem in Box 3-12 of Chapter 3 (Ernst and Newell, 1969), as well as the problems shown in Box 3-13 (Ernst and Newell, 1969) and Box 3-14 (Newell and Simon, 1972).

To derive a precise description of the solution process for such problems, a first step is to analyze the performance of a subject solving a problem. As the subject solves the problem, he or she is asked to describe the mental processes involved. Thus, computer simulations of thinking may begin with what is called a "thinking aloud protocol"—a transcript of a subject's running description of what is going on inside her head as the problem is being solved. Box 7-2 provides part of a subject's protocol for the DONALD + GERALD = ROBERT problem. Newell and Simon (1972) devote an entire chapter to this subject's behavior, including 18 pages of raw protocol and almost 100 pages in all. Can you see any strategy or set of procedures

BOX 7–1

```
P:   Men are all alike.
MD:  In what way?
P:   They're always bugging us about something or other.
MD:  Can you think of a specific example?
P:   Well, my boyfriend made me come here.
MD:  Your boyfriend made you come here?
P:   He says I'm depressed much of the time.
MD:  I am sorry to hear you are depressed.
P:   It's true. I am unhappy.
MD:  Do you think coming here will help you not be unhappy?
P:   I need some help, that much seems certain.
MD:  What would it mean to you if you got some help?
P:   Perhaps I could learn to get along with my mother.
MD:  Tell me more about your family.
P:   My mother takes care of me.
MD:  Who else in your family takes care of you?
P:   My father.
MD:  Your father.
P:   You are like my father in some ways.
MD:  What resemblance do you see?
P:   You are not very aggressive but I think you don't want me to notice that.
MD:  What makes you think I am not very aggressive?
P:   You don't argue with me.
MD:  Why do you think I don't argue with you?
P:   You are afraid of me.
MD:  Does it please you to believe that I am afraid of you?
P:   My father is afraid of everybody.
MD:  What else comes to mind when you think of your father?
P:   Bullies.
MD:  Does that have anything to do with the fact that your boyfriend made
     you come here?
```

From Weizenbaum (1968)

the subject is using? Newell and Simon note that in step 5 the subject is substituting the given into the equation, in step 7 the subject is making an inference based on having two numbers in a column, and in steps 10 and 12 he is using a strategy of searching for "known" letters, and so on. By carefully observing the general procedures used by individual subjects, Newell and Simon were able to produce a computer program that solved similar cryptarithmetic problems in a way apparently similar to human methods.

What other types of "thinking" can computers engage in? The ever-expanding list now includes:

Solving algebra story problems (Bobrow, 1968).

Solving geometry problems (Gelernter, 1960; Greeno, 1978).

Generating logical proofs (Newell, Shaw, and Simon, 1957).

BOX 7–2   Protocol for a Subject on the DONALD + GERALD = ROBERT Problem

---

Problem

DONALD	Find a number for each letter, given that D = 5, every number
+ GERALD	between 0 and 9 has a corresponding letter, and each letter had a
ROBERT	unique number.

Protocol

1. Each letter has one and only one numerical value. . . .
2. (E: One numerical value.)
3. There are 10 different letters.
4. And each of them has one numerical value.
5. Therefore, I can, looking at the two D's . . .
6. each D is 5;
7. therefore, T is zero.
8. So I think I'll start by writing that problem here.
9. I'll write T, T is zero.
10. Now, do I have any other T's?
11. No.
12. But I have another D.
13. That means I have a 5 over on the other side.
14. Now I have 2 A's
15. and 2 L's
16. that are each
17. somewhere
18. and this R
19. 3 R's

(Continues for 321 units.)

From Newell and Simon (1972)

Playing chess (Newell, Shaw, and Simon, 1958; Newell and Simon, 1972).

Playing checkers (Samuel, 1963).

Concept learning (Gregg and Simon, 1967; Simon and Kotovsky, 1963).

Solving analogy problems (Evans, 1968; Reitman, 1965).

Producing Rogerian therapy and neurotic personality (Colby, 1965; Colby, Watt, and Gilbert, 1966; Weizenbaum, 1968).

General problem solving (Ernst and Newell, 1969).

Solving logical and deductive problems (Newell and Simon, 1972).

Understanding problem descriptions (Hayes and Simon, 1974, 1977; Simon and Hayes, 1976).

Understanding natural language (Winograd, 1972).

Understanding simple pictures (Winston, 1975).

Understanding electronic circuit diagrams (Sussman and Stallman, 1975).

Diagnosing medical symptoms (Shortliffe, 1976; Pople, 1977).

Diagnosing errors in children's arithmetic procedures (Brown and Burton, 1978).

Analyzing chemical structure from mass spectrograms (Buchanan, Sutherland, and Feiganbaum, 1969).

Teaching computer-programming strategies (Papert and Solomon, 1971).

Teaching as a Socratic tutor (Stevens and Collins, 1980).

COMPUTER SIMULATION DEFINITION OF THINKING

The computer-simulation approach to thinking assumes that a problem solver solves problems by applying operators to problem states. An *operator* is any move that the problem solver deems to be legal, and the operator may be applied physically such as moving a disk from one peg to another or may be applied mentally by thinking about the move. A *problem state* is a description of the elements in the problem, such as saying that all the disks are on peg 1. When you apply an operator you change the problem from one state to another. Thus, problem solving or thinking can be represented in one of two ways:

A sequence of mental processes or operations performed on information in a subject's memory.

A sequence of internal states or changes in information that progress toward the goal.

The goal of the computer-simulation psychologist is to define precisely the strategy that the problem solver uses to generate a sequence of moves.

In a sense the computer-simulation approach is a refinement of the associationist view of thinking as selecting the correct response from a response hierarchy, since the problem solver applies a sequence of moves until the problem is solved. Yet, there is also a sense in which the computer simulation approach is not a theory at all but rather a method for precisely describing the strategies used in the problem-solving process. As such, it offers a method of describing and testing competing views of thinking.

Simon (1978, 1979), who was earlier a pioneer in the computer-simulation approach, has suggested that any discussion of problem must deal with three major components:

The problem solver—which he calls the "information processing system."

The problem—which he calls "the task environment."

The problem representation—which he calls a "problem space."

Problem solving occurs when a problem solver translates a problem into an internal problem representation and then searches for a path through the problem space from the given to the goal state. This chapter considers some key ideas proposed by Simon's conception of problem solving. First, we consider the idea that the same theoretical approach can be applied to problem solvers who happen to be humans as well as to problem solvers who happen to be computers. Then, we investigate two key techniques for talking about problem solving: (1) representation of problems as problem spaces and (2) solution of problems as search strategies through the problem space.

CYBERNETICS

The cybernetic revolution (Weiner, 1948), which involves the idea of feedback and machine servomechanisms, plus the rapid development of sophisticated computers and computer programs have heavily influenced the information-processing approach to thinking. This approach is based on two computer metaphors: (1) the *human-machine* analogy, in which the human being may be viewed as a complex computer, and (2) the *thinking-program* analogy, in which the thought processes used by humans to solve a problem may be viewed as a computer program.

The primary ideas from the cybernetic-computer approach that have been useful in developing a theory of problem solving are:

1. *Feedback loops and homeostatis*—the idea that an adaptive system continually monitors the difference between its current state and its desired state and performs actions to reduce any differences that may be detected.

2. *Hierarchical structure*—the idea that any complex process or behavior can be represented as hierarchy of simple interlocking component processes.

Feedback Loops and Homeostatis

Miller, Galanter, and Pribram (1960) introduced a popular example of a feedback system to describe the cognitive processes involved in hammering a nail (see Box 7-3). The plan shown in the box is called a TOTE, for Test-Operate-Test-Exit, and is simply a hierarchy of operations with feedback. Written as a computer program, the processes should be in the form of a list to be read top down:

BOX 7–3   A Hierarchical Plan for Hammering Nails

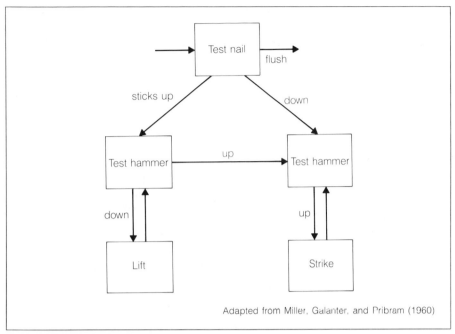

Adapted from Miller, Galanter, and Pribram (1960)

1. Test nail. If it sticks up, go to 2; otherwise stop.

2. Test hammer. If down, lift; otherwise go to 3.

3. Strike nail.

4. Go to 1.

Although it may seem peculiar that psychologists are so interested in how to hammer a nail, techniques such as flow charts and programs are important because they allow psychologists to specify their theory of cognitive processes for a certain intellectual task with precision.

Unfortunately, these kinds of representations make no major distinctions between human and nonhuman thought processes. For example, Box 7-4 shows the thought processes of a thermostat. The flow chart could also be represented as a program:

1. Test temperature. If under 70°, go to 2, if over 72°, go to 5; otherwise go to 1.

2. Test furnace. If on, go to 1; otherwise go to 3.

BOX 7–4   A Plan for Regulating Temperature

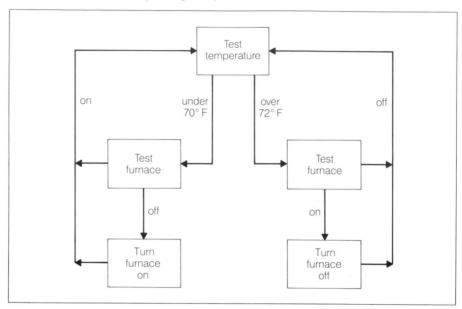

3. Turn furnace on.

4. Go to 1.

5. Test furnace. If off, go to 1; otherwise go to 6.

6. Turn furnace off.

7. Go to 1.

The development of such ways of describing internal cognitive processes is, obviously, heavily dependent on the computer analogy and focuses particularly on the role of feedback.

Hierarchical Structure

Miller, Galanter, and Pribram (1960) argued that TOTEs are the building blocks of all kinds of complex behaviors. For example, there can be TOTEs inside of TOTEs. The hammering a nail TOTE is part of a larger plan for building a cabinet, which is part of a larger plan for building a kitchen, and so on. Thus, complex behavior can be described as a hierarchy of simple component behaviors.

In an enthralling essay, "The Architecture of Complexity," Simon (1969) similarly argued that the behavior of complex systems can be described as a hierarchy of simple parts. As an example of the advantages of hierarchical structure, Simon presented a parable about two watchmakers. Tempus and Hora are both fine and popular craftsmen, who build watches consisting of 1000 parts. Tempus builds his watches as a single assembly of 1000 parts: thus, if he is interrupted in the middle of a job by one of his many customers, the partially assembled watch will fall back into its original parts. Hora's watches are just as complex, but he builds his in units, each consisting of 10 pieces. Thus, 10 single parts make a unit, 10 units make a larger unit, and 10 of the larger units make the entire watch. If Hora is interrupted, he loses only a small portion of the unfinished watch. Thus, Hora's method of watch building is more efficient; for example, Simon estimated that Tempus will lose an average of 20 times as much work per interruption as Hora. Further, Simon suggested that the efficiency of hierarchical structure can be seen in biological systems, in social systems, and in human problem-solving behavior.

More recently, Hofstadter (1980) has emphasized the importance of *recursion* — the nesting of stories within stories, action sequences within action sequences, or computer programs within computer programs. For example, suppose you wanted to learn about problem solving. To solve this problem you must read this chapter. However, in order to read this chapter you must first find a large chunk of time. To solve this problem you could decide to stay up late at night. However, you need to prevent yourself from falling asleep. To solve this problem you may drink lots of hot coffee. This ''problem'' involves embedding problems within problems; it is an example of recursion. Many of the problems described in this chapter involve this kind of recursion. Hofstadter has suggested that the most interesting examples of recursion involve *strange loops* — rules that can act upon and change other rules. Indeed, principles of computer programming demonstrate that complex and novel behavior can be generated through a hierarchy of simple parts that respond to feedback and that can act upon themselves.

LOGIC OF COMPUTER SIMULATION

Why would anyone want to spend the time to program a computer to solve problems? The motives probably vary, but the reason given for many of the early attempts was to see if machines could solve problems. The development of computer programs that display intelligence by solving problems or engaging in conversation is generally referred to as the field of *artificial intelligence*. A subfield of particular interest to cognitive psychologists is the development of computer systems that display the same problem-solving behavior as humans—that is, behavior that simulates human behavior. This field is referred to as *computer simulation*. If you were interested in building a machine that could serve as an encyclopedia and answer any spoken question, such as R2D2 in *Star Wars* or COMPUTER in *Star Trek*, you probably would not care if its memory storage system and language perception system were the same as in people as long as the machine worked. Your interest would be in artificial intelligence. However, if you had a particular theory of how human beings solve a problem (not necessarily the best or most logical method), you could use the computer simulation to test the theory. The logic of computer simulation is simple: if a computer program produces the same problem-solving behavior as a human, then the series of operations are an accurate representation of the human thought processes.

The experimental method used with computer simulation generally involves asking subjects to solve problems aloud while giving a running description of their thought process and their behavior. From careful analyses of the obtained *protocols* (the transcript of all the subject's comments) the experimenter may derive a description of the mental processes a subject used to solve the problem. By specifying these as a computer program, the experimenter has a precise description that can be tested by feeding it to a computer and observing how closely the computer's protocol matches the subject's. If the match is close, the experimenter may conclude that the program's description of the problem-solving process is accurate; if not, it is necessary to make up a new program and try again.

Although computer simulation offers a new tool for generating and testing theories of human thinking, much popular attention has been directed towards a complementary issue: how can we know whether a machine thinks? Years before the technology for computer simulation existed, the mathematician Turing (1950) wrote an article entitled, "Can Machines Think?" in which he proposed the following test—now called the Turing Test. Put two teletypewriters and a person to act as judge in a room. The judge may ask any questions he likes by typing. One teletype is connected to a person in another room who communicates by typing his answers and one is connected to a computer that also types out its answers. If the human judge cannot tell which teletype is connected to the human, then the computer is thinking.

There is, of course, an interesting flaw in the "logic" of computer simulation. Just because a computer and a human give the same behavioral output, does that really mean they are using the same cognitive processes? In addition, protocol states may not accurately reflect internal states. The idea seems particularly absurd in light of the fact that computers use entirely different components than the human brain. Yet a computer program is a very precise and testable way to state a theory of human thinking and as such offers an opportunity to go beyond the vague theories of the Gestaltists. Talking about programs and states may be no more absurd than talking about thoughts or ideas—all are abstractions that must ultimately be described in a way that provides clear tests.

THE PROBLEM SOLVER

What does the problem solver bring to the problem-solving situation? Lindsay and Norman (1972) have distinguished among several types of knowledge that are used in problem solving:

> *facts* —basic propositions that are immediately available to the subject.
>
> *algorithms* —sets of rules that automatically generate answers.
>
> *heuristics* —rules of thumb or general plans of actions or strategies.

For example, generating a solution to the question "What is 8 × 4?" involves a fact; generating a solution for "What is 262 × 127?" involves an algorithm; and a heuristic would be an estimate of the correct answer by rounding to manageable numbers.

Algorithms guarantee specific answers since they simply apply a past set of rules to a new situation. The set of rules can be stored as a *subroutine,* thus saving memory load. Heuristics, on the other hand, may not always generate a solution for a problem. For example, the heuristic of finding a related or analogous problem or breaking the problem into subgoals may help, but does not guarantee solution. A major heuristic is *means-ends analysis,* discussed later in this chapter.

Ernst and Newell (1969) have provided a simplified description of how the problem solver is involved in the problem-solving process (see Box 7-5). The *input* —that is, the problem—is acted upon by a *translator* that converts it into an *internal representation* (including the initial state, the goal state, and a means of telling which problem states are closer to the goal state) that is acted upon by *problem-solving techniques* that generate the *solution.* In spite of the contribution of the assimilation theory of thinking and the idea of functional fixedness from the gestalt theory, very little attention has been paid to the translation process. The internal representation of a problem can take many forms including the problem-space representation we discussed earlier, and the problem-solving techniques may be represented as operators, facts, subroutines, and heuristics.

Greeno (1973) has proposed the memory model for problem solving shown in Box 7-6. The three main components of interest in describing problem solving are:

> *Short-term memory* (STM)—through which the external description of the problem is input.
>
> *Long-term memory* (LTM; semantic and factual memory)—which stores past experience with solving problems such as facts, algorithms, heuristics, related problems, and so on.
>
> *Working memory* (WM)—in which the information from STM and LTM interact and the solution route is generated and tested.

BOX 7–5   The Problem-Solving Process

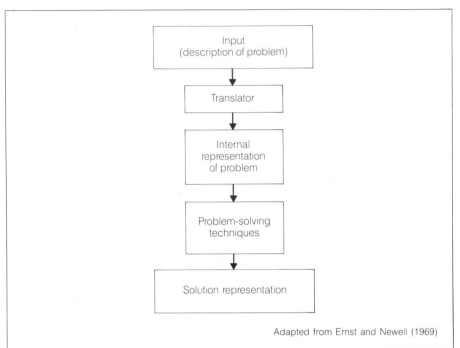

Adapted from Ernst and Newell (1969)

A description of the problem, including the initial state, the goal state, and the legal operators, comes into working memory by way of short-term memory as represented by arrows from STM to WM; and past experience about how to solve the problem enters working memory from LTM, as represented by the arrow from LTM to WM. The arrows from WM to STM and LTM to STM suggest that more information from the outside world may be required as problem solving progresses (the solver may pay attention to different aspects of the presented information) and the arrow from WM to LTM suggests that the generation of new problem states in WM may require more old information from past experience. The concept of working memory, first introduced by Feigenbaum (1970), has special importance in Greeno's model: the internal representation of the problem occurs there, the construction of links between givens and unknowns occurs there, and relevant past experience is used to modify the structures held in WM.

For example, Hayes and Simon (1974, 1977; Simon and Hayes, 1976) have developed a program called UNDERSTAND that can be used on isomorphs of the disk problem such as the monster problems in Box 7-7. The description of the problem is translated into an internal representation by the UNDERSTAND pro-

BOX 7–6   Components of Memory

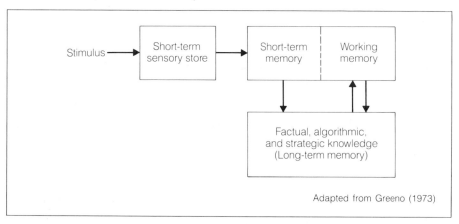

Adapted from Greeno (1973)

gram, which involves a language interpreter for breaking down each sentence into its parts of speech and a construction process that builds a unified description of the problem from this information. For example, a sentence from the problem would be read into working memory. Then, the language interpreter would be activated in long-term memory so that it could manipulate the parts of the sentence in working memory. The same process would take place for the next sentence, and so on. For the construction phase, the interpreted sentences in working memory would be further manipulated by the construction rules activated in long-term memory. The output of the UNDERSTAND program is a description of the problem consisting of a definition of the goal state, initial state, legal operators, and so on. For example, monster problem 1 might be translated as a disk problem. Once the problem has been represented internally, then the problem-solving processes can be applied.

If you look carefully at the two problems in Box 7-7, you might notice that they suggest two different ways of describing the problem. In monster problem 1, the monsters seem fixed and the globes seem movable; thus, the legal operators seem to involve moving a globe, which is similar to moving a disk in the disk problem. In monster problem 2, the globes seem fixed while the monsters can change; thus, the legal operators involve changing the monsters, which is similar to changing the pegs in the disk problem. In a series of experiments, Hayes and Simon (1977; Simon and Hayes, 1976) found that people tended to translate problems in ways similar to how the UNDERSTAND program translated problems. For example, problems like monster problem 1 were translated into a representation that had "move globe" operators, while problems like monster problem 2 were translated into a representation that had "change monster" operators. As you might suspect, the "move" kind of representation was easier to work with than the "change" type of represent-

BOX 7–7 Two Monster Problems

Monster Problem 1 (Move)

Three five-handed extraterrestrial monsters were holding three crystal globes.
Because of the quantum-mechanical peculiarities of their neighborhood, both monsters and globes come in exactly three sizes with no others permitted: small, medium, and large.

The medium-sized monster held the small globe; the small monster held the large globe; and the large monster held the medium-sized globe.

Since this situation offended their keenly developed sense of symmetry, they proceeded to teleport globes from one monster to another so that each monster would have a globe proportionate to his own size.

Monster etiquette complicated the solution of the problem since it requires:

1. that only one globe can be transmitted at a time,
2. that if a monster is holding two globes, only the larger of the two can be transmitted, and
3. that the globe may not be transmitted to a monster who is holding a larger globe.

By what sequence of transmissions could the monsters have solved this problem?

Monster Problem 2 (Change)

The same three monsters from problem 1 found themselves in an identical situation: The medium-sized monster was holding the small globe; the small monster was holding the large globe; and the large monster was holding the medium-sized globe.

Since this situation offended their sense of symmetry, they proceeded to shrink and expand themselves so that each monster would hold a globe proportionate to his own size.

Monster etiquette complicated the solution of the problem, which required:

1. that only one monster may change at a time
2. that if two monsters are of the same size, only the monster holding the larger globe can change, and
3. that a monster may not change to size of a monster who is holding a larger globe.

By what sequence of changes could the monsters have solved this problem?

Adapted from Hayes and Simon (1977)

ation. Also, subjects had difficulty in solving two problems if the second one involved a representation—that is, move versus change—different from the first problem. Similarly, Reed, Ernst, and Banerji (1974) found that subjects who solved a missionaries and cannibals problem were not better at solving an analogous problem about ''jealous husbands and wives'' unless they were given explicit instruction on the relationship between the problems. Simon and Hayes (1976, p.

89) conclude that ''the way in which the subject names objects and the way in which he structures the internal problem representation are determined pretty directly by the language in which the problem instructions are written. . . . This is precisely what the UNDERSTAND program predicts.''

THE PROBLEM SPACE

One of the major theoretical contributions of the computer simulation approach to problem solving is the idea of *problem space*. The problem space refers to the problem solver's internal representation of:

Initial state—in which the given or starting conditions are represented,

Goal state—in which the final or goal situation is represented,

Intermediate problem states—consisting of states that are generated by applying an operator to a state,

Operators—the moves that are made from one state to the next.

Ernst and Newell (1969) and Simon (1978) have pointed out that problem space is the set of all states (or all possible sequences of operators) that the problem solver is aware of. Simon also points out that the *basic problem space*—the problem space generated by a perfect problem solver—may not be identical to a particular person's *problem space*. For example, an individual problem solver can generate a problem space that contains errors or is seriously incomplete.

Consider the disk problem (also called the tower of Hanoi problem) that we discussed in Box 4-3 . Remember that the problem is to move the disks from peg 1 to peg 3 by moving them to any peg one at a time and never placing a larger disk on top of a smaller disk. Thus, when there are three disks, the problem consists of:

Initial state—the three disks are on peg 1 with the largest on the bottom and the smallest on the top.

Goal state—the disks are on peg 3 with the largest on the bottom and the smallest on the top.

Operators—the top disk from one peg is placed on another peg that does not contain a smaller disk.

Part of the problem space for this problem is given in Box 7-8. The initial state (labeled 1) is on the left, the goal state (labeled 8) is on the right. The intermediate states are in between, with the most efficient path through the problem space indicated along the top of the problem space (states 2 through 7).

Each box or node in the problem space represents one possible state of the

170

BOX 7–8 Problem Space for Disk Problem

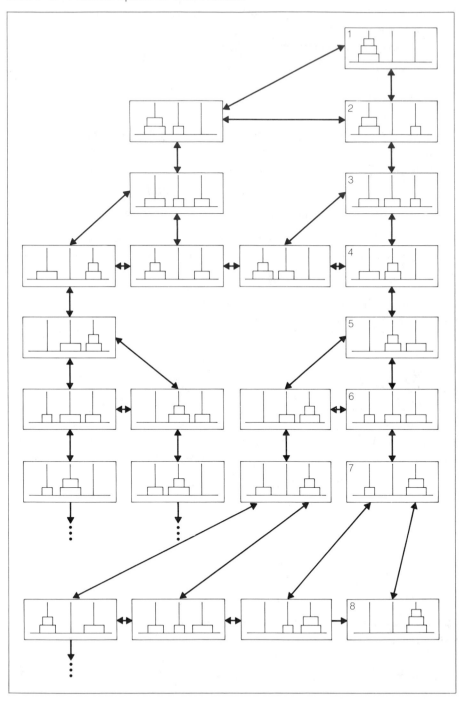

problem, and each branch or arrow represents a legal action that could be taken from that state. For example, if you are in state 1, there are two actions that can be taken—moving the small disk to peg 3 (resulting in state 2) or moving the small disk to peg 2. If you are in state 2, there are three possible actions—moving the medium disk from peg 1 to peg 2 (resulting in state 3), moving the small disk from peg 3 to peg 2, or moving the small disk from peg 3 back to peg 2 (resulting in a return to a previous state). You can move from an intermediate state back to a previous state in the problem space.

Another example of the problem space is the hobbits and orcs problem in Box 3-12. In that example, the initial state has 3 hobbits, 3 orcs, and the boat on the left; the right side is empty. The goal state is the opposite: 3 hobbits, 3 orcs, and the boat on the right side with the left side empty. The legal operators are to move 1 hobbit, 2 hobbits, 1 orc, 2 orcs, or 1 hobbit and 1 orc from the side with the boat to the other side along with the boat as long as the hobbits are never outnumbered by orcs on either side of the river. As you can see in Box 3-12, there are few alternatives from each state to the next.

Solving a problem can be viewed as finding the correct path or route through a problem space. In Box 3-12, the path is fairly obvious since there is usually only one new move that can be made from each state. In Box 7-8, paths through the lower part of the space are likely to create much difficulty.

Wickelgren (1974) and Polya (1968) have suggested several techniques for "pruning the tree," for making the problem space easier to work with:

Macroactions—the space can be reduced by thinking in terms of "macro-actions" in which different sequences of actions often result in the same problem state. For example, the arrows on the problem space can represent several equivalent sequences of smaller actions.

Subgoals—the space can be broken down into several smaller subgoals, that is, it can be converted into several smaller problem spaces each ending in a subgoal state.

Working backward—the number of alternative paths in a space can sometimes be reduced by working backward from the goal state toward the initial state.

Related problem spaces—the correct path can be suggested by remembering how you solved similar or analogous problems in the past.

Thus, as you can see, one of the major contributions of the information-processing approach to problem solving is the development of a technique for representing problems—namely, the problem space. However, the problem-space technique seems best applied to MOVE problems—problems with clearly defined given states, goal states, and operators.

SEARCHING THROUGH THE PROBLEM SPACE

The previous section demonstrates how the information-processing approach can provide a concrete representation of what it means to "understand the problem"—that is, building a problem space. Although the problem-space representation allows you to describe the problem, you also need a technique for finding a path through the problem space. Hayes (1978) and Wickelgren (1974) have suggested several *search strategies*—methods for finding a way from the initial state to the goal state. Three search strategies —*random trial and error, hill climbing,* and *means-ends analysis*—are discussed here.

Random Trial and Error

The most straightforward technique is to randomly apply legal operators until you have generated the goal state. Thus, if you are in a certain state, you may randomly choose any legal move as your next move. For example, in the disk problem in Box 7-8, if you are in state 3, you randomly choose among the three possible moves, for example, to state 2, to state 4, or to the unnumber state. The trouble with random searches is that they have many wasted moves. Although humans may use it for unfamiliar problems or when they are under great stress, random search does not seem to be a good candidate for complex problem-solving behavior.

Hill Climbing

A more systematic search that retains much of the simplicity of random search is hill climbing. In hill climbing you continually try to move from your present state to a state that is closer to the goal. Thus, if you are in a certain state, you evaluate the new state you would be in for each possible move, and you select the move that creates the state that moves you closest to the goal. For hill climbing, you need some state evaluation procedure, that is, your own system for evaluating how far any state in the problem space is from the goal state. For example, in the disk problem (as in Box 7-8), your rule for state evaluation could be that the more disks you have on peg 3, the closer you are to the goal. For the hobbits and orcs problem (as in Box 3-12) the rule for state evaluation could be that the more characters you have on the right side of the river, the closer you are to the goal. The main drawback to hill climbing is that it can take you to a "local high," a state in the problem that is closer to the goal than any adjacent state in the problem space. For example, in the disk problem in Box 7-8, state 3 represents a local high since moving the small disk off the third peg (which is required for solving the problem) could be evaluated as moving away from the goal. Similarly, in the hobbits and orcs problem in Box 3-12, state 110 represents a local high because taking two characters from the right to the left could be evaluated as moving away from the goal. Thus, hill climbing will not work well in problems that have hills and valleys, that is, problems that occasionally require that you move away from the goal in order to ultimately reach the goal.

Atwood and Polson (1976) provide some experimental evidence that subjects sometimes use a strategy similar to hill climbing. They gave subjects the following version of a water jug problem (called the water jar problem by the Luchins, Chapter 3):

> You have three jugs, which we will call A, B and C. Jug A can hold exactly eight cups of water, B can hold exactly five cups, and C can hold exactly three cups. A is filled to capacity with eight cups of water. B and C are empty. We want to find a way of dividing the contents of A equally between A and B so that both have four cups. You are allowed to pour water from jug to jug.

Thus, in this problem the initial state is eight cups of water in jug A and none in jugs B and C, the goal state is four cups of water in jug A and four in jug B, and the legal operators are to pour from one jug to another.

Box 7-9 provides a partial problem space for the problem. Let's suppose that you evaluate each state by determining how different jug A is from four cups and how different jug B is from four cups; the closer these two jugs are to four cups each, the better is the evaluation of that state. Using this hill-climbing procedure, which move do you think a person would take: pouring A into B or pouring A into C? As you can see, pouring into B creates state 9, which is just two cups different from the goal (jug A and jug B are each one cup off); however, pouring into C creates state 2, which is five cups different from the goal (jug A is one off and jug B is four off). As the researchers predicted, twice as many subjects opted for state 9 rather than state 1. As you look at the states from 9 to 15, do you see any moves that tend to go against the hill-climbing strategy? For example, consider the move from state 11 to state 12. Here, you must move from a state that is four cups different from the goal to one that is eight cups different from the goal; according to a hill-climbing strategy you are losing ground. Atwood and Polson found that subjects were likely to deviate from the correct path at such junctions as state 11. For example, subjects preferred a move from state 11 that seemed closer to the goal (such as pouring A into C) but which actually prolonged the course of the problem.

Means-End Analysis

So far we have found that random search is too costly in terms of wasted moves, and hill climbing is too shortsighted because it strands the problem solver at local highs. What is needed is a search strategy that retains the simplicity of random search and the order of hill climbing, without the disadvantages of wasteful or shortsighted problem solving. Thus, we need to be able to describe a search strategy that is both powerful and simple, that corresponds to human problem-solving characteristics as

BOX 7–9   Problem Space for a Water Jug Problem

Adapted from Atwood and Polson (1976)

well as being amenable to computer implementation. By far, the most popular and widely used strategy fitting these descriptions is means-ends analysis.

In *means-ends analysis*, the problem solver always works on one goal at a time. If you are in a certain state, you set a goal of creating the goal state. If that goal cannot be directly achieved, you set a subgoal of removing any barriers to directly achieving the goal, and so on. The problem solver in means-ends analysis is continually asking three questions: What is my goal, what obstacles are in my way, and what operators are available for overcoming these obstacles? Simon (1969, p. 112) summarizes means-ends analysis as follows: "Given a desired state of affairs and an existing state of affairs, the task of an adaptive organism is to find the difference between these two states and then to find the correlating process that will erase the difference."

Do humans actually use means-ends analysis in problem solving? Let's consider the problem space for the hobbits and orcs problem again, as shown in Box 3-12. Greeno (1974) has provided a means-ends analysis of the task and found that human performance fits this description with some interesting exceptions. For example, subjects spend a lot of time at state 110 (Thomas, 1974) and seem to run into trouble possibly because they must violate a hill-climbing strategy by moving away from the goal. However, subjects seem to be able to jump rapidly from state 020 to the conclusion, while means-ends analysis still requires a lot of goal setting and comparing. Several researchers have observed that subjects do not seem to be setting as many subgoals as suggested by a strict form of means-ends analysis in river-crossing problems (Jeffries, Polson, Razran, and Atwood, 1977; Simon and Reed, 1976). Apparently, subjects' performance on river crossing problems can be described as a sort of compromise between means-ends analysis and hill climbing. In another series of studies, Larkin, McDermott, Simon, and Simon (1980) have found that introductory physics students seem to solve textbook problems using means-ends analysis but experienced physicists use a much more streamlined procedure that avoids setting so many goals.

A CLOSER LOOK AT MEANS-ENDS ANALYSIS

Since means-ends analysis is the major problem-solving strategy used in many computer simulations of thinking, let's take a closer look at how it works. The main ideas that you need to understand are: *subgoals, goal stack, table of connections, goal structure*, and *production system*.

Subgoals

Newell and Simon (1972) have described three types of subgoals that are involved in means-ends analysis, as shown in Box 7-10. The transform goal involves comparing the present state of the problem to the goal state and listing any differences between the two. The input for the transform goal is a description of the present state (called A) and the goal state (called B); the output is a description of the difference (called D) between the two states. For example, in the disk problem, the first goal

BOX 7–10 Three Kinds of Subgoals in Means-Ends Analysis

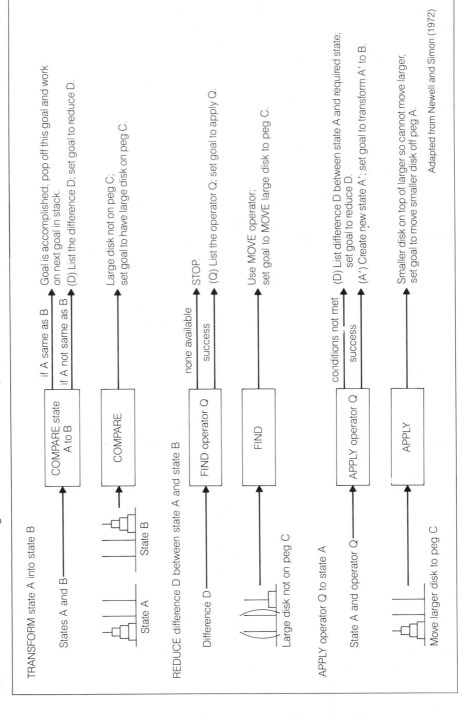

TRANSFORM state A into state B

States A and B

State A   State B

COMPARE state A to B

if A same as B → Goal is accomplished; pop off this goal and work on next goal in stack.

if A not same as B → (D) List the difference D; set goal to reduce D.

COMPARE

Large disk not on peg C; set goal to have large disk on peg C.

REDUCE difference D between state A and state B

Difference D

Large disk not on peg C

FIND operator Q

none available → STOP.

success → (Q) List the operator Q; set goal to apply Q.

FIND

Use MOVE operator; set goal to MOVE large disk to peg C.

APPLY operator Q to state A

State A and operator Q

Move larger disk to peg C

APPLY operator Q

conditions not met → (D) List difference D between state A and required state; set goal to reduce D.

success → (A') Create new state A'; set goal to transform A' to B.

APPLY

Smaller disk on top of larger so cannot move larger, set goal to move smaller disk off peg A.

Adapted from Newell and Simon (1972)

could be a transform goal: transform the initial state (state 1) into the goal state (state 8). The outcome of this goal is the identification of a difference between the two states, for example, the large disk is not on peg C.

The reduce goal involves finding an operation that can be applied to reduce a certain difference. The input for the reduce goal is a description of the difference D; the output is an appropriate operator (called Q) that would reduce or eliminate that difference. For example, in the disk problem, the next goal could be a reduce goal: reduce the difference by finding an operator that will get the large disk on peg C. The outcome of this goal is the identification of an operator, for example, move the large disk to peg C.

The apply goal involves applying the operator Q to state A to produce a new state (called A'). The input for the apply goal is a description of the operator Q and the state A to which it is to be applied. The output is either a new state A' if the operator Q can be directly applied to A or a description of the difference D between state A and the required state if Q cannot be directly applied to A. For example, in the disk problem, the goal could be to apply the move operator to state A (that is, move the large disk to peg C). However, the outcome of this goal is the identification of a difference between the present state (A) and required state for this operation, namely, there must not be any disks on top of the large disk on peg A.

Box 7-10 summarizes the transform, reduce, and apply goals; the box shows the needed input, the possible outputs, and an example of each kind of goal. When more than one goal is needed to solve a problem, the goals are called "subgoals." Thus, solving any move problem involves establishing a series of subgoals made up of these three basic types shown in the box.

Goal Stack

With these three goals, you can solve a wide variety of problems. However, in means-ends analysis you may work on only one goal at a time; the other goals are "stacked" for future use. Assume that you start with a "push-down, pop-up stack," as shown in Box 7-11. You put the first goal in that stack; for example, your first goal might be "transform state 1 into state 8" for the disk problem. However, this goal cannot be directly attained so a subgoal is created (such as "reduce difference"), and this goal 2 is pushed down on top of goal 1; since goal 2 cannot be directly accomplished, goal 3 is created and pushed down on top; for the same reasons goal 4 and 5 are added to the stack. The goal on top is always the goal that is being worked on. Let's suppose that the stack has goals 1, 2, 3, 4, and 5 in it. If goal 5 can be achieved it pops off, as does goal 4 if it can now be achieved. This brings us back to goal 3, which still cannot be achieved; thus, new subgoals are created and pushed down on top (goals 6 and 7). These are achieved and pop off; but two new goals must still be added to the stack (goals 8 and 9). As these are

BOX 7–11   Goal Stack in Means-Ends Analysis

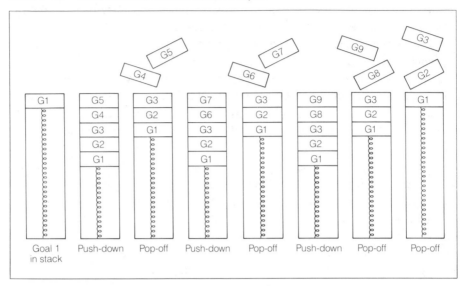

accomplished, they allow all of the goals to pop off, returning us to goal 1. The goal stack consists of all subgoals that have not yet been achieved. It begins with the top goal (transform the give state into the goal state) and ends when this goal is achieved; in between, many subgoals must be pushed on and eventually popped off.

Table of Connections

In the means-ends analysis, each time you fail to transform state A into state B, you must find a difference D; when you find a D, you must select an operator Q that can be used to reduce that difference. How does the computer (or the problem solver) know which operators should be used for reducing each difference? In many computer simulations, the computer must be given a "table of connections"—a list of all of the possible differences along with the appropriate operators to be performed for each. Box 7-12 provides an example of a partial table of connections for the disk problem. For example, if you come across a difference such as "the large disk is not on peg C but it should be there," the appropriate operator to use is "MOVE the large disk to peg C." Thus, for each possible difference that may be located in the course of solving the disk problem, the table of connections provides an operator that should be tried. As you can see, there is a sense in which the table of connections contains all of the information needed to solve the problem.

BOX 7–12   Table of Connections for Three Disk Problem

Difference (D)	Operator (Q)
Large disk not on peg C	MOVE large disk to peg C
Medium disk not on peg C	MOVE medium disk to peg C
Small disk not on peg C	MOVE small disk to peg C
Small disk on top of to-be-moved disk	MOVE small disk to another peg
Medium disk on top of to-be-moved disk	MOVE medium disk to another peg
Small (or medium) disk on peg C when attempt is made to move large disk to peg C	MOVE small (or medium) disk off peg C to another peg
Small disk on peg C when attempt is made to move medium disk to peg C	MOVE small disk off peg C to another peg

Goal Structure

In the solution of a problem, various changes in the goal stack represent the goal structure of the problem. In other words, the order in which goals are pushed on and popped off the stack represent the goal structure for a problem. For example, Box 7-13 shows a goal structure for the disk problem. The first goal (G1) is to transform state 1 into state 8. However, this goal's outcome is to locate a difference: the large disk (disk 3) is on peg C. Thus, a second goal (G2) is added to the stack: reduce the difference. The outcome is the location of an operator: move the large disk to peg C. Thus, goal 3 (G3) is added to the stack: apply the operator. When we try to apply the operator in goal 3, we find another difference: there is a small disk on top of the large disk so the large disk cannot be moved. We add a fourth goal (G4) to the location of an operator: move the small disk to peg C. Thus goal 5 (G5) is added to the stack: apply the operator. This is successful since the small disk can be moved; a new state is created (state 2) and goal 5 pops off the stack. Also, goal 4 is achieved and is popped off. But goal 3 (to move the large disk to peg C) is still not possible. The outcome of reinstating goal 3 is a difference: the medium disk is on top of the large disk. A new goal must be set (goal 6): to reduce the difference by getting rid of the medium disk. The outcome is the identification of an operator: move the medium disk to peg C. Goal 7 is added to the stack: apply this operator. Since this goal is successful, state 3 is created and goals 7 and 6 pop off the stack. However, when we return to state 3, we find another difference that will not allow us to move the large disk to peg C: the little disk is on peg C. More goals must be added and eventually popped off, as shown in the rest of Box 7-13. This analysis suggests that some moves such as from state 5 to state 6 require much goal stacking and are

BOX 7–13   Goal Structure for Means-End Analysis

Current Goal	Goals in Stack	Type of Goal	Outcome
G1	G1	TRANSFORM current state to goal state	DIFFERENCE: Disk 3 not on peg C
G2	G2, G1	REDUCE difference—So disk 3 is on peg C	Use MOVE operator
G3	G3, G2, G1	APPLY operator—Move disk 3 to peg C	DIFFERENCE: Disk 1 on top of disk 3
G4	G4, G3, G2, G1	REDUCE difference—So disk 1 is not on top of disk 3	Use MOVE operator
G5	G5, G4, G3, G2, G1	APPLY operator—Move disk to peg B	Success: Now in state 2
G3	G3, G2, G1	APPLY operator—Move disk 3 to peg C	DIFFERENCE: Disk 2 on top of disk 3
G6	G6, G3, G2, G1	REDUCE difference—So disk 2 is not on top of disk 3	Use MOVE operator
G7	G7, G6, G3, G2, G1	APPLY operator—Move disk 2 to peg B	Success: Now in state 3
G3	G3, G2, G1	APPLY operator—Move disk 3 to peg C	Difference: Disk 1 is on peg C
G8	G8, G3, G2 G1	REDUCE difference—So disk 1 is not on peg C	Use MOVE operator
G9	G9, G8, G3, G2, G1	APPLY operator—Move disk 1 to peg B	Success: Now in state 4

therefore difficult, while other moves such as from state 6 to state 7 require less stacking and are therefore easier.

Production System

The means-ends analysis strategy for the disk problem is summarized in the goal structure of Box 7-13. However, another way to describe the means-ends strategy is in a production system, which consists of a list of productions (Newell and Simon, 1972; Winston, 1977). A production is simply a condition-action pair, with a description of the state of affairs on the left and a description of some action on the right. For example, Newell and Simon suggest the following production system for crossing a street:

Current Goal	Goals in Stack	Type of Goal	Outcome
G3	G3, G2, G1	APPLY operator—Move disk 3 to peg C	Success: Now in state 5
G1	G1	TRANSFORM current state to goal state	Difference: Disk 2 not on peg C
G10	G10, G1	REDUCE difference—So disk 2 is on peg C	Use MOVE operator
G11	G11, G10, G1	APPLY operator—Move disk 2 to peg C	Difference: Disk 1 on top of disk 2
G12	G12, G11, G10, G1	REDUCE difference—So disk 1 is not on top of disk 2	Use MOVE operator
G13	G13, G12, G11, G10, G1	APPLY operator—Move disk 1 to peg A	Success: Now in state 6
G11	G11, G10, G1	APPLY operator—Move disk 2 to peg C	Success: Now in state 7
G1	G1	TRANSFORM current state to goal state	Difference: Disk 1 not on peg C
G14	G14, G1	REDUCE difference—So disk 1 is on peg C	Use MOVE operator
G15	G15, G14, G1	APPLY operator—Move disk 1 to peg C	Success: Now in state 8
G1	G1	TRANSFORM current state to goal state	Success: Problem is solved

1. If the traffic light is red ⟶ stop (and eliminate move goal).
2. If the traffic light is green ⟶ set a goal to move.
3. If your goal is "move" and your left foot is on the pavement ⟶ step with right foot.
4. If your goal is "move" and your right foot is on the pavement ⟶ step with left foot.

In such a production system, if more than one condition is met, you always give priority to the one that is higher on the list. Thus, if the light is red you always stop, even if one of the lower conditions might be met.

Box 7-14 provides a possible production system for the disk problem. The first production says that if you are in the goal state, then you can stop working on the

BOX 7–14   Production System for Disk Problem

Production Number	Condition	Action
(1)	Disks 1, 2, and 3 are on peg C	⟶ Stop
(2)	Disk 3 not on peg C	⟶ Set Goal: "Move disk 3 to peg C"
(3)	Goal is "Move disk 3" and no disk is in the way	⟶ Move disk 3 to peg C and erase goal
(4)	Goal is "Move disk 3" and a disk is in the way	⟶ Move the disk that is in the way
(5)	Disk 3 is on peg C and disk 2 is not on peg C	⟶ Set Goal "Move Disk 2 to peg C"
(6)	Goal is "Move disk 2" and no disk is in the way	⟶ Move disk 2 to peg C and erase goal
(7)	Goal is "Move disk 2" and a disk is in the way	⟶ Move the disk that is in the way
(8)	Disk 2 and 3 are on peg C and disk 1 is not on peg C	⟶ Set Goal "Move disk 1 to peg C"
(9)	Goal is "Move disk 1" and no disk is in the way	⟶ Move disk 1 to peg C and erase goal

problem. The second production says that if the large disk is not on peg C, then you should set a goal to move the large disk. The third production says that if the goal is to move the large disk and there are no barriers, then you should move the large disk and erase the goal. As you see, nine such productions are listed in the system.

Let's assume that this production system represents a person's strategy for solving the disk problem. Further, let's assume that this person always starts at the top of the list and looks for the first condition to be met; after carrying out the action, the person returns to the top of the list and works down again, and so on. In the disk problem, the first production to "fire"—when the conditions are met—is P2. Thus, you set your goal to move and return to the top of the list. Now, the next production to fire will be P4; the small disk is in the way so you move it to another peg. You return to the top of the production list, and P4 again will fire; this time the medium disk is on top of the larger disk that you want to move. You carry out the action (move the medium disk off of peg A) and return to the top of the list. Again P4 fires since there is now a small disk on peg C that is in your way; the action is to move that disk off of peg C. Now when you go the production system, P3 can fire—so you move the large disk to peg C. When you go the production system again, P5 will fire, and so on. Thus, the production system summarizes the means-ends analysis for the disk problem. Since production systems are made up of simple elements (similar in some ways to stimulus-response associations), it is easy to represent productions in computer programs. Thus, the strategy that a person uses to solve a problem can be represented precisely, using simple building blocks.

GPS: AN EXAMPLE

One of the best-known and most general problem-solving programs is general problem solver or GPS (Ernst and Newell, 1969). GPS was intended as a demonstration that certain general problem-solving techniques are involved in a wide spectrum of problems, and that it is possible to state explicitly what these general procedures are in a computer program able to solve a wide variety of different problems.

GPS, like other programs, begins by translating a statement of the problem into an internal representation of the initial state, goal state, and set of operators. In addition, GPS has stored in its memory a table of connections for each problem it will solve; the table of connections contains all possible problem states for that problem with a listing of how far apart any two states are from one another. Problem solving involves *breaking a problem down into subgoals* and then achieving each subgoal by *applying various problem-solving techniques,* each of which changes the problem state in the direction of the subgoal. For example, the program can try a technique and then test whether it changes the problem state to one that is closer to the subgoal by checking the difference on the table of connections. If the technique succeeds the program uses that technique and the process starts over, but if it fails the program tries another technique. Thus, when GPS solves a problem it performs the following:

Translates the problem into initial state, goal state, and legal operators.

Holds the appropriate table of connections in memory in order to tell the differences between the states.

Breaks the problem down into a hierarchy of goals and subgoals, each of which brings the problem closer to solution.

Applies problem-solving techniques based on the principle of means-ends analysis (reducing the difference between the present state and the desired subgoal state).

Moves on to the next subgoal when one is achieved, until the problem is solved.

The entire process is presided over by the "problem-solving executive," which determines the order in which operators will be applied, attempts to achieve subgoals by using means-ends analysis and develops a new subgoal structure if one does not work.

GPS can also solve a variation of the hobbits and orcs problem (missionaries and cannibals); the tower of Hanoi problem, water jar problems, letter series completion problems, calculus problems, and half a dozen other different tasks. For example, the previous sections show how a GPS-like technique can be applied to the disk, or Tower of Hanoi, problem.

EVALUATION

The computer-simulation approach is an attempt to study theories of human problem solving in a precise and scientifically testable manner. The approach requires that the theories be stated precisely, in a formal computer program, and provides for the use of sophisticated lab equipment, computers, in testing theories. Thus, computer simulation offers a breakthrough in the psychology of thinking which may ultimately produce a precise reformulation and integration of Gestaltist, associationist, and other ideas. However, the computer-simulation approach also has certain basic drawbacks. The human-machine analogy, the description of mental operations as computer operations, is not a perfect analogy. Psychology has been heavily influenced by developments in other sciences, including the breakthroughs in computer technology. However, the information-processing view of human beings as machinelike processors of information—through a currently popular view—is limited and may act to limit present views of thinking. In addition, there is a flaw in the logic of computer simulation: although a program may simulate human thinking behavior, this does not mean it simulates the underlying cognitive processes. Finally, current simulation programs require something like a table of connections—a list of every possible problem state and a measurement of its distance from the goal. Thus, in a way, the solution is given and the thinking process involves what the Gestaltists would call reproductive thinking. But the chapter on computer simulation is a continuing one, and it remains to be seen how far technology and humans may go in simulating human thought.

Suggested Readings

Newell, A., and Simon, H. A. *Human problem solving.* Englewood Cliffs, N.J.: Prentice-Hall, 1972. A giant, 900-page book that offers an information processing theory and computer simulation of problem solving in cryptarithmetic, logic, and chess.
Simon, H. A. *Models of thought.* New Haven, Conn.: Yale University Press, 1979. A collection of essays about computer models of human cognition.
Wickelgren, W. A. *How to solve problems: Elements of a theory of problem solving.* San Francisco: W. H. Freeman and Company, 1974. A short, basic introduction to the information processing approach to problem solving and how it can be applied to solve numerous interesting problems.
Winston, P. H. *Artificial intelligence.* Reading, Mass.: Addison-Wesley, 1977. A textbook about artificial intelligence.

CHAPTER 8

MENTAL CHRONOMETRY: Thinking as a Series of Mental Operations

Suppose you are seated in front of a panel that contains a light bulb and a response button. When the light comes on, you are required to press the button as quickly as possible. This simple task, summarized in Box 8-1, is called a *simple reaction time task*. It normally requires about 50 to 250 milliseconds to complete, depending on such task characteristics as the intensity of the bulb and on such subject characteristics as attentiveness, eyesight, and so forth. Notice that in simple reaction time tasks you have one stimulus and one response.

The situation could be made a little more complicated. Suppose you are seated in front of a panel with five light bulbs and one response button. When the target light—the one designated as correct—comes on, you should press the button, but should not when any of the other bulbs light up. This task is called a *discrimination reaction time task* because you must discriminate *which* particular light comes on. This task normally requires more time than simple reaction time tasks when all other variables are held constant. The *discrimination reaction time task* is summarized in Box 8-1. Notice that there are several possible stimuli but only one response.

Finally, we could complicate the task even further by setting you in front of five light bulbs, each of which has its own response button. In this case, you must press the button corresponding to the light that comes on, as shown at the bottom of Box 8-1. This is called a *choice reaction time task* because you must also choose the appropriate response. All other factors being equal, this task normally takes even longer than the other two.

THE DONDERS EXPERIMENT

F. C. Donders ([1868] 1969) performed experiments using reaction time tasks in 1868. His work represents the first attempt to analyze and measure the component processes of a simple task. Donders' reasoning was that different series of mental processes were required for each of the three types of task just described. Box 8-2 shows the stages that might be involved in the three tasks, with processes represented as rectangles and decisions represented as diamonds. A simple reaction time task requires perception and motor stages—time to perceive the stimulus and execute the response. In contrast, a discrimination reaction time task requires the same perception and motor stages plus a discrimination stage—time to distinguish which light was on. Finally, a choice reaction time task requires the same perception, discrimination, and motor stages plus a choice stage—time to decide which response to perform. As expected, choice tasks take more time than discrimination tasks, and simple tasks take the least amount of time. Using a subtraction technique, it was possible for Donders to calculate the time required for each stage:

Perception and motor time = time required for simple task.

Discrimination time = time for discrimination task minus time for simple task.

Choice time = time for choice task minus time for discrimination task.

Donders' reasoning was straightforward—more stages should require more time—and his method of analyzing the cognitive components of his tasks is similar to methods currently used in cognitive psychology for more complex tasks.

Until Donders' work, many scientists had assumed that the mental operations involved in responding to a stimulus occurred instantaneously. For example, a nineteenth-century physiologist, Muller, proclaimed that the speed of neural transmission was so fast that it could not be measured. Shortly thereafter, Helmholtz

BOX 8–1   Some Reaction Time Tasks

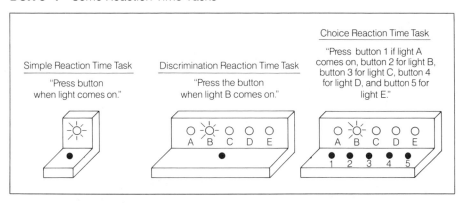

measured the speed, both in humans and lab animals, at a rather slow 100 meters per second. For example, transmission from a sense receptor in the periphery to the brain could take as long as 20 milliseconds not to mention time for processing within the brain. Thus, Donders deserves to be remembered for (1) showing that tasks could be broken down into elementary mental processes, (2) finding that each process takes a certain amount of time to occur, and (3) devising the subtraction technique as a means of measuring the time of mental events.

MENTAL CHRONOMETRY

Donders' work is interesting because it offers a means of describing what is going on "inside the black box" by analyzing cognitive activity into separate stages. However, Donders' work was rejected by early experimental psychologists such as Wundt, and strong interest in his work rematerialized only during the past twenty years. The rebirth of interest in developing cognitive models of processes involved in performing tasks can be marked by the appearance in 1960 of a remarkable book by Miller, Galanter, and Pribram called *Plans and the Structure of Behavior*. As discussed in Chapter 7, Miller and his colleagues argue that simple tasks may be represented as plans—a series of elementary mental processes.

Posner (1978) has called Donders' techniques "mental chronometry"—studying the time it takes to perform elementary cognitive operations. This approach makes several assumptions:

Components—any task can be described as a set of separate, elementary mental processes.

BOX 8-2   Component Processes in Reaction Time Tasks

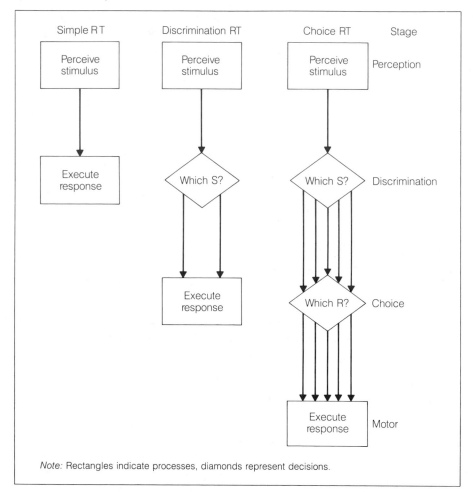

Note: Rectangles indicate processes, diamonds represent decisions.

Time —each elementary process takes a certain, measurable amount of time.

Serial —the processes are carried out one at a time, in order.

Additive/subtractive —the time for component processes may be legitimately added or subtracted.

Although objections may be raised to each of these assumptions (Posner, 1978), let's hold our judgment until we explore some of the applications of the stage analysis approach.

As a theory of problem solving, the mental chronometry approach is based on the idea that problem solving involves a series of mental operations, such as manipulating or operating on information in memory. The goal of this approach is to determine the elementary mental operations that are used in basic cognitive tasks and thus to establish a catalogue of the building blocks of human thought. In this chapter, we will explore how the mental chronometry approach has been applied to four cognitive tasks: letter matching, memory scanning, image rotating, sentence-picture verification.

LETTER-MATCHING TASKS

Consider the following task. For each pair of letters, say Yes if they are physically identical and No if they are not:

A   A
A   a
a   a
A   B

This is called a *physical match task;* the correct answers are yes, no, yes, no.

Now, for each of the following letter pairs, say Yes if both letters have the same name and No if they do not:

A   A
A   a
a   a
A   B

This is called a *name match task;* the correct answers are yes, yes, yes, and no.

Posner and his colleagues (Posner, 1969, 1978; Posner and Mitchell, 1967; Posner, Lewis, and Conrad, 1972; Posner, Boies, Eichelman, and Taylor, 1969) developed tasks like these in order to measure the speed of mental processes involved. The subject sits in front of a screen, and two letters are presented. For a physical match task, the subject presses the button marked "same" when both letters are physically identical and the button marked "different" when they are not. A similar setup is used for a name match task.

Consider the cognitive processes involved in a name match and physical match. Does your list look anything like those listed in Box 8-3? For example, the physical match may involve encoding, comparing, and responding; the name match involves these same stages as well as one more, namely, finding the name of each letter in long-term memory. Thus, if we subtract the time to make a physical match from the time to make a name match, we have an estimate of the time for the finding process.

The results of a typical study (Posner and Mitchell, 1967) indicate that the response time was 549 milliseconds for the physical match task (for example, AA)

BOX 8–3   Component Processes for Physical Match and Name Match Tasks

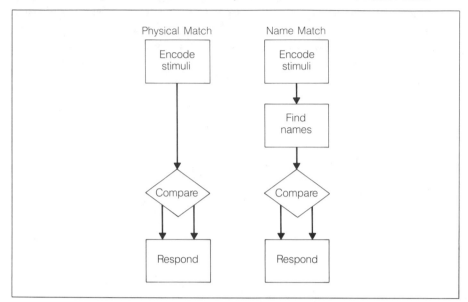

but 623 milliseconds for the name match task (Aa). Thus, using the subtraction technique, you might conclude that the time to search for a letter name in memory is 74 milliseconds. However, the times for component processes may be affected by several factors such as the physical similarity of the letters or the particular letter name (Posner, 1969, 1978).

In a related study by Posner, Lewis, and Conrad (1967), subjects were asked to judge whether two words were physically identical (such as *ELM-ELM*) or had the same name (such as *ELM-elm*). Results indicated that the time for a physical match was 555 milliseconds, and the time for a name match was 674 milliseconds. This suggests that the time to find the name of a simple word in memory is about 119 milliseconds. Similarly, when the task involves using a rule, response times are even longer. For example, the time to judge whether two letters are both vowels is 699 milliseconds. Some of these results are summarized in Box 8-4.

How can we be sure that name matches involve finding a letter's name in long-term memory while physical matches do not? Pachella and Miller (1976) suggest that if the model by Posner is correct, then using familiar letters will make the finding process easier, thus reducing the name match time. However, since the finding process is not part of the physical match task, using familiar letters should not affect physical match time. As predicted, increasing the familiarity of letters had no effect on physical match time but greatly reduced name match time. Similarly,

BOX 8–4 Response Times for Several Matching Tasks

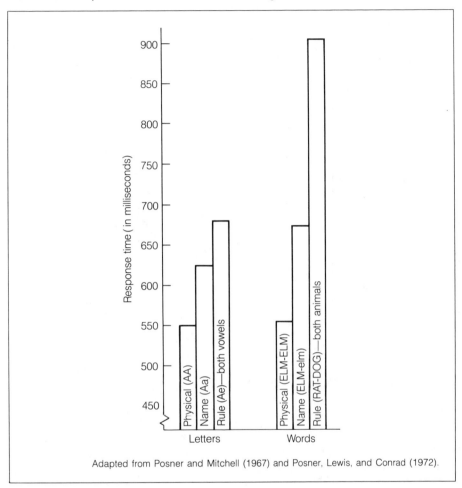

Adapted from Posner and Mitchell (1967) and Posner, Lewis, and Conrad (1972).

Posner (1978) points out that manipulations on the physical characteristics of the stimuli such as intensity, size, color, and contrast have strong effects mainly on physical matches. Thus, the subtraction technique seems to have been successful in locating and measuring the component processes in stimulus-matching tasks.

MEMORY-SCANNING TASKS

Suppose I gave you a set of digits to remember such as 2 4 7 3. Read each of these numbers aloud so that you keep them in your short-term memory. Now, suppose I

BOX 8–5   Component Processes in Memory-Scanning Task

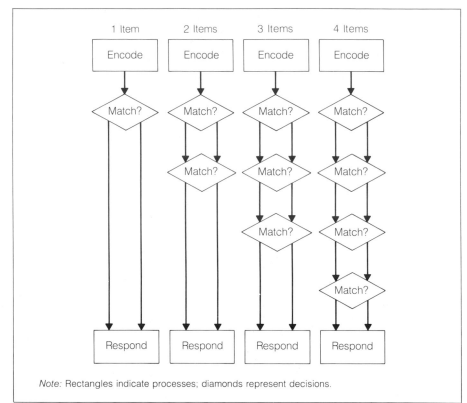

Note: Rectangles indicate processes; diamonds represent decisions.

gave you a probe and asked whether that probe was one of the numbers in your memory set. The probe is 7. Your answer, of course, should be Yes since there was a 7 in the memory set (2 4 7 3).

Sternberg (1966, 1969, 1975) used this task, called "memory scanning," to study cognitive processes in short-term memory. In a typical experimental trial, the subject read a set of one to six digits that were presented for two seconds; then, after a two-second delay, a probe digit was presented. The subject's job was to press the "yes" button if the probe matched one of the digits in the memory set and press the "no" button if it did not. On some trials there was just one digit in the memory set, on others there were two to six digits.

If you were a subject in a memory-scanning experiment, what cognitive processes do you think you would be using? You would have to encode and remember the memory set, you would have to compare the probe to each digit in your memory, and you would have to respond. Box 8-5 summarizes the processes that might be

BOX 8–6   Response Times for Various Memory Set Sizes in Memory-Scanning Task

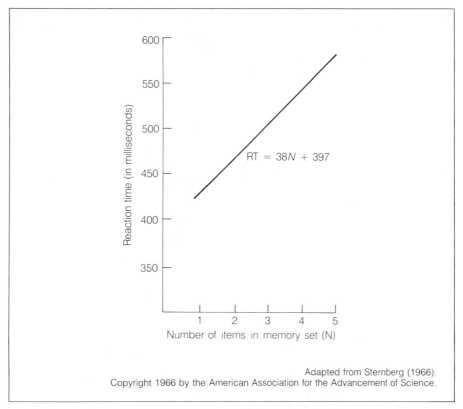

RT = 38N + 397

Reaction time (in milliseconds)

Number of items in memory set (N)

involved for memory sets of size 1, 2, 3, and 4. This analysis suggests that adding one more item to the memory set results in the need for one more mental comparison process.

Box 8-6 summarizes the average response times for memory sets ranging from one to six. For each additional digit in the memory set, response time increases approximately 38 milliseconds (Sternberg, 1966). Thus, by the subtraction method, we can conclude that each mental comparison takes about 38 milliseconds.

The sequence of processing stages indicated in Box 8-5 contains two assumptions that may seem peculiar to you. First, the model assumes that the probe is compared to each digit in the memory set sequentially, that is, one at a time; this is called *serial processing*. It seems more efficient to compare the probe to several digits in the memory set simultaneously; this is called *parallel processing*. Serial processing predicts an increasing response time as memory set is increased, such as is shown in Box 8-6, while parallel processing predicts a flat line. Thus, Sternberg

BOX 8–7   Scanning Rates for Various Stimuli

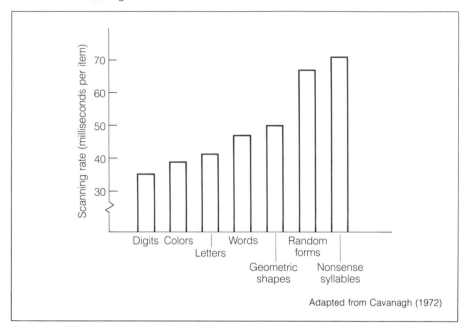

Adapted from Cavanagh (1972)

is able to point out that the observed data are most consistent with serial processing. However, there is some evidence that highly practiced subjects can search multiple targets as easily as searching for one target (Neisser and Lazar, 1964; Neisser, Novick, and Lazar, 1963).

A second assumption is that the subject compares the probe to each and every digit in the memory set, even if a match has already been found. This is called an *exhaustive search* because all comparisons are made. A more efficient alternative is a *self-terminating search,* the idea that you stop searching as soon as you find a match. The self-terminating search predicts that times to answer "yes" will be faster than for "no" since less comparisons need to be made on the average; the exhaustive search idea predicts no difference between "yes" and "no" response times. Again, Sternberg points out that the data support the predictions of exhaustive search, namely no difference between "yes" and "no" response times. However, there is some troubling evidence that response times are faster when the probe matches the first digit in the memory set and longer when it matches the last digit in the memory set (Burrows and Okada, 1971; Clifton and Birenbaum, 1970; Raeburn, 1974).

In a recent summary, Sternberg (1975) has addressed many of the issues raised by the serial exhaustive search model. Such problems should remind you that the

BOX 8–8   Examples of Stimuli Used in Letter Rotation Task

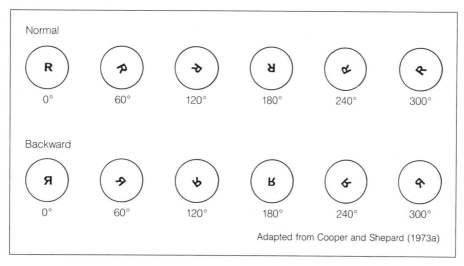

Normal

| 0° | 60° | 120° | 180° | 240° | 300° |

Backward

| 0° | 60° | 120° | 180° | 240° | 300° |

Adapted from Cooper and Shepard (1973a)

neat diagrams shown in Box 8-5 are not the only possible stage models. Under certain experimental situations or for certain subjects, entirely different processes and arrows might be needed. For example, Box 8-7 summarizes the average processing times for various kinds of stimuli (Cavanagh, 1972). Using random forms or nonsense syllables instead of digits in a memory scanning task seem to almost double the time required for each comparison stage.

MENTAL ROTATION TASKS

The mental chronometry approach has also been successfully applied to the study of how people manipulate visual images in memory. For example, Cooper and Shepard (1973a, 1973b) presented a single letter or digit to subjects on each trial. Each letter or digit was either normal or a mirror image (called *backward*); in addition, each letter or digit was presented either in its normal orientation or was rotated clockwise every 60 degrees. Examples of normal and backward stimuli in each of these orientations are given in Box 8-8. For each letter or digit, the subject's job was to press a button marked ''normal'' if the letter was normal and press a button marked ''backward'' if the letter was backward.

If you were a subject in this experiment, what mental processes would you have to perform for each task? First, you would have to encode the presented stimulus—

BOX 8–9   Component Processes in Image Rotation Task

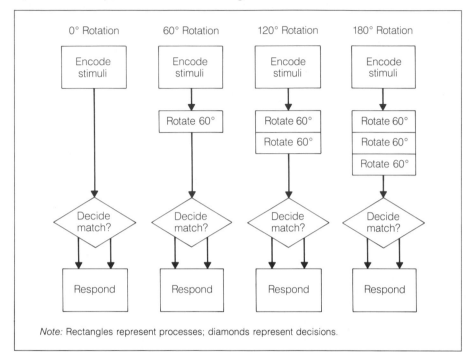

Note: Rectangles represent processes; diamonds represent decisions.

that is, represent the letter in your short-term memory. Then, you might rotate this representation until it was at an upright (0 degree) orientation. Your next step might be to decide whether the letter is normal or backward, and your final step is to press the appropriate button. Box 8-9 summarizes the sequence of processes you might go through for the 0 degree, 60 degree, 120 degree, and 180 degree tasks. As you can see, all tasks require encoding, deciding, and responding stages. However, the 60 degree task requires an additional stage—rotating 60 degrees—compared to the 0 degree task; similarly, the 180 degree task requires three times as much rotation as the 0 degree task. Thus, the time to make a 60 degree rotation may be determined in several ways, such as subtracting the time for the 0 degree task from the time for the 60 degree task.

The average response time for each task is given in Box 8-10. As you can see, response time is lowest when the stimulus is upright (0 degree or 360 degree), and longest when it is upside down (180 degree); there is a systematic increase in response time for tasks requiring more rotation. Although these results are consistent with the analysis in Box 8-9, there are several problems that may occur to you. First,

BOX 8–10   Box Times for Letter Rotation Task

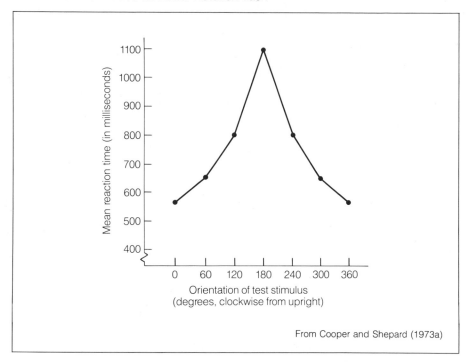

From Cooper and Shepard (1973a)

you may have noticed that the difference in response time between the 0 and 60 degree orientation is not the same as the difference between the 120 and 180 degree orientation; this discrepancy could be due to many factors, including some hesitancy concerning which way to rotate the upside down stimulus. Second, you can see that the response times for the 240 and 300 degree orientations corresponded nicely with those for 120 and 60 degree orientations, respectively; apparently, subjects are able to decide whether a clockwise or counterclockwise rotation is more efficient, so a direction decision state could be added to the models in Box 8-9 immediately after the encoding stage.

Similar analyses have also been conducted using three-dimensional stimuli by Metzler and Shepard (1974; Shepard, 1975). In a typical study (Metzler and Shepard, 1974), subjects are shown two figures such as those shown in Box 8-11. Some pairs (such as the A pair in Box 8-11) are identical except one figure must be rotated on the same plane as the picture. Other pairs (such as the B pair) are also identical except that one figure must be rotated perpendicularly to the picture plane. Finally, other pairs are not identical, although you must rotate one to see that clearly.

BOX 8–11   Examples of Stimuli Used in Figure Rotation Tasks

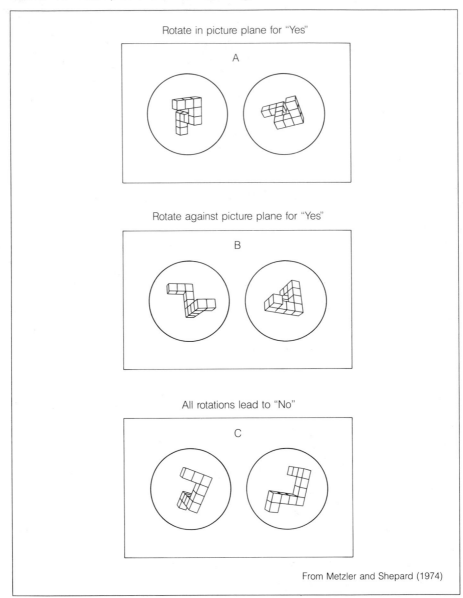

Rotate in picture plane for "Yes"

A

Rotate against picture plane for "Yes"

B

All rotations lead to "No"

C

From Metzler and Shepard (1974)

The amount of rotation required to match the two figures in any trial was either 0, 20, 40, 60, 80, 100, 120, 140, 160, or 180 degrees. A 0 degree rotation means the two objects are in the same orientation, and a 180 degree rotation means one is

BOX 8–12   Response Times for Figure Rotation Task

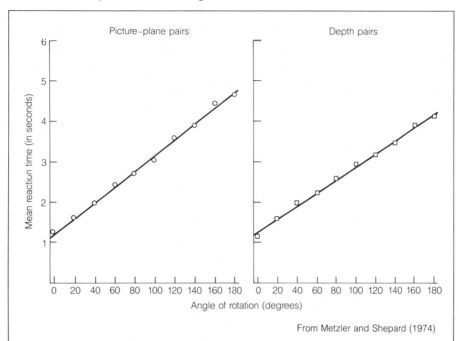

From Metzler and Shepard (1974)

upside down relative to the other; those in Box 8-11 all show an 80 degree rotation. The subject's task is to press a button labeled "same" if the two figures are identical and to press the button labeled "different" if they are not identical.

Consider the processing stages involved in this task. You must encode the stimuli, rotate one of them until it is in the same orientation as the other, decide if they match, and then respond. These stages are quite similar to those outlined in Box 8-9 for the letter rotation task. For example, the time to rotate a figure 20 degrees may be determined by subtracting the time for 0 degree orientation from that when the orientation is 20 degrees.

The response time results for the three-dimensional task are summarized in Box 8-12. Response times increase about 20 seconds for each additional 20 degrees of rotation that is required. These results are consistent with the stage models described earlier; for example, the 80 degree orientation task requires the same processes as the 60 degree task, plus one more stage—rotating an image 20 more degrees. These studies have been followed up (Cooper, 1975, 1976) and provide a convincing demonstration that the mental chronometry approach may be applied to nonverbal tasks.

SENTENCE-PICTURE VERIFICATION TASKS

Another important question that has generated considerable research concerns the information-processing stages involved in the comprehension of a sentence. The basic experimental method has been to present a simple sentence along with a picture and ask the subject whether the two are consistent.

For example, Clark and Chase (1972) presented sentences such as "star is above plus" simultaneously with symbol pictures, such as $^{*}_{+}$. The subjects were asked to press the "true" button if the sentence matched the picture, as it does in this example, or the "false" button if it did not. Four types of questions were asked, and examples of each are given below:

true-affirmative (TA):	star is above plus $^{*}_{+}$
false-affirmative (FA):	plus is above star $^{*}_{+}$
false-negative (FN):	star isn't above plus $^{*}_{+}$
true-negative (TN):	plus isn't above star $^{*}_{+}$

The answers to these four examples are true, false, false, true.

Just and Carpenter (1971) used sentences that involved the color of dots along with a picture of dots that were either red or black; examples follow:

true-affirmative (TA):	dots are red (picture of red dots)
false-affirmative (FA):	dots are black (picture of red dots)
false-negative (FN):	dots aren't red (picture of red dots)
true-negative (TN):	dots aren't black (picture of red dots)

As you try to solve a sentence-picture verification problem, can you determine what steps must be involved in each task? Do some problems require more processes than others? First, let's consider how the picture and sentence may be encoded. One way to represent the picture and sentence is to express each as a string consisting of features (in parentheses) and a sign (in front of the parentheses). For example, the sentence "the star is above plus" would be represented as AFF (star above plus), or "the star isn't above plus" would be represented as NEG (star above plus) or the picture $^{*}_{+}$ would be represented as AFF (star above plus), where AFF means "affirmative" and NEG means "negative." Actually, we can assume that AFF strings do not need to be marked, but NEG strings must be marked.

Four basic stages that may be involved in comparing sentences with pictures are:

Reading and response time—the time to encode each picture and sentence and time to execute a response.

Negation time—extra time needed to encode a sentence that has a negative in it.

Features mismatch time —extra time required when the features of two encoded strings do not match (for example, a sentence says ''red dots'' but the picture shows black dots).

Sign mismatch time—extra time required when the signs of two encoded strings do not match (the sentence is negative but the picture is affirmative, for example).

Models have been suggested (Clark and Chase, 1972; Chase and Clark, 1972) based on these stages in which sentences and pictures are encoded and their features and signs are then compared.

Box 8-13 gives a flow chart based on these stages. The first step is to set the ''truth index'' to ''true,'' which means that if there are no mismatches the subject will answer ''true.'' Then, in stages 2, 3, and 4, the presented items must be encoded into strings of the form ''sign (features)'' for the sentence and ''sign (features)'' for the picture. If no negatives are involved, there is no need to include a sign since AFF is understood, but, if the sentence contains a negative, extra time is required to incude the NEG sign in the representation (stage 3). The next decision (stage 5) involves comparing the features of the two strings: if they match, the subject goes on to the next stage without delay, but if not, the subject must change the truth index, which takes extra processing time. The final decision (stage 6) involves comparing the signs of the two strings: if they match, the subject goes on to the final stage (stage 7), but if they do not, the subject must first reverse the truth index. Thus there are three stages that can add extra time: if the sentence contains a negative (stage 3), if the features do not match (stage 5), or if the signs do not match (stage 6).

This model predicts that true-affirmative problems (TA) require time for each of the steps but not extra time, which we will call K stages. False-affirmative problems (FA) require time for each of the same steps plus extra time at step 5a since the features do not match—the stages are K + 5a. False-negatives (FN) require all the same steps as TA as well as extra time at 3a and 6a because of the negative—the stages are K + 3a + 6a. Finally, the true-negative problems require all the basic steps as well as all three extra steps—the stages are K + 3a + 5a + 6a. Thus, TA requires only the time to go through the 7 basic stages, FA requires that time plus time for one more process, FN requires K plus two more processes, and TN requires K plus three more processes. These predictions are summarized at the bottom of Box 8-13.

Some typical response times for each of the four types of problems are given in Box 8-14. As both graphs show, the time to respond increases for questions that require more processing stages. In a review of sentence-picture verification studies, Carpenter and Just (1975) listed 10 experiments, all of which obtained similar results. In all cases, the response time increased from lowest to highest in the order

BOX 8–13   Component Processes in Sentence-Picture Verification Task

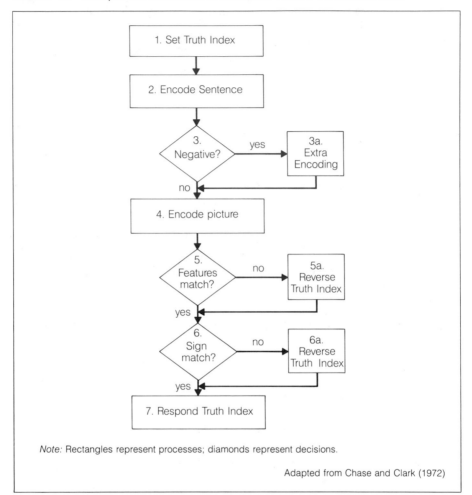

Note: Rectangles represent processes; diamonds represent decisions.

Adapted from Chase and Clark (1972)

TA, FA, FN, TN, as predicted by the process model in Box 8-13. Carpenter and Just (1975) have developed a more sophisticated flowchart model that gives more specific predictions.

In follow-up experiments, Just and Carpenter (1976) examined the sentence-picture verification task by recording the eye fixations of subjects as they answered four types of questions (TA, FA, FN, TN). For example, a typical question (in this case, TA) is shown in Box 8-15. Just and Carpenter measured the length of the initial gaze at the sentence in the middle (perhaps a measure of encoding time), subsequent gazes at the sentence, looks at the location that was named by the sentence such as

BOX 8–14   Response Times for Four Types of Sentence-Picture Verification
Problems

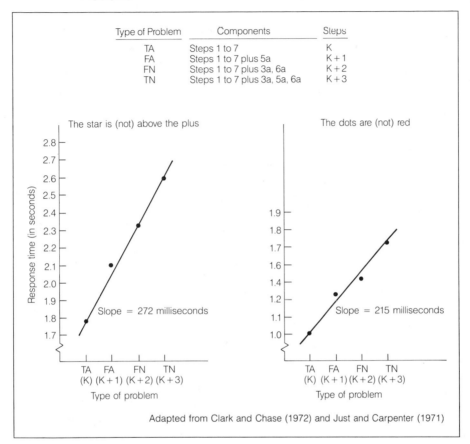

Type of Problem	Components	Steps
TA	Steps 1 to 7	K
FA	Steps 1 to 7 plus 5a	K + 1
FN	Steps 1 to 7 plus 3a, 6a	K + 2
TN	Steps 1 to 7 plus 3a, 5a, 6a	K + 3

The star is (not) above the plus

Slope = 272 milliseconds

The dots are (not) red

Slope = 215 milliseconds

Response time (in seconds)

TA   FA   FN   TN
(K) (K + 1) (K + 2) (K + 3)
Type of problem

TA   FA   FN   TN
(K) (K + 1) (K + 2) (K + 3)
Type of problem

Adapted from Clark and Chase (1972) and Just and Carpenter (1971)

"north" (perhaps a measure of processing time), and gazes at all other locations. An average of 57 milliseconds more was spent gazing at a negative sentence— "isn't north," for example—than an affirmative sentence—"is north"—perhaps indicating added encoding time for negatives. Also, length of gaze at the indicated location increased from TA to FA to FN to TN, perhaps indicating additional comparisons at the rate of 135 milliseconds per comparison. Thus, length of initial gaze at the sentence seems correlated with encoding time, and length of gaze at the indicated location is related to match-mismatch processing, while the other two measures indicate random activity that is constant for all questions. These results are

BOX 8–15   Duration of Eye Fixations for Four Types of Sentence-Picture Verification Problems

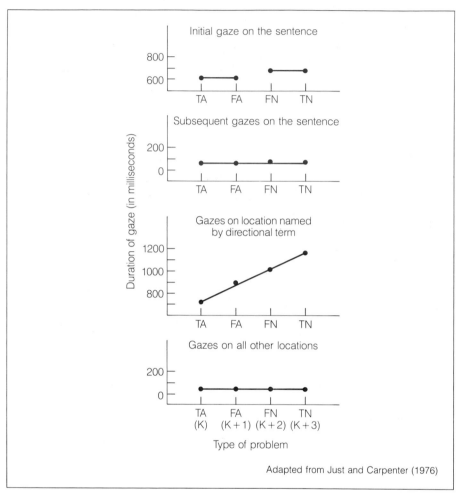

Adapted from Just and Carpenter (1976)

encouraging because they provide support for the stage model by using an entirely different experimental procedure.

There are, however, some problems with the stage analysis in sentence-picture verification as just given. For example, there is evidence that different people use different techniques for representing information in the sentence-picture verification tasks (Pellegrino and Glasser, 1979; Hunt and MacLeod, 1979). These differences are discussed more fully in Chapter 12; however, this research suggests that it may not be possible to find one flow chart model that fits all people for a given task.

EVALUATION

In this chapter you have seen how stage analysis techniques, or mental chronometry, may be applied to four simple cognitive tasks: letter matching, memory scanning, image rotation, and sentence-picture verification. In all four situations, the same procedure was followed. First, several related versions of a task were broken down into a series of components. Then, response times were obtained for each version of the task. As predicted, response times were related to the number of stages involved in the task. Times for individual stages were determined by using the subtraction method: subtracting the time for one task from the time for a task that involves all of the same processes plus one more. In this way, it can be found that mental images are rotated at the rate of 60 milliseconds per 60 degrees, letters can be scanned in memory at the rate of about 38 milliseconds per letter, the time to find a letter name in memory is about 75 milliseconds or the time to encode a negative is about 100 milliseconds.

On the surface, such techniques appear to be successful. However, there are serious problems with the assumptions of the stage analysis approach. For example, the assumption that a task can be broken down into stages is open to challenge because different researchers may invent different models for the same task, different subjects may behave quite differently on the same task, a given subject may shift from one series of stages to another with practice, and components may not be separable. Similar problems have been raised concerning the assumptions of serial processing, the legitimacy of the subtraction method, and the time assumptions (Posner, 1978; Sternberg, 1975).

Finally, the stage analysis approach may be criticized for having too narrow a goal. For example, it is not clear whether stage analysis models tell us more about how the human mind works or about the nature of the specific tasks. Suppose that in twenty-five years we have neat stage models for all of the major cognitive tasks. Would we have a complete theory of human problem solving? We would have a list of the "primitive processes" involved in intellectual tasks—processes such as compare, increment, set a counter, encode, and so on. Yet we would still need information concerning the strategies that people use in deciding how to solve a problem, as well as how people represent the problem. Thus, the stage analysis approach is a component in a larger theory of problem solving.

Suggested Reading

Posner, M. I. *Chronometric explorations of mind.* Hillsdale, N.J.: Erlbaum, 1978. An introduction to research and theory using the mental chronometry approach.

CHAPTER 9

SCHEMA THEORY:
Thinking as an Effort After Meaning

Schema Theory Definition of Thinking

Bartlett's Schema Theory

Understanding of Sentences

Understanding of Passages

Reading Task

Suppose I asked you to read a prose passage, such as a short story or a textbook lesson. How are you able to understand and remember the passage? Let's assume that you read each word and that you are familiar with the meaning of each word. Further, let's assume that you carefully read each sentence and that you are familiar with the rules of English sentence structure. Is this all you have to know to be able to understand a passage?

In order to get a better feeling for what is involved in the understanding process, please read the passage in Box 9-1. All of the words are fairly common, and you should know what each one means. All of the sentences follow the grammatical rules of English, with which you are familiar. You are able to read each word, and each sentence, with little effort. However, when you try to understand the passage, does it make sense to you? How would you rate your understanding on a scale of 1 to 7?

BOX 9–1   The Balloons Passage

If the balloons popped, the sound would not be able to carry since everything would be too far away from the correct floor. A closed window would also prevent the sound from carrying since most buildings tend to be well insulated. Since the whole operation depends on a steady flow of electricity, a break in the middle of the wire would also cause problems. Of course the fellow could shout, but the human voice is not loud enough to carry that far. An additional problem is that a string could break on the instrument. Then there could be no accompaniment to the message. It is clear that the best situation would involve less distance. Then there would be fewer potential problems. With face to face contact, the least number of things could go wrong.

From Bransford and Johnson (1972)

1	2	3	4	5	6	7

I understand   I don't understand

When Bransford and Johnson (1972) gave this passage to subjects, most found it rather difficult to understand, and most performed quite poorly on retention of the passage.

Now, look at the illustration in Box 9-2, which goes along with the passage. Reread the passage in Box 9-1. Do you understand it better now? How would you now rate your understanding?

1	2	3	4	5	6	7

I understand   I don't understand

When Bransford and Johnson (1972) provided this illustration along with the passage, subjects were able to understand and remember it much better.

Why is the passage easier to understand when it is accompanied by the illustration? What does the illustration provide? The passage in Box 9-1 appears out of context and has no apparent theme. The illustration in Box 9-2 provides a context for the passage, what Bransford (1979) and others call a "schema." A schema provides a general structure for the passage and allows you to hold the information together in an overall organization.

SCHEMA THEORY DEFINITION OF THINKING

Chapters 3 and 4 on Gestalt theory presented the idea that a person's understanding of a problem depends on how the problem is represented in the memory of the individual. Further, these chapters on Gestalt psychology emphasized the role of "understanding the problem" as the key to problem solving. This chapter follows the same memory representation approach, but emphasizes how prose sentences and passages are understood and represented in memory. As you will see, understanding

BOX 9–2   A Picture for the Balloons Passage

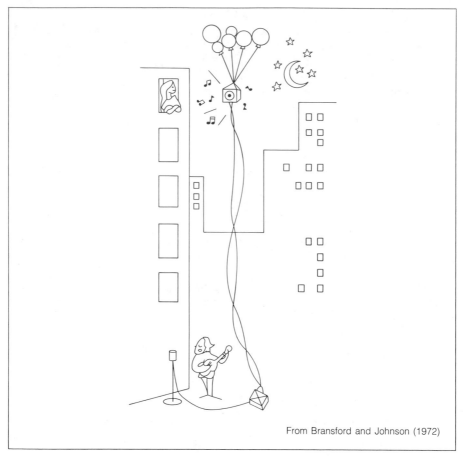

From Bransford and Johnson (1972)

sentences is a problem-solving process in which you must apprehend relations among elements and construct an integrated representation. For example, Greeno (1978, p. 243) has noted: "A close analogy can be made between the process of solving a . . . problem and the process of understanding a sentence."

The schema theory presented in this chapter views problem solving as the process of understanding. Schema theory is an advance because it offers a more precise description of the understanding process than Gestalt theory. According to schema theory, understanding involves the construction of a schema and the assimilation of incoming information to the schema. For example, in reading the passage in Box 9-1 you must: (1) construct a schema such as realizing that the story is about a serenade and (2) assimilate facts from the story to that schema such as focusing on information about the characters and location.

Although each theorist offers a slightly different view of schemata, a general definition of *schema* would contain the following points:

General—a schema may be used in wide variety of situations as a framework for understanding incoming information.

Knowledge—a schema exists in memory as something that a person knows.

Structure—a schema is organized around some theme.

Comprehension—a schema contains "slots" that are filled in by specific information in the passage.

Thus, a schema is a general knowledge structure used in comprehension. A schema serves to select and organize incoming information into an integrated, meaningful framework. The precise nature of this framework and its role in comprehension is the focus of schema theory and this chapter.

BARTLETT'S SCHEMA THEORY

Bartlett (1932) was one of the first psychologists to address the question of what processes people use to remember. As an example, consider "The War of the Ghosts" in Box 9-3. Read it over once, at your normal pace, then put the text away and try to reproduce on paper, from memory, what you have just read.

This example comes from the pioneering work of Bartlett and is summarized in his delightful little monograph, *Remembering* (1932). In his experiments, Bartlett used a version of the child's game of "telephone," in which a message is passed along a chain of people, changing a bit in each retelling. Bartlett called his procedure the "method of serial reproduction," and employed it as follows: he presented folk stories (or pictures) from unfamiliar cultures to British college students, asking Subject 1 to read the story, put it aside, reproduce it from memory, and to pass this reproduction on to Subject 2, who would in turn read the reproduced version, put it aside, reproduce his own version and pass it on to Subject 3, and so on.

Bartlett noticed that something quite curious happened in these studies. The stories (and pictures) changed as they were passed along but they changed in systematic ways. The version of the story reproduced by Subject 10, given in Box 9-3, is one of many examples on which Bartlett based the following observations:

Leveling or flattening. Most of the details such as proper names (Egulac, Kalama), titles (The War of the Ghosts), and the individual writing style tended

BOX 9–3 Three Versions of *The War of the Ghosts*

Original Version

The War of the Ghosts

One night two young men from Egulac went down to the river to hunt seals, and while they were there it became foggy and calm. Then they heard war-cries, and they thought: "Maybe this is a war-party." They escaped to the shore, and hid behind a log. Now canoes came up, and they heard the noise of paddles, and they saw one canoe coming up to them. There were five men in the canoe, and they said:

"What do you think? We wish to take you along. We are going up the river to make war on the people."

One of the young men said: "I have no arrows."

"Arrows are in the canoe," they said.

"I will not go along. I might be killed. My relatives do not know where I have gone. But you," he said, turning to the other, "may go with them."

So one of the young men went, but the other returned home.

And the warriors went on up the river to a town on the other side of Kalama. The people came down to the water, and they began to fight, and many were killed. But presently the young man heard one of the warriors say: "Quick, let us go home: that Indian has been hit." Now he thought: "Oh, they are ghosts." He did not feel sick, but they said he had been shot.

So the canoes went back to Egulac, and the young man went ashore to his house, and made a fire. And he told everybody and said: "Behold I accompanied the ghosts, and we went to fight. Many of our fellows were killed, and many of those who attacked us were killed. They said I was hit, and I did not feel sick."

He told it all, and then he became quiet. When the sun rose he fell down. Something black came out of his mouth. His face became contorted. The people jumped up and cried.

He was dead.

Version Reproduced by First Subject

The War of the Ghosts

There were two young Indians who lived in Egulac, and they went down to the sea to hunt for seals. And where they were hunting it was very foggy and very calm. In a little while they heard cries, and they came out of the water and went to hide behind a log. Then they heard the sound of paddles, and they saw five canoes. One canoe came toward them, and there were five men within, who cried to the two Indians, and said: "Come with us up this river, and make war on the people there."

to be lost. Bartlett attributed this loss to the fact that British college students had no prior experience with folk tales native to other cultures or to spirits and ghosts; thus, since learning in this case required assimilating new material to existing concepts, the students were at a loss. According to Bartlett (1932, p. 172): "Without some general setting or label as we have repeatedly seen, no material can be assimilated or remembered."

But one of the Indians replied: "We have no arrows."

"There are arrows in the canoe."

"But I might be killed, and my people have need of me. You have no parents," he said to the other, "you can go with them if you wish it so; I shall stay here."

So one of the Indians went, but the other stayed behind and went home. And the canoes went on up the river to the other side of Kalama, and fought the people there. Many of the people were killed, and many of those from the canoes also.

Then one of the warriors called to the young Indian and said: "Go back to the canoe, for you are wounded by an arrow." But the Indian wondered, for he felt not sick.

And when many had fallen on either side they went back to the canoes, and down the river again, and so the young Indian came back to Egulac.

Then he told them how there had been a battle, and how many fell and how the warriors had said he was wounded, and yet he felt not sick. So he told them all the tale, and he became weak. It was near daybreak when he became weak; and when the sun rose he fell down. And he gave a cry, and as he opened his mouth a black thing rushed from it. Then they ran to pick him up, wondering. But when they spoke he answered not.

He was dead.

Version Reproduced by the Tenth Subject

The War of the Ghosts

Two Indians were out fishing for seals in the Bay of Manpapan, when along came five other Indians in a war-canoe. They were going fighting.

"Come with us," said the five to the two, "and fight."

"I cannot come," was the answer of the one, "for I have an old mother at home who is dependent upon me." The other said he could not come, because he had no arms. "That is no difficulty," the others replied, "for we have plenty in the canoe with us"; so he got into the canoe and went with them.

In a fight soon afterwards this Indian received a mortal wound. Finding that his hour was coming, he cried out that he was about to die. "Nonsense," said one of the others, "you will not die." But he did.

From Bartlett (1932)

Sharpening. A few details may be retained and even exaggerated. Apparently subjects can store a schema plus a few selected details.

Rationalization. Passages tended to become more compact, more coherent, and more consistent with the readers' expectations. All references to spirits and ghosts faded away, and the story became one of a simple fighting trip. Bartlett called this process *rationalization* and argued that the reader was actively engaged in "an effort after meaning"—an attempt to make the story fit in with the individual's expectations. Since mystical concepts are not a major factor in Western culture, the mystical aspects of the story were not well remembered; instead, many subjects tended to tack on a "moral," which was a widely accepted practice in other stories they were familiar with.

Although Bartlett's work lay dormant for many years as the behaviorist movement swept across the study of psychology in the United States, he is now recognized as the major forerunner of modern cognitive psychology because he suggested two fundamental ideas about human mental processes:

Learning and memory. The act of comprehending new material requires "an effort after meaning." In reading a complex text, or acquiring any new information, humans must assimilate the new material to existing concepts or schemata. The outcome of learning—what is stored in memory—does not duplicate exactly what was presented, but rather depends on both what was presented and the schema to which it is assimilated. People change the new information to fit their existing concepts, and in the process, details are lost and the knowledge becomes more coherent to the individual.

Remembering and memory. The act of remembering requires an active "process of construction"; during recall, an existing schema is used to generate or construct details that are consistent with it. Memory is not detailed but rather is schematic, that is, based on general impressions. Although recall produces specific details that seem to be correct, many of them are, in fact, wrong.

Carmichael, Hogan, and Walter (1932) provided complementary evidence for Bartlett's theory by using pictorial figures and providing subjects with a method for interpreting them. They showed their subjects a series of 12 figures like those in Box 9-4 and gave each one a name. Before presenting Figure 1, for example, the experimenter might say, "This figure resembles eyeglasses," or "This figure resembles a dumbbell." For Figure 4, the experimenter might suggest "a gun" or "a broom." When the subjects were asked to reproduce these figures from memory, their drawings tended to be influenced by the labels they had been given during the presentation. These results were consistent with Bartlett's idea that memory for figures or passages involves assimilation to schemata—in this case, the labels may have served as schemata.

Bartlett's work was tantalizing because it demonstrated that memory is "schematic"—that both learning and remembering are based on general schemata rather than specifics. However, Bartlett's work did not yield clear or powerful predictions; for example, it could not predict which details would "fall out" of a passage or in what ways a subject would make a passage more coherent. In a sense, the work of

BOX 9-4   Effects of Verbal Labels on Memory for Ambiguous Figures

Figure presented to subjects	Figure reproduced by subjects with label list 1		Figure reproduced by subjects with label list 2	
⚬—⚬	eyeglasses	⚬⚬	dumbbell	⚬—⚬
✕	hourglass	✕	table	✕
⌐7	seven	7	four	4
▷—	gun	▷—o—	broom	🧹

Adapted from Carmichael, Hogan, and Walter (1932)

modern cognitive psychologists has been to clarify the ideas of Bartlett and the Gestalt psychologists and to test and refine their theories. The basic method that has been used for this is known as the "recall method" in which subjects are presented with complex verbal material and are then asked questions about it.

UNDERSTANDING OF SENTENCES

Chomsky's Theory

The modern rebirth of interest in psycholinguistics, and especially in the study of how sentences are comprehended and stored, was touched off by Chomsky's "generative" theory of language (1957, 1959, 1965, 1968). Although Chomsky's complex theory is a linguistic theory rather than a tested psychological theory, it includes three basic ideas that have attracted psychologists:

The distinction between surface structure and deep structure—the surface structure of a sentence is the way it is written or spoken; its deep structure is the way it is represented in memory. For example, the sentence "The ball was hit by John" may be stored in deep structure as "John hit ball." Thinking, apparently, is based on the deep structure of language.

Transformation rules—language consists of a set of rules for converting surface structure into deep structure (comprehension) and deep structure into surface structure (recall and communication).

Universal grammar—some general characteristics are shared by all language users.

Chomsky's cognitive approach to language came as an alternative to the idea B. F. Skinner expressed in his book, *Verbal Behavior* (1957), that language is a learned behavior subject to the laws of conditioning. By introducing the idea of deep structure and transformation rules, Chomsky suggested that memory structure— how sentences are stored and used—is not necessarily the same as surface structure. Unfortunately, Chomsky's theory was not based on psychological research, but rather on logical arguments. For example, consider the sentence: "They are eating apples." According to Chomsky, the meaning of this sentence depends on how one transforms it to deep structure; if one assumes that "they" refers to people, the deep structure is quite different than if "they" refers to the apples. (I spotted a similar example hanging in a laundromat: "Not responsible for clothes you may have stolen.") The importance of such examples is that they show the same surface structure may lead to different deep structures; apparently, the study of surface structure or verbal behavior alone may not adequately explain human comprehension of language.

Another important distinction with respect to sentences is between *syntax*—the order of language units, as specified by grammatical rules—and *semantics*—the meaning or referents of a sentence. Considerable research has been done on the importance of both syntax and semantics in comprehending and recalling sentences.

For example, Miller and Selfridge (1950) investigated the role of syntax in memory for sentences by varying the "approximation to English" sentences for strings of words. Word strings were constructed based on a random sampling of words (zero-order approximation), a random sampling of words from a typical passage (first-order), an actual text lifted from a typical passage (text), or by making a second-, third-, fourth-, fifth-, or seventh-order approximation to English. The procedure for developing the second-order, for instance, was to ask a subject to complete a sentence starting with a word supplied by the researchers. A second subject in turn was asked to complete a sentence starting with the word that immediately followed the one that had been supplied for the first subject. Then the second subject's first new word was passed on to a third subject, and so on. The first new words produced by each successive subject were put together into a string that was called second-order approximation to English; to obtain third-order, Miller and Selfridge took the first two words given by each subject, and so on. Examples are given in Box 9-5.

Lists of 10, 20, 30, or 50 words were constructed using these methods; new subjects were asked to listen to the string and then recall it in order. The results shown in Box 9-5 indicate that as the word strings more closely approximated English, more words were recalled. Miller and Selfridge concluded that in reading

BOX 9-5   Memory for Word Strings That Are Approximations to English

Word Strings (10-Word Lists)

0 order approximation: by way consequence handsomely financier flux cavalry swift-
ness weatherbeaten extent

1st order approximation: abilities with that beside I for waltz you the sewing
2nd order approximation: was he went to the newspaper is in deep and
3rd order approximation: tall and thin boy is a biped is the best
4th order approximation: saw the football game will end at midnight on January
5th order approximation: they saw the play Saturday and sat down beside him
7th order approximation: recognize her abilities in music after he scolded him
before

Text: the history of California is largely that of a railroad

Percentage of Words Recalled for Different Word Strings

From Miller and Solfridge (1950).
Copyright 1950 by the University of Illinois Press.

normal prose, people use their knowledge of syntax (grammatical rules) as an aid in comprehension and remembering rather than simply storing and recalling each word individually.

There has also been much work on the role of semantics in remembering sentences. For example, Miller (1962) has suggested that comprehending and storing a sentence involves transforming it into a "kernel" sentence (K) plus a mental "footnote" about the syntactic structure. This theory predicts that a sentence such as "The boy hit the ball" would serve as the kernel (along with some footnote) for passive (P) surface structures, such as "The ball was hit by the boy," for inter-rogative (Q) surface structures, such as "Did the boy hit the ball?," for negative (N) surface structures, such as "The boy did not hit the ball," or for any combination of passive, interrogative, and negative structures.

In a promising study, Mehler (1963) presented lists of sentences in kernel form, sentences transformed into passive, interrogative, and negative forms, and all com-binations of these. Recall was best for the lists of kernel sentences and worst for the passive-interrogative, interrogative, and passive-interrogative-negative sentences. This result seemed consistent with Miller's and Chomsky's idea that sentences are converted into a deeper structure like K sentences. However, when Martin and Roberts (1966) replicated the Mehler study but controlled for sentence length, they obtained the opposite results and concluded that Mehler's findings could be ex-plained by the fact that K sentences were shorter and thus easier to recall.

After reviewing the studies of sentence memory, Adams (1976, p. 355) con-cluded: "There is no evidence that Miller's hypothesis about sentences, derived from generative theory, is valid . . . Generative theory may have a short the-oretical life in psychology because it is not a psychological theory." In other words, although the concept of deep structure has been useful to psychologists, the partic-ular theory that the kernel sentence represents the meaning of a sentence is based on logical or linguistic analysis rather than on psychological study. It is now the task of psychologists through empirical studies to determine exactly how a sentence is represented in memory. Or, to put it another way, the search continues for the schema of a sentence.

Memory for Sentences in Text

Cognitive psychologists have recently been trying to study more carefully Bartlett's idea that subjects *abstract* the general meaning from prose during reading, and *construct* their answers during recall. In an already classic study, Bransford and Franks (1971) read the sentences shown in the first part of Box 9-6 to the subjects and then asked the recognition questions shown in the second part of the box. Take a few minutes now to read the sentence list and then take the recognition test. In the original study the subjects were asked to rate on a 5-point scale how sure they were that the test sentence had been in the original list, but you can skip the rating for your test.

To make up the sentences given in the top of Box 9-6, Bransford and Franks used four basic "idea sets":

"The scared cat running from the barking dog jumped on the table."

"The old car pulling the trailer climbed the steep hill."

"The tall tree in the front yard shaded the man who was smoking his pipe."

BOX 9-6   The Bransford and Franks Experiment: A Typical Set of Sentences

Sontence	Question
Acquisition sentences: Read each sentence, count to five, answer the question, go on to the next sentence.	
The girl broke the window on the porch.	Broke what?
The tree in the front yard shaded the man who was smoking his pipe.	Where?
The hill was steep.	What was?
The cat, running from the barking dog, jumped on the table.	From what?
The tree was tall.	Was what?
The old car climbed the hill.	What did?
The cat running from the dog jumped on the table.	Where?
The girl who lives next door broke the window on the porch.	Lives where?
The car pulled the trailer.	Did what?
The scared cat was running from the barking dog.	What was?
The girl lives next door.	Who does?
The tree shaded the man who was smoking his pipe.	What did?
The scared cat jumped on the table.	What did?
The girl who lives next door broke the large window.	Broke what?
The man was smoking his pipe.	Who was?
The old car climbed the steep hill.	The what?
The large window was on the porch.	Where?
The tall tree was in the front yard.	What was?
The car pulling the trailer climbed the steep hill.	Did what?
The cat jumped on the table.	Where?
The tall tree in the front yard shaded the man.	Did what?
The car pulling the trailer climbed the hill.	Which car?
The dog was barking.	Was what?
The window was large.	What was?
STOP. Turn the page and read the sentences in the box. Without looking back at the sentences above, decide if each sentence appeared in the list above (old) or if it is a new sentence.	

"The girl who lives next door broke the large window on the porch."

Each idea unit was broken down into four single ideas (called ones), such as:

"The cat was scared."

"The dog was barking."

"The cat was running from the dog."

"The cat jumped on the table."

The ones could be combined to form twos, such as: "The scared cat jumped on the table." The ones could be combined to form threes, such as: "The scared cat was running from the barking dog." Finally, the ones could also be combined to form an entire idea unit, like the examples just given, and called a four.

BOX 9-6, continued

Sentence	Question
Test set . . . Check "old" or "new."	
The car climbed the hill.	(old ____ , new ____)
The girl who lives next door broke the window.	(old ____ , new ____)
The old man who was smoking his pipe climbed the steep hill.	(old ____ , new ____)
The tree was in the front yard.	(old ____ , new ____)
The scared cat, running from the barking dog, jumped on the table.	(old ____ , new ____)
The window was on the porch.	(old ____ , new ____)
The barking dog jumped on the old car in the front yard.	(old ____ , new ____)
The cat was running from the dog.	(old ____ , new ____)
The old car pulled the trailer.	(old ____ , new ____)
The tall tree in the front yard shaded the old car.	(old ____ , new ____)
The scared cat was running from the dog.	(old ____ , new ____)
The old car, pulling the trailer, climbed the hill.	(old ____ , new ____)
The girl who lives next door broke the large window on the porch.	(old ____ , new ____)
The tall tree shaded the man.	(old ____ , new ____)
The cat was running from the barking dog.	(old ____ , new ____)
The cat was old.	(old ____ , new ____)
The girl brok the large window	(old ____ , new ____)
The scared cat ran from the barking dog that jumped on the table.	(old ____ , new ____)
The scared cat, running from the dog, jumped on the table.	(old ____ , new ____)
The old car pulling the trailer climbed the steep hill.	(old ____ , new ____)
The girl broke the large window on the porch.	(old ____ , new ____)
The scared cat which broke the window on the porch climbed the tree.	(old ____ , new ____)
The tree shaded the man.	(old ____ , new ____)
The car climbed the steep hill.	(old ____ , new ____)
The girl broke the window	(old ____ , new ____)
The man who lives next door broke the large window on the porch.	(old ____ , new ____)
The tall tree in the front yard shaded the man who was smoking his pipe.	(old ____ , new ____)
The cat was scared.	(old ____ , new ____)

STOP. Count the number of sentences judged "old."
    See text for answer.

The subjects heard a long list of sentences consisting of some ones, twos, and threes but no fours from the idea sets, presented in random order.

Now comes the surprise. In your test, the sentences in the second part of Box 9-6 are all "new," so each "old" you checked is a "false recognition"—you thought you had seen it in the original list but it was not there. In a related study,

BOX 9–7 Recognition of Old and New Sentences

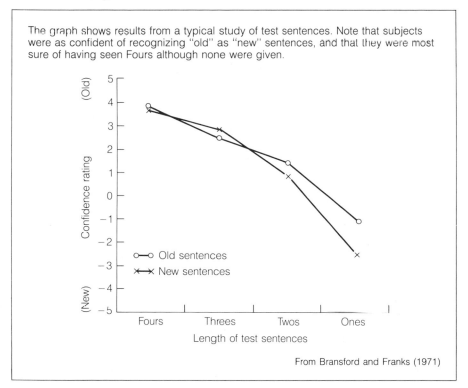

The graph shows results from a typical study of test sentences. Note that subjects were as confident of recognizing "old" as "new" sentences, and that they were most sure of having seen Fours although none were given.

From Bransford and Franks (1971)

Bransford and Franks presented the same kind of study sentences, but this test consisted of some sentences that had been in the original list (old), some that had not been in the original list but could be inferred from one of the idea sets (new), and some (called noncase) that were based on putting parts of different idea sets together.

The ratings of the subjects for the test sentences are given in Box 9-7. As you can see, they could not tell the difference between sentences that had actually appeared in the original list and those that were simply consistent with an idea set. In fact, they were most confident about having seen fours although no fours were ever presented. Bransford and Franks concluded that during reading the subjects abstracted the four general linguistic ideas and that during recall they used these general abstract ideas, but had no memory of the specific sentences from which they were abstracted.

Further evidence for abstract memory of prose was obtained by Sachs (1967). She asked subjects to read a passage about the invention of the telescope like the one

BOX 9–8 Memory for the Meaning of Text

The Passage

Subjects read the following passage and were asked a question about the italicized sentence either immediately after it was presented (0 syllables), 80 syllables later, or 160 syllables later.

> There is an interesting story about the telescope. In Holland, a man named Lippershey was an eyeglass maker. One day his children were playing with some lenses. They discovered that things seemed very close if two lenses were about a foot apart. Lippershey began experiments and his "spyglass" attracted much attention. *He sent a letter about it to Galileo, the great Italian scientist.* (0 syllable test here.) Galileo at once realized the importance of the discovery and set out to build an instrument of his own. He used an old organ pipe with one lens curved out and the other curved in. On the first clear night he pointed the glass towards the sky. He was amazed to find the empty dark spaces filled with brightly gleaming stars! (80 syllable test here.) Night after night Galileo climbed to a high tower, sweeping the sky with his telescope. One night he saw Jupiter, and to his great surprise discoverd with it three bright stars, two to the east and one to the west. On the next night, however, all were to the west. A few nights later there were four little stars. (160 syllable test here.)

The Results

The proportion of correct response for each type of recognition question is given in the chart below.

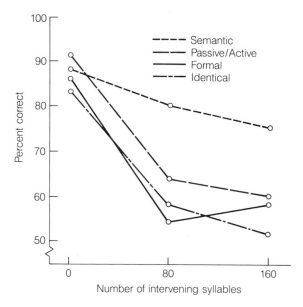

From Sachs (1967)

shown in Box 9-8, then she presented a test sentence and asked them to tell whether or not it had occurred verbatim in the text. The test sentence was based on a sentence from the text and the test was given immediately after a subject had read the sentence (0 syllables), after the subject had read 80 syllables beyond the sentence, or 160 syllables beyond the sentence. The test sentence contained either a change in meaning (semantic change), a change in voice (active or passive change), a change in wording that did not alter meaning (formal change), or no change (identical) from the text sentence. For example, the text sentence, "He sent a letter about it to Galileo, the great Italian scientist," was presented in the test in one of the following forms:

Identical: same text sentence.

Formal change: He sent Galileo, the great Italian scientist, a letter about it.

Active or passive change: A letter about it was sent to Galileo, the great Italian scientist.

Semantic change: Galileo, the great Italian scientist, sent him a letter about it.

The results of the experiment are given in Box 9-8. If the subjects had just read the sentence (0 interpolated syllables), they performed well in saying Yes to the identical sentence and No to each of the changed sentences. However, if the test came after the subject had read 80 or 160 syllables beyond the target sentence, then performance fell sharply for detecting formal or voice changes, but the subjects were still fairly accurate at noticing a change in meaning. In other words, once a sentence had been "digested" by the subject, the subject retained little information about the original grammatical form of the sentence, but did retain the general meaning. Sachs concluded that in the course of reading a passage, a subject abstracted the general meaning but not the specific grammatical details.

Paivio (1971) has suggested that subjects may have formed mental images as a way of abstracting meaning of sentences in Sachs's study. Since Sachs, as well as Bransford and Franks, used sentences that were relatively concrete, the subjects could have easily formed images that retained the meaning but destroyed the grammatical form of the presented text. In order to test this idea, Begg and Paivio (1969) replicated Sachs's study using some passages that tended to evoke vivid images and some that used abstract words that did not tend to evoke imagery. For example, typical sentences were: "The vicious hound chased a wild animal" (concrete), or "The absolute faith aroused an enduring interest" (abstract). For the concrete, high-imagery sentences, Begg and Paivio obtained results similar to Sachs's finding: subjects noticed a semantic change more easily than a change in sentence structure; however, for the abstract, low-imagery sentences, the reverse trend was found, with better recognition of lexical changes than semantic changes. Based on such findings, Paivio (1971) developed a "two-process theory of memory"—the idea that knowledge may be stored using imagery codes or verbal codes. Although most of the models of memory described in this chapter assume verbal coding for stored knowledge, Paivio's work has helped to reintroduce the idea that some types of representations may be nonverbal.

UNDERSTANDING OF PASSAGES

Levels Effects

The results of Bransford and Franks and of Sachs complement those of Bartlett and help to extend the idea that memory for prose is schematic. However, another important question is whether we can predict in advance what a person will remember about a passage. Johnson (1970) investigated this question by breaking a story down into "idea units" and asking a group of subjects to rate the idea units for their importance to the story. Then another group read the story and were asked to recall it. As predicted, the new subjects remembered more of the important units, even when the experimenter controlled study time for each with a slide projector.

Johnson's results are interesting because they imply that certain ideas in a passage are more important than others and that it is possible to predict in advance what these well-remembered ideas will be. In addition, similar results have been obtained in some cases that used different material (Meyer and McConkie, 1973; Meyer, 1977). More recently, other researchers have attempted to devise methods of *text analysis,* procedures for analyzing a text into a hierarchical structure. Structural variables were discussed in the previous chapter as affecting memory for word lists. For the study of remembering passages, those results suggest as a working hypothesis that ideas high in the structural hierarchy are more likely to be remembered than ideas low in the hierarchy.

In a review of the advances in text analysis, Meyer (1975, p. 1) described the goal of her research as follows: "After reading a passage, people are unable to recall all the information that it contained. When a number of people read or hear the same passage, some ideas are recalled by almost everyone whereas other ideas are recalled by very few. The goal . . . is to determine whether certain variables can account for these differences in recall."

In an exploratory study, Meyer (1975) broke a 500-word prose passage from *Scientific American* into idea units and then arranged them into a hierarchical outline, which she called a "tree structure" or "content structure." Independent judgments by one group of subjects produced almost identical tree structures from the same materials, thus indicating that objective text analysis may be possible. When new subjects were asked to read and recall the passage, there was a clear relationship between the "height" of an idea in the structure and the likelihood of its being recalled—ideas high in the structure were recalled better than those low in the structure. Apparently, findings based on subjective ratings of "importance," such as those used by Johnson, may be accounted for by Meyer's concept of "height" in a content structure. Unfortunately, one problem with interpreting the results of Meyer's study is that the "height" of an idea in the structure is often closely related (or confounded) with its serial order. High, important ideas more often come first, and verbal learning research on the serial position effect (see Chapter 9) indicates that subjects are more likely to recall the first few items in a list.

Meyer (1975) attempted to overcome this problem in a subsequent study that used three passages of approximately 575 words each. The passages dealt with topics such as "breeder reactors," "schizophrenia," and "parakeets." A target paragraph was selected from each passage, and two similar versions of each passage were constructed. The same target was inserted in the same place in both versions, but in one version the ideas in the target paragraph were high on the content structure, that is, important to the theme and to other ideas presented in the passage; for the other passage they were low. Subjects recalled much more about the target paragraph if it was high in the structure than if it was low. One important problem in interpreting these results is that the "high" and "low" passages might not have been equally difficult; this problem was mitigated partially by the fact that Meyer did make sure they were similar in number of words, number of idea units, and number of levels in the content structure.

Kintsch (1974, 1976) has developed a method for dividing a text into a hierarchy of propositions called the *text base*. The system is similar to that used by Meyer to generate *content structure* and is inspired by the case grammars we discussed earlier in this chapter. Each proposition consists of two or more words that are related to one another; the propositions generally consist of verbs and arguments that relate to the verb. For example, consider the text:

> Turbulence forms at the edge of a wing and grows in strength over its surface, contributing to the lift of a supersonic aircraft.
>
> This text can be analyzed into a text base as follows:

1. Turbulence forms		(Verb Frame)
2. at the edge		(Location)
3. of a wing		(Part of)
4. Turbulence grows in strength		(Verb Frame)
5. over the surface		(Location)
6. of a wing		(Part of)
7. Turbulence contributes to the lift of an aircraft		(Verb Frame)
8. The aircraft is supersonic		(Characteristic)

Note that the system for building a text base is based on finding the main verbs and using them as basic frames around which to place the arguments such as location, part of, characteristic, and others. Each indentation represents a lower level in the text base, so that proposition 1 is at level 1, propositions 2, 4, and 7 are at level 2, propositions 2, 5, and 7 are at level 3, and proposition 6 is at level 4. When the arguments are read, they can be added after the proposition at the above level; for example, Proposition 1 is "Turbulence forms," Proposition 2 involves "Turbulence forms at the edge," and Proposition 3 involves "Turbulence forms at the edge of a wing."

Kintsch's notation is different from that just given but is based on the same principles. A proposition is represented within a set of parentheses, and the first word gives the verb or the relation involved; "loc" refers to location. For example, in Kintsch's notation, the text base is:

1. (Form, turbulence)
2.   (Loc: at, 1, edge)
3.   (Part of, wing, edge)
4.   (Grow, turbulence, strength)
5.   (Loc: over, 4, surface)
6.   (Part of, wing, surface)
7.   (Contribute, turbulence, lift, aircraft)
8.   (Supersonic, aircraft)

The numbers refer to the propositions.

Kintsch's system for analyzing text yields several interesting predictions if one assumes, as Kintsch does, that the text base for a passage is an indication of how the information is represented in a subject's memory. For example, one prediction is that if propositions—as defined by Kintsch's system—are the basic units of comprehension and memory, then reading time ought to depend on the number of propositions. To test this idea, passages were constructed that contained equal numbers of words but varied in the number of propositions; reading time increased as the number of propositions increased even though the same number and kind of words were processed (Kintsch, 1976).

In a related study, subjects were asked to read and recall a passage from *Scientific American* that contained 70 words and 25 propositions; time required to read the passage was a direct linear function of the number of propositions that were recalled. These results, summarized in Box 9-9, indicate that each proposition that was recalled added 1.26 seconds to the reading time on the average.

In a striking test of the idea that certain propositions are more central than others, Kintsch (1976) measured the percentage of propositions recalled at each level in the text base. Box 9-10 shows that subjects recalled about 80 percent of the level 1 propositions and that lower level propositions were less likely to be recalled. Similar procedures for organizing folk stories have been proposed, and there is some evidence that higher level features of the story are best remembered (Rumelhart, 1975).

BOX 9–9   Relationship Between Reading Time and Number of Propositions Recalled

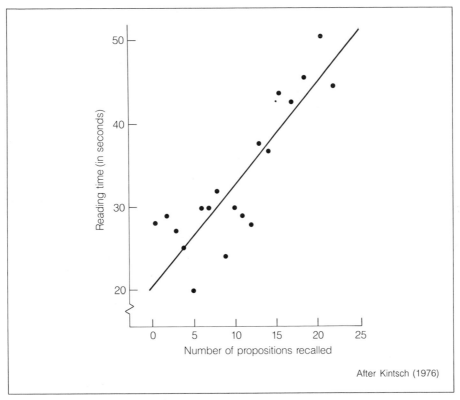

After Kintsch (1976)

These findings add support to Meyer's findings and reveal an advance in our attempt to extend Bartlett's original work.

Case and Story Grammars

The foregoing research suggests a new way of describing a schema—a hierarchical framework with specific slots. For example, Kintsch (1974) and Meyer (1975) suggest that the verb in any proposition tends to involve *case relations,* which are simply arguments that normally go with particular verbs. For example, the verb *to hit* usually suggests an agent (someone to do the hitting), an object (someone or something to get hit), and an instrument (an object to hit with). When you hear the word *hit,* you expect to fill in slots for a specific agent, object, and instrument. Thus, the sentence "Sue hit the pesky fly with a fly swatter" allows you to fill in the agent

BOX 9–10   Recall of Propositions as a Function of Different Levels in the Text
Base Hierarchy

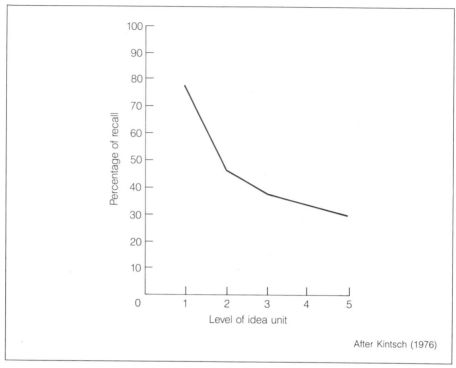

After Kintsch (1976)

as *Sue,* the object as *fly,* and the instrument as *swatter.* A representation of the
schema for this sentence is given in Box 9-11, and some other common case
relations are listed in Box 9-12. Meyer and Kintsch report evidence that subjects
tend to "remember" case relations, even when they are not presented. For example,
if a passage says that a careless smoker started a fire, most subjects remember that
the instrument was a match even if that fact is never stated. Apparently, many
cognitive processes may be viewed as filling in or finding slots in a case structure.

More recently, Rumelhart (1975) and Thorndyke (1977) have found a system for
organizing the parts of a story into what they call a *story grammar.* For example,
when you read a story you may expect four main slots to be filled: the setting, the
theme, the plot, and the resolution. The setting may consist of several parts such as
characters, location, and time. The theme consists of a topic and a goal. The plot's
series of episodes contain goals, attempts, and outcomes. An event or a state
constitutes the resolution. According to Thorndyke (1977), subjects attempt to fill

BOX 9-11   A Framework for a Sentence

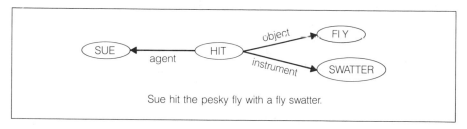

Sue hit the pesky fly with a fly swatter.

BOX 9-12   Some Case Relations

Agent: Instigator of an action.

Instrument: Something used by an agent to perform an action.

Vehicle: Something that conveys an object.

Object: Who or what is directly affected by an action.

Benefactive: Someone or something on which the action has a secondary effect, good or bad.

Range: Location or path of an action.

Adapted from Meyer (1975)

in these slots as they read a story, beginning with the main four parts and working down.

Thorndyke asked subjects to listen to a story like the "Old Farmer" in Box 9-13. When subjects recalled this story, they tended to remember events and states from the top of the story grammar hierarchy (such as setting, theme, resolution) better than those lower (such as characters' specific actions). In addition, if the theme—in this case, getting the donkey into the barn—was left out of the story, recall was much poorer. Apparently, subjects try to build a framework for the story and then fill in the slots. If the theme is unclear, subjects may not be able to find the right schema or framework for the story. These findings are summarized in Box 9-14.

As another example of a story grammar, Schank and Abelson (1977) have suggested the "restaurant script" summarized in Box 9-15. Schank and Abelson propose that people have scripts such as these for many generalized events. When people think about such an episode, they expect to fill in the slots for that script, such as the specifics of entering and ordering in the restaurant script. Work on story grammars and scripts represents an attempt to more specifically describe what Bartlett might have meant by the term *schema*.

BOX 9–13   List of Events and States for "The Old Farmer and the Donkey"

1. There was once an old farmer.
2. who owned a very stubborn donkey.
3. One evening the farmer was trying to put his donkey into its shed.
4. First, the farmer pulled the donkey,
5. but the donkey wouldn't move.
6. Then the farmer pushed the donkey,
7. but still the donkey wouldn't move.
8. Finally, the farmer asked his dog
9. to bark loudly at the donkey
10. and thereby frighten him into the shed.
11. But the dog refused.
12. So then, the farmer asked his cat
13. to scratch the dog
14. so the dog would bark loudly
15. and thereby frighten the donkey into the shed.
16. But the cat replied, "I would gladly scratch the dog
17. if only you would get me some milk."
18. So the farmer went to his cow
19. and asked for some milk
20. to give to the cat.
21. But the cow replied,
22. "I would gladly give you some milk
23. if only you would give me some hay."
24. Thus, the farmer went to the haystack
25. and got some hay.
26. As soon as he gave the hay to the cow,
27. the cow gave the farmer some milk.
28. Then the farmer went to the cat
29. and gave the milk to the cat.
30. As soon as the cat got the milk,
31. it began to scratch the dog.
32. As soon as the cat scratched the dog,
33. the dog began to bark loudly.
34. The barking so frightened the donkey
35. that it jumped immediately into its shed.

From Thorndyke (1977)

Effects of Prior Knowledge

As, the foregoing section suggests, we use schemas in learning and remembering new meaningful information. How can we encourage people to use their existing schema when confronted with new information? As an example, consider the passage in Box 9-16. Bransford and Johnson (1972) read this passage to subjects and either gave them a title ("Washing Clothes") before they read, after they read, or not at all. Subjects are asked to rate the passage on "comprehension" (with 1

BOX 9–14   Recall of the Story Structure for Two Groups

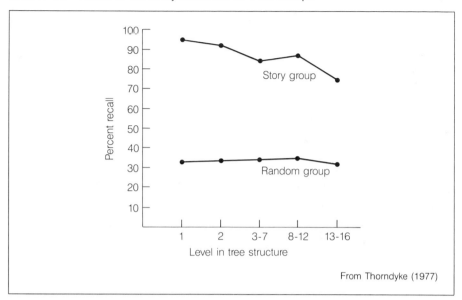

From Thorndyke (1977)

indicating low and 7 indicating high) and to recall it. As shown in Box 9-16 subjects in the no-topic and topic-after groups rated the passage low in comprehension and recalled little of the information, while subjects in the topic-before group recalled more than twice as much information.

Similarly, Bransford and Johnson (1972) asked subjects to read the "Balloons Passage" in Box 9-1 with no picture, a picture given before, or the picture given after reading. Box 9-17 shows that comprehension ratings and amount recalled were about twice as high in the "before" group compared to the other groups. Dooling and Lachman (1971) and Dooling and Mullet (1973) obtained similar results; presenting a title before an ambiguous passage aided recall but presenting the title after the passage did not. Apparently, the title provides a context so that the reader can relate the new information to appropriate previous experience.

A study by Wittrock, Marks, and Doctorow (1975) suggests that subjects try to find familiar elements in the passage. For example, subjects were asked to read or listen to stories and then were given retention tests. For some subjects the major words in the story were all high frequency, familiar words. For other subjects, low frequency, unfamiliar words were substituted for the familiar words in the passage. For example, a familiar sentence was: "I saw that the flowers and leaves of the

BOX 9–15   The Restaurant Script

Schema: Restaurant.

Characters: Customer, hostess, waiter, chef, cashier.

Scene 1: Entering.
    Customer goes into restaurant.
    Customer finds a place to sit.
        He may find it himself.
        He may be seated by a hostess.
            He asks the hostess for a table.
            She gives him permission to go to the table.
    Customer goes and sits at the table.

Scene 2: Ordering
    Customer receives a menu.
    Customer reads it.
    Customer decides what to order.
    Waiter takes the order.
        Waiter sees the customer.
        Waiter goes to the customer.
        Customer orders what he wants.
    Chef cooks the meal.

Scene 3: Eating.
    After some time the waiter brings the meal from the chef.
    Customer eats the meal.

Scene 4: Exiting.
    Customer asks the waiter for the check.
    Waiter gives the check to the customer.
    Customer leaves a tip.
        The size of the tip depends on the goodness of the service.
    Customer pays the cashier.
    Customer leaves the restaurant.

From Rumelhart (1977)

mirror were moving.'' The same sentence with unfamiliar words: "I saw that the blossoms and leaves of the mirror were stirring.'' On the subsequent retention test, subjects performed twice as well if they had read the familiarly worded passage compared to the unfamiliarly worded passage. Apparently, the unfamiliar words prevented subjects from finding an appropriate schema or context for interpreting the story.

As another example, consider the passage in the top of Box 9-18. As you read this passage, you may notice that it could have two different themes—it could be a story about a card game or a story about a musicians' jam session. Anderson, Reynolds, Schallert, and Goetz (1977) presented this passage to two groups of subjects: physical education majors and music majors. Results shown in the bottom of Box 9-18 indicated that the music students tended to interpret it as about music

BOX 9–16 The Washing Clothes Passage

The Passage

The procedure is actually quite simple. First you arrange items into different groups. Of course one pile may be sufficient depending on how much there is to do. If you have to go somewhere else due to lack of facilities that is the next step; otherwise, you are pretty well set. It is important not to overdo things. That is, it is better to do too few things at once than too many. In the short run this may not seem important but complications can easily arise. A mistake can be expensive as well. At first, the whole procedure will seem complicated. Soon, however, it will become just another facet of life. It is difficult to foresee any end to the necessity for this task in the immediate future, but then, one never can tell. After the procedure is completed one arranges the materials into different groups again. Then they can be put into their appropriate places. Eventually they will be used once more and the whole cycle will then have to be repeated. However, that is part of life.

Comprehension and Recall Scores for the Passage

	No Topic	Topic After	Topic Before	Maximum Score
Comprehension ratings:	2.29	2.12	4.50	7.00
Number of idea units recalled:	2.82	2.65	5.83	18.00

From Bransford and Johnson (1972)

BOX 9–17 Comprehension and Recall of the Balloons Passage

	No Context (1 Repetition)	Context After	Context Before	Maximum Score
Comprehension ratings:	2.30	3.30	6.10	7.00
Number of idea units recalled:	3.60	3.60	8.00	14.00

Adapted from Bransford and Johnson (1972)

---

and remembered things that were consistent with a jam session, while the other subjects were more likely to take the card game perspective and remembered items consistent with card playing. For another passage that could be interpreted as a

BOX 9–18   Two Ambiguous Passages

Card/Music Passage

Every Saturday night, four good friends get together. When Jerry, Mike, and Pat arrived, Karen was sitting in her living room writing some notes. She quickly gathered the cards and stood up to greet her friends at the door. They followed her into the living room but as usual they couldn't agree on exactly what to play. Jerry eventually took a stand and set things up. Finally, they began to play. Karen's recorder filled the room with soft and pleasant music, Early in the evening, Mike noticed Pat's hand and the many diamonds. As the night progressed the tempo of play increased. Finally, a lull in the activities occurred. Taking advantage of this, Jerry pondered the arrangement in front of him. Mike interrupted Jerry's reverie and said, "Let's hear the score." They listened carefully and commented on their performance. When the comments were all heard, exhausted but happy, Karen's friends went home.

Prison/Wrestling Passage

Rocky slowly got up from the mat, planning his escape. He hesitated a moment and thought. Things were not going well. What bothered him most was being held, especially since the charge against him had been weak. He considered his present situation. The lock that held him was strong but he thought he could break it. He knew, however, that his timing would have to be perfect. Rocky was aware that it was because of his early roughness that he had been penalized so severely—much too severely from his point of view. The situation was becoming frustrating; the pressure had been grinding on him for too long. He was being ridden unmercifully. Rocky was getting angry now. He felt he was ready to make his move. He knew that his success or failure would depend on what he did in the next few seconds.

Mean Percentage Correct on Multiple Choice Tests

| | Subject's Background | |
Passage	Physical Education	Music
Prison/Wrestling	64%	28%
Card/Music	29%	71%

wrestling match or a prison episode, physical education students were more likely than music majors to remember elements that were consistent with the wrestling theme. Apparently, subjects come to the experiment with individual schemata that may differ from person to person. Similar results have been reported by other researchers (Pichert and Anderson, 1977; Schallert, 1976; Bransford, 1979).

The foregoing results demonstrate that sometimes a passage may be difficult to understand because the underlying schema is not obvious or because the perspective of the writer is different from the perspective of the reader. In a recent study, Pichert

BOX 9–19   The House Passage

The two boys ran until they came to the driveway. "See, I told you today was good for skipping school," said Mark. "Mom is never home on Thursday," he added. Tall hedges hid the house from the road so the pair strolled across the finely landscaped yard. "I never knew your place was so big," said Pete. "Yeah, but it's nicer now than it used to be since Dad had the new stone siding put on and added the fireplace."

There were front and back doors and a side door which led to the garage which was empty except for three parked 10-speed bikes. They went in the side door. Mark explaining that it was always open in case his younger sisters got home earlier than their mother.

Pete wanted to see the house so Mark started with the living room. It, like the rest of the downstairs, was newly painted. Mark turned on the stereo, the noise of which worried Pete. "Don't worry, the nearest house is a quarter of a mile away," Mark shouted. Pete felt more comfortable observing that no houses could be seen in any direction beyond the huge yard.

The dining room, with all the china, silver and cut glass, was no place to play so the boys moved into the kitchen where they made sandwiches. Mark said they wouldn't go to the basement because it had been damp and musty ever since the new plumbing had been installed.

"This is where my Dad keeps his famous paintings and his coin collection," Mark said as they peered into the den. Mark bragged that he could get spending money whenever he needed it since he'd discovered that his Dad kept a lot in the desk drawer.

There were three upstairs bedrooms. Mark showed Pete his mother's closet which was filled with furs and the locked box which held her jewels. His sisters' room was uninteresting except for the color TV which Mark carried to his room. Mark bragged that the bathroom in the hall was his since one had been added to his sisters' room for their use. The big highlight in his room, though, was a leak in the ceiling where the old roof had finally rotted.

From Pichert and Anderson (1977)

and Anderson (1977) manipulated readers' perspectives. Subjects were asked to read the passage about a house shown in Box 9-19. Some subjects were told to take the perspective of a potential homebuyer; other subjects were told to take the perspective of a burglar; others were given no special instructions concerning how to read the passage. Results indicated that subjects' recall was influenced by their perspectives. Details that may be important for one perspective—such as where Dad keeps his coin collection—are not important for other perspectives. Thus, the pattern of recall depended both on the information in the passage and on the reader's perspective.

EVALUATION

The term *schema* has become increasingly popular in explanations of how people understand and remember verbal information. Many early theorists such as Piaget and Bartlett popularized the term, but seldom provided complete definitions. Recently, other theorists have invented their own terms such as *scripts* (Schank and Abelson, 1977), *frames* (Minsky, 1975), and *anchoring ideas* (Ausubel, 1968) to refer to various specialized meanings.

In spite of the widespread use of the jargon of schema theory, you could well ask, Has work on schema theory, such as that reviewed in this chapter, served to clarify earlier notions such as Bartlett's ''schema'' or the Gestaltists' concept of ''structure''? Critics claim that the answer is no. For example, ''I do not think that talking about 'schema' or 'schemata' or 'frameworks' does much that 'tuning' does not or that 'gestalt' did not'' (Scriven, 1977; p. 60). Some critics even claim that the empirical support for schema theory is lacking and ''is best forgotten'' (Zangwill, 1972).

In response to these criticisms of a lack of precise definition and lack of empirical support, schema theory may plead guilty to the first charge but must certainly protest its innocence to the second. As Klatzky (1980, p. 216) has pointed out in a recent review: ''Whether we call them scripts, frames, or schemata, evidence for knowledge structures representing complex events is compelling.'' This chapter has reviewed some of the consistently clear results of research on schema theory. People tend to remember (1) the gist of a passage rather than the verbatim content, (2) important information better than unimportant information, and (3) information that is consistent with their perspective better than information that does not fit their perspective. These kinds of findings help show that humans do not learn and remember like machines; we are not passive tape recorders or computer memories that copy the exact words as presented. Instead, the act of understanding involves an act of problem solving—what Bartlett called ''an effort after meaning.'' Thanks to recent research on schema theory, we now know more about what is involved in ''effort after meaning'' than we did twenty years ago. In addition, ongoing work on computer simulation of schemata may allow for even more precise descriptions.

Suggested Readings

Anderson, R. C., Spiro, R. J., and Montague, W. E. *School and the acquisition of knowledge.* Hillsdale, N. J.: Erlbaum, 1977. A collection of papers written by leading schema theorists.

Bartlett, F. C. *Remembering.* London: Cambridge University Press, 1932. Presents the work that was the forerunner of modern cognitive psychology, including "The War of the Ghosts" study.

Bransford, J. D. *Human cognition: Learning, understanding and remembering.* Belmont, Calif.: Wadsworth, 1979. Clearly written introduction to modern research on comprehension and learning from prose.

Schank, R. C., and Abelson, R. P. *Scripts, plans, goals and understanding.* Hillsdale, N.J.: Erlbaum, 1977. Describes a project concerning the computer simulation of knowledge structures and the understanding process.

CHAPTER 10

QUESTION ANSWERING:
Thinking as a Search of Semantic Memory

Semantic Memory Theory Definition of Thinking

Models of Semantic Memory

Structure of Semantic Categories

Language and Thought

Question Answering Task

How do people understand and retrieve the answers to questions? Look at the following question and then try to describe how you went about answering it.

> Query: In the house you lived in three houses ago, how many windows were there on the north side?

Rumelhart, Lindsay, and Norman (1972) found that most people are able to solve this problem; they do so by first visualizing their present dwelling, then moving back in time to visualize their previous homes, determining the north wall, and counting the windows.

Although this example may tap a trivial piece of information, it does point to the amazing ability we have to use our memories to answer questions. Let's try another one.

Query: What were you doing on Monday afternoon of the third week of September two years ago?

A hypothetical set of responses given by Lindsay and Norman (1972) is shown in Box 10-1. How does this protocol mesh with yours? The interesting aspect of such examples is that human beings are capable of answering a wide variety of complex questions and that we do so not always by direct recall but by working on a series of subquestions that bring us progressively closer to the answer. In observing the process of question answering, Lindsay and Norman were struck by the observation that their subjects engaged in productive thinking, and thus it was possible to discuss "retrieval as problem solving." The problem for psychologists, of course, is to describe how this process of answering questions occurs.

Let's try one last question.

Query: Draw a diagram of the floor plan of your place of residence.

In a typical study conducted by Kovarsky and Eisenstadt (cited by Anderson and Bower, 1973), the errors made by graduate students who had occupied the same apartments for years did not occur randomly but were systematic. A common error was for the students to include structural features that were part of most apartments but not of their own particular dwelling. One possible conclusion that may be reached is that in recall we tend to rely primarily on our general experiences or knowledge rather than entirely on specifics. Were there any such errors in your diagram?

SEMANTIC MEMORY THEORY DEFINITION OF THINKING

Chapters 9 and 10 are both concerned with the role of memory structures in problem solving. Both chapters deal with the structure of knowledge in memory, and the idea of schematic memory representation. Chapter 9 emphasized thinking as the formation of a schematic representation, but this chapter emphasizes thinking as a search and retrieval from the store of meaningful knowledge that we call *semantic memory*.

Since problem solving depends heavily on how knowledge is organized in memory, the nature of memory representation is a particularly important issue. When we ask people a question on a subject on which they are knowledgeable, there are several aspects of the recall task that we as psychologists may be interested in: How is the information represented in memory, and how is it retrieved? Thus, in this chapter we can view problem solving as a process in which people search their existing knowledge in response to a problem.

This chapter focuses mainly on how people organize and process information about categories of things. Previously we explored how people learn concepts, or learn to form categories, but we did not describe how category information is stored or processed in memory. This chapter is an extension of earlier work in concept

BOX 10–1   Hypothetical Protocol for the Query, "What Were You Doing?"

1. Come on. How should I know? (Experimenter: Just try it anyhow.)
2. O.K. Let's see. Two years . . .
3. I would be in high school in Pittsburgh . . .
4. That would be my senior year.
5. Third week in September—that's just after summer—that would be the fall term . . .
6. Let me see. I think I had chemistry lab on Mondays.
7. I don't know. I was probably in the chemistry lab . . .
8. Wait a minute—that would be the second week of school. I remember he started off with the atomic table—a big fancy chart. I thought he was crazy, trying to make us memorize that thing.
9. You know, I think I can remember sitting . . .

From Lindsay and Norman (1972, p. 379)

learning; however, the focus in this chapter is on how category information is stored in memory and how it is processed when answering questions.

MODELS OF SEMANTIC MEMORY

Tip-of-the-Tongue Phenomena

This section focuses on recall of one's general knowledge. Consider the following dictionary definition and try to think of the word it defines:

> "A navigational instrument used in measuring angular distances, especially the altitude of the sun, moon, and the stars at sea."

If the answer does not immediately come to you, try to answer the following questions: What is the first letter of the word? How many syllables does the word have?

If you are ready to give up, the answer is *sextant*.

Brown and McNeil (1966) gave a series of these problems to subjects in a laboratory setting and found that sometimes the answer came right away, sometimes the subjects had no idea what to say, and in a number of cases subjects were "seized" by a tip-of-the-tongue (TOT) state. In this state the subjects felt that they were on the verge of finding the answer, but had not yet found it; they were in a "mild torment, something like the brink of a sneeze." Brown and McNeil were particularly interested in these cases of TOT, and, in fact, were trying to induce them as a way of studying the structure of human memory and the process of answering questions. The subjects were asked to describe their thought processes aloud; in addition, they were asked the two specific questions given earlier while they were in the TOT state: What is the first letter of the word? How many syllables does it have?

In a typical study, 57 instances of the TOT state were induced, and while the subjects "could not for the life of them" state the specific word, they were amazingly accurate at "guessing" the first letter (51 percent correct) and the number of syllables (47 percent correct). Brown and McNeil concluded that in the course of searching one's memory for a piece of information, *generic* recall (or a general memory) may precede the *specific* recall of a word, especially when specific recall is felt to be imminent. (Note the similarity to Duncker's "funneling" view of problem solving we discussed in Chapter 3.)

This type of task, which we could call *question answering,* provides another important approach to understanding human thinking and problem solving. By emphasizing the role of memory structure, this approach views problem solving as a search of one's meaningful memory. The goal suggested by this view is to develop a theory of how complex information is organized in meaningful fashion in human memory and what processes are used to retrieve it to answer questions.

Since Brown and McNeil obtained their intriguing results, a number of psychologists have proposed very detailed and precise theories of how human beings organize particular sets of knowledge about the world. These theories have been called *models of semantic memory* because they try to represent how meaningful— that is, semantic—knowledge is stored and used. The basic types of models of semantic memory are:

> *Network models,* which are based on the idea that memory is made up of elements and the associations among them; this view goes beyond the early associationist ideas in that (a) the relations may be of many types, (b) the units are meaningful concepts, and (c) the theories can be tested.

> *Feature models,* which are based on the idea that memory is made up of features that belong to sets and sets that belong to larger or supersets, and so on.

The basic method used to test these theories is called the *reaction time method* in which subjects are asked to press a Yes or No button in response to questions about their general knowledge, for example, Is a collie a dog? The time to respond is measured in milliseconds (thousandths of a second), and the results are interpreted on the basis of the simple idea that more times means more processes or deeper processes were performed.

Network Models of Semantic Memory

One of the first popular network models was called the *teachable language compre- hender* or TLC (Collins and Quillian, 1969, 1972). Although these researchers have

BOX 10–2   Hypothetical Adult's Knowledge About Animals: A Network Hierarchy

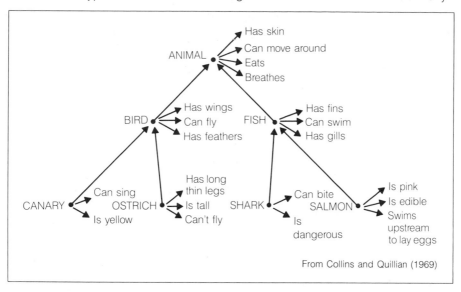

From Collins and Quillian (1969)

revised and amended the specifics of their original model, their goal has been to develop a computer program that simulates how human beings answer factual questions. (The computer simulation approach is discussed more fully in Chapter 6.) According to one version of TLC, the structure of semantic memory is based on:

Units —words that represent one thing or subject.

Properties —words that represent characteristics of the unit.

Pointers —associations of various types among units and properties.

An example of the knowledge a hypothetical adult has about certain animals is given in Box 10-2. In this case, words such as *animal, bird,* and *canary* represent units, whereas word combinations such as *is yellow, has wings, has skin* represent properties, and the arrows represent pointers. According to this hierarchical structure, the properties or characteristics of a unit at any one level apply to things connected by pointers at lower levels. In other words, a bird has wings and so does a canary, but the property of having wings is stored only with the higher unit, bird; it cannot be stored with animals because some animals do not have wings.

According to TLC, the process a hypothetical person uses to respond to the truth or falsity of a statement such as ''A canary has skin'' is a search process:

1. Find the unit for the target word, *canary.*

2. Check to see if the property, *has skin,* is stored with that unit; if not, follow

BOX 10-3   Reaction Times for Answering Questions About Animals

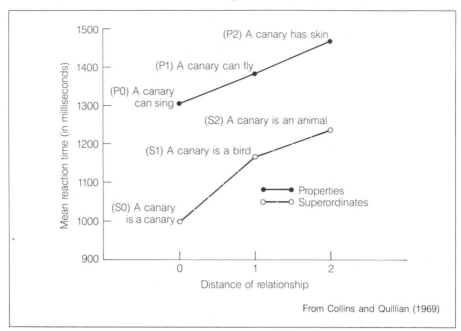

From Collins and Quillian (1969)

the pointer to the next higher level on the hierarchy, *bird,* and continue as needed to *animal.*

3. When the pointers lead to a unit that has the target property, respond Yes.

It is a bit more difficult to describe how subjects decide how to respond No to a sentence such as "A canary has fins," but one idea is that subjects terminate their search and give the No answer if they fail to reach the unit with the target property within a certain time period.

While formal models like Collins and Quillian's are elegant and plausible, in order to be useful they must also be testable. Fortunately, this model does offer certain predictions; for example, sentences that require working on just one level of the hierarchy (a canary can sing) should require less processing time than two-level problems (a canary can fly), and a three-level problem (a canary has skin) should take the longest processing time. In order to test these predictions, Collins and Quillian asked their subjects to press a button labeled True or False in response to sentences based on hierarchies such as are shown in Box 10-3. Both true and false statements were presented, but of primary interest was the time it took subjects to respond to various true sentences. You can see that the more levels there were, the longer the response time; it took a particularly long time to answer False.

The results just described can be called a *category size effect* because response time for questions like "Is an X a Y?" increase as you increase the size of the Y category. Although the network model of Collins and Quillian is consistent with the category size effect, it is certainly not the only explanation for such findings. For example, Landauer and Meyer (1972) were able to replicate the category size effect, but they argued that the results could be explained by a theory of feature sets. More features must be tested when you retrieve from a larger category. One piece of evidence that seems to support the feature theory is that more time is required to answer false sentences if they involve a large category—for example, "A cliff is an animal"—than if they involve a small category—"A cliff is a dog." This alternative theory is described in the next section.

There are also several serious problems with the predictions of the Collins and Quillian model. First, the model proposes a logical hierarchy and predicts that response time will be longer for such statements as "A collie is an animal" than for "A collie is a mammal." However, the opposite seems to be the case (Rips, Shoben, and Smith, 1973). Apparently, the fact that collies belong to the mammal category is not as well established in most people's memories as it is in the logical hierarchy of Collins and Quillian. Second, Collins and Quillian propose a "cognitive economy" in which a feature will be stored only at the highest possible level in the hierarchy. For example, a feature like *can move* should be stored with *animal* rather than at lower levels such as *dog* or *collie*. However, Conrad (1972) showed that subjects could answer questions about features like *can move* equally quickly for various levels in the hierarchy. Third, Collins and Quillian predict that response time should be the same for all questions that involve the same number of levels such as "A robin is a bird" and "An ostrich is a bird." But Rips, Shoben, and Smith (1973) and Rosch (1973) found that response time was faster for typical examples (such as *robin*) than for nontypical ones (such as *ostrich*). Thus, there is evidence that contradicts almost all of the basic assumptions of the Collins and Quillian model.

Does this mean that Collins and Quillian's model was a failure? To the contrary, their model helped generate a great deal of research and helped give birth to the alternative theories discussed in the next section. In addition, Collins and Loftus (1975) have been able to modify the original model so that it can now account for each of the phenomenon just considered. The new revised network model is called a *spreading activation model*. Although the new model is still made up of nodes and relations, as are all network models, the rigid hierarchical structure has been eliminated. In addition, the links may vary in type and in importance. Question answering involves starting at the nodes that are mentioned in the question, and slowly spreading out from those nodes.

More recently, Anderson (1976) has created a model of human cognition called ACT. His model deals with two distinct kinds of knowledge: *declarative knowledge*, such as a factual sentence, and *procedural knowledge*, such as a list for how to do some task. Some of the actions involved in procedural knowledge involve modifying the nodes or relations in one's declarative knowledge. Although a complete description of ACT is beyond the scope of this book, the ACT model has already demonstrated that it can account for many of the inferences and inductions that people make.

Feature Models of Semantic Memory

Although network models are currently the most numerous, there are other ways of representing semantic memory. For example, Meyer (1970) proposed a model of how subjects answer questions about semantic memory that was not based on networks at all; rather, Meyer assumed that each concept was stored in memory as a list of subsets (or features). When subjects were asked to respond to such statements as "All females are writers" or "Some females are writers," they appeared to go through the following two stages:

> *Stage 1:* Determine all the subsets of "writer," including male and female, and all the subsets of "female," and see if there is any overlap, that is, if there are any subsets in common. If there are no common features (as in a sentence such as "Some typhoons are wheat") answer False; if there are some common features (for example, writers and females), answer True if the statement calls for "some," and go on to Stage 2 if it calls for "all."
>
> *Stage 2:* Is each subset of "writer" also a subset of "female"? If yes, answer True; if no, answer False.

Meyer's theory predicted that it would take longer for the subjects to respond to problems of the form "All S are P" than "Some S are P" because two stages were required for the former and only one stage for the latter. Like Collins and Quillian, Meyer predicted that response time would increase if the size of category P was increased because the list of subsets was now longer. Meyer used experiments similar to those of Collins and Quillian and obtained results consistent with his (as well as Collins and Quillian's) model. However, while the Meyer model based on sets may be just as powerful as Collins and Quillian's network model, neither model can explain results such as why it would take longer to answer questions about whether a dog is a mammal than about whether a dog is an animal.

Rips, Shoben, and Smith (1973; Shoben, Smith, and Rips, 1974) have developed a set model of semantic memory that accounts for such findings. The main new ingredient in their model was based on a skepticism of Collins and Quillian's assumption that "memory structure mirrors logical structure." In one study, Rips, Shoben, and Smith asked a group of subjects to rate pairs of words in terms of how closely related they were to one another, in order to derive a measure of "semantic

BOX 10–4   Adults' Knowledge About Animals: A Semantic Distance Chart

The following chart is based on subjects' ratings of how closely pairs of words are related. Short distances represent high relatedness.

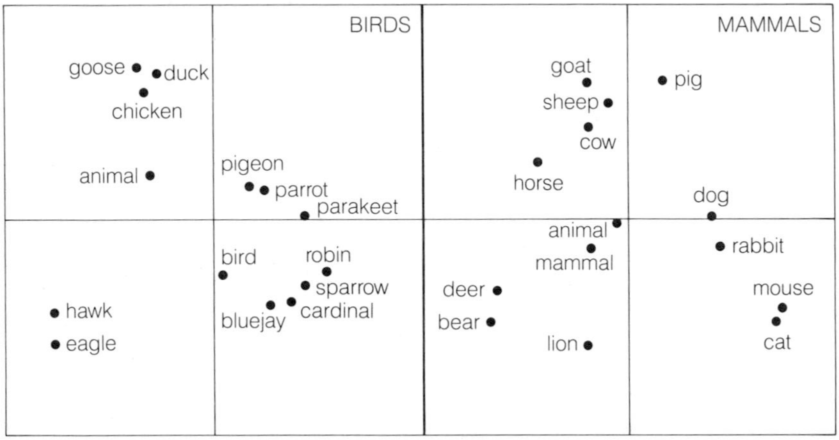

From Rips, Shoben and Smith (1973)

distance.'' For example, they asked the subjects to rate how closely related various kinds of birds were to each other, to the category ''bird,'' and to the category ''animal'' or how closely related various mammals were to each other, to the category ''mammal,'' and to the category ''animal.'' The chart that is shown in Box 10-4 was derived from the ratings; note that high relatedness is represented by short distance.

This method of representing semantic memory predicts that reaction time judgments like those used by Collins and Quillian should be related to semantic distance, and these predictions have been upheld. In other words, according to the semantic distance idea, the reason it takes longer to press the True button for Robin-Animal than Robin-Bird or longer for Dog-Mammal than Dog-Animal is that the actual semantic distance is greater from Dog to Mammal than from Dog to Animal (regardless of logical structure) or from Robin to Animal than from Robin to Bird. These researchers have further argued that semantic distance is basically a function of how many semantic features the two concepts have in common, or of how much overlap there is between the list of features that make up the sets.

According to the *feature comparison model* proposed by Smith, Shoben, and Rips (1974), each concept in our memory is associated with a list of features. Some features, called *defining features,* are crucial to the meaning of the concept. For example, ''has wings'' and ''has feathers'' may be defining features of birds since they are important aspects of the category's definition. Other features, called *characteristic features,* are less important. For example, ''eats worms'' or ''builds nests'' may be characteristic features of birds since many but not all birds possess these features. An example of some of the features of the concepts ''bird,'' ''robin,'' and ''ostrich'' are given in Box 10-5.

What happens when you answer a question such as ''Is a robin a bird?'' According to the feature comparison model, you go through two stages as indicated in Box 10-5. First, you find the list of features in your memory for the two words in the question, such as the features for *bird* and for *robin.* Then, you compare the lists. If they are very similar (as they would be for *robin* and *bird*) you answer Yes; if they are very different (as they would be for *dog* and *robin*) you answer No. However, if there is just a moderate degree of overlap, you need to process more completely by comparing the defining features of both words. For example, a question like ''Is an ostrich a bird?'' might create only moderate overlap, but when you look only at defining features you can answer Yes. This model overcomes each of the problems of the Collins and Quillian model described earlier. However, some researchers (such as Rosch, 1973, 1975) have questioned the need to make a distinction between defining and characteristic features.

STRUCTURE OF SEMANTIC CATEGORIES

The network and set feature models represent two different views of how we use categories in our thinking. More recently, Rosch (1978) has extended the set feature approach by focusing on the nature of the categories we use in our everyday lives. Rosch (1978) argues that categories are used to help us process information more effectively. This same line of argument was proposed by Bruner, Goodnow, and Austin (1956, p. 1) as an introduction to some of the first research on human concept learning:

> We begin with what seems a paradox. The world of experience of any normal man is composed of a tremendous array of discriminably different objects, events, people, impressions. There are estimated to be more than 7 million discriminable colors alone . . . But were we to utilize fully our capacity for registering the differences in things and to respond to each event encountered as unique, we would soon be overwhelmed by the complexity of our environment. Consider only the linguistic task of acquiring a vocabulary fully adequate to cope with the world of color differences. The resolution of this seeming paradox—the existence of discrimination capacities which, if fully used, would make us slaves to the particular—is achieved by man's capacity to categorize.

BOX 10–5 Feature Comparison Model

Knowledge in Subject's Memory

Birds: flies, eats worms, is small, has feathers*, has wings*, builds nests, lives in trees

Robin: flies, eats worms, is small, has feathers*, has wings*, has red breast*, chirps, builds nests

Ostrich: can put head in the sand*, is tall, is clumsy, has wings*, has feathers*

*indicates defining feature.

Feature Comparison Process

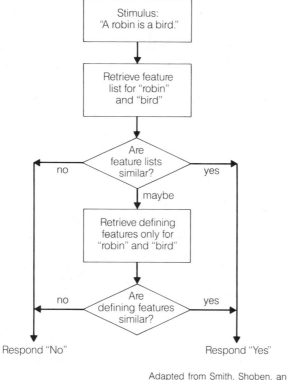

Adapted from Smith, Shoben, and Rips (1974)

Previous work on concept learning provided some information about how people categorize artificial stimuli like geometric shapes or dot patterns. In this section, we explore how the categorization process may be applied to objects in our natural environment.

Goodness of Fit

The categories that we normally use in our everday lives—let's call these *natural categories*—are different from the categories we learn about in mathematical set theory. For example, a precise mathematical set like the set of all squares includes every figure that corresponds to the definition of square; every figure is either in this category or not in it, and all squares are equally members of the category. However, natural categories do not seem to have such firm boundaries; instead, the border lines of a natural category are what Rosch (1973) calls "fuzzy." For example, think of the category for fruit. Some examples, like apple or orange, seem to fit right into the category. Other examples, such as avocado or coconut, may not seem to be as typical. Thus, when we answer questions about natural categories, we are not dealing with mathematically precise sets, but rather with fuzzy sets. The "goodness-of-fit" of a concept refers to how well it fits into a category.

To study the structure of natural categories, Rosch presented subjects with a category name along with names for possible examples of the category. For example, in one study (Rosch, 1975) the examples for fruit were orange, coconut, and all the other words listed in part of Box 10-6. The subjects' job was to rate each word according to "how good an example of a category" it was on a scale of 1 to 7; they considered how typical "apple" was for the category "fruit," and so on. Subjects rated 50 to 60 words for each of 10 categories such as vegetable, tool, bird, and sport. Results of the rating task for fruit and furniture categories are given in Box 10-6. Some words were rated as being good examples of a category while others were not typical. Thus, unlike mathematical sets, all members of a natural category do not seem to be equal. In addition, Rosch found that subjects were able to perform the rating task with a very high level of agreement, suggesting that there is social consensus about the structure of common categories.

What effect does the fuzzy nature of categories have on performance in answering questions? To study this issue, Rosch (1973) asked children and adult subjects to answer questions of the form, "Is an apple a fruit?" For some questions, the example was a typical one (such as "apple") and for others the example was not typical (such as "coconut"). As you can see in Box 10-7 the time to respond was faster for good examples than for poor examples. The effect was strongest for children but was also clearly present in adults. In another study, Rosch (1975) presented two words on each trial and asked subjects to tell whether the words belonged to the same category or to different categories. Some pairs contained words that were good examples of the category (for example, *table* and *bed*), some were medium (*lamp* and *stool*), and some were poor examples (*rug* and *fan*). As in the previous study, more time is required when the words are not good examples of their category. Thus, these experiments show that people are faster at answering questions

BOX 10–6   Goodness-of-Example Ratings for Furniture and Fruits

Member	Goodness of Example Rank	Specific Score		Goodness of Example Rank	Specific Score
			Furniture		
chair	1.5	1.04	chaise longue	24	2.26
sofa	1.5	1.04	lamp	31	2.94
couch	3.5	1.10	stool	32	3.13
easy chair	5	1.33	piano	35	3.64
dresser	6.5	1.37	cushion	36	3.70
coffee table	8	1.38	cupboard	39	4.27
rocker	9	1.42	stereo	40	4.32
chest of drawers	11	1.48	mirror	41	4.39
desk	12	1.54	television	42	4.41
bed	13	1.58	bar	43	4.46
davenport	15.5	1.61	wastebasket	47	5.34
end table	15.5	1.61	radio	48	5.37
bookcase	22	2.15	sewing machine	49	5.39
lounge	23	2.17	stove	50	5.40
			Fruit		
orange	1	1.07	lemon	20	2.16
apple	2	1.08	watermelon	23	2.39
banana	3	1.15	cantaloupe	24	2.44
peach	4	1.17	lime	25	2.45
apricot	6.5	1.36	papaya	27	2.58
tangerine	6.5	1.36	fig	29	2.86
plum	8	1.37	mango	30	2.88
grapes	9	1.38	pomegranate	32	3.05
strawberry	11	1.61	date	37	3.35
grapefruit	12	1.77	raisin	39	3.42
cherry	14	1.86	persimmon	41	3.63
pineapple	15	1.19	coconut	43	4.50
blackberry	16	2.05	avocado	44	5.37
raspberry	19	2.15	tomato	46	5.58

Note: 1 means highly typical, 7 means least typical.

From Rosch (1975). Copyright 1975 by the
American Psychological Association. Reprinted by permission of the author.

about typical members of a category than they are about members that are at a category's fuzzy boundaries.

Family Resemblance

Let's return to our comparison of natural categories and artificial sets. In an artificial set, such as the set of all squares, there is one rule that defines the members of the

BOX 10–7   Response Time for Category Judgments

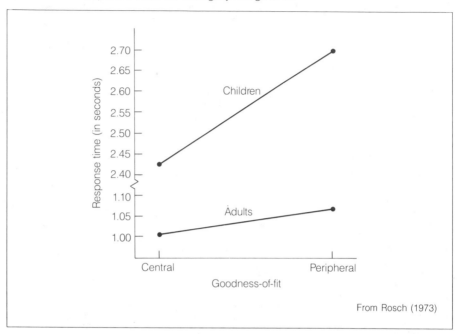

From Rosch (1973)

set. Every example must have the same set of features, such as "four sides," "all sides of equal length," and "all angles at 90 degrees." There is less agreement among attributes of all members in a natural category. What are the attributes that all fruits, all birds, or all pieces of furniture have in common? Instead of one list of common features, members of a category seem to share what Rosch and Mervis (1975) call "family resemblance." By this they mean that a basic core of features for the category exists such that each example may possess some but not all of the features. For example, not all birds have the characteristic of "flying" or "small-ness" or "singing" but these are features present in many birds.

Rosch and Mervis (1975) studied the idea of family resemblance by selecting 6 categories with 20 examples in each category. One group of subjects was asked to list all of the attributes they could think of in 90 seconds for each of the words. Another group of subjects was asked to rate how typical each example was for its category. Results of the task of listing attributes indicated that rarely did one or two attributes define all of the members of a category. Instead of some critical features that were common to all members, Rosch and Mervis found there was a group of attributes that were present in some but not all category members. In addition, if Rosch and Mervis focused on the most typical examples in each category, there was much overlap in their attributes; if they focused on the least typical examples in each

BOX 10–8 Number of Attributes in Common to Five Most and Five Least Typical Members of Six Categories

Category	Most Typical Members	Least Typical Members
Furniture	13	2
Vehicle	36	2
Fruit	16	0
Weapon	9	0
Vegetable	3	0
Clothing	21	0

category, there were few or no attributes in common. This result is summarized in Box 10-8. Additionally, there was a strong correlation between ranking how typical a word was and ranking how many family resemblance attributes the word had. Apparently, words that had many features in common with the category were rated as more typical.

Basic Level Categories

Finally, let's consider another aspect of natural categories—the notion that some levels of categorization are easier to think about than others. For example, Rosch, Mervis, Gray, Johnson and Boyes-Braem (1976) have suggested that there are at least three category levels:

Superordinate level—such as "furniture."

Basic level—such as "table."

Subordinate level—such as "kitchen table."

The basic level offers a way of dividing the world that provides the most information with the least cognitive effort. This level also allows us to reduce differences among all the objects in our environment without wiping out the important differences among objects.

Rosch (1978) has summarized a variety of evidence to support the idea of basic level categories. First, if subjects are asked to list the attributes of superordinate, basic, and subordinate categories, they list very few attributes for the superordinate category, many for the basic level, and not significantly more for the subordinate level. Apparently, the basic level is the one at which we store information about attributes of categories; getting more specific (at the subordinate level) did not add any more information about features. Second, if subjects are asked to describe motor behaviors that could be performed with objects, the basic level again elicits the largest number of responses. Apparently, our motor behaviors are coordinated with objects at the basic level. Finally, if subjects juxtapose drawings of objects, the ratio of overlap to nonoverlap is strongest at the basic level. In addition, Rosch et al. (1976) argue that sorting tasks are easier if the basic level is used and that children begin to learn classification at the basic level.

More recently, Newport and Bellugi (1978) have provided an interesting analysis of American Sign Language. Usually, a single sign is used for basic level terms such as "apple" or "car" or "piano." Superordinate categories like "fruit" or "vehicle" or "musical instrument" require compounding of several simple signs, such as signing "apple-orange-banana . . . " to mean "fruit." Similarly, signs for subordinate categories require compounding signs. For example, "kitchen chair" requires the sign for "cook" and "chair." Apparently, when we use a language that has a restricted vocabulary, humans prefer words that refer to objects at the basic level.

LANGUAGE AND THOUGHT

So far this chapter has shown that humans can think in terms of categories, like "bird" and "robin." However, you may be wondering where these categories come from. In particular, you might wonder whether the words in the language you speak influence the way you break the world into categories. Although psychologists have not provided much data on this issue, linguists and anthropologists have proposed the concept of "linguistic relativity"—the idea that the language one speaks influences the way one learns and thinks about the world (Sapir, 1960; Whorf, 1956). For example, based on an anthropological study of the language and culture of non-Western language speakers (for example, the Hopi Indians of the southwestern United States), Whorf proclaimed the doctrine of linguistic relativity: "Every language and every well-knit technical sublanguage incorporates certain points of view and certain patterns resistant to widely divergent points of view" (p. 247). Further, the concepts and categories that we learn and use are also supposed to be influenced and limited by our native tongue: "We cut up and organize the spread and flow of events as we do, largely because, through our mother tongue we are parties to an agreement to do so and not because nature itself is segmented in exactly that way for all to see" (p. 240).

These ideas have profound implications for the study of human learning and cognition. One of the first experimental studies of the Whorfian hypothesis was conducted by Brown and Lenneberg (1954) and reported in their now famous paper, " A Study of Language and Cognition." Brown and Lenneberg began by selecting 240 color chips from the *Munsell Book of Color,* a catalog similar to the color charts for house paint colors. Then they asked 5 judges to pick the best examples of red, orange, yellow, green, blue, purple, pink, and brown from the set of 240 colors.

There was high agreement among the judges. Brown (1976, p. 131), reminiscing about the experiment, reports that the colors looked quite familiar: "I remember thinking that there was something uncanny about the 8 best instances, and indeed, about the chips in the immediate neighborhood of each. I can see them still, that good Gulf orange, that Ticonderoga pencil yellow, that blood red; they all of them shine through the years like so many jewels." To these colors, Brown and Lenneberg added 16 "filler" color chips, which were spaced as evenly as possible within the other 8. Of these filler colors, however, Brown reports that he has no vivid visual memory.

Armed with the full array of 24 colors (8 distinctive and 16 filler), Brown and Lenneberg presented them to college subjects and asked them to name the colors. For each of the 8 basic colors, the subjects tended to use a single word and they tended to agree on the word; for the other colors, they used modifiers, such as "light green," and there was much less agreement among them. Codability scores were determined for each color and then new, different subjects were given a recognition task. They were shown a color chip (or a set of them) for a few seconds, then after some delay, were asked to point out the color from an array of 120 colors. The results indicated a moderately high correlation between codability and recognition: the colors that could be easily named were also easier to remember.

These results seemed to support the Whorfian notion of linguistic relativity because the availability of names for colors apparently influenced a cognitive task such as remembering stimuli. The colors used in the experiment formed a natural continuum based on wavelength, but language artificially "cut up" the colors into categories like those shown in Box 10-9.

In an attempt to further explore the Whorfian hypothesis, Heider (1970, 1972; Heider and Oliver, 1972) investigated the color memory task in different cultures. For example, the Dani tribe of Indonesian New Guinea are a Stone Age people with only two basic color words—"mili" for dark or cold colors and "mola" for bright and warm colors. The Dani people can, of course, talk about other colors, but they must use longer descriptive phrases. According to the Whorfian idea, two colors that happen to fall in different categories in English should be easier for the Dani to remember if they also fall in the two separate Dani categories rather than in the same category; results, however, indicated no difference. A more striking disconfirmation of the Whorfian hypothesis comes from a study of several non-European languages. Colors that were easy to name in English were easier to remember for English speakers (as Brown and Lenneberg had found) but they were also easier to remember for speakers of every other language, including languages like Dani, even though no specific words for the colors existed.

The chart in Box 10-10 gives a list of the order in which color names appear in languages based on a study of 98 different languages (Berlin and Kay, 1969). The figure shows that although languages differ in how many basic color terms are

BOX 10–9 Frequency of Names Given by English Speakers to Various Color Chips

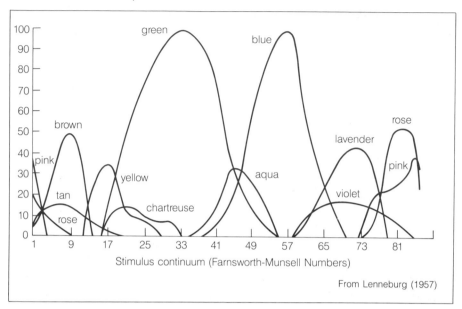

Stimulus continuum (Farnsworth-Munsell Numbers)

From Lenneburg (1957)

provided (ranging from 2 to 12), there is a universal pattern: if 2 words are used, they signify black and white; if 3 are used, red is added; if 5 are used, green and yellow are added, and so on, up to 12 basic color words used frequently in English. These 12 are called "focal" colors and Heider's (now called Rosch's) results show that focal colors are remembered better than others regardless of whether the learner's language has specific names for them. As Brown (1976) pointed out in a recent review of this work, the Whorfian hypothesis has been turned inside out—apparently, at least for colors, there are "natural categories that are shared by all humans with normal color vision." Languages reflect these categories in that they all divide up the world of color in the same way, with some languages going into more detail.

Although the current state of our understanding casts doubt on the Whorfian hypothesis, there is certainly much more to language than "color names." At least one research study (Carmichael, Hogan, and Walter, 1932) has shown that "labeling" a picture influences how it is remembered. What is particularly important and to some extent unique about the study of color categories is this: it demonstrates that cross-cultural differences in cognition can be studied experimentally and that such investigations promise to increase our understanding of our common human capacity to think and to learn.

BOX 10–10   Universal Order of Evolution of Color Terms in 98 Languages

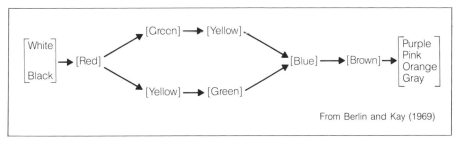

From Berlin and Kay (1969)

EVALUATION

The network models and feature models represent two popular attempts to describe specifically how people structure knowledge and answer questions. Because these models are both detailed and broad, they are useful in testing various ideas about human question answering. As this chapter has shown, the rapidly growing research literature in semantic memory has already challenged the basic tenets of each of these theories. The perfect theory of semantic memory is still evolving.

The more recent research on natural categories and on language categories has provided a new approach to the study of semantic memory. Apparently, rules of learning and memory established for artificial, laboratory materials must be modified in light of current research on more natural categories. The movement to more commonplace situations is a promising one that may ultimately provide the key to a unified theory of semantic memory.

Suggested Readings

Anderson, J. R. *Language, memory and thought.* Hillsdale, N.J.: Erlbaum, 1976. An updated theory of how knowledge is represented and processed.

Clark, H. H., and Clark, E. V. *Psychology and language.* New York: Harcourt Brace Jovanovich, 1977. A general introduction to language structures and processes.

Rosch, E., and Lloyd, B. B. *Cognition and categorization.* Hillsdale, N.J.: Erlbaum, 1978. Summarizes current work by prominent researchers in the natural categories field.

PART FOUR

IMPLICATIONS AND APPLICATIONS

The following four chapters introduce you to some of the basic applications of cognitive psychology to actual problems. Up to this point, most of this book has dealt with artificial problem solving in artificial laboratory tasks—such as anagrams, matchsticks, concept learning, syllogisms, disk problems, mental rotation, and class inclusion questions. In this final section of the book, we now progress to tasks and issues that have more practical significance. These issues include the development of thinking in children (Chapter 11), the nature of individual differences in thinking ability (Chapter 12), whether or not creative thinking can be taught (Chapter 13), and classroom problem solving in mathematics (Chapter 14). Each of these issues entails an understanding of the theories and research described in previous chapters, and each builds on these previous chapters.

Chapters 11 through 14 each start with a practical issue and then see whether existing theories of cognition can shed light on that issue. In these chapters the study of problem solving is driven by practical demands of real issues. These chapters try to extend theories that have been developed in previous chapters to broader arenas. The focus is on using what we know about human cognition to answer practical questions.

In Chapters 11 to 14 you will see how theories of cognitive psychology can be applied to practical issues in human development, individual differences, cognitive training, and mathematical learning. Although these are practical tasks, you would be mistaken to view this work as narrowly applied rather basic research. Instead, when faced with extending our theories to real issues, we are challenged to build better, broader, and more useful theories. Thus, in Part Four you can see how good applied research and good basic research are really two sides of the same coin—actual situations challenge psychologists to build useful theories, and useful psychological theories may be applied to real situations. The ultimate test of a theory of problem solving is a test that goes beyond the laboratory toward the real world.

CHAPTER 11

COGNITIVE DEVELOPMENT: Thinking as Influenced by Growth

Box 11-1 presents words for a free association task. Your job is to read each word, individually and separately, and after each write down the first word that comes to your mind. You may cover the words with a piece of paper and move it down the page one word at a time, giving your association for each word as you come to it. When you have given associations for all the words, look at Box 11-2.

This type of task has been given to subjects of varying ages, and several interesting differences in the responses related to age have been noted. For example,

BOX 11–1   Free Association Test

Give your first word association for each of the following words:

Table   _____

Dark   _____

Man   _____

Deep   _____

Soft   _____

Mountain   _____

BOX 11–2   Word Associations for Adults and Children

Stimulus	Response	1000 Children	1000 Adults
Table	Eat	358	63
	Chair	24	274
Dark	Night	421	221
	Light	38	427
Man	Work	168	17
	Woman	8	394
Deep	Hole	257	32
	Shallow	6	180
Soft	Pillow	138	53
	Hard	27	365
Mountain	High	390	246
	Hill	91	184

Based on data from Woodrow and Lowell (1916)

Box 11-2 gives the number of children and the number of adults who made each of two basic responses (Woodrow and Lowell, 1916). Don't worry if your responses seem closer to the children's norms or are so bizarre they don't appear on the table—things may have changed a bit since 1916. As Box 11-2 shows, the children tended to give words that would occur with the stimulus word in a sentence (phrase completion) and hence were generally different parts of speech, while the adults tended to give words with the same or opposite meaning and were thus from the same part of speech. More recently, similar differences were obtained by Ervin (1961), Palermo (1963), Palermo and Jenkins (1963), and Brown and Berko (1960).

BOX 11–3   The Corplum Problem

See if you can tell what a "corplum" is:

A corplum may be used for support.

Corplums may be used to close off an open space.

A corplum may be long or short, thick or thin, strong or weak.

A wet corplum does not burn.

You· can make a corplum smoother with sandpaper.

The painter used a corplum to mix his paints.

From Werner and Kaplan (1952).
Copyright 1952 by The University of Chicago Press.

As an example, Palermo and Jenkins asked for associations to such words as *deep, mutton, red, live, lift, make;* the norm responses for children were, respectively, *hole, button, color, house, heavy,* and *it;* the respective norms for adults were *shallow, sheep, white, die, carry,* and *build.* Brown and Berko (1960), in noting a similar pattern in their data, suggested that the children tended to give "heterogeneous-by-part-of-speech" responses and the adults tended to give "homogeneous-by-part-of-speech" responses. The systematic differences between the responses of children and adults imply that there is a basic difference in the way words (and perhaps all concepts) are stored in memory. The fact that children tend to complete phrases suggests that they store strings of words exactly as they would be used in ordinary speech whereas adults tend to classify words both by meaning and by part of speech. Such findings suggest that the cognitive processes of children and adults differ, not just in a quantitative way in that adults know more, but also in a qualitative way in that children may not think the same way that adults do.

Take a look at the six sentences in Box 11-3. Read each sentence and after each try to define *corplum.* Note how your definition is clarified with each new sentence and count how many sentences are required for you to "know" the meaning of *corplum.* Older children and adults are readily able to abstract the meaning of new words based on their context but Werner and Kaplan (1952) found that younger children behaved differently. They had much more difficulty in figuring out the word meaning; their definitions tended to be tied very closely to the context of the sentence with the meanings of new words completely changing for each new sentence. A typical younger child listened to the sentence, "People talk about the *bordicks* of others and don't like to talk about their own," and then gave the following definition of *bordicks* (faults): "Well, *bordick* means people talk about others and don't talk about themselves, that's what *bordick* means." Apparently, the younger children viewed each sentence separately, with the word meaning changing from sentence to sentence, while the older children and adults could consider several contexts at once, abstracting the common meaning from all.

COGNITIVE DEVELOPMENT DEFINITION OF THINKING

According to the theories of cognitive development, thinking depends on how a person represents the world and in what ways a person can manipulate or act upon this internal representation. A major contribution of the cognitive development approach is that different ways of representing the world and different ways of manipulating those representations are present at different stages in development—for example, the way a four-year-old child represents the world is quite different from the way an adult does.

As you may have noticed, the idea that internal mental structures are the substance of our cognitive processes is closely related both to Bartlett's idea of the schema and to the Gestalt idea of organization. In fact, the best known figure in the area of cognitive development, Jean Piaget, calls the internal mental structures or representations "schemata," and he refers to the ways we manipulate them when thinking as "operations." However, in Piaget's theory, schemata are continually growing and developing rather than remaining fixed. Describing thinking at various stages thus becomes a problem of trying to define the schema (or mental structure) and the operations (or internal actions) that a problem solver is using.

PIAGET'S THEORY: INTRODUCTION

Piaget is neither a psychologist by training nor an American, yet he has made a tremendous impact, perhaps because of his unusual perspective, on American developmental psychology. Piaget is a French-speaking Swiss, a zoologist by training and a philosopher by interest, and since 1927 he and his associates in Geneva have published the world's largest existing source of information and theories on cognitive development.

Piaget's main interest is in "genetic epistemology"—the study of the growth of knowledge in humans. As Elkind (1967) has pointed out concerning Piaget, "He is not fundamentally a child psychologist concerned with the practical issues of child growth and development. He is rather, first and foremost, a genetic epistemologist concerned with the nature of knowledge and with the structures and processes by which it is acquired (p. xviii)." However, instead of making armchair theories of how knowledge accumulates in the mind of a human being, he decided he would study the process empirically. Starting with the newborn infant, who presumably had very little knowledge, Piaget studied how knowledge came to be represented in the mind and how it changed with growth. Thus Piaget's study of cognitive development was intended to provide information on an important philosophical question; its effect has also been to stimulate the development of whole new areas in psychology.

Piaget's method of study began as being mainly *clinical* —that is, he has care-fully observed how children behave in various "real world" situations and, based on these observations, has developed his theories of cognitive growth. He kept detailed diaries on the early life of each of his three children, which eventually became the basis for his books, *The Origins of Intelligence in Children* (1952), *Play, Dreams and Imitation in Childhood* (1951), and *The Construction of Reality in the Child* (1954). Piaget's method has received a great deal of criticism on two basic accounts:

> *Method* —The clinical method is too loose and lacks good experimental control. For example, Rosenthal and Jacobson (1968) have shown that the experimenter can influence subjects in subtle ways such as by facial expression without being aware of it. In addition, Piaget's method depends heavily on language concepts which young children may not use in the same way as adults.
>
> *Theory* —The theories are too general and vague. Like many of Freud's theories, they are sometimes not even testable in a clear experiment, and those theories which are testable have often been shown not to hold up [Gelman, 1969, p. 69].

Yet the dozens of books and hundreds of articles by Piaget and his associates continue to stimulate and influence our view of human cognitive growth, including human thinking. Let us now turn to a brief summary of those ideas.

PIAGET'S THEORY: STAGE INDEPENDENT

Piaget's theory may be roughly divided into two parts—the enumeration of the stages of human cognitive development and the general concepts that are indepen-dent of stages.

The premise from which Piaget begins his stage-independent theory is that human beings are alive, striving to survive and to function successfully in their environments. In order to survive, they must take in information from their environ-ments; however, out of all the possible information that exists, only a small part can be taken in by an individual since all new knowledge must be related to exist-ing knowledge. Information from the outside world that differs greatly from a person's existing knowledge will not be understood or encoded because there is no way to relate it to the existing knowledge, just as information that is exactly the same as existing knowledge will have no influence since it adds nothing new. However, outside information that is similar, but not identical, to the existing knowledge structures will be taken in (or assimilated) by the existing mental structures. There will also be some changes in mental organization to fit (or accommodate) the new knowledge. The resulting mental structure will be a bit more sophisticated since it includes more knowledge and thus will be able to assimilate even more complex information, restructure to fit the new knowledge, and so on. All cognitive growth, according to this view, depends on our taking in information that is slightly different from what we already know and then restructuring our knowledge to integrate both the old and new information; this process produces an improved cognitive structure, which will help us to survive and function better.

As can be inferred from this brief description, Piaget's theory is based on several fundamental ideas:

It is life-based—the accumulation of better and better modes of representing reality is accomplished to help us survive and get along in our environment.

Knowledge is mediate rather than immediate—our view of reality is not passively registered but is actively constructed by continually relating new information to existing knowledge.

Motivation for cognitive growth is intrinsic—living things naturally seek out information that is just slightly more complex than their existing knowledge.

It is dialectic—there is a continual interaction between the desire to have a well-organized bank of knowledge (accommodation) and the need for more information (assimilation) which is continuously disrupting existing organizations and evoking slightly more sophisticated ones.

The main terms that Piaget uses to explain his stage-independent theory are given in Box 11-4. The theory is often hard for American psychologists to understand, partly because it borrows heavily from unfamiliar biological concepts, partly because it is translated from French, and partly because it is massive, sometimes vague, and difficult. However, a good understanding of some of the basic ideas he uses will help you to understand Piaget's theory. We shall discuss the following terms: *structures* and *schemata; functions, organization,* and *adaptation; equilibration, assimilation,* and *accommodation.*

According to Piaget, the way a person represents the world—the internal mental structures or schemata—changes systematically with development. If the structures did not change, there could be no development for there could be no growth in knowledge. For example, the infant structures information based on how the information relates to such actions as sucking. Piaget refers to the ''sucking schema'' to suggest that knowledge about the world is stored in the form of how objects respond to sucking.

Although cognitive structures change—we hope that adults do not represent the world solely in terms of how things taste or feel—our function as living beings remains invariant. There are two basic functions common to all biological systems: the need to stay alive and survive in our environment—*adaptation*—and the need to have well-organized and orderly internal structure—*organization.* In terms of cognitive structure, this means that we have a constant need for our representation

BOX 11–4 Piaget's Stage-Independent Theory

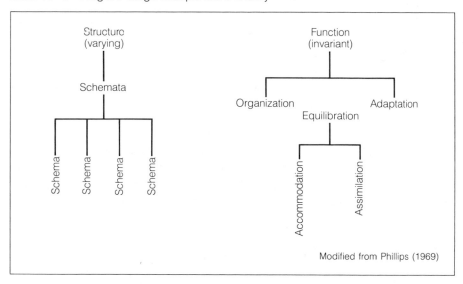

Modified from Phillips (1969)

of the world to be well organized, internally consistent, and orderly while at the same time we have a need to bring in new information that will disrupt the internal organization but will help us better to survive and adapt to the reality of the external world.

The mechanisms for balancing this conflict between the need for organization and the need for adaptation are equilibration, assimilation, and accommodation. Assimilation and accommodation are called "functional invariants" because they are constantly involved in the growth of any biological system—including the growth of knowledge. Assimilation occurs whenever something from outside the system is taken in and incorporated; the most obvious example is the ingestion of food in which something from the environment becomes part of us. In short, input is changed to fit the existing internal structure. Accommodation is the complementary process that always must accompany assimilation—the changing of the existing internal structure to fit the newly assimilated input. Cognitive growth involves continually assimilating new knowledge and accommodating existing knowledge. Piaget cites imitation as a temporary imbalance in which accommodation overpowers assimilation and playing as a situation in which assimilation overpowers accommodation.

Most of the time, however, in a normally functioning person there is a striving for a balance between assimilation and accommodation; this balancing process is called *equilibration* and it is actually responsible for all cognitive growth. When new information is assimilated to existing structures, a process of equilibration begins.

BOX 11-5   Piaget's Stage-Dependent Theory

Sensorimotor period	0–2 years
Preoperational period	2–7 years
Concrete operation period	7–11 years
Formal operations period	11–adult

It results in a new cognitive structure—one that incorporates some of the new information but also retains some of the prior information all organized in a more efficient way. Thus equilibration is never finished because as soon as new information is assimilated the process begins again, resulting in progressively better representations of the world.

PIAGET'S THEORY: STAGE DEPENDENT

The progressive changes in cognitive structure may vary in rate from person to person, but they follow an invariant sequence, always moving in the same order, and the progressive changes in the way children organize information can be characterized as a sequence of stages. The four main periods of cognitive growth are shown in Box 11-5, although in some writings preoperations and concrete operations are considered to be a single period. The ages shown are averages based on Piaget's observations, but they are only approximate and subject to large individual differences. However, the order of the four periods is fixed, and according to the theory, all human beings progress through them in the same order.

The stages are based on two aspects of cognitive life: (1) *structure* —how the child represents the world and (2) *operations* —how the child can act upon this representation. The sequence of stages thus represents progressively better cognitive structures accompanied by progressively more powerful cognitive operations.

Sensorimotor Period

For approximately the first two years of life, children progress through the six stages of the *sensorimotor period*. Most of Piaget's research on this period came from diaries of careful observations of his own three children—Laurent, Lucienne, and Jacqueline—which were later summarized in his classic books such as *Origins of Intelligence in Children* (1952). At this stage the child represents the world in terms of actions—sucking, shaking, looking, dropping, and so on—and performs operations or manipulations on actual objects rather than on internal representations. The reason for the peculiar name, sensorimotor, is that during this period infants learn to coordinate their senses with motor behavior such as adapting the sucking reflex to search for a nipple before sucking, coordinating the movement of the hand to the mouth, or visually following an object moving through the environment.

One of the most interesting accomplishments achieved during the sensorimotor period involves the progressive development of the concept of object permanence. At birth, the infant has no concept of object permanence: when objects are out of the visual field they no longer exist; the only reality is the ongoing sensory stimulation. For example, newborn infants will not search for an object that leaves their field of vision (see the first entry in Box 11-6). Later, the concept begins to develop as an infant will actively search for a vanished object but cannot yet follow a sequence of displacements as is described in the second entry of Box 11-6. Eventually, the child further refines the concept of objects and is able to follow an object through a series of displacements (third entry) and finally to represent the displacements mentally (fourth entry). The ability to represent objects mentally and to move them from place to place mentally (as required in the fourth entry) marks the end of the sensorimotor period.

Another interesting accomplishment of the sensorimotor period is a progressive ability to control and investigate the environment. At first, infants have only reflexes like sucking and grasping, which become adapted to the environment (first entry of Box 11-7). Primary circular reactions are attempts by the infant to gain sensorimotor coordination by repeating movements such as hand to mouth, following objects with the eyes, and so on, over and over again. These movements are circular because they are repeated several times; they are primary because they involve a single simple act that is not intentionally initiated by the infant (second entry). Secondary circular reactions are repeated efforts to control the environment that are initiated by the infant—an example is given in the third entry of Box 11-7. Tertiary circular reactions are advances over the previous two because the child actively initiates a series of systematic manipulations such as dropping objects from different heights (fourth entry). Finally, the beginning of representational thought occurs when, as in the final entry, Lucienne represents the matchbook as her mouth and derives a solution.

Preoperational Period

At the end of the sensorimotor and the beginning of the *preoperational period,* the child has made some startling advances, including sensorimotor coordination, the ability to represent objects rather than just actions and sensations, and the rudiments of symbolic problem solving. Yet children at this stage deal with static, concrete images and are limited by the following six problems (Phillips, 1969):

Concreteness—the child can deal only with concrete objects that are physically present here and now.

BOX 11–6   Development of Object Permanence in the Sensorimotor Period

On the basis of careful observations of his three children—Lucienne, Laurent, and Jacqueline—Piaget concluded that the concept of object permanence develops during the first two years of life. Excerpts are given below:

7 months, 30 days. (No special behavior.)
Lucienne grasps a small doll which I present to her for the first time. She examines it with great interest, then lets go (not intentionally); she immediately looks for it in front of her but does not see it right away. When she has found it, I take it from her and place a coverlet over it, before her eyes (Lucienne is seated); no reaction.

9 months, 17 days. (Active search for vanished objects without taking account of a sequence of visual displacements.)
Laurent is placed on a sofa between a coverlet A on the right and a wool garment B on the left. I place my watch under A; he gently raises the coverlet, perceives part of the object, uncovers it, and grasps it. The same thing happens a second and a third time. . . . I then place the watch under B; Laurent watches this maneuver attentively, but at the moment the watch has disappeared under B, he turns back toward A and searches for the object under that screen. I again place the watch under B; he again searches for it under A. . . .

11 months, 22 days. (Taking account of visual displacements.)
Laurent is seated between two cushions A and B. I hide my watch alternately under each; Laurent constantly searches for the object where it has just disappeared, that is, sometimes under A and sometimes under B, without remaining attached to a privileged position as during the [above] stage. . . . At 12 months, 20 days, he also searches sequentially in both my hands for a button I am hiding. Afterward he tries to see behind me when I make the button roll on the floor (on which I am seated) even though, to fool him, I hold out my two closed hands.

18 months, 8 days. (Internally representing the visual displacements.)
Jacqueline throws a ball under a sofa. Instead of bending down at once and searching for it on the floor she looks at the place, realizes that the ball must have crossed under the sofa, and sets out to go behind it. . . . She begins by turning her back on the place where the ball disappeared, goes around the table, and finally arrives behind the sofa at the correct place. Thus she has closed the circle [of displacements] by an itinerary different from that of the object.

From Piaget (1954). Copyright 1954 by Basic Books, Inc.

Irreversibility—the child is unable to rearrange objects mentally or to conceive of them in some other arrangement.

Egocentrism—the child believes that everyone sees the world through his or her eyes and that everyone experiences what the child is experiencing.

Centering—the child can attend to only one dimension or aspect of a situation at a time.

States versus transformations—the child focuses on states, on the perceptual way things look rather than on the operations that produced that state.

Transductive reasoning—the child reasons that if A causes B then B causes A.

BOX 11-7 Development from Reflexes to Reactions to Thought

0 months, 20 days. (Adaptation of reflexes.)
He bites the breast which is given him, 5 centimeters from the nipple. For a moment he sucks the skin when he lets go in order to move his mouth about 2 centimeters. As soon as he begins sucking again he stops . . . when his search subsequently leads him accidentally to touch the nipple with the mucosa of the upper lip (his mouth being wide open), he at once adjusts his lips and begins to suck.

1 month, 1 day. (Primary circular reactions.)
. . . his right hand may be seen approaching his mouth. . . . But as only the index finger was grasped, the hand fell out again. Shortly afterward it returned. This time the thumb was in the mouth. . . . I then remove the hand and place it near his waist. . . . after a few minutes the lips move and the hand approaches them again. This time there is a series of setbacks . . . [but finally] the hand enters the mouth. . . . I again remove the hand. Again lip movements cease, new attempts ensue, success results for the ninth and tenth time, after which the experiment is interrupted.

3 months, 5 days. (Secondary circular reactions.)
Lucienne shakes her bassinet by moving her legs violently (bending and unbending them and so on), which makes the cloth dolls swing from the hood. Lucienne looks at them, smiling, and recommences at once. . . . Lucienne, at four months, 27 days, is lying in her bassinet. I hang a doll [from the hood] over her feet which immediately sets in motion the schema of shaking. But her feet reach the doll right away and give it a violent motion, which Lucienne surveys with delight. Afterward she looks at her motionless foot for a second, then recommences.

10 months, 11 days. (Tertiary circular reactions.)
Laurent is lying on his back . . . He grasps in succession a celluloid swan, a box, and so on, stretches out his arm and lets them fall. He distinctly varies the positions of the fall. Sometimes he stretches out his arm vertically, sometimes he holds it obliquely, in front or behind. . . . When the object falls in a new position (for example, on his pillow), he lets it fall two or three times more in the same place . . . then he modifies the situation.

1 year, 4 months, 0 days. (Beginning of thought.)
I put [a] chain into a box and reduce the opening to 3 millimeters. It is understood that Lucienne is not aware of the functioning of the opening and closing of the matchbox. . . . She only possesses the two preceding schemata: turning the box over . . . and sliding her fingers into the slit to make the chain come out. It is, of course, this last procedure that she tries first; she puts her fingers inside and gropes to reach the chain, but fails completely. A pause follows during which Lucienne manifests a very curious reaction. . . . She looks at the slit with great attention; then, several times in succession, she opens and shuts her mouth, at first slightly, then wider and wider! . . . [Then] Lucienne unhesitatingly puts her finger in the slit and, instead of trying as before to reach the chain, she pulls so as to enlarge the opening. She succeeds and grasps the chain.

From Piaget (1954). Copyright 1954 by Basic Books, Inc.

Examples of these are given in Box 11-8. Children are struck by the perceptual way the world looks and are "preoperational" because they cannot perform mental operations on their representations and cannot change their representation of the world unless the perceptual world also changes.

BOX 11-8 Examples of Preoperational Thought

Irreversibility

A four-year-old subject is asked:

"Do you have a brother?" He says, "Yes."

"What's his name?" "Jim."

"Does Jim have a brother?" "No."

From Phillips (1969)

Transductive Reasoning

At two years, 14 days, Jacqueline wanted a doll dress that was upstairs. She said "Dress," and when her mother refused to get it, "Daddy get dress." As I also refused, she wanted to go herself "To mommy's room." After several repetitions of this she was told that it was too cold there. There was a long silence, and then: "Not too cold." I asked, "Where?" "In the room." "Why isn't it too cold?" "Get dress."

From Piaget (1951)

Egocentrism

After interviewing children on how they play the game of marbles, Piaget concludes: ". . . how little children from the same class at school, living in the same house, and accustomed to playing with each other, are able to understand each other at this age. Not only do they tell us of totally different rules . . . but when they play together they do not watch each other and do not unify their respective rules even for the duration of the game. The fact of the matter is that neither is trying to get the better of the other: each is merely having a game on his own, trying to hit the marbles in the square, that is, trying to 'win' from his point of view. [In other situations, such as sitting around the sandbox] one can observe in children between 2 and 6 a characteristic type of pseudo-conversation or 'collective monologue' during which children speak only for themselves . . . and each is concerned only with himself."

From Piaget (1965)

Centering

When the child is asked to put a set of sticks which vary in length in order, the following arrangement is constructed:

Apparently, the child "centers" on only one aspect of the problem (for example, the tops of the sticks) and cannot simultaneously consider other aspects (for example, the bottoms of the sticks).

From Piaget (1952)

Concreteness, Irreversibility, Centering, and States

A four-year-old is asked: "Have you got a friend?"

"Yes, Odette."

"Well look, we're giving you, Clairette, a glass of orangeade (A1, 3/4 full), and we're giving Odette a glass of lemonade (A2, also 3/4 full). Has one of you more to drink than the other?"

"The same."

"This is what Clairette does: she pours her drink into two other glasses (B1 and B2, which are thus half filled). Has Clairette the same amount as Odette?"

"Odette has more."

"Why?"

"Because we've put less in." (She points to the levels in B1 and B2 without taking into account the fact that there were two glasses.)

(Odette's drink was then poured into B3 and B4.) "It's the same."

"And now?" (Pouring Clairette's drink from B1 and B2 into L, a long thin tube, which is then almost full.)

"I've got more."

"Why?"

"We've poured it into the glass (L) and here (B3 and B4) we haven't."

"But were they the same before?"

"Yes."

"And now?"

"But where does the extra come from?"

"From in there." (B1)

From Piaget (1952)

Concrete Operations

At about age seven, as children enter into the period of *concrete operations,* Piaget noted a basic change in the children's mental structures and operations. By the end of the preoperational period, a child has achieved or begun to achieve the ability to reverse or decenter (that is, to simultaneously consider two or more dimensions at a time), to focus on transformations rather than static perceptual states, and has begun to lose her egocentrism and transductive reasoning. The world comes to be represented not as a set of static perceptual images but rather as concrete objects that can be mentally acted upon and changed in logical ways. Reversibility is a newly acquired mental operation that frees the child from being dominated by how things look. The name, *concrete operations,* comes from this newly acquired ability to mentally operate or change a concrete situation and to perform logical operations on a situation in one's head.

These new mental operations are displayed in a series of small experiments on what Piaget calls *conservation,* including conservation of number, conservation of substance, and conservation of quantity. For example, consider the conservation of number situation shown in the top of Box 11-9. If Piaget showed a handful of pennies, for example, to preoperational children, they would base their judgment of quantity on perceptual appearance. A child might say there are "more" pennies when they are spread out than when they are bunched together. Even if children are asked to count the pennies under each arrangement, they still insist there are more when they are spread out. The children are centering on the dimension of length and cannot mentally reverse the operation of bunching or spreading out the pennies. However, a slightly older child who has acquired concrete operations is certain that it is the same amount of pennies regardless of how they are arranged. When asked how he knows, the child responds that although one arrangement may look bigger he knows he could move them and get the other arrangement, that is, he can mentally reverse the situation and rearrange the pennies in his head.

The second panel of Box 11-9 gives an example of conservation of substance. A plasticene ball is shown to a child, and then it is stretched out to form a sausage before the child's eyes. The preoperational child generally claims that when the ball is made into a sausage it is now "more" (sometimes the ball is seen as "more" than the sausage shape). In these cases the child is centering on just one dimension such as length (or width), and lacks the ability to perform the mental operation of reversibility—of mentally changing the ball into sausage or sausage into ball. The older child in concrete operations, however, is able to say that the "same" amount of plasticene is part of each shape. Children in this period are not overcome by how things look and may decenter—consider both length and width simultaneously—and reverse—mentally reshape the plasticene.

BOX 11–9 Typical Conservation Tasks

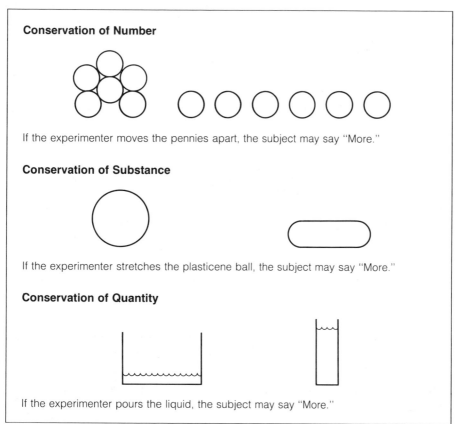

Conservation of Number

If the experimenter moves the pennies apart, the subject may say "More."

Conservation of Substance

If the experimenter stretches the plasticene ball, the subject may say "More."

Conservation of Quantity

If the experimenter pours the liquid, the subject may say "More."

The lower panel in Box 11-9 gives an example of conservation of quantity. When liquid is poured from a short-fat glass into a tall-thin glass, the preoperational child may say that there is "more" (or "less") liquid in the tall glass than when it is in the short glass. The child focuses, or centers on the dimension of height (or width) to base the decision and is unable to reverse. However, the slightly older child who has acquired concrete operations says that the amount of liquid is the "same"; this child can decenter—realize that height and width compensate for one another—and can reverse—can mentally pour the liquid from one glass to another.

Box 11-10 gives an example of the change in egocentrism that occurs at this period—the three mountain problem (Piaget and Inhelder, 1956). A set of three mountains, in three-dimensional relief, is placed on a table as shown. The child sits in one chair and a doll is placed on a chair with a different perspective. The child

BOX 11-10   The Three Mountain Problem

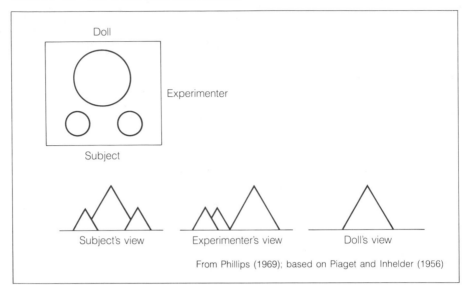

From Phillips (1969); based on Piaget and Inhelder (1956)

is asked to draw what the doll "sees" from where it is sitting. The preoperational child draws how the scene looks from her own perspective regardless of where the doll is seated while the concrete operational child is capable of drawing the "correct" perspective. Apparently, the new mental operations acquired during this period allow children to view the world from many possible perspectives rather than the single static image they are currently receiving.

There are, of course, many other examples of the new mental operations that begin to emerge throughout the period of concrete operations. However, even these advances have their shortcomings. For example, the child in this period, while freed from the perceptual image of how things look, is still tied to concrete objects thought about and manipulated in the here and now. The concrete operational child, while possessing the powerful operations of reversibility and decentration, is unable to apply them to abstract situations.

Formal Operations

By early adolescence, about age eleven, the *formal operations period* begins and with it comes a progressively more sophisticated ability to perform mental operations not only on concrete objects but also on symbols. Although most of Piaget's work has centered on the leap from preoperational to concrete operational thought, the formal operations stage is of some interest because it consists of the mental op-

BOX 11–11   The Oscillation Problem

Given a pendulum, the subject may vary the length of the string, the weight of the suspended object, the height of the released object, and the force with which the object is released. Which of these influences the rate of oscillation—how fast the pendulum swings?

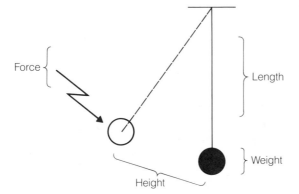

Piaget reports on the performance of a typical adolescent (15 years, 1 month):
". . . after having selected 100 grams with a long string and a medium length string, then 20 grams with a long and a short string, and finally 200 grams with a long and a short, concludes: 'It's the length of the string that makes it go faster or slower; the weight doesn't play any role.' She discounts likewise the height of the drop and the force of her push."

From Inhelder and Piaget (1958)

erations that normal human adults have. During this period the child develops the ability to think in terms of the hypothetical, in terms of probabilities, in terms of the possible rather than the concrete here and now. Given a situation, all possible alternatives can be discovered, and scientific reasoning in its most systematic and sophisticated form begins to emerge.

Box 11-11 shows the pendulum problem, which Piaget used to investigate the development of formal operational thought. A pendulum was constructed by hanging an object from a string, and the subject had to discover how four factors influenced the frequency of oscillation: the length of the string, the weight of the ball, how high the weight was when it was started, and how hard it was pushed. A typical response is also shown in Box 11-11. Children in the formal operational stage are able to systematically vary conditions—similar to the tertiary circular reactions but more organized—in such a way as to solve the problem.

It may be no coincidence that the cognitive stage of formal operations—the adult ability to think in terms of the hypothetical—is accompanied by social and emotional changes including uncertainty over the meaning of life, the identity crisis, and adolescent idealism. In any case, formal operations is adult thought, and Piaget's theory posits no additional stages.

THE BIG LEAP: BRUNER'S THEORY

Perhaps Piaget's greatest contribution is the idea of a qualitative change in cognitive processing between preoperational and concrete operational thought, at about the age of five to seven. Although Piaget relied heavily on the processes of reversibility and decentration as descriptions of new mental powers that occur, there have been many alternative views.

The work of Bruner and his associates (summarized in Bruner, 1964, 1973; Bruner, Olver, and Greenfield, 1966) provides a major supplement to Piaget's theory. For example, instead of four periods of cognitive development, Bruner suggested there are three different modes of representing the world:

Enactive—representing the world in terms of actions (similar to the sensori-motor period).

Iconic—representing the world in terms of static perceptual images (similar to the preoperational period).

Symbolic—the use of language and symbols (similar to operational thinking).

The leap from iconic representation to symbolic representation (or form pre-operational to concrete operational thought) is indicated in conservation experiments, but Bruner and Piaget differ on how to explain it. Piaget emphasizes the importance of mental operations such as reversibility as a prerequisite for conservation and suggests that the child's recognition that identical material must also be equivalent is a side effect. Bruner emphasizes the importance of the child's concept of identity and the linking of identity with equivalence (if it's the "same" it must be "equal") as a prerequisite for conservation, and suggests that reversibility is a side effect. Although Bruner's theory closely resembles Piaget's, it differs on how to characterize the periods of development (three modes of representation versus four periods) and in how to explain conservation (identity versus reversibility).

Bruner and Kenney (1966) provided an example of the change at about age six from iconic to symbolic representation. Children who were aged five, six, and seven were shown a 3×3 matrix of nine glasses with each row getting progressively wider from left to right and each column getting progressively taller from bottom to top, as shown in Box 11-12. A child was asked to look at the matrix, and then the experimenter scrambled all the glasses and asked the child to "make something like what was there before." Once the child had successfully reproduced the original

BOX 11–12   The Nine-Glass Problem

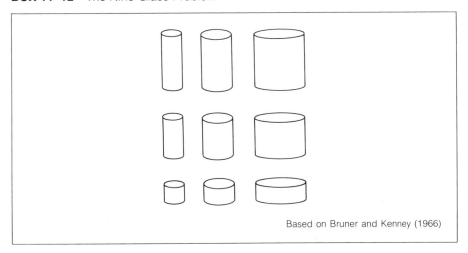

Based on Bruner and Kenney (1966)

array, the experimenter scrambled the glasses again except that the short, thin glass from the lower left corner was now placed in the lower right corner. The child was again asked to "make something like what was there before" but to leave the one short, thin glass in the lower right corner. On the first task (reproduction) there were no differences in errors among the three age groups with all the children performing quite well, although the older children were a bit faster. However, on the second task (transposition) almost none of the younger children and almost all of the older children solved the problem. More careful analysis of the children's comments indicated that the five-year-olds were more likely to represent the matrix iconically—as a spatial image—while the seven-year-olds used language symbols such as height and width.

An experiment by Frank (1966) illustrates Bruner's contention that identity, rather than reversibility, is the basis of conservation. Four-, five-, six-, and seven-year-old children were given a standard task of conservation of quantity as a pretest using two standard beakers equally filled with water (the children said they were the same). The water was poured from one into a differently shaped beaker (for example, short and wide) and the child was asked if the amount of water was still the same. As you can see in Box 11-13, the ability to conserve, indicated by the child's saying that the amount was still the same, increased with age. Next, Frank performed a similar demonstration, except that all the beakers were placed behind a screen for the pouring so that only the tops of the beakers were showing. In this case, as is shown in Box 11-13, 50 percent of the four-year-olds and 90 to 100 percent of the older children predicted that the amount of water in the newly poured beaker

BOX 11–13   A Conservation Experiment

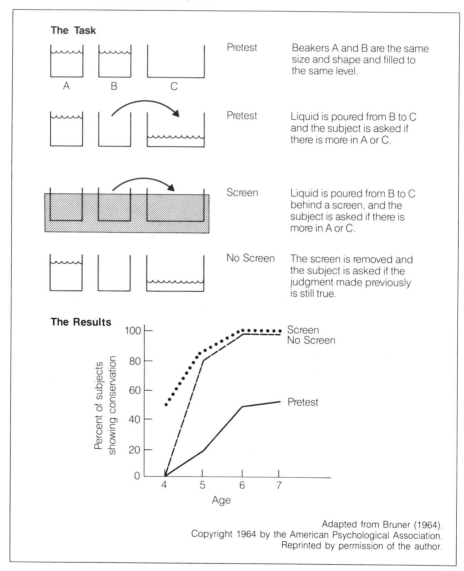

The Task

Pretest — Beakers A and B are the same size and shape and filled to the same level.

Pretest — Liquid is poured from B to C and the subject is asked if there is more in A or C.

Screen — Liquid is poured from B to C behind a screen, and the subject is asked if there is more in A or C.

No Screen — The screen is removed and the subject is asked if the judgment made previously is still true.

The Results

Adapted from Bruner (1964).
Copyright 1964 by the American Psychological Association.
Reprinted by permission of the author.

was the same. When the screen was removed, all the four-year-olds changed their minds. Apparently the perceptual display overwhelmed them, and they decided the wider beaker contained less liquid. However, none of the older children changed their judgments. As one seven-year-old explained, "It looks like more to drink but it is only the same because it is the same water and was only poured from here to there." On a posttest, in which water was poured into a tall, thin beaker along with a standard one without a screen, no four-year-olds conserved but the number of older children who conserved increased greatly (see Box 11-13). Apparently, subjects can be correct on reversibility (with screen) but wrong on conservation (without screen); nonconservers may rely on perceptual factors while conservers rely on internal symbolic representations.

Nair (1963, cited in Bruner, 1964) provided a further example of the importance of the concepts of identity and equivalence in conservation. First, children were given a standard pretest for conservation of quantity involving pouring water from one beaker to another. Then, to test for the concepts of identity and equivalence, she added a small toy duck that floated on the water; she said that it was moving to a new lake taking its water with it as she poured the water from a tall, narrow beaker into a short, wide one. The children were asked whether the duck now had the same water (identity) and whether it had the same amount of water (equivalence). All the children who conserved in the pretest answered the question about identity correctly; furthermore, reminding the children that the duck was taking its water with it (identity) helped conservation, and reminding them that the new lake must have the same water in it (equivalence) added further help.

Another example of the shift from visual or iconic mode of representation to symbolic came from Olver and Hornsby (1966). Children ranging in age from 6 to 18 were asked to tell the similarities and differences among words (for example, banana, peach, potato, and so on) or among pictures (bee, balloons, airplanes). The results indicated that the younger subjects tended to base their judgments on perceptual features such as color, size, and pattern and would say for banana, peach, and potato, "They are curved," while the older children tended to classify objects by their function and would say, in this case, "You can eat them."

THE BIG LEAP: OTHER APPROACHES

Bruner's theory accounts for the "big leap" in cognitive processing that occurs at about age five to seven, partly by emphasizing the increased power that language provides—that is, the shift from iconic to symbolic representation. There are, however, other sources of evidence concerning the big leap from preoperational to concrete operational thought or from iconic to symbolic representation. Many theorists, like Bruner, emphasize the role of language development rather than Piaget's concept of reversibility and other mental operations.

For example, the introductory section of this chapter provided evidence for a major shift in the way language concepts are stored that occurs at about age six— from heterogeneous to homogeneous word associations (Brown and Berko, 1960). In addition, the work of the Kendlers, discussed in Chapter 5, revealed that reversal shifts were easier for children over six and nonreversal shifts were easier for labo-

BOX 11–14   An Inference Problem

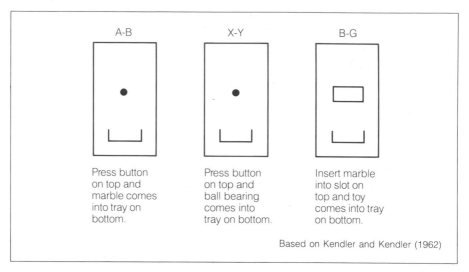

A-B	X-Y	B-G
Press button on top and marble comes into tray on bottom.	Press button on top and ball bearing comes into tray on bottom.	Insert marble into slot on top and toy comes into tray on bottom.

Based on Kendler and Kendler (1962)

ratory animals and children under six. The Kendlers suggested that a set of internal symbols such as language acts as a mediator for the verbal children (for example, "Pick the large ones") while single perceptual associations are made by the younger children.

In another experiment, Kendler and Kendler (1956, 1962) compared kindergartners and third-grade children on making inferences, as shown in Box 11-14. First, the A-B panel was presented and the children were taught that pressing a button yielded a marble, then panel A-B was put away and panel X-Y was presented in which pressing a button (X) yielded a ball bearing (Y). Next when X-Y panel was put away, the B-G panel was presented along with a pile of marbles and ball bearings in which putting a marble in the slot produced a toy but putting in a ball bearing produced nothing. After learning how each of the three panels worked separately, the child was given all three panels together. Six percent of the younger children and 50 percent of the older children gave the correct A-B, B-G response. Apparently the ability to mediate—to see the marble as both a result of pressing a button and as a tool for getting the prize—develops with age.

A different kind of evidence comes from the work on eidetic imagery, such as is shown in Box 11-15 (Haber, 1969). When children were shown a picture and then asked about details when the picture was removed, some were able to "see" it in almost perfect detail and to answer questions about it. In a large-scale study, about 8 percent of elementary school children possessed this ability—called *eidetic imagery*—while almost no adults had it. One explanation (Doob, 1964) is that our society demands that we encode information verbally rather than visually and that as the ability to read and write increases the use of image representation falls.

Sheldon White (1965) has compiled a list of over 20 changes that occur between the ages of five and seven, including several of those mentioned above. In addition, White notes changes in the following areas:

Resistance to classical conditioning. Susceptibility to classical conditioning—a very simple form of response learning—increases up to age six and decreases thereafter (Razran, 1933; Braun and Geiselhart, 1959).

Far transposition. After learning a simple discrimination task, such as choosing the larger of two squares, older children also succeed in applying the principle to very different situations (squares that are many times larger) while younger children cannot (Reese, 1962; White, 1963).

Discrimination learning. Improvement in discrimination learning increases up to age six and then declines, perhaps because older children develop more complex hypotheses (Weir and Stevenson, 1959; White, 1963).

Development of personal left-right. Children become able to discriminate their left and right sides at about the age of six (Piaget, 1926; Benton, 1959). Since many children with language problems also have trouble distinguishing left and right, this too may be tied to language.

Apparently, there is a major difference in the way the preverbal child and the older child think. The difference is not just a quantitative one, with the older child being "smarter," but rather a qualitative difference in the way thinking occurs. The reason for the differences is still not well understood; for example, it is not clear whether the onset of language is the cause of or the result of these emerging new cognitive powers. As White (1965, p. 216) observed, "Surely the move does not take place in one giant step, but the coincidence or sequencing of all the little steps has not yet been investigated and needs to be."

MODIFICATIONS OF PIAGET'S THEORY

So far we have seen that Piaget's theory is the most comprehensive and general theory of cognitive development. However, even a general theory as powerful as Piaget's should not be seen as an unchangeable monument to a great scientist. On the contrary, it is a compliment to Piaget's theory that so many researchers have sought to test and modify the theory. Presently no alternative theory matches the grand scale of Piaget's theory; rather, researchers have sought to carefully test specific aspects of the theory to clarify and, if necessary, modify a portion of the theory.

BOX 11–15   Eidetic Imagery

In experiments with eidetic subjects, Haber (1969) reported an example of a typical 10-year-old eidetic child who has just seen a color version of the illustration from *Alice in Wonderland* shown here; the picture has been taken away and the child is trying to revisualize it on a blank surface in front of him. What follows is the dialogue between the child and the experimenter.

Experimenter: Do you see something there?
       Subject: I see the tree, gray tree with three limbs. I see the cat with stripes around its tail.
E: Can you count those stripes?
S: Yes (*pause*). There's about 16.

In this section we will explore recent research that differs from Piaget's work in two important ways: first, recent work has attempted to describe cognitive development by using information-processing models such as computer simulation or process models; second, recent work has focused on well-controlled experimentation rather than Piaget's clinical method of informally testing and observing children. In a sense, recent work has attempted to recast cognitive developmental psychology into the language and methods of modern information processing.

To build a theory of cognitive development that is more consistent with the information processing approach, Case (1978a) has suggested two major modifications of Piaget's theory: strategies and working memory.

Piaget argues that development involves the acquisition of logical and mathematical systems, including the idea of reversibility discussed earlier in this chapter. Thus, development can be described in terms of the formal properties of mathe-

F: You're counting what? Black, white or both?

S: Both.

E: Tell me what else you see.

S: And I can see the flowers on the bottom. There's about three stems, but you can see two pairs of flowers. One on the right has green leaves, red flower on bottom with yellow on top. And I can see the girl with a green dress. She's got blonde hair and a red hair band and there are some leaves in the upper left-hand corner where the tree is.

E: Can you tell me about the roots of the tree?

S: Well, there's two of them going down here (*points*) and there's one that cuts off on the left-hand side of the picture.

E: What is the cat doing with its paws?

S: Well, one of them he's holding out and the other one is on the tree.

E: What color is the sky?

S: Can't tell.

E: Can't tell at all?

S: No. I can see the yellowish ground, though.

E: Tell me if any of the parts go away or change at all as I'm talking to you. What color is the girl's dress?

S: Green. It has some white on it.

E: How about her legs and feet?

(The subject looks away from the easel and then back again.)

E: Is the image gone?

S: Yes, except for the tree.

E: Tell me when it goes away.

S: (*pause*) It went away.

matics and logic. Building on the work of Simon (1962) and Pascaul-Leone (1970), Case proposes that cognitive development involves the acquisition of information-processing strategies. These strategies can be described in terms of computer-simulation models or process models. In development, simple strategies become automatic through use and then are modified into more powerful strategies.

In Piaget's theory, the overall level of cognitive development is reflected in the level of "operativity"—how many mental operations the child can use in an integrated way. In Case's theory, following the work of Pascaul-Leone (1970), development level is reflected in the child's level of working memory—how many different pieces of information the child can hold in active memory at one time. Higher levels of development require that more information be held in working memory.

As an example of the role of strategies and working memory capacity, Case cites

BOX 11–16   Juice Mixture Problems

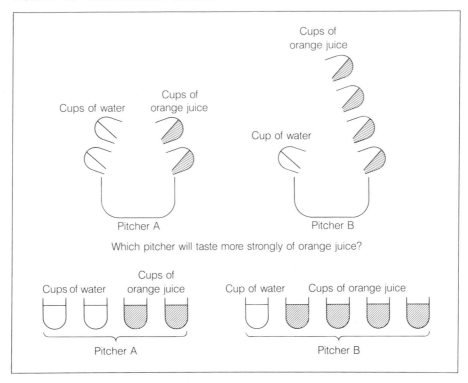

a study by Noelting in which children are shown two empty pitchers. Then, the experimenter explains that he will pour some cups of water and some cups of orange juice into each pitcher. The child's job is to predict which pitcher will taste more strongly like orange juice. For example, suppose the experimenter said that he will pour two cups of water and two cups of juice into pitcher A, and he will pour one cup of water and four cups of juice into pitcher B. Which pitcher will taste more strongly of orange juice? In this case, the answer is pitcher B. The top portion of Box 11-16 summarizes the procedure for this mixing experiment.

Box 11-17 summarizes four kinds of juice ratio problems:

1. In type 1 problems, one pitcher gets some juice while the other pitcher does not.

2. In type 2 problems, one pitcher receives more cups of juice than the other, and the number of cups of water is not relevant.

3. In type 3 problems, one pitcher has an excess of cups of juice over cups of water while the other pitcher does not.

BOX 11–17   Four Types of Juice Mixture Problems

Problem type	Example	Strategy name	Number of steps in strategy	Memory demand for strategy
1		1. Isolated centration	2	1
2		2. Unidimensional comparison	3	2
3		3. Bidimensional comparison	7	3
4		4. Bidimensional comparison with quantification	7	4

After Case (1978a)

4. In type 4 problems, both (or neither) pitchers get an excess of juice over water cups, but one gets a greater excess; the specific ratio is not relevant.

In Noelting's experiments a group of children, ranging in age from 3 to 10, were asked to solve juice problems of these four types. Results of the experiment revealed that there were four basic strategies (see Box 11-18), with younger children using the simplest and older children using more complex strategies.

Strategy 1: Isolated Centration (ages three to four-and-one-half years). The simplest strategy is to base your decision on whether or not orange juice will be poured into a pitcher: if a pitcher contains any orange juice, then it will taste of orange juice. As you can see, this strategy will generate correct answers only if one pitcher gets some orange juice while the other gets none; if both pitchers get orange juice, the child has no strategy for determining which is more concentrated. Children using strategy 1 (those three- to four-and-one-half-years old) show a pattern of correct answers for problem type 1 only. According to Case, this strategy requires two steps and demands only one item be held in working memory (for example, whether or not there is juice in pitcher A).

Strategy 2: Unidimensional Comparison (ages four-and-one-half to six years). Slightly older children use a more sophisticated strategy that focuses on the number of juice cups in each pitcher. In this strategy, you choose the pitcher that has the greatest number of cups of juice, ignoring the number of cups of water in each pitcher. This strategy will generate correct answers only when one side has more cups of juice but proportionately equal or fewer cups of water, that is types 1 and

2. According to Case, this study requires three steps and demands that a maximum of two items be held simultaneously in working memory (the number of juice cups in pitcher A and the number of juice cups in pitcher B).

Strategy 3: Bidimensional Comparison. Seven- to eight-year-old children notice the number of cups of juice and the number of cups of water that go into each pitcher. In this case, you pick the side that has more juice than water. As you can see, this strategy fails when both sides have more cups of juice than water, fewer cups of juice than water, or when both sides have equal differences between cups of juice and water. Thus, problem types 1, 2, and 3 can be solved using strategy 3. This strategy involves seven steps and a maximum memory load of three items (excess of juice cups to water cups in pitcher A, number of juice cups in pitcher B, and number of water cups in pitcher B).

Strategy 4: Two-dimensional Comparison with Quantification. The most sophisticated strategy, observed in the oldest children, aged 9 to 10, involved noticing the exact difference between the number of cups of juice and water for each pitcher. In this case, you subtract the number of water cups from the number of juice cups on each side, then you simply choose the pitcher that yields the highest answer. This strategy succeeds for all four problem types in Box 11-17, but will fail for problems in which the ratio must be taken into account. Case shows that this strategy requires seven steps and a maximum of four items held simultaneously in working memory.

In Case's revision of Piagetian theory, the level of the child's strategy depends on the amount of attentional energy available in working memory—what Pascaul-Leone calls "M-space" (Case, 1974). Early in development, even a simple strategy requires much attentional energy because each step must be monitored. Thus, a child does not have attentional energy available for holding many items in working memory. However, once a strategy has become automatic, through much practice, it no longer requires as much attention. Thus, there is more attentional energy available for holding more items in working memory so a child may move on to a more complex strategy, and so on. Increasingly sophisticated strategies develop because simple strategies become automatic, freeing space in working memory for more use in monitoring more complex strategies.

Case's modifications of Piaget's theory rely heavily on the idea that cognitive growth is restricted by limitations of the capacity of working memory. One important question is whether the holding capacity of working memory increases with age, or whether capacity remains constant while techniques for effectively using that capacity increase with age.

The typical test of the holding capacity of working memory is a test of memory span. For example, in a test of digit span, a list of digits is read, and the subject must then recite the digits in order. A child's digit span is measured as the longest string of digits that he or she can recall without error. In general, digit span increases with age, from about four items recalled by five-year-olds to about eight recalled by

BOX 11–18 Four Strategies for Solving Juice Mixture Problems

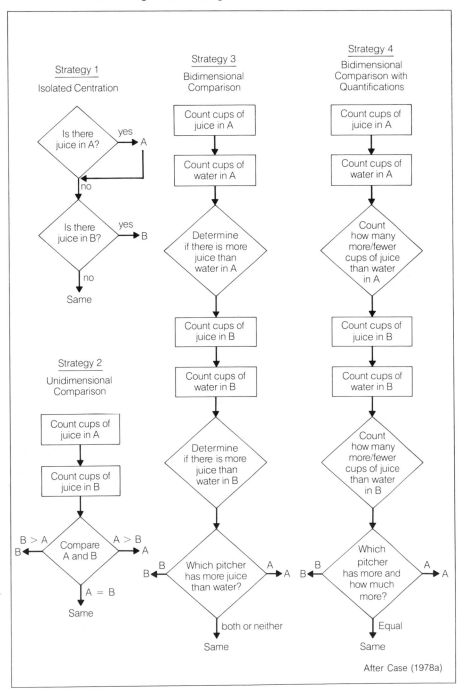

After Case (1978a)

BOX 11–19   Recall Performance by Children and Adults

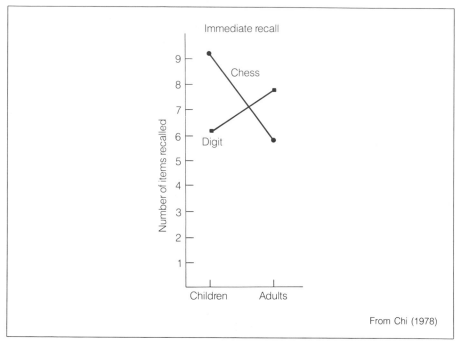

From Chi (1978)

adults (Chi, 1976, 1978). Does this increase in digit span with age imply that the holding capacity of memory increases with age? Does it mean that adults have structurally larger working memories than children? To help answer this question, Chi (1978) gave tests of digit recall and tests of recall of chess pieces to a group of children who were knowledgeable about chess and a group of adults who were not chess players. The average age of the children was ten-and-one-half years. The digit recall test consisted of asking subjects to recall lists of 10 digits. The results were similar to those described earlier: recall of digits was greater for adults than for children. In the chess piece test, a chess board with several pieces from a real game were presented for 10 seconds, and the subject had to reconstruct the board from memory; in this test, the children outperformed the adults. Box 11-19 summarizes the results of the digit and chess tests. These results cast serious doubt on the idea that the size of working memory increases with age. Instead, Chi's work suggests an alternative explanation for the observed increases in digit span performance with age: older subjects may have more knowledge and experience with techniques for grouping items. To an adult, a set of two or three numbers may be held as a single unit; to a chess player, a configuratiion of several pieces may be held in memory as

BOX 11–20   The Balance Beam Problem

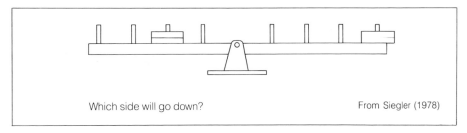

Which side will go down?   From Siegler (1978)

a single unit. These results suggest that increases in memory span performance are due to experience in grouping items.

Like Case, Siegler (1976, 1978) has suggested that cognitive development may be viewed as the acquisition of increasingly sophisticated strategies. In particular, Siegler has shown that performance on Piagetian tasks can be described in terms of changes in the information-processing strategies used by children.

For example, Box 11-20 shows Siegler's version of the balance beam problem, used originally by Inhelder and Piaget (1958) to study the development of scientific reasoning in formal operations. In this task, the child is shown a balance beam with four equally spaced pegs on either side of the fulcrum. Then weights are placed on pegs on each side of the fulcrum, while the beam is held in place. The child's task is to predict which side of the beam will go down.

Siegler used six types of balance beam problems, as shown in Box 11-21:

1. In *balance problems,* the same configuration of weights is placed on both sides; the beam is balanced.

2. In *weight problems,* there are more weights on one side than the other, and the distance between the weights and the fulcrum is the same on both sides.

3. In *distance problems,* an equal number of weights are placed on both sides, but they are placed closer to the fulcrum on one side.

4. In *conflict-weight problems,* one side has more weights but the other side has the weights placed further from the fulcrum; however, the side with more weights goes down.

5. In *conflict-distance problems,* one side has more weights but the other side has the weights placed further from the fulcrum; however, the side with the more distant weights goes down.

6. In *conflict-balance problems,* one side has more weights but the other side has the weights placed further from the fulcrum; the beam remains balanced.

BOX 11–21   Six Types of Balance Beam Problems

	Strategy			
Problem-type	1	2	3	4
Balance	100	100	100	100
Weight	100	100	100	100
Distance	0 (Should say "Balance")	100	100	100
Conflict-weight	100	100	33 (Chance responding)	100
Conflict-distance	0 (Should say "Right down")	0 (Should say "Right down")	33 (Chance responding)	100
Conflict-balance	0 (Should say "Right down")	0 (Should say "Right down")	33 (Chance responding)	100

From Siegler (1978)

If you were given the balance beam problems, how would you go about solving them? According to Siegler (1978), four basic strategies can be described and represented as flow charts. These four strategies are summarized in Box 11-22.

Strategy 1: One Decision. The simplest model involves noticing only if one side has more weights than the other; if both sides have an equal number of weights, then you say that the beam will be balanced; if one side has more weights, then you say that side will go down. This strategy involves only one decision and generates correct answers for balance, weight, and conflict-weight problems.

Strategy 2: Two Decisions. The next strategy contains the same decision as strategy 1, but also adds a second decision concerning whether or not the weights are placed at equal distances from the fulcrum. If one side has more weights than the other, then you say that side will go down (just as in strategy 1). If both sides have an equal number of weights, then you check their distance from the fulcrum. You say that the side with weights the greater distance from the fulcrum will go down. This strategy involves two decisions and generates correct answers for balance, weight, distance, and conflict-weight problems.

Strategy 3: Three Decisions. This strategy incorporates the two decisions from strategy 2—noticing the distribution and distance of weights—as well as a third decision. If both sides are equal, then you say they will balance. If one side has more weights but both sides have equal distance, then you say the side with more weights will go down. If both sides have the same weight but one has greater distance, then you will say the side with greater distance will go down. However, when one side has more weight and the other side has more distance, you must guess. This strategy generates correct answers for balance, weight, and distance problems and change level answers for the other problems.

Strategy 4: Four Decisions. The fourth strategy builds on strategy 3, by including a decision concerning the cross products (weight × distance). Thus, when one side has more weights and the other side has more distance, the answer is determined by computing the cross product for each side. This strategy involves four decisions and generates correct answers for all problems.

In a typical experiment, Siegler (1976, 1978) gave problems like the six in Box 11-21 to children of ages 7 through 17. The errors generated by each child were matched against the pattern of errors predicted by each of the four strategies. Almost all of the children could be easily fit into one of the four strategy groups—that is, the performance of a given child usually matched perfectly with the performance predicted by one of the strategies. There was also a pattern in which older children preferred the more sophisticated strategies while younger children used the simpler strategies. These results are consistent with those described by Case in which developmental changes in performance may be described in terms of increasingly more complex strategies of information processing.

Additional support for the idea that development involves requiring more sophisticated strategies comes from a study by Klahr (Klahr, 1978; Klahr and Wallace, 1976). In information-processing theories of problem solving, planning—such as "means-ends" analysis—is an important strategy in solving "move" problems. In means-ends analysis, a problem solver establishes subgoals whenever a desired goal

BOX 11–22 Four Strategies for Solving Balance Beam Problems

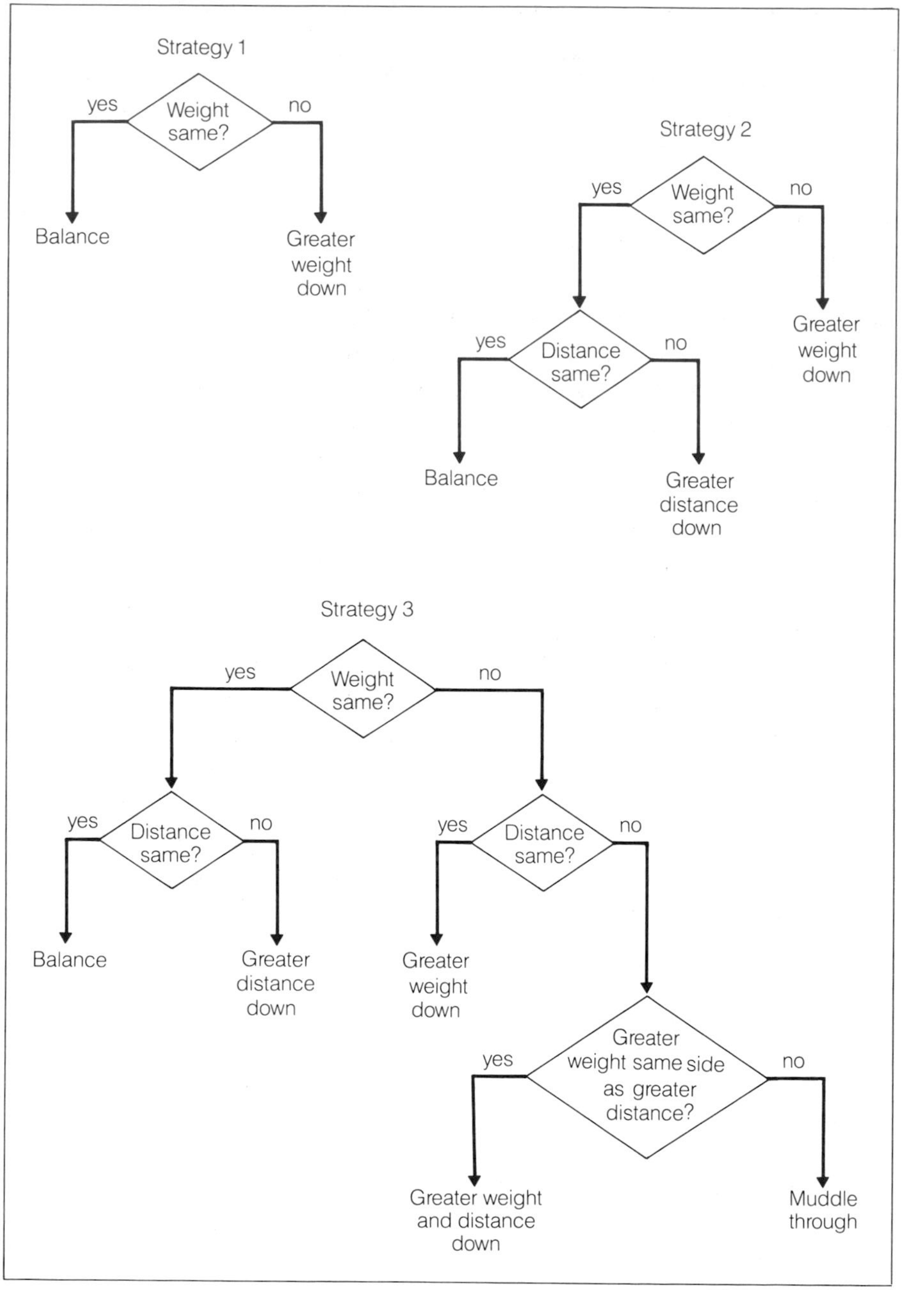

Strategy 1

yes — Weight same? — no

Balance

Greater weight down

Strategy 2

yes — Weight same? — no

Distance same?

Greater weight down

yes — Distance same? — no

Balance

Greater distance down

Strategy 3

yes — Weight same? — no

yes — Distance same? — no

yes — Distance same? — no

Balance

Greater distance down

Greater weight down

yes — Greater weight same side as greater distance? — no

Greater weight and distance down

Muddle through

BOX 11–22, *continued*

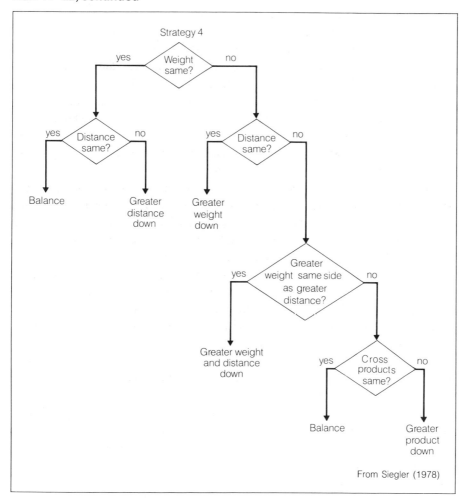

From Siegler (1978)

cannot be directly accomplished. For example, Klahr (1978, pp. 181–182) presents the following example of the use of subgoal stacking in children:

Scene: Billy and Daddy are in the yard. Billy's playmate appears on a bike.

Billy: "Daddy, will you unlock the basement door?"
Daddy: "Why?"
Billy: "'Cause I want to ride my bike."
Daddy: "Your bike is in the garage."
Billy: "But my socks are in the dryer."

In this case, Billy's top goal is to ride his bike. However, this goal cannot be achieved directly because he needs to be wearing his shoes (subgoal 1). However, he cannot directly achieve the goal of getting his shoes on because he needs to put on his socks (subgoal 2). Again, he cannot directly achieve his goal because his socks are in the dryer (subgoal 3). He cannot get to the dryer directly because the basement door leading to the dryer is locked (subgoal 4). Unlocking the door cannot be directly accomplished because Daddy always has the keys for everything (subgoal 5). Thus, Billy determines that he must ask his dad to open the basement door. Once this goal is accomplished, all the others can be executed in turn. Thus, in this example Billy has shown that he can "stack subgoals"—that is, set up subgoals when a top goal cannot be directly accomplished.

Similarly, Klahr (1978) asked children to solve versions of the tower of Hanoi, or disk, problem. To appeal to children, Klahr developed the monkey can problem shown in Box 11-23. In this problem children are told that the cans are monkeys and the pegs are trees. The large can is the daddy, the medium size can is the mommy, and the small can is the baby. The monkeys are able to jump from tree to tree (peg to peg), but a smaller can may never be put on top of a larger can. One configuration is given on the experimenter's side of the puzzle; the child's job is to move the monkeys so they will be in the same configuration as on the experimenter's side.

Klahr presented this problem to children ranging in age from three to five years. The youngest children in the group were able to solve only very short problems that did not require any setting of goals. For example, one simple problem begins with one can on each peg and ends with them all stacked on the same peg. Older children were able to solve longer problems that required some moderate amount of goal setting. Klahr developed computer simulation models at six levels of sophistication in order to describe different levels of performance among the children.

The work of Case, Siegler, and Klahr gives examples of how the information-processing approach can be applied to describing cognitive development. As you can see, one persistent modification of Piaget's theory is that developmental progressions may be described as the acquisition of increasingly more sophisticated strategies.

CAN COGNITIVE DEVELOPMENT BE TAUGHT?

One of Piaget's major contributions is his proposal of a series of stages of cognitive development through which all humans progress in a fixed order. Although the order is fixed, the rate of development is not fixed in Piaget's theory. Thus, much research has been aimed at the question of whether or not the rate of development may be speeded up, that is, whether it is possible to teach children who are in one stage of development to move on to the next stage.

BOX 11–23 The Monkey Can Problem

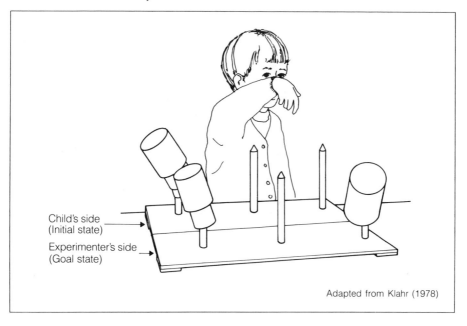

Child's side
(Initial state)

Experimenter's side
(Goal state)

Adapted from Klahr (1978)

Conservation-Training Studies

During the past 20 years there have been literally hundreds of conservation-training studies (Murray, 1978; Bcilin, 1971; Brainerd, 1974; Glaser and Resnick, 1972; Goldschmidt, 1971; Kuhn, 1974; Strauss, 1972). Conservation training studies begin with children who do not conserve on standard Piagetian conservation tasks; they receive training on how to perform, and finally the children are retested to see whether they have learned to conserve. Although various teaching techniques have been used by different researchers, there is presently "no longer any doubt that conservation can be taught" (Murray, 1978, p. 421). However there are also many cases in which training is not effective. For example, Murray points out that training is most effective for children who are already close to the criterion behavior. In addition, training is most effective when it involves social interaction—such as nonconservers having to come to a group consensus with conservers—and role playing or imitation—such as when a nonconserver must try to act like a conserver.

As an example, let's consider a major conservation training study by Gelman (1969; also discussed in Gelman and Gallistel, 1978). In this study, children were taught about conservation of number and conservation of length, as discussed earlier in this chapter. Subjects were given practice on 32 problem sets with 6 problems in each set. Box 11-24 shows a typical problem set for conservation of number and one

BOX 11–24   Training Procedure for Conservation of Number and Length

Point to the line with more dots (length).

Trial	Number	Length
1		
2		
3		
4		
5		
6		

Adapted from Gelman (1969)

for conservation of length. On each problem, the child is shown three sets of dots (or three lines) and asked to indicate which one is different. On the first problem in each set and the last problem in each set, the dots (or lines) are arranged to elicit a correct response. However, on problems 2 through 5, the child must learn to overcome irrelevant features of the display such as the placement of the dots (or lines). Children are given feedback on each trial. According to Gelman, the training is aimed at focusing the learner's attention on the relevant aspects of the display and away from the irrelevant aspects. Box 11-25 shows the results for a group of trained subjects. As you can see, at the beginning the children make many errors; however, after about 16 problem sets, the rate of performance approaches 100 percent.

Siegler (1978) was able to influence the problem-solving performance of children on the balance beam task described earlier by providing training. Two types of training were used: feedback and encoding. In feedback training, children were given systematic feedback concerning their predictions about which side of the

BOX 11-25 Percent Correct on Conservation Task for Various Amounts of Training

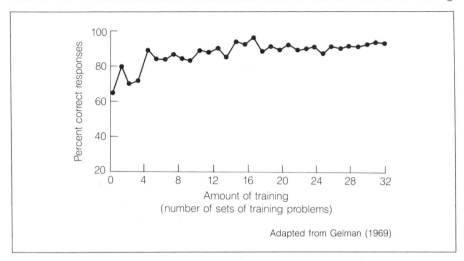

Amount of training
(number of sets of training problems)

Adapted from Gelman (1969)

balance would go down. In encoding training, children had to note the number of weights and the configuration of weights on each side to be able to reproduce the exact number and configuration on another balance beam. These two techniques tended to help some children learn more systematic strategies, although instruction was most beneficial for children who were already in transition.

Logical Reasoning Training Studies

Let's consider some other Piagetian tasks. For example, in a "transitive inference" task, like the linear reasoning tasks discussed previously the child is shown that stick A is taller than stick B, and stick B is taller than stick C. Piaget (1952) noted that most children in the group of four- to six-year-olds fail on tests of transitive inference, such as "Is stick A taller than C?" Piaget's theory attributes this failure to a lack of the appropriate logical operations.

Trabasso and his colleagues (Bryant and Trabasso, 1971; Riley and Trabasso, 1974; Riley, 1976) have offered a modification of Piaget's theory of transitive inference. In a typical study, Bryant and Trabasso used a series of five colored sticks labeled A, B, C, D, and E. The children in the study, aged four to six, were shown only adjacent pairs, such as A and B. For each pair, the child learned which stick was longer. The test of transitive inference involved the B-D pair. Children who were able to correctly solve the inference problem (B > D) also tended to remember the premises (B > C, C > D), while children who did not perform well on the inference task tended to forget one or more of the premises. Thus, failure to perform on an inference task may result from forgetting the premises rather than a lack of logical operations. When training techniques were used that ensure memory for the premises, transitive inference performance was improved (Riley, 1976; Riley and Trabasso, 1974). Similarly, performance on class inclusion problems can be improved by systematically teaching each step in the problem solving process (Trabasso, Isen, Dolecki, McLanahan, Riley, and Tucker, 1978).

Learning Training

A related area that has received much research attention concerns children's ability to learn a rote list. In a typical study, children are shown a list of pictures of objects and then must try to recall them. Young children in the preschool years tend to be unable to predict how well they will do on a recall task while older children are far more accurate (Flavell and Wellman, 1977). In addition, young children do not tend to use encoding strategies such as organizing the list into taxonomic categories or rehearsing the list when the pictures are no longer present (Worden, 1974; Kail, 1979); older children do use such strategies. Brown and DeLoache (1978) have provided a review of training studies in which young children are taught to use organizing and rehearsal strategies. In general such training can be effective in improving recall performance, that is, in making four-year-olds learn like seven-year-olds. Such training is aimed at what has been called ''metamemory'' skills— knowledge of how to learn and how to think.

Implications of Training Studies

Apparently, children's performance on almost any sort of task can be improved with appropriate training or by changing the format of the task. Does this mean that Piaget's theory is wrong in stating that cognitive development involves a fixed sequence of stages? Do training techniques shorten the natural development process and deprive children of learning how to learn on their own? If it is possible to improve performance on Piagetian tasks, does that mean that we *should* do so?

The implications of training studies are far from clear. However, almost all of the improvements that have been demonstrated in training studies would likely have occurred within the children given the normal course of time. There is little evidence from training studies that the final level of development as an adult can be influenced by speeding the developmental process. As for Piaget's theory, training studies also provide some support: they tend to show that effects are strongest for children who are at the borderline between stages, and they support the idea that cognitive development is always in a state of flux. However, there is a sense in which training studies obscure the original purpose of Piagetian research and research on development in general. As Gelman and Gallistel state: "The idea is to look for ways to compare, as well as to contrast, the preschooler with his older sibling" (1978, p. 24).

EVALUATION

The cognitive development approach provides a unique theory of human thinking and the only one explicitly based on the idea that humans are living beings striving to survive and function successfully. Like the information-processing approach, which is strongly influenced by developments in computer technology, the cognitive development approach was heavily influenced by biological concepts. To the extent that the biological analogy is not perfect, theories of human thought based on it are limited.

The cognitive development approach, particularly the work of Piaget, has been criticized on several grounds. Many of Piaget's theories are so vague or ambiguous that they cannot be tested. Some of the theories that are testable fail to be confirmed. Piaget's "experiments" are poorly controlled, lack statistical analysis, and could easily be biased by the experimenter's expectations or by the use of language. In addition, recent information-processing approaches to cognitive development have posed challenges to some of the fundamental ideas in Piaget's theory. However, the unique approach of the cognitive developmentalists offers an emerging source of information that ultimately must be assimilated into the wider area of the psychology of thinking.

Suggested Readings

Flavell, J. F. *Cognitive development.* Englewood Cliffs, N.J.: Prentice-Hall, 1977. A summary of Piagetian and related theories.

Ginsburg, H., and Opper, S. *Piaget's theory of intellectual development.* Englewood Cliffs, N.J.: Prentice-Hall, 1969. Summary and interpretation of Piaget's theory for the introductory reader.

Kail, R. *The development of memory in children.* San Francisco: W. H. Freeman and Company, 1979. Summary of modern research on development of cognitive processing.

Phillips, J. L. *The origins of intellect: Piaget's theory.* San Francisco: W. H. Freeman and Company, 1975. Another summary and interpretation of Piaget's theory.

Piaget, J. *Six psychological studies.* New York: Random House, 1967. A collection of some of Piaget's papers, organized and introduced by an American Piagetian psychologist, David Elkind.

Siegler, R. S. *Children's thinking: What develops.* Hillsdale, N.J.: Erlbaum, 1978. An anthology of recent papers concerning the information-processing approach to cognitive development.

CHAPTER 12

INTELLIGENCE: Thinking as a Measurable Ability

Intelligence

Psychometric Approach

Cognitive Correlates Theory

Cognitive Components Theory

Expert-Novice Differences

Most people are familiar with tests of mental ability. What may surprise you, however, is that there are so many different kinds of tests of mental ability. For example, try the problems in Box 12-1.

These test items are from the *Kit of Factor-Referenced Cognitive Tests* (Ekstrom, French, and Harman, 1976). This set of 72 tests is designed to measure 23 different mental factors. These tests have been used in research since the *Kit* was introduced in 1963. By now, there are hundreds of studies involving these tests. Where did these tests and these factors come from? The developers of the *Kit* selected commonly used types of test items and employed them in testing large groups of people. Some tests seemed highly correlated—that is, people who scored high (or low) on one

BOX 12–1 Some Tests of Mental Ability

Flexibility of Closure (CF)

Definition: The ability to hold a given visual percept or configuration in mind to disemble it from other well-defined perceptual material.

Example from "Hidden Figures Test": Which one of the five simple figures can be found (in the same size and orientation) in the more complex figure?

A   B   C   D   E

A B C D E

Induction (I)

Definition: This factor identifies the kinds of reasoning abilities involved in forming and trying out hypotheses that will fit a set of data.

Example from "Letter Sets Test": Draw an X through the set of letters that is different.

1. NOPQ   DEFL   ABCD   HIJK   UVWX

2. NLIK   PLIK   QLIK   THIK   VLIK

Visualization (V)

Definition: The ability to manipulate or transform the image of spatial patterns into other arrangements.

Example from "Surface Development Test": Which of the lettered edges on the object correspond to the numbered edges on the sheet? Numbers 1 and 4 are already marked for you.

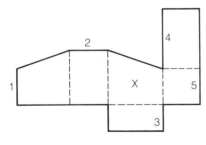 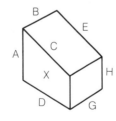

1:	H
2:	
3:	
4:	C
5:	

General Reasoning (RG)

Definition: The ability to select and organize relevant information for the solution of a problem.

Example from "Arithmetic Aptitude Test": Circle the best answer.

1. How many candy mints can you buy for 50 cents at the rate of 2 for 5 cents?

a. 10   b. 20   c. 25   d. 100   e. 125

BOX 12–1, *continued*

Logical Reasoning (RL)

Definition: The ability to reason from premise to conclusion, or to evaluate the correctness of a conclusion.

Example from "Nonsense Syllogisms Test": If the conclusion drawn from the statements shows good reasoning, circle the letter G. If the conclusion drawn from the statements shows poor reasoning, circle the letter P.

1. Some swimming pools are mountains. All mountains
   like cats. Therefore all swimming pools like cats.   G   P

2. All swimming pools are mountains. All mountains
   like cats. Therefore all swimming pools like cats.   G   P

Giving examples of 5 of the 23 factors, all items are selected from the *Kit of Factor-Referenced Cognitive Tests* (Ekstrom, French and Harman, 1976).

Answers:
Flexibility of Closure: D.   Induction: DEFL, THIK.   Visualization: 1-H, 2-B, 3-G, 4-C, 5-H.
General Reasoning: B.   Logical Reasoning: P, G.

---

were likely to score high (or low) on the others. The researchers assumed that highly correlated tests measure the same factor. For example, "flexibility of closure" is a factor that is measured by three tests in the *Kit:* hidden figures (as in Box 12-1), hidden patterns, and a copying test. The tests within a factor are more strongly correlated with each other than with tests for other factors. Thus, tests for flexibility of closure are more closely correlated with each other than with tests for general reasoning or word fluency.

Of course, the 72 tests in the *Kit* are not the only ones available. There are hundreds of mental tests (Buros, 1978). Not all psychologists agree on the existence of exactly 23 separate mental factors. As you will see in the next section of this chapter, some psychologists have proposed the existence of up to 120 different factors. However, the *Kit* is a useful introduction to the measurement of mental ability because it contains representative examples of most major test items. A typical test of intelligence has an assortment of many of the types of test items similar to those in the *Kit.* A variety is given because intelligence tests are supposed to measure general mental ability, that is, the ability to perform on a wide spectrum of cognitive tasks.

The challenge facing cognitive psychologists is to determine what these tests measure. Other chapters explore studies on induction and logical reasoning, as well as tests of creativity (including flexibility of use, ideational fluency, and word fluency) and mathematical problem solving (such as number and general reasoning). In this chapter, we will explore the idea that people may differ in various ways, and we will explore techniques for describing differences in mental ability.

INTELLIGENCE

To start, it would be useful to define what is meant by *intelligence* or mental ability. Unfortunately, there is little agreement among psychologists concerning such a definition. For example, common definitions of intelligence include the ability to learn, to adapt to new situations, to represent and manipulate symbols, and to solve problems. The confusion concerning a definition of intelligence led Boring (1923) to conclude that intelligence is "what these tests measure."

A complete definition of *intelligence* (or any mental ability) is still a goal rather than a reality in psychology. Furthermore, there is a sense in which the main goal of cognitive psychology is to define intelligece. When we understand the basic cognitive processes and structures responsible for individual differences in intellectual performance, we will have solved many of the current problems in cognitive psychology. In the meanwhile, however, let's tentatively consider a general definition that has three parts:

Internal cognitive characteristics—Intelligence concerns the nature of the human cognitive system.

Related to performance—Intelligence is related to peformance on tasks such as solving problems.

Individual differences—Differences in intelligence are related to differences in internal cognitive characteristics and performance.

Thus, intelligence refers to internal cognitive characteristics that are related to individual differences in problem-solving performance.

A quarter of a century ago, Cronback (1957) pointed out that scientific psychology seemed to have developed as two distinct and separate disciplines: the *psychometric approach,* which focused on individual differences among people's performances without much interest in underlying cognitive processes and structures, and the *experimental psychology approach,* which focused on analyzing general cognitive processes without much interest in individual differences. Psychometricians focused on part of the definition of intelligence—measuring individual differences in performance—while experimental psychologists focused on a different part of the definition—analyzing the basic processes in cognition and learning.

In the past few years, however, there has been an amazing rapprochement between the two traditions. For example, Carroll (1976) has selected basic tests of mental ability and has shown how an individual's performance on them may be related to internal cognitive processes, such as manipulating information in short-term memory or recognizing a stimulus.

After a brief overview of the psychometric approach, this chapter presents three new approaches to individual differences in the experimental psychology tradition:

BOX 12–2   Factor Theory

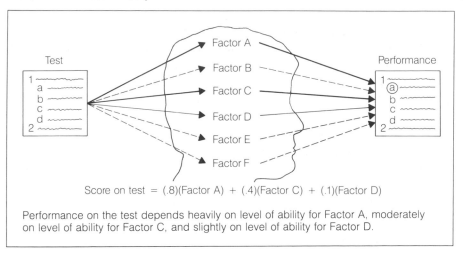

Score on test = (.8)(Factor A) + (.4)(Factor C) + (.1)(Factor D)

Performance on the test depends heavily on level of ability for Factor A, moderately on level of ability for Factor C, and slightly on level of ability for Factor D.

cognitive correlates, cognitive components, and expert-novice differences. These three new approaches are attempts to unify scientific psychology once again; they focus on all parts of the definition of intelligence.

PSYCHOMETRIC APPROACH

The first approach to the study of mental ability is the psychometric approach. This approach is based on the idea that we should list the basic mental abilities and then develop tests to measure each of them, rather than focus on trying to define each mental ability in words. The underlying theme of the psychometric approach is that humans are endowed with a set of factors, or traits, that there are individual differences along each factor, and that individual differences in these factors are related to differences in intellectual performance. Thus, performance on a test of ''general intelligence'' or some other mental ability such as verbal, quantitative, or spatial ability is mediated by a set of underlying factors or traits. A summary of the factor theory of mental ability is presented in Box 12-2. In the remainder of this section, you will see how psychometricians have attempted to determine what the major mental factors are and how to measure them.

    Galton (1869, 1883) was one of the first to systematically study individual differences in mental ability. His hypothesis was that differences in general performance were due to differences in many smaller, basic processes, such as how fast a person responds to a stimulus, how well she judges which of two balls weighs

BOX 12–3 Normal Distribution

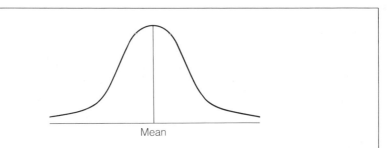

Mean

Some of the characteristics of the normal distribution are:

1. Half the people score above the mean and half score below.
2. The curve is symmetrical, that is, for each score a distance below the mean there is a score the same distance above the mean.
3. The curve is bell shaped, because most people score near the mean and very few people score at the upper or lower extremes.

more, her sensitivity to pain, and so on. To test this idea, he gave a battery of 17 tests to 9337 people. In addition to large individual differences among people, he found that differences in many mental abilities seemed to be normally distributed, as shown in Box 12-3. A person's level of ability could be described in terms of how much that person deviates above or below the mean. Thus, early in the course of scientific observation, Galton showed that people differ from one another.

Findings of individual differences by Galton and by others seem to have serious implications for the "one size fits all" approach to public education. In 1905 the French Minister of Public Instruction asked Alfred Binet to develop a simple test for use in schools. The purpose of the test was to locate "mentally deficient" students so they could be given special instruction. In essence, Binet was asked to develop a test that would predict success in school. Binet quickly found that the basic tasks used by Galton such as response time and sensory acuity were not related to school success. Instead, Binet decided to observe what an average child could do at each age level. After observing large groups of children at each age, he was able to generate a list as shown in Box 12-4. To test mental ability, Binet simply noted which tasks a child could do. If an eight-year-old, for example, could perform the tasks listed for that age, but could not perform any tasks for older ages, that child was average. If an eight-year-old child could perform the tasks listed for that age as well as many of the tasks for nine-year-olds, that child scored above average. Binet's test, modified for "normal" children, became enormously popular and in many ways formed the basis for many subsequent intelligence tests.

Binet's work is important for several reasons. First, he launched the highly

BOX 12–4 Typical Test Items on Stanford-Binet Test

Age Two

1. Three-hole Form Board. Placing three geometric objects in form board.
2. Delayed Response. Identifying placement of hidden object after 10-second delay.
3. Identifying Parts of the Body. Pointing out features on paper doll.
4. Block Building Tower. Building four-block tower by imitating examiner's procedure.
5. Picture Vocabulary. Naming common objects from pictures.
6. Word Combinations. Spontaneous combination of two words.

Age Six

1. Vocabulary. Correctly defining 6 words on 45-word list.
2. Differences. Telling difference between two objects.
3. Mutilated Pictures. Pointing out missing part of pictured object.
4. Number Concepts. Counting number of blocks in a pile.
5. Opposite Analogies II. Items of form "Summer is hot; winter is _____."
6. Maze Tracing. Finding shortest path in simple maze.

Age Ten

1. Vocabulary. Correctly defining 11 words on same list.
2. Block Counting. Counting number of cubes in three-dimensional picture, some cubes hidden.
3. Abstract Words I. Definition of abstract adverbs.
4. Finding Reasons I. Giving reasons for laws or preferences.
5. Word Naming. Naming as many words as possible in one minute.
6. Repeating Six Digits. Repeating six digits in order.

Average Adult

1. Vocabulary. Correctly defining 20 words.
2. Ingenuity I. Algebraic word problems involving mental manipulation of volumes.
3. Differences between Abstract Words. Differentiating between two related abstract words.
4. Arithmetical Reasoning. Word problems involving simple computations.
5. Proverbs I. Giving meaning of proverbs.
6. Orientation: Direction II. Finding orientation after a verbal series of changes in directions.
7. Essential Differences. Giving principal difference between two related concepts.
8. Abstract Words III. Meanings of abstract adverbs.

successful field of testing, perhaps today the major application of scientific psychology in our society. Second, he based his definition of mental ability on success in schools; thus, from the beginning of such testing, mental ability has been related to performance in real-world tasks. Finally, as you read over the items in Box 12-4, you may notice that Binet seems to be measuring the basic knowledge of the student rather than some primary memory processes; the theme that successful problem solving requires specific knowledge will be repeated again later in this chapter.

One question raised by work such as Binet's concerns whether intelligent performance is due to a single general factor or whether instead there are many small specific factors. Spearman (1904, 1927) addressed this question by collecting scores on many different tests from a large number of people. If there was one single factor that determined performance in all mental tests, he proposed that scores of all the tests should be related to one another. In other words, if a certain person did well on one, he should do well on the others; if a person did poorly on one, he should do poorly on the others. However, if each test measured a single, specific ability, then test scores should be unrelated. Using some newly developed statistical techniques, Spearman was able to find some support for both ideas: all of the tests seemed to be related to one another although they were not perfectly related. This led Spearman to propose a ''two-factor theory'' of intelligence: there is a general factor (called *g*) as well as many smaller specific factors (called *s*) that come to influence performance on any given test. For example, verbal analogy tests may require the g factor as well as s factors such as vocabulary and verbal fluency; a pictorial analogy test may require the same g factor as well as different s factors such as visualization and imagery fluency.

Later, Thurstone (1938) modified the statistical techniques used by Spearman and found that there seemed to be seven ''primary mental abilities'': verbal comprehension, number, memory, perceptual speed, space, verbal fluency, and inductive reasoning. Thus, where Spearman found one general factor, Thurstone found seven factors.

In light of the conflicting findings of Spearman and Thurstone, Guilford (1959, 1967) adopted a different approach, called the ''structure of the intellect.'' Guilford began by suggesting that any mental ability could be classified in terms of the following three dimensions:

Operation—such as evaluation, convergent production, divergent production, memory and cognition.

Product—such as units, classes, relations, systems, transformations, and implications.

Content—such as figural, symbolic, semantic, and behavioral.

There are 5 × 6 × 4 or 120 mental abilities, corresponding to each possible combination of the three categories. Box 12-5 gives a summary of the structure of intellect theory as well as examples of some of the 120 factors. Although there are now tests available for most of the 120 factors, some factors are not yet measurable.

Where does the psychometric approach leave us? It leaves us with ample evi-

BOX 12–5 Guilford's 120 Mental Factors and Some Sample Test Items

Structure of the Intellect

Operations
Evaluation
Convergent thinking
Divergent thinking
Memory
Cognition

Products

Units
Classes
Relations
Systems
Transformations
Implications

Figural
Symbolic
Semantic
Behavioral

Contents

1. Scrambled Words (Cognition–Symbolic–Units)
   Rearrange the letters to make real words:

   R   A   C   I   H

   T   V   O   E   S

   K   L   C   C   O

2. Oddity Problems (Cognition–Semantic–Classes)
   Which object does not belong?   clam   tree   oven   rose

3. Analogy Problems (Cognition–Semantic–Relations)
   Poetry is to prose as dance is to (1) music (2) walk (3) sing (4) talk.

4. Sentence Production (Divergent–Symbolic–Systems)
   Write as many sentences as you can of the form:

   W_____   c_____   e_____   n_____ .

5. Completion Task (Convergent–Symbolic–Relations)

   pots   stop   bard   drab   rats   _____

6. Deduction Task (Convergent–Symbolic–Relations)

   Charles is younger than Robert.
   Charles is older than Frank.
   Who is older? Robert or Frank?

Answers: 1. CHAIR, STOVE, CLOCK   2. oven   3. walk   4. We covered every notch (and so on).   5. stars   6. Robert

Diagram adapted from Guilford. Copyright 1959 by the American Psychological Association.
Reprinted by permission of the author.

dence that humans differ in intellectual performance and that these differences can be systematically measured. However, what is missing from the psychometric approach is a clear description of what differences in ability really mean. For example, what does someone who is high in "verbal ability" or "analogical reasoning" have in her head that is different from someone who scores low on the same tests? In the next three sections of this chapter, we explore three techniques for describing differences in ability.

COGNITIVE CORRELATES THEORY

The cognitive correlates approach begins by selecting some ability that can be measured using psychometric tests, such as verbal ability. The goal is to describe individual differences in that ability in terms of differences in general information-processing capacities or techniques. The cognitive correlates theory is based on two ideas:

Information-processing system—All humans come equipped with an information-processing system, such as a long-term memory for storing information permanently, a short-term memory for holding information we are actively thinking about, and processes for acting on that information.

Individual differences—People may differ with respect to the particular capacities of each memory process, and these are the building blocks of intelligent behavior.

As you can see, the cognitive correlates approach attempts to answer questions such as, "What does it mean to be high in some ability?" In a series of papers, Hunt and his colleagues (Hunt, Frost, and Lenneborg, 1973; Hunt, Lenneborg, and Lewis, 1975; Hunt, 1978) have introduced the cognitive correlates approach by investigating the information-processing capacities that may be related to verbal ability. They use the term "information processing" or "mechanics of ability" to describe their theory.

In order for you to get a better understanding of this approach, let's consider a question raised by Hunt, Lenneborg, and Lewis (1975), namely, "What does it mean to be high verbal?" They found a group of college students who had scored very well on a standardized achievement test of verbal ability (like the SAT verbal scale) and a group who had scored low on the same test. The goal of Hunt, Lenneborg, and Lewis was to determine whether differences between high and low verbal students could be described in terms of differences in basic information-processing capacities.

BOX 12–6   An Information-Processing System

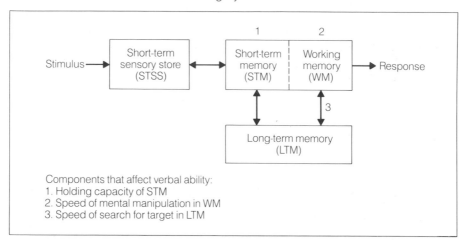

Components that affect verbal ability:
1. Holding capacity of STM
2. Speed of mental manipulation in WM
3. Speed of search for target in LTM

Their first step was to describe the information processing system that all humans process. Box 12-6 shows a simple version of the information-processing system, consisting of memory stores and memory processes. The rectangles in Box 12-6 refer to memory stores: large amounts of information may be present in the outside world, large amounts of information may be stored permanently in long-term memory, and limited amounts of information may be temporarily held in short-term memory (such as information we are currently thinking about in a problem). The arrows in Box 12-6 refer to memory processes, such as searching for a specific piece of information in long-term memory or making a comparison decision in short-term memory. Thinking can be viewed as performing a series of manipulations of information that is held in short-term memory.

The next step in analyzing verbal ability was to try to locate basic memory processes that are required for verbal tasks such as reading. For example, Hunt and his colleagues suggest several processes, including the following:

Decoding information from long-term memory—Decoding refers to finding a specific piece of well-learned information in long-term memory, such as recognizing that the printed letter *A* refers to the first letter of the alphabet. In the normal course of reading, you must decode letters or strings of letters thousands of times. People may differ in the speed with which they can decode, that is, find the name of a printed symbol in long-term memory.

Holding information in short-term memory—Holding refers to actively thinking about and remembering information at one instance, such as hearing a list of letters and being able to recite them back in order. In reading, you must hold combinations of letters in short-term memory until you can figure out what the word is, or you must hold a string of words until you can understand the entire sentence. People may differ in the amount of information that they can actively hold in their minds at one time.

Manipulating information in short-term memory—Manipulating refers to performing a simple operation on information that is being held in short-term memory, such as comparing two letters to determine whether they are the same. Reading requires many such operations in working memory, and people may differ in their speeds for comparing and deciding.

Hunt has thus suggested some basic information processes that may be the building blocks of verbal ability.

The next step in Hunt's plan was to measure the basic memory processes in high- and low-verbal students, and to see whether differences in verbal ability are related to differences in these basic processes. Let's examine decoding from long-term memory, holding information in short-term memory, and manipulating information each in turn.

To measure the speed of decoding processes, Hunt modified a procedure developed by Posner and his colleagues (Posner and Mitchell, 1976; Posner, Boies, Eichelman, and Taylor, 1969; Posner, 1978) called a "letter-matching task." (This task is discussed in Chapter 8.) A subject sits in front of a computer terminal screen on which two letters appear. If they are the same, the subject presses the "same" button; if they are different, the subject presses the "different" button. Two kinds of trials are used: physical match and name match. On physical match trials, the subject is asked to base the "same-different" judgment on whether the two letters are physically identical, such as AA is "same," but Aa is "different." On name match trials the subject is asked to judge whether the two letters have the same name; in this case, Aa is "same" and AB is "different."

To find the decoding time, you must use a "subtraction method" (Posner, 1978) as follows. Let's assume that the physical match requires the following processes: encoding the letters, comparing the letters, deciding on a response, and executing the response. The name match task requires all of these processes plus finding the name of the letters in long-term memory; these processes are: encoding the letters, finding their names in long-term memory, comparing the names, deciding on a response, and executing the response. Thus, if we take the time for a name match and subtract the time for physical match, we will have an estimate of the time for "decoding," or finding the name of letters in long-term memory.

Box 12-7 shows the average response times for high- and low-verbal subjects on physical and name matches. Both groups performed at similar levels for physical matches; thus, there is no evidence that high-verbal subjects are just faster in responding. However, the name match task adds 64 milliseconds for the high verbals

BOX 12–7   Performance of High and Low Verbal Subjects on Name and Physical Identity Problems

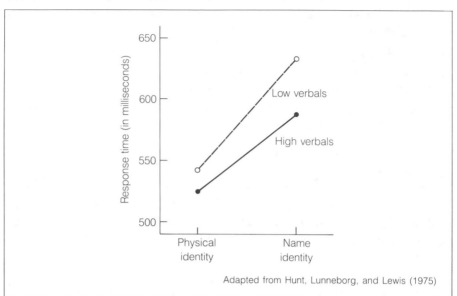

Adapted from Hunt, Lunneborg, and Lewis (1975)

and 89 milliseconds for the low verbals. Apparently, the time to look up the name for a letter is less for high-verbal subjects. Although the extra speed of the high-verbal subjects is just a small fraction of a second, you must remember that reading requires thousands of such decoding processes. In a study by Goldberg, Schwartz, and Stewart (1977), subjects made judgments about homophones such as deer-deer and deer-dear. The high verbals had a one-third of a second advantage when the task required looking up the meaning of a word in long-term memory. Thus, there is evidence that differences in verbal ability may be described in terms of differences in basic processes such as decoding.

Hunt used a memory span task modified from Peterson and Peterson (1959). Their procedure, summarized in Box 12-8, was designed to measure the holding capacity of short-term memory. Four letters were displayed on a screen, one at a time, for 400 milliseconds each. Then, 1 to 36 digits were presented on the screen and the subject had to recite them; this digit shadowing task of repeating digits aloud was included to prevent the subject from rehearsing the four letters. Next, the subject was asked to recall the four letters in order.

Box 12-9 shows that high-verbal subjects made fewer errors in recall than low-verbal subjects. The fact that high-verbal subjects were better able to remember letters in order suggests that they have better techniques for keeping large amounts of information in short-term memory. For example, one way to keep information in

BOX 12–8   Measurement of STM Capacity Using a Modified Peterson Task

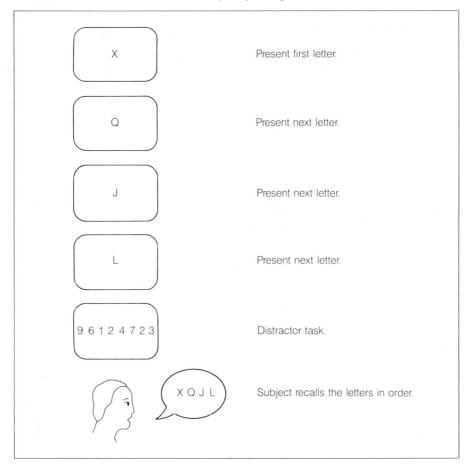

X — Present first letter.

Q — Present next letter.

J — Present next letter.

L — Present next letter.

9 6 1 2 4 7 2 3 — Distractor task.

X Q J L — Subject recalls the letters in order.

active memory is to "chunk" the information. A letter sequence like SPTR could be remembered as a single group—SPuTteR. One explanation of the superior performance of high-verbal subjects is that they make better use of techniques such as grouping. In any case, results indicate that high-verbal subjects are able to hold more verbal information in active memory at once than low-verbal subjects.

Finally, Hunt, Lenneborg, and Lewis (1975) modified Sternberg's (1966, 1975) memory-scanning task in order to measure the time needed to manipulate information in short-term memory. (This task is discussed in Chapter 8). A subject is seated in front of a screen and sees a memory set of one to five letters, presented one at a time. Then a probe letter comes on the screen, and the subject must decide whether that probe letter was one of the letters just presented. Let's consider what the subject

BOX 12–9   Performance of High and Low Verbal Subjects on STM Task

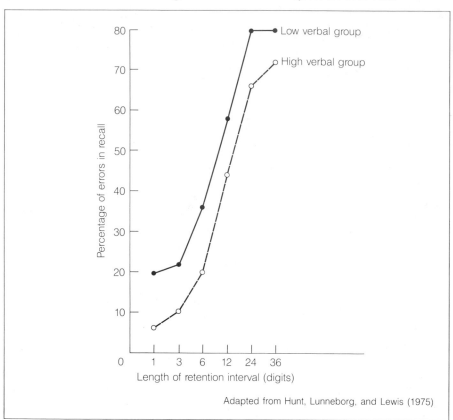

Adapted from Hunt, Lunneborg, and Lewis (1975)

must do when one letter is in the target set: encode one letter, hold that letter in memory, encode the probe letter, compare it to the one letter in memory, decide on a response, and respond. When two letters are in the target set, the subject must encode and store two letters instead of one and make an additional mental comparison. Each time a letter is added to the memory set, the subject must engage in one more mental comparison.

In an earlier study, Hunt, Frost, and Lenneborg (1973) found that adding a letter to the target set tended to add about 60 milliseconds to the response of high-verbal subjects and 80 milliseconds to low-verbal subjects. Thus, it appears that the time to make a mental comparison is less for high-verbal than for low verbal subjects. Again, a simple mental process can be used to describe differences in verbal ability.

Unfortunately, there are several problems with the cognitive correlates approach, including empirical and theoretical issues. First, some of the data have been difficult to replicate. For example, Hunt (1978) notes that it has not been possible to replicate the findings concerning the memory-scanning task and that Sternberg (1975) found no relation between scanning speed and intelligence. As a response to this criticism, note that when more demanding versions of the task are used, large individual differences again emerge. Thus, Hunt (1978) suggests that tasks must allow individuals to give all of their attention to the task.

As another example, Hogaboam and Pellegrino (1978) were unable to find any relation between verbal SAT scores and performance on a task involving making judgments about whether a word (or picture) belonged to a given category. Although this task is similar to the letter matching task used by Hunt, Lenneborg, and Lewis (1975), Hogaboam and Pellegrino were forced to the opposite conclusion: "Verbal ability in our college sample was totally unrelated to the speed of making simple semantic category decisions" (1978, p. 192). However, Hunt (1980) has presented new data showing that differences between high- and low-verbal subjects may be obtained under certain circumstances.

A second major criticism of the cognitive correlates approach is that it emphasizes differences in the speeds of basic mental processes while it should emphasize differences in strategies for manipulating these basic processes. In other words, intelligent behavior requires both being able to apply information processing procedures efficiently *and* deciding which procedures to use, monitoring those procedures, and determining when to change. For example, early work by Galton was aimed at finding simple processes—such as the time needed to respond to a stimulus—that might be related to individual differences in intellectual ability. However, such measures proved useless for later development of intelligence tests. Pellegrino and Glaser (1979, p. 68) fear that cognitive correlates research may lead to "overemphasis on the mechanics of thought and return us to the position of Galton."

More recently, Hunt and his colleagues (MacLeod, Hunt, and Mathews, 1978; Hunt and MacLeod, 1979) have begun to incorporate "strategies" into their approach. For example, they used a sentence-picture verification task (see Chapter 8) in which subjects see a sentence such as "The star is not above the plus" and a picture such as $\overset{*}{+}$. The subject must answer "true" if the sentence and picture are consistent, and "false" if they are not (as is the case in the example cited here). MacLeod, Hunt, and Mathews (1978) found that for one group of subjects— apparently those using verbal encoding strategies—performance differences correlated highly with verbal ability but not with spatial ability. For the other subjects, using visual encoding strategies, differences in response time were correlated highly with spatial ability but not with verbal ability. Thus, as work in the cognitive correlates tradition continues, increased attention is being paid to differences in the general strategies used by subjects.

BOX 12–10   Some Analogy Problems

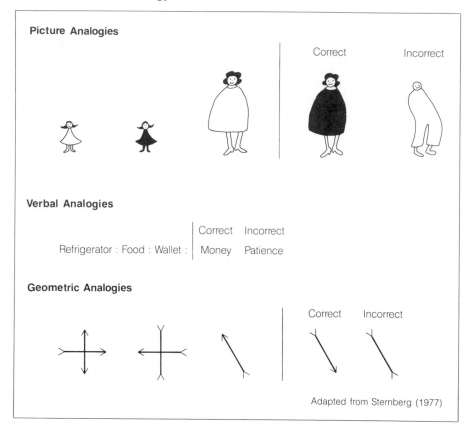

Picture Analogies

Correct   Incorrect

Verbal Analogies

Correct   Incorrect

Refrigerator : Food : Wallet :   Money   Patience

Geometric Analogies

Correct   Incorrect

Adapted from Sternberg (1977)

COGNITIVE COMPONENTS THEORY

The theory of cognitive components provides an alternative way of describing differences in intellectual ability. This theory consists of two basic ideas:

Task analysis—for any given intelligence test item, the task of solving that problem can be broken down into a list of component processes.

Isolation of critical components—the goal of research is to determine which of the component processes are related to individual differences in performance.

The cognitive components approach attempts to answer questions like, "What does an intelligence test measure?" In his book *Intelligence, Information Processing, and Analogical Reasoning*, Robert Sternberg (1977) presented a theory and data

BOX 12–11   Component Process in Analogy Task

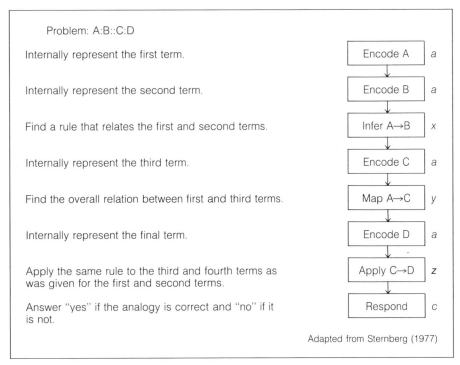

Problem: A:B::C:D

Internally represent the first term.	Encode A	a
Internally represent the second term.	Encode B	a
Find a rule that relates the first and second terms.	Infer A→B	x
Internally represent the third term.	Encode C	a
Find the overall relation between first and third terms.	Map A→C	y
Internally represent the final term.	Encode D	a
Apply the same rule to the third and fourth terms as was given for the first and second terms.	Apply C→D	z
Answer "yes" if the analogy is correct and "no" if it is not.	Respond	c

Adapted from Sternberg (1977)

that launched the cognitive components theory. He used the term "componential theory" to describe his theory; Pellegrino and Glaser (1979) used "cognitive components" in referring to it.

The first step in the cognitive components approach was to choose a problem that is commonly found on IQ tests or other tests of intellectual ability. For example, consider the analogy problems given in Box 12-10. In Sternberg's version of the analogy task, you are given four items in the form "A is to B as C is to D." Your job as a subject is to answer Yes or No; if the rule linking A and B also applies to the relation between C and D the answer is yes, otherwise you answer no. As you can see in Box 12-11, Sternberg used a variety of analogies including pictorial, verbal, and geometrical analogies. Since analogies are often used on IQ tests, understanding individual differences in solving analogies could tell us about individual differences in intelligence.

Once Sternberg selected a problem, such as the analogies in Box 12-11, his next step was to perform a task analysis (see Greeno, 1976; Resnick, 1976; Gagné,

BOX 12–12   Procedure for Analogy Experiments

Situation	Cue Phase	Solution Phase
C-0		A:B::C:D
C-1	A	A:B::C:D
C-2	A:B	A:B::C:D
C-3	A:B::C	A:B::C:D

1968). He determined that an analogy problem can be broken down into the following major components. Consider this analogy: red is to stop as green is to go, or red:stop::green:go.

Encoding (a)—Each of the four stimulus item is translated into an internal representation. For example, "red," "stop," "green," and "go" are represented in memory.

Inference (x)—A rule is found that relates the A term of the analogy to the B term. For example, a red traffic light is a signal to stop.

Mapping (y)—A higher order rule is found that relates the A term with the C term. For example, red and green are colors of traffic signals.

Application (z)—A rule is applied to C in order to generate a final term D. For example, green is the signal for go. If this answer matches the answer given for the D term, the answer regarding the analogy is yes; otherwise, the answer is no.

Preparation-response (c)—This includes all the remaining time that is used in preparing to solve the analogy and carrying out the response.

This task analysis of a verbal analogy problem into component processes is summarized in Box 12-11; it is simpler than Sternberg's actual model.

Sternberg's next major step was to collect data concerning how long it takes people to perform each of the component processes in analogy solving, namely, encoding, inference, mapping, application, and preparation response. He conducted a long series of experiments using a large number of subjects; each subject participated in many sessions. On each trial the subject was asked to look at a screen, then the first part of the problem (called a "cue" phase) was given—such as A:B. When the subject was ready for the rest of the problem, he or she pressed a button, and the entire problem (called the "solution" phase) was given—such as A:B::C:D. If the analogy was correct, the subject pressed a "yes" button and a "no" if the D term was inappropriate. On some trials the cue phase consisted of the first three terms, such as A:B::C, and this was called C-3. The cue phase when it was called C-2 consisted of the first two terms, such as A:B. When only one term was given

BOX 12–13 Response Times for Analogy Experiment

		Components	Response Time (in milliseconds)
Cue Phase	C-0		530
	C-1	1a	755
	C-2	2a, x	952
	C-3	3a, x, y	1147
Solution Phase	C-0	4a, x, y, z, c	1423
	C-1	3a, x, y, z, c	1328
	C-2	2a, y, z, c	947
	C-3	1a, z, c	681

in the cue phase, such as A, this was called C-1. Finally, on some trials, no information was given during the cue phase, and this was called C-0. In all cases, the entire analogy with all four terms was presented in the second half of each trial during the solution phase. This procedure is summarized in Box 12-12.

Sternberg assumed that during the cue phase of each trial, the subject was able to accomplish some of the component processes. For example, for the C-3 situation, the subject could encode three of the four terms, make an inference, and make a mapping. For the C-2 situation, the subject encodes two of the three terms and makes an inference. For C-1, the subject encodes one term. For C-0, nothing happens. Thus, on the solution phase, what is left to be done? For subjects who had three terms in the cue phase, all they have to do during the solution phase is encode one term and make an application as well as a preparation and response. For the C-2 situation, the solution involves encoding two terms, making a mapping, and making an application as well as a preparation and response. For the C-1 situation, a solution uses all of the component processes except one encoding; for C-0, a solution involves every component process. Sternberg assumed that each component is independent and additive; that is, if you carry out a component process during the cuing phase you need not bother with it during the solution phase. These assumptions are summarized in Box 12-13.

Let's assume that each component process takes a certain amount of time. Further, let's assume that solution for the C-0 situations take all the processes involved in C-1 plus one more, and the solution for C-1 situations take all the processes involved in C-2 plus one more, and so on. This is what Sternberg means by his assumption that the components are independent and additive. The average response times for the cuing phase and the solution phase of each situation are given in Box 12-14. As expected, reaction takes longer when more component processes must be carried out: C-3 takes more time than C-0 on the cuing phase, but C-0 takes

BOX 12–14   Estimated Time for Each Component in an Analogy Problem

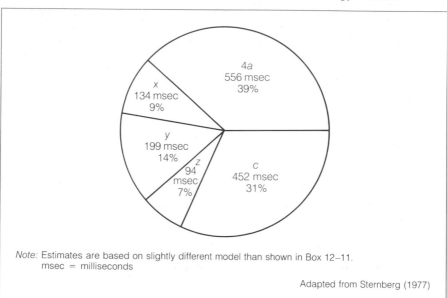

Note: Estimates are based on slightly different model than shown in Box 12–11.
msec = milliseconds

Adapted from Sternberg (1977)

more time than C-3 on solution. By subtracting the time of one situation from another, we can begin to get a rough idea of how long each component process takes. For example, the difference between C-3 and C-2 on the solution phase is that C-3 contains two more component processes—mapping and encoding of one term. Thus, the difference in response time between C-3 and C-2 gives a rough estimation of the time needed to perform a mapping and one encoding.

Using this subtraction method along with statistical regression techniques that we will not describe here, Sternberg was able to find average response latency values for each component. As you can see in Box 12-14, most of the time required to solve a typical pictorial analogy consists of encoding and preparing a response (a and c, respectively).

Finally, the last step in Sternberg's work was to give his subjects standardized tests of intellectual ability, such as tests of reasoning and perceptual speed. A high correlation would indicate if performance on these tests is related to one of the components in the analogy test. You might expect that reasoning ability should be related to inference, mapping, and application. However, as Box 12-15 shows, performance on tests of reasoning was most strongly related to the preparation and response component. Although these results are for pictorial analogies, similar results were obtained for other types of analogies. Thus, Sternberg was able to

BOX 12–15   Correlations Between Component Times and Ability Tests

	Component				
	a	*x*	*y*	*z*	*c*
Reasoning	.32	−.13	−.31	−.19	.71*
Perceptual speed	−.22	−.16	.08	−.19	−.22

*Significant correlation at $p<.01$.

Adapted from Sternberg (1977)

isolate the components that are most strongly related to individual differences in intellectual ability.

Sternberg's componential analysis implies that we will be able to describe intelligence in a new way. Instead of saying, "Intelligence is what an intelligence test measures," the cognitive components approach allows us to say, "Intelligence involves individual differences on component processes X, Y, and Z." The advance of this approach over the psychometric approach is that we are able to give precise definitions of what we mean by component processes X, Y, and Z.

The componential analysis approach of Sternberg has been criticized mainly on two grounds: methodological and theoretical (Pellegrino and Lyon, 1979). First, the method of Sternberg's research has been criticized because very simple analogy tasks were used. These problems were so easy that there were few errors. Subjects seem to be able to use automatic processes on such problems. However, if more complex analogies had been used, there may have been more evidence of individual differences in strategies and decision tactics. This point is important if differences in intelligence are more closely related to differences in how people use strategies than to how well they use automatic procedures.

As a response to this criticism, note that componential analysis has now been applied to a wide range of intellectual tasks. These include linear and syllogistic reasoning, reasoning on spatial tasks, reasoning on series completion tasks, and memory span (see Sternberg, 1979, 1980; Pellegrino and Glaser, 1979). Thus, this criticism is actually a call for expanded research, a call that is sure to be heeded in years to come.

The second criticism is that the theory does not emphasize the role of planning and decision making in problem solvers. For example, there is reason to believe that some subjects use visual encoding and some use verbal encoding in certain tasks (Hunt and McLeod, 1979). Similarly, Campione and Brown (1979) have pointed to the role of "executive control" in intelligence, that is, how people choose which strategy is appropriate.

As a response to this criticism, Sternberg (1979, p. 259) has revised his theory to include *metacomponents:* "Metacomponents supplement components by supplying the decision making and planning that are necessary to carry out their functions. Whereas components solve problems, metacomponents decide how the problems will be solved, and even what problems need to be solved in the first place." Thus, current work on componential, or cognitive component, analysis of intelligence is aimed at locating both the automatic information-processing procedures (the components) and the strategic techniques for managing those components (the metacomponents) that are related to intelligence. One promising new approach concerns teaching component processes or strategies to people (Holtzman, Pellegrino and Glaser, 1976; Campione and Brown, 1979).

EXPERT-NOVICE DIFFERENCES

The previous sections have explored some ways of describing individual differences among people in problem-solving ability. Another way to explore the issue of individual differences in thinking ability is to compare how experts and novices perform on a certain task. What do experts possess that novices lack? Consider the performance of a grand chess master, for example. Such a person is able to remember past board positions from much earlier in the game and is able to see many moves ahead. We might well ask what expert chess players possess that novices lack.

To answer this question, Chase and Simon (1973) found a master chess player, a good chess player, and a beginning chess player. The stimuli for the experiment were two kinds of chess board positions: *actual board positions* from either the middle of a real game (24 to 26 pieces on the board) or the end of an actual game (12 to 15 pieces on the board) and *random board positions* generated by taking a position from a game and then randomly rearranging all of the pieces on the board. In the experiment, each subject saw a board position consisting of a chess board with some chessmen on it for 5 seconds. Then the board was covered. Subjects were given a clear board with a set of the appropriate pieces and were asked to reconstruct what they had just seen.

The results indicated that masters performed very well on reconstructing board positions from actual games, averaging 16 out of 24 for the middle game boards after viewing the board for only 5 seconds. Beginners fared much worse, remembering where to put only about 4 of the pieces. However, for the random board positions, both masters and beginners performed at the same level; about 4 pieces could be correctly placed by each subject. These findings are summarized in Box 12-16.

BOX 12–16 Performance on Reconstruction of Actual and Random Chess Board Positions

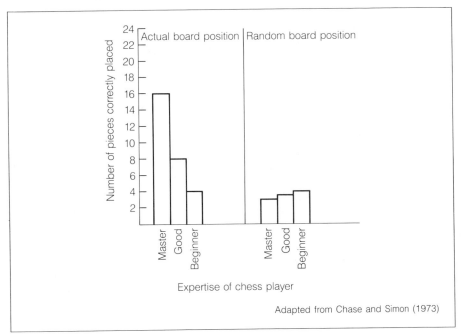

Expertise of chess player

Adapted from Chase and Simon (1973)

This study provides some interesting suggestions concerning differences between expert and novice chess players. Apparently, experts do not have better memory capacities or superior cognitive skills; if so, they would have performed much better on memory for random board positions. What allows them to plan so many moves ahead in a game or to remember board positions from early in the game? Chase and Simon (1973) suggest that experts have a large vocabulary of recognizable configurations of chess pieces, that is, they can see a configuration of many pieces as a single meaningful chunk. Thus, in the experiment, when the expert looks at a board with 24 pieces, he is able to see 3 or 4 major chunks of chessmen, each with a clear meaning. Such a vocabulary is built up over years of practice, playing hundreds of games, and doing little other than playing or thinking about chess. Simon (1980) estimates a master possesses 50,000 chunks. This study suggests that experts have a greater domain of specific knowledge—for example, a large vocabulary of recognizable configurations—rather than some superior memory capacity.

More recently, there has been much study of expert and novice solvers of physics problems (Larkin, McDermott, Simon, and Simon, 1980; Simon and Simon, 1978,

BOX 12–17   A Simple Physics Problem

A bullet leaves the muzzle of a gun at a speed of 400 meters per second. The length of the gun barrel is 0.5 meter. Assuming that the bullet is uniformly accelerated, what is the average speed within the barrel?

speed = 400 meters per second

distance = 0.5 meters

Some Potentially Relevant Formulas:

$v = v_0 + aT$
$\bar{v} = \frac{1}{2}(v_0 + v)$
$S = \bar{v}T$

where S is distance, $\bar{v}$ is average velocity, T is time, v is terminal velocity, v_0 is velocity at origin, a is acceleration.

Adapted from Larkin et al. (1980)

1979; Larkin, 1979a). For example, consider kinematics problems such as those shown in Box 12-17. Kinematics problems like these are often covered in an early chapter of a basic physics book. Larkin et al. (1980) suggest that such a chapter might contain about 11 formulas, expressing relations among such variables as time, distance, average velocity, initial velocity, and acceleration.

Larkin and her colleagues (Larkin et al., 1980; Larkin, 1979, 1980) presented simple physics problems to novices (for example, students who were just beginning in introductory physics) and experts (professors and advanced graduate students). Subjects were asked to "think aloud"; that is, they were asked to tell what was going on in their heads as they solved the problems. Of course, one of the most obvious differences between experts and novices concerned time to solution: novices took about four times longer than the experts to solve the problems. However, a careful analysis of the thinking aloud protocols, or transcript of what subjects said, revealed several interesting differences between experts and novices. The two most important differences between experts and novices concerned the way in which knowledge is organized in memory and the strategies that are used in problem solving.

First, let's look at differences between the way experts and novices seemed to organize knowledge. In solving physics problems, you can express most of the information as equations. For example, suppose that you are given a problem in which you must find the value for C; the values for A, X, Y, and K are given. Novices act as if they have knowledge in small units such as $C = A + B$, $B = K \div L$, $L = X \times Y$. To solve for C they must substitute one equation into another and so on. However, experts seem to have the solution procedure available as one large equation, such as $C = A + K \div (X \times Y)$. Larkin (1979) calls this "a large functional unit." Thus, while novices have to go step by step with a lot of checking, experts are able to solve all at once using a more automatic procedure.

Second, let's consider differences in the solution strategies used by experts and novices in solving physics problems. Larkin et al. (1980) note that novices tend to work backward from the unknown to the givens. For example, if they want to find the value of C, they try to solve the equation in which C is the dependent variable, $C = A + B$. If they cannot solve that equation because they don't know the value for one of the variables (in this case, B), they then set up a goal of finding the value of B, through such an equation as $B = K \div L$. Since L is not known they must set a goal of finding L through the equation $L = X \times Y$. This generates a value for L, which can be used to find the value of B, and this can be used to find the value of C. Experts, on the other hand work forward from the givens to the goal. For example, they fill the values of A, K, X and Y into the equation $C = A + K \div (X \times Y)$; this generates the value of the unknown, C. Thus, experts begin by noticing what kind of problem is being asked and then finding the solution equation to solve it. Novices use a much more gradual process of continuously setting goals and then seeing if they know an equation that will generate the answer they want. These differences are summarized in Box 12-18.

As a way of validating these observations, Larkin et al. (1980) produced computer programs that simulate the problem-solving performance of experts versus novices. The expert program works forward and uses large-scale functional units, while the novice program works backward and uses smaller units of knowledge. The main output of the programs is the order in which equations are used; the expert program seems to follow the order used by human experts and the novice program seems to follow the order used by novices. This is one independent validation of the differences in knowledge organization and strategies used by experts and novices.

EVALUATION

The two disciplines of scientific psychology—the psychometric approach and the experimental psychology approach—seem to be moving together again at last. The psychometric approach has succeeded in measuring individual differences, but has failed in interpreting processes and structures that underlie those differences. The experimental psychology approach has succeeded in describing the general processes and structures in humans, but has failed to deal adequately with individual

BOX 12–18   Differences Between Experts and Novices in Physics Problem Solving

Problem

The problem gives values for four variables, A, K, X, and Y. The problem asks you to find the value of one variable, C. (Based on your knowledge of physics, let's assume the following equations are relevant: $C = A + B$, $B = K/L$, $L = X*Y$.)

Novices	Experts
Knowledge is in small units	Knowledge is in large units

$$C = A + B$$
$$B = K/L$$
$$L = X*Y$$

$$C = A + K/(X*Y)$$

Solve by working backward	Solve by working forward

In order to find C, I must use the formula $C = A + B$.
I know the value for A but I must find the value for B.
To find the B, I must use the formula $B = K/L$.
I know the value of K, but I must find the value of L.
In order to find L, I must use the formula $L = X*Y$.
I know X and Y so now I find L.
Since I know L and K, I can now solve the equation for B.
Since I know B and A, I can now solve the first equation for C.

I recognize that this is a problem that requires the solution formula:
$C = A + K/(X*Y)$.
I plug in the values of A, K, X, and Y. Then, I can compute the value for C.

---

differences. Yet, this chapter has pointed to several new techniques that promise to join the study of individual differences with the study of internal cognitive characteristics.

Although the cognitive correlates approach, the cognitive components approach, and the expert-novice approach are all quite new, they each have already contributed to our understanding of mental ability. In this chapter, we have pointed to the problems of each approach as well as its major findings to date. A common theme of all three approaches is that differences between good performers and poor performers may someday be categorized in terms of differences in specific knowledge, automatic processes, and general strategies. Of particular interest is the emerging idea that a good portion of observed differences may be due to differences in learned strategies for controlling the problem-solving process. Such findings are exciting because they imply that areas of intelligent behavior may be teachable. This issue is dealt with directly in Chapter 13.

Suggested Readings

Resnick, L. B. *The nature of intelligence.* Hillsdale, N.J.: Erlbaum, 1976. Contains many useful papers describing how cognitive psychologists study individual differences in intellectual abilities.

Sternberg, R. J. *Intelligence, information processing, and analogical reasoning.* Hillsdale, N.J.: Erlbaum, 1977. Provides an excellent historical review and summarizes a research project on the analysis of intelligence.

CHAPTER 13

CREATIVITY TRAINING: Thinking as a Learnable Skill

Creativity

The 1930s and 1940s: Creativity Training in Industry

The 1950s: Remediation of Problem Solving in College Students

The 1960s: Teaching Productive Thinking to School Children

The 1970s: Specific Training in Strategies

The 1980s: Specific Knowledge Versus General Skills

Suppose you read the following advertisement from the Eastside Mind Builders Club:

> Tired of having a puny mind? Do you have trouble solving simple problems at home, at work, or at school? We have the solution for you! Take our simple 10 week mind-building course. We have a series of simple mind-building exercises planned just for you. We guarantee that when you finish our course you will have trimmed hours off the time it takes you to solve problems, and you will have added valuable points to your IQ and SAT scores. Call 961-2472 for your first exercise appointment.

Certainly, this advertisement is offered as a joke. However, there are numerous commercial programs that seriously offer to increase your scores in tests like the SAT or various graduate school examinations, to increase your problem-solving effectiveness as a business executive, or to increase your ability to get good grades in school. Are such programs really helpful? Would you actually "get smarter" by taking such courses? If so, how do they work?

These questions are addressed in this chapter. In particular, we will explore the various approaches to creativity training that have been developed since the first such course was introduced in the 1930s.

How much do you think you could increase your IQ score through 10 to 20 hours of practice on typical test problems? Take a minute to write down the thinking skills that *you* think would be useful to teach. Then, see if your list corresponds to the various techniques presented in this chapter.

CREATIVITY

Definition

If we want to teach people to be creative problem solvers we must first define what we mean by "creativity." For purposes of this chapter, let's define *creativity* as a cognitive activity that results in novel solutions for a problem. Thus, creativity training involves teaching people how to generate new ideas for a given situation.

Measurement

Guilford (1959, 1967) viewed aptitude for creative thinking as a trait that is related to several factors:

Fluency—the ability to generate many solutions that all fit some requirement such as listing all the synonyms for a certain word.

Flexibility—the ability to change approaches to a problem such as being able to solve a series of tasks that each require a different strategy.

Originality—the ability to generate unusual solutions such as coming up with unique answers.

In describing basic mental traits, Guilford made a distinction between two types of thinking:

Convergent thinking—thinking that proceeds toward a single answer, such as "$33 \times 14 = \underline{\hspace{1cm}}$."

Divergent thinking—thinking that moves outward from the problem in many possible directions such as "list all the uses for a brick."

Guilford noticed that most of the factors that made up creative problem solving seemed most closely related to *divergent thinking*. Since there are many standard

BOX 13–1   Some Creativity Problems

Problem 1

List all of the questions you can think of concerning the figure shown below. Ask all of the questions you need to know for sure what is happening. Do not ask questions that can be answered just by looking at the drawing. (Give yourself three minutes to list your questions.)

Problem 2

Suppose that all humans were born with six fingers on each hand instead of five. List all the consequences or implications that you can think of. (Give yourself three minutes.)

Adapted from Torrance (1978). Figure from Examples and rationales of test tasks for assessing creative abilities by E. P. Torrance, *Journal of Creative Behavior*, 1968, Volume 2, No. 3, published by The Creative Education Foundation, Buffalo, New York.

tests of divergent thinking, it is convenient for psychologists to equate creativity with divergent thinking. Thus, to measure creativity, one need only administer several divergent-thinking tests.

Box 13-1 presents two standard tests of divergent thinking. In each test, subjects are given a problem and are asked to generate as many solutions as they can to the problem, within a limited amount of time. Notice that in divergent thinking the goal is to produce many possible answers rather than logically deduce the single solution.

To measure how well you did in divergent thinking, we need to examine several characteristics of your answer. First, the *quantity* of your answers can be measured by counting how many different answers you came up with. Second, the *originality* of your answers can be measured by seeing how many other people gave the same answer or by getting judges to rate each of your answers for originality. Third, the *importance* (or usefulness) of your answers can be measured by seeing whether they work or by asking judges to rate how effective each answer is.

For example, suppose your answers for the problem about six fingers were: (1) We would need to make gloves with six fingers, (2) we would need to redesign handgrips on bicycle handlebars, (3) we would be able to invent new obscene gestures, (4) we would be able to give a new secret handshake, (5) we would say "Give me six" instead of "Give me five," and (6) we would use a base 12 number system instead of base 10. To measure the quantity, we can just count the six answers. With respect to originality, we can see that when we give this test to many individuals, answer 1 is given by almost all of them. Thus, it is low in originality. However, if answer 4 is given by only a few people, it is high in originality. Finally, if judges rate each answer for importance, answer 6 might receive a high rating while answer 3 receives a lower one. Any training in divergent thinking may focus on quantity, originality, or the importance of answers.

Creativity and IQ

What is the relationship between creativity and intelligence? Can someone be intelligent but not be creative? Can someone be creative without being intelligent? To help answer these questions, Getzels and Jackson (1963) gave tests of intelligence and creativity to secondary school students. To measure intelligence, they used a standard IQ test. To measure creativity, they used the following five tests suggested by Guilford's work:

Word association—Give as many definitions as possible to a common word such as "bark," "bolt," or "sack." The score was based on the number of definitions and number of different categories of definitions.

Uses test—Give as many uses as possible for such common objects as a brick or paper clip. The score was based on the number of uses and the originality of each answer.

Hidden shapes—Find a given geometric shape that was hidden in a more complex pattern.

Fables test—Compose different endings for an unfinished fable, including a moralistic, humorous, and sad ending. The score was based on appropriateness and originality of the endings.

Make-up problems—Make up algebra story problems using a base of information provided by the experimenter. The score was based on the number, appropriateness, and complexity of the problems.

As you can see, each creativity test involved generating many solutions to a given situation within a given amount of time; in other words, these tests were tests of divergent thinking.

Out of a sample of 449 students, Getzels and Jackson were able to find some students who scored very high in IQ but not in creativity, and some students who scored very high in creativity but not in intelligence. As you might expect, there were small correlations (r) between IQ score and scores on the creativity tests $(r = .12$ to $r = .39)$, but the relation was by no means perfect. Similarly, in a study of 989 New York high school students, Anastasi and Schaefer (1971) found low correlations between tests of creativity and IQ $(r = .10$ to $r = .27)$.

Getzels and Jackson observed that both the high creative and the high IQ group performed very well in school, but the teachers preferred the students in the high IQ group. The high IQ students tended to gauge success by conventional standards, to behave as teachers expected them to, and to seek careers that conform to what others expect of them. The high creative students used unconventional standards for determining success; their behavior and career choices did not conform to people's expectations. You can get some idea of the differences between the high IQ and high creative students by examining the answers shown in Box 13-2. Getzels and Jackson conclude that most educational training favors logical or convergent thinking and does not nurture creative (or divergent) thinking. The remainder of this chapter explores some techniques that are purported to enhance creativity.

THE 1930s AND 1940s: CREATIVITY TRAINING IN INDUSTRY

The first structured courses in creative thinking and problem solving appeared in the 1930s and 1940s. As Davis (1973) points out, these courses were aimed mainly at improving the creativity of engineers, managers, product designers, and other members of industry. For example, Crawford (1954) is credited with initiating the first creativity training course in 1931, aimed at increasing the creativity of professionals. In order for you to get a better idea of how the creativity training began, let's briefly explore three major industry-oriented programs: Crawford's "attribute listing," Osborn's "brainstorming," and Gordon's "synectics."

One of the major ideas in Crawford's original 1931 course, and in his revised courses, is the use of "attribute listing." This procedure involves listing the critical attributes of a product and then listing some modifications that may be made to each attribute or suggesting the transfer of attributes of one object onto another. For example, Davis (1973) suggests the following problem: "What can be done to improve an ordinary piece of classroom chalk?" First, you should list the important attributes of the object, such as its shape, size, color, hardness, and so on. Next, consider how you could modify the attributes, such as using colors other than white, or extra large-sized chalk. You should also consider importing other attributes such as including a device to hold the chalk similar to a cigarette holder. In *Techniques of Creative Thinking* (1954, p. 96), Crawford summarizes his approach as follows:

BOX 13–2   Creative and Noncreative Answers to a Picture Interpretation Problem

---

Problem

Write a short description of a picture. The picture shows a man sitting in an airplane's reclining seat as if he was returning from a business trip.

Answer from High IQ Student

Mr. Smith is on his way home from a successful business trip. He is very happy and he is thinking about his wonderful family and how glad he will be to see them again. He can picture it, about an hour from now, his plane landing at the airport and Mrs. Smith and their three children all there welcoming him home again.

Answer from High Creative Student

This man is flying back from Reno where he just won a divorce from his wife. He couldn't stand to live with her anymore, he told the judge, because she wore so much cold cream on her face at night and her head would skid across the pillow and hit him in the head. He is now contemplating a new skid-proof face cream.

Adapted from Getzels and Jackson (1969)

"Each time we take a step, we do it by changing an attribute or a quality of something, or else by applying that same quality or attribute to some other thing." Following Crawford's lead, several other training programs have emphasized "idea checklists." For example, Osborn (1963) has a list of 73 "idea spurring questions" such as "What to add?" or "How about a blend?" or "New ways to use it as is?"

Osborn is credited with popularizing the use of brainstorming techniques, beginning in the 1940s. According to Osborn's *Applied Imagination* (1963), "brainstorming" involves group problem solving, in which the following four rules are followed:

1. *No criticism.* Participants are instructed to obey the "principle of deferred judgment," that is, to postpone all critical comments until after the initial brainstorming session.

2. *Quantity is wanted.* Participants are instructed to generate as many ideas as they can, without regard to the quality of the ideas.

3. *Originality is wanted.* Participants are encouraged to generate wild and unusual ideas, rather than trying to be practical.

4. *Combination and improvement are wanted.* Participants are encouraged to build on the previous suggestions given during the session.

Thus, in brainstorming, the goal is to generate as many unusual ideas as possible without criticizing any ideas. Osborn claims: "You can think up almost twice as many good ideas in the same length of time if you defer judgment" (Vervalin, 1978, p. 82). Brainstorming techniques can also be used by an individual in solving problems.

Gordon (1961) has suggested a program based on "synectics"—the joining together of apparently unrelated elements. In his book *Synectics* (1961), the main goal is to teach people to make use of analogies in problem solving. For example, Gordon describes a group session in which the problem is to design a new roof that would turn white in summer to reflect heat and black in winter to absorb heat. Can you think of an analogy in nature? In Gordon's group, they hit upon the idea that the flounder can change colors to match its surroundings as it swims near the ocean bottom. This is accomplished by chromatophores, tiny sacks of black pigment, that contract to push to the skin surface or relax to retract. After some discussion of this biological device, the group designed an all-black roof that was impregnated with little white plastic balls. These balls expand when the roof is hot, thus making it lighter, and contract when the roof is cold, thus making it darker.

Edwards (1968) reported on creativity training programs at dozens of American corporations, consulting firms, and colleges. Several companies claim that training courses have saved money, increased development of new products, and increased profit. The oldest course has been taught at the State University of New York at Buffalo since 1949. Edwards' survey suggests that creativity programs are definitely a part of many industrial training efforts.

As you can see from this brief description, there is a substantial history of creativity training programs, beginning in industry in the 1930s and 1940s. However, much of this work has been ignored by researchers in the field of problem solving. As Davis and Scott (1978, p. ix) recently pointed out: "Although representatives of the business world have drawn freely from creativity research and theory in psychology, this line of communication has been astonishingly one-way." In fact, it would be useful for us to know whether such creativity programs really work; if they do work, it would be useful to study how they work.

Unfortunately, the grand claims concerning the effectiveness of industrial creativity courses have not always been substantiated by controlled research. For example, Bouchard (1971) notes that the brainstorming technique that began in the 1930s was a "firmly entrenched idea" by the 1950s. However, the attractiveness of the techniques was greatly diminished by a study in which four people working separately generated more unique ideas than four people working as a group (Taylor, Berry, and Block, 1958). As Bouchard points out, there were many replications of this finding. In addition, several studies of brainstorming sessions showed that instructions to generate unusual ideas are less productive than instructions to generate practical ideas (Weisskopf-Joelson and Eliseo, 1961) or that deferred judgment instructions are not effective (Dunnette, Campbell, and Jaastad, 1963). In summary, much careful research is needed before we can know whether creativity programs work, and more importantly, why they work.

THE 1950s: REMEDIATION OF PROBLEM SOLVING IN COLLEGE STUDENTS

The first major effort to improve the problem-solving performance of college students was carried out at the University of Chicago by Bloom and Broder (1950). To obtain the bachelor's degree, students had to pass a series of comprehensive examinations in various subjects. Students could take the exams whenever they felt they were ready; each exam consisted of a wide variety of problems covering the subject. As you might suppose, some students performed quite well on the exams while others were unable to pass in spite of their high scholastic ability and conscientious study.

Bloom and Broder selected a group of "remedial" students, that is, those who performed poorly on the comprehensive exams. The researchers were careful to select remedial students who scored high in scholastic aptitude (such as is measured by the SAT), who claimed to study hard, and who asserted that the exam did not reflect what they knew. Thus, the remedial students seemed to have the ability, motivation, and knowledge to do well in solving test problems, but for some reason they performed quite poorly. In addition, Bloom and Broder selected a group of "model" students, those who had the same general scholastic ability as the remedial students but who had scored high in solving examination problems.

How could Bloom and Broder boost the problem-solving performance of remedial students? To answer this question, they addressed two issues: what to teach and how to teach. In determining what to teach, Bloom and Broder were forced to make the following distinction:

> *Products of problem solving* —whether the student arrives at the correct final answer or not.
>
> *Process of problem solving* —the strategy that people use on their way to getting the answer.

Bloom and Broder argued that previous research had placed too much emphasis on the products of problem solving, instead of emphasizing the processes involved in creative problem solving. Two people might come up with the same answer and use entirely different approaches to get them. For example, Box 13-3 shows a typical problem and the answers given by three students. The students generated the same product in that the final answers are the same, but their descriptions of process are

BOX 13–3 How Three Students Solved the Inflation Problem

Problem

Some economists feel that there is danger of an extreme inflationary boom after the war. It is the opinion of such economists that the government should control the boom in order to prevent a depression such as the one following the stockmarket crash of 1929.

Below are a number of specific suggestions. For each of the following items, *blacken*

>   answer space 1—if it would be *consistent* with the policy of controlling the boom;
>   answer space 2—if it is directly *inconsistent* with the policy.

26. Lower the reserve that banks are required to hold against deposits

27. Reduce taxes considerably

28. Encourage the federal reserve banks to buy securities in the open market

Mary's Answer

>   Mary W. (Score 2): (Read the statements and the directions.)
>   (Read item 26.) "Look down to see what I'm supposed to do.
>   (Re-read the statements and the directions.) "Not quite sure what I'm doing so re-read for the third time. (Re-read the statements and the directions.)
>   (Re-read item 26.) "Not sure of this, so on to second one.
>   (Read item 27.) "Say inconsistent, because if there is inflationary boom, if people make more money, taxes have to keep up with it to take away the money so they can't spend it.
>   (Read item 28.) "Try to figure out what bearing that had exactly.
>   (Re-read item 26.) "I'm a time waster, say 26 would be consistent—no, that I know, banks have reserve—idea is to get people to deposit as much as possible—not answer 28.
>   (Re-read item 28.) "Say inconsistent, I feel it is."

Diagnosis: unsystematic, jumps around, uses "feelings" rather than "reasoning," not
       confident.

quite different. Thus, Bloom and Broder decided that instruction in problem solving should not focus on reinforcing students for getting the right final answers but rather on teaching the problem-solving strategies that are useful in generating answers. They asserted that the "habits of problem solving, like other habits, could be altered by appropriate training and practice" (1950, p. 67).

The second problem facing Bloom and Broder was to develop techniques for teaching the process of problem solving. To find out which strategies were used by successful problem solvers, they asked their model students to solve some typical exam problems by thinking aloud in a session. In such a session, students are asked to describe what is going on in their minds as they approach a problem and work through it. The comparison of the thinking aloud procedures of model solvers with the procedures used by remedial students showed important differences. Thus, as a

James' Answer

James S. (Score 2): (Read the statements.) "In other words, the OPA and such. (Read the directions.) "Taken for granted they're going to control the boom. (Read item 26. Re-read item 26.) "That would be inconsistent.

(Read item 27.) "That would be inconsistent, because you can't have too great a boom as long as you have taxes, at least in my interpretation of boom—although if taxes go up, prices go up—no, I'll stick to my answer.

(Read item 28.) "Consistent—however, I think I need more subject-matter back-ground to tell how I thought it out—more of a guess—don't think inconsistent, so put consistent."

Diagnosis: translates problem into something more familiar (OPA), lacks subject-
matter knowledge, guesses.

Dora's Answer

Dora Z. (Score 2): (Read the statement and the directions—emphasizing the key words.)

(Read item 26.) "Lower the reserve, raise the amount of money in circulation—if you raise the money in circulation—inconsistent. By raising the money in circulation you don't control a boom.

(Read item 27.) "Also inconsistent for the same reason.

(Read item 28.) "Open market—think what the open market is. Think would take money out of circulation, therefore would be consistent."

Diagnosis: focused on key ideas, reduced three items to a single problem, attempted
to determine how money supply is affected by each item, attacks problem
on basis of single role on principle, higher-order problem solving.

From Bloom and Broder (1950). Copyright 1950 by The University of Chicago Press.

method of instruction, Bloom and Broder decided to teach remedial students to imitate and make use of the processes used by model students.

In a typical experiment, for example, remedial students were asked to solve a problem like the one in Box 13-3, using a thinking aloud technique. Then, the students were given a transcript of the procedure that a model student had used for the same problem. Each remedial student was asked to list in his or her own words all of the strategies used by the model student that the remedial student had not used; the experimenter helped to stimulate discussion. The remedial students were then given another problem so that the new techniques could be practiced. The procedure was repeated for new problems. Box 13-4 shows the differences that students found between how they answered questions and how the model student answered them. After 10 to 12 training sessions in which they continuously compared their problem-

BOX 13–4   Student's Lists of Differences Between Model and Self

Jean's List

1. I didn't think it necessary to formulate the general rule.
   Generalization too broad.
   Verbalization reversed actually.
2. Lack of understanding of given terms.
   Define and illustrate as alternatives.
   I looked for "true" and "false"—others looked for "best." Didn't interpret directions properly.
   I looked for answer—didn't have an answer before I looked. Higher degree of inaccuracy. (I get this O.K. with syllogisms.)
3. He associated and brought in intermediary event with dates. I did the same with the second part, but didn't know country.
4. He employed an illustration for proof.
   Should set up criteria for an answer; if not enough, set up illustrations and examples.
5. Didn't get essential terms of what I was looking for before I began reading alternatives.
   Jumped to conclusion without carrying illustrative reasoning through.
   Did read terms thoroughly but didn't keep them in mind; reversed them.
6. Didn't define terms of statements. Got it right through outside example.
7. Should pull out main words. Got it right, though.
8. Didn't establish relations between terms. Got it right, though.
   Careless about selecting right alternative.
   Keeping directions in mind. I think in terms of "true" and "false" instead of "scientific study," etc.

Ralph's List

1. Find a rule or formula that applies to problem under consideration.
2. Apply rule and formulate answer, then check with offered answers.
3. Progress into problem by formula which has been generalized through application.
4. Rules should deal with specific problem.
5. Try to read directions clearly the first time.
6. Do not answer by guessing or supposition.
7. Think before the formulation of answer.
8. Direct thought in stream which has been pointed in the direction of the problem at hand.
9. Emphasis on the major ideas in the problem, not all ideas.
10. Box off ideas into main question in the problem.
11. Reason from known knowledge or examples.
12. In graphs formulate a specific picture.

From Bloom and Broder (1950). Copyright 1950 by The University of Chicago Press.

solving strategies to those of model students on specific problems, the remedial students were ready to take their exams. Later experiments used groups of remedial and model students, but the same general methods were employed.

The results of the study are encouraging. Students who participated in the training tended to score an average of .49 to .68 grade points higher on the exam that matched groups who did not take the training. In addition, students who took the training expressed high levels of confidence and optimism concerning their newly acquired problem-solving abilities. However, Bloom and Broder caution that it would be wrong to conclude that general problem-solving strategies can be taught. Rather, they conclude: "It became clear that some specific information was necessary for the solution of the examination problems and that a certain amount of background in the subject was indispensable. It became apparent that methods of problem solving, by themselves, could not serve as a substitute for the basic knowledge of the subject matter" (1950, pp. 76–77). Thus, Bloom and Broder's major contributions are the emphasis on process rather than product, the refinement of "thinking aloud" techniques, and the finding that both specific knowledge and general strategies are needed to be a successful problem solver in a given domain.

THE 1960s: TEACHING PRODUCTIVE THINKING TO SCHOOL CHILDREN

While the 1950s were highlighted by modest studies such as Bloom and Broder's project, there was a dramatic increase in the size and number of such projects in the 1960s, a decade marked by innovation and experimentation in American education. Numerous programs were designed to teach problem-solving skills in classrooms across the nation. Some of the best known projects:

Productive-Thinking Program was aimed at increasing the general problem-solving skills of fifth- and sixth-graders through practice in solving mystery and detective stories (Covington, Crutchfield, and Davies, 1966; Covington, Crutchfield, Davies, and Olton, 1974).

Inquiry Training was designed to teach problem solving in science by asking students to react to a filmed or live demonstration (Suchman, 1960, 1966, 1969).

Thinking Creatively was a workbook taking the form of a humorous discussion among several cartoon characters (Davis and Houtman, 1968).

Myers-Torrance Idea Books consisted of workbooks for elementary children and involved practice in solving creativity problems (Myers and Torrance, 1964).

Purdue Creativity Program (Feldhusen, Treffinger, and Bahlke, 1970) was a set of tape-recorded programs with printed exercises designed to foster divergent thinking in fourth-graders.

Parnes Program was based on Osborn's (1963) brainstorming techniques (Parnes, 1967).

BOX 13–5   Excerpt from the Productive-Thinking Program

The TV Announcer: "Following the robbery, things moved quickly. The captain of the boat called the Elmtown police. When the boat docked in Elmtown, the police were already on guard there. No one was allowed on or off the boat except the police and our reporter and TV cameraman.

"Here is the police chief on the boat, telling our reporter what has happened so far:"

Let's take a closer look at the productive-thinking program, since it has been the most studied project. Like Bloom and Broder's program, the productive-thinking program focuses on teaching problem-solving processes and uses imitation of models as a technique for teaching. But unlike Bloom and Broder's project, the productive-thinking program is a self-paced and self-administered set of booklets rather than interpersonal dialogues. It is aimed at elementary school children rather than college students, and it emphasizes different detective problems rather than examination problems.

The productive-thinking program consists of 15 cartoonlike booklets, each about 30 pages in length. Each booklet presents a single mystery or detective story for the child to solve. The stories involve two children, Jim and Lila, as well as Jim's Uncle John and Mr. Search. Each story presents a series of clues or facts, and the student

Before Lila tells her idea, what thoughts do you have about other possible suspects? Use your Reply Notebook to write down all the ideas you can think of.

What persons besides Louie might be the thief?

There are several people besides Louie who might have stolen the money. You may have thought of the steward who called Mr. Burk to the phone, or perhaps you even considered the riverboat captain.
Lila has another possible suspect in mind.   *(continued)*

is required to answer questions aimed at "restating the problem in his own words," "formulating his own questions," and "generating ideas to explain the mystery" (Covington and Crutchfield, 1965, p. 3). After the student has generated some answers or ideas, Jim or Lila give theirs. Thus, Jim and Lila act as models to be emulated. Like all realistic models, they make some mistakes at first, but they eventually learn to solve the caper. The adults in the story provide hints, point out positive and negative features of Jim and Lila's strategies, and try to maintain high levels of enjoyment. Thus, as students read the booklets, they become engaged in solving a case, and feedback is presented to them regularly.

Box 13-5 gives a few pages from one of the first lessons in the program, "The Riverboat Robbery." As you read the lesson you are given some information and asked to make a response. Then, you get feedback by seeing how Jim and Lila

BOX 13–5, *continued*

Uncle John is right. You can always think of more ideas. And you should never be afraid to talk about your ideas.

From Covington, Crutchfield, Davies, and Olton (1974)

respond. Finally, Uncle John provides guidance and analysis of Jim and Lila's strategies. (If you read the entire booklet carefully, you will discover that the culprit was Mr. Larkin—the bank manager.)

Each lesson is designed to teach several basic problem-solving strategies, which are listed in Box 13-6. For example, "The Riverboat Robbery" attempts to teach strategies 4, 5, 6, 9, 11, and 15.

Is the productive-thinking program effective in improving the problem-solving skills of school children? This question has been addressed in over a dozen studies, involving hundreds of students (Mansfield, Busse, and Krepelka, 1978). For example, in an early study by Olton and Crutchfield (1969), one class of 25 fifth-graders was given intensive training in productive-thinking, while no such training was given to another class of fifth-graders matched for IQ, age, and achievement. All students took the same battery of pretests (given before the program), the same posttests (given immediately after the training program), and the same follow-up

BOX 13-6   Some Problem-Solving Skills Taught in the Productive-Thinking Program

1. Take time to reflect on a problem before you begin to work. Decide exactly what the problem is that you are trying to solve.
2. Get all the facts of the problem clearly in mind.
3. Work on the problem in a planful way.
4. Keep an open mind. Don't jump to conclusions about the answer to a problem.
5. Think of many new ideas for solving a problem. Don't stop with just a few.
6. Try to think of unusual ideas.
7. As a way of getting ideas, pick out all the important objects and persons in the problem and think carefully about each one.
8. Think of several general possibilities for a solution and then figure out many particular ideas for each possibility.
9. As you search for ideas, let your mind freely explore things around you. Almost anything can suggest ideas for a solution.
10. Always check each idea with the facts to decide how likely the idea is.
11. If you get stuck on a problem, keep trying. Don't be discouraged.
12. When you run out of ideas, try looking at the problem in a new and different way.
13. Go back and review all the facts of the problem to make sure you have not missed something important.
14. Start with an unlikely idea. Just suppose that it is possible, and figure out how it could be.
15. Be on the lookout for odd or puzzling facts in a problem. Explaining them can lead you to news ideas for solution.
16. When there are several puzzling things in a problem, try to explain them with a single idea that will connect them all together.

Adapted from Covington, Crutchfield, Davies, and Olton (1974)

tests (given six months later). Box 13-7 presents a typical test, and Box 13-8 summarizes some of the tests that were given to the students. Many of the test problems resemble the mystery and detective stories in the instructional booklets.

The results seem to demonstrate the effectiveness of the program. As expected, there were no differences between the two groups on solving problems in the pretest, thus indicating that both groups began with the same level of problem-solving ability. However, the trained group scored significantly better than the untrained group on the posttest (55 percent versus 37 percent correct) and on the follow-up test (57 percent versus 34 percent correct).

In interpreting these results, however, you should keep three things in mind. First, this was an evaluation study aimed mainly at evaluating the effectiveness of an instructional program; it was not a theoretical study aimed at telling us *why* or *how* the training works. Second, since the tests covered problems that were similar to the mystery story format of the instructional lessons, there is no evidence that the

BOX 13–7   The Poverty Problem: A Test Used To Measure the Effectiveness
of the Productive-Thinking Program

A problem of poverty in a land of plenty:

When Americans travel abroad, they are sometimes asked how can it be that the United States, the richest nation in the world, is faced with such a great problem of poverty among many of its people.

Some people in other nations say they are puzzled by the fact that in spite of the great wealth of our nation, many of our cities have great slum areas, many of our people are dependent for their support on relief and welfare funds, and many of our people do not share in the American dream of enjoying a high standard of living.

Now, suppose that you and your family are visiting a foreign country this summer. Some children your age in that country ask you about why the United States is faced with such a problem of poverty. What would you say?

Take time to think about this; then write below what you would say to them about this puzzling problem of poverty in a land of plenty. (There are several additional blank pages attached to this page, so you may write as much as you wish.)

From Olton and Crutchfield (1969)

training will transfer to novel, actual situations. Third, as in any evaluation study, you should question whether there are other possible explanations for the results; these include the possibility that subjects in the training group tried harder because they knew they were supposed to do better, that the teacher in the experimental group was so enthusiastic about the project that the students were motivated, or that students were simply learning what the teacher meant by certain questions. (A good creative problem-solving task would be to list all the possible criticisms of this study.)

Finally, you should ask whether other evaluation studies provide support as strongly as this study. In studies that use larger samples and stronger methodological controls, the effects are sometimes much weaker. In small studies, where teachers and students can be carefully selected and trained, and where everyone knows they are participating in a special project, it is easier to get strong results. In a careful review of 12 studies, Mansfield, Busse, and Krepelka (1978, p. 522) concluded that in many cases there is evidence that the productive-thinking program improves performance on problems like those in the lessons; however, "it is unclear whether the effects of training are sufficiently generalizable to be useful in real-life problem-solving situations."

In addition, most of the other widely adopted programs seem to enhance performance mainly on the kinds of problems that each teaches how to solve (Mansfield, Busse, and Krepelka, 1978). Thus, Mansfield and his associates have summarized such studies by noting that "most evaluation studies of creativity-training programs seem to support the view that creativity can be trained," but

BOX 13–8   Selected Tests Given To Study the Effectiveness of the Productive-Thinking Program

Pretests

Controlling the weather   Student thinks of various consequences of man's future ability to change the weather.

Project for a village   Student puts himself in the shoes of a Peace Corps volunteer who must first acquaint himself with the customs and mores of a tribal village. Then, without offending such customs, he must figure out ways the inhabitants can earn money for their village needs.

Posttests

Transplanting organs   Student thinks of various consequences of man's future medical ability to transplant bodily organs from one person to another.

"Black House" problem   Student attempts to solve a puzzling mystery problem in which he must make an insightful reorganization of the elements of the problem.

Follow-Up Tests

The missing jewel problem   Student attempts to solve a puzzling mystery problem in which he must make an insightful reorganization of the elements of the problem.

The nameless tomb   Student works on a hypothetical problem in archeology in which he must discover which of 10 possible suspects is buried in a nameless ancient tomb.

From Olton and Crutchfield (1969), from *Trends and issues in developmental psychology*, edited by Paul Mussen, Jonas Langer, and Martin Covington. Copyright © 1969 by Holt, Rinehart and Winston, Inc. Reprinted by permission of Holt, Rinehart and Winston, CBS College Publishing, a division of CBS, Inc.

"there is only limited and inconsistent evidence of transfer to dissimilar problems" (1978, p. 531).

Torrance (1972) reviewed 142 studies on the effectiveness of various creativity-training programs. Of the packaged programs such as those listed at the beginning of this section, some improvement in creativity was found in 38 out of 47 studies. However, as Torrance points out, the programs tended to work well only when a teacher was heavily involved; furthermore, most of the studies used test problems such as those shown in Box 13-1 from the Torrance Tests of Creative Thinking (Torrance, 1966). Thus, there was no strong evidence concerning whether courses enhanced creativity in solving real problems.

Such equivocal results, however, do not seem to eliminate the interest in creativity-training programs in schools. For example, Treffinger and Gowan (1971) have collected a list of hundreds of active creativity training programs and materials. What is needed, of course, is a basic theory of how people use strategic information in problem solving. The beginning of such a theory is discussed later in this chapter.

THE 1970s: SPECIFIC TRAINING IN STRATEGIES

One of the best known problem-solving courses of the 1970s is Rubinstein's (1975, 1980) *Patterns Problem Solving* course. This is an actual college course (Engineering 11) taught at the University of California at Los Angeles since 1969. The course attracts a yearly enrollment of 1200 students with 12 sections operating each quarter. Modified versions of the course are in use at several other colleges, as well.

The course is based on Rubinstein's textbook, *Patterns of Problem Solving* (1975). The first half of the book is devoted to problem-solving tools such as how to use tree diagrams or flow charts to represent a problem, how to use mathematical models to represent a theory, and how to work with probability. The remainder provides examples of solving specific problems, taken mainly from physics and engineering.

For example, Rubinstein discusses how to use tree diagrams in logic problems. Suppose you have two statements (let's call them p and q) and each can be either true or false (let's call those T or F). This means there are four combinations for the various truth values of p and q, as shown in Box 13-9. In addition, students are asked to solve problems using their newly acquired skills, such as solving a logic problem that involves use of a tree diagram.

During the 10-week course, students read the textbook, solve exercises, perform independent projects, and meet in groups to discuss and improve problem-solving strategies. Thus, like other instructors who focus on *process* in problem solving, Rubinstein seems to believe that there are certain general strategies and specific strategies that can be described and taught. This course starts with general strategies and later focuses on strategies specific to certain domains such as engineering.

What do students learn from the course? Unfortunately, we cannot adequately answer that question. As Reif (1980) has pointed out, there has not been an attempt to objectively evaluate the course, in spite of its lengthy history. Rubinstein (1980, p. 32) offers student testimonials such as the observation that "students find the course very enlightening." However, such testimonials are notoriously unreliable. The only hard data offered by Rubinstein (1980) is a summary of an unpublished study conducted by a colleague using a similar course at another college; the study claims that the course was responsible for substantial gains in IQ score as measured by comparing pretest and posttest scores. However, you should be very skeptical of

BOX 13–9   An Example of a Tree Diagram

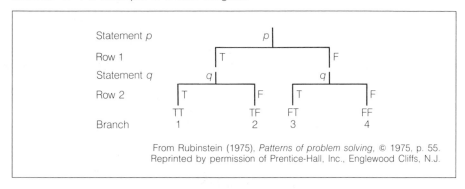

From Rubinstein (1975), *Patterns of problem solving,* © 1975, p. 55.
Reprinted by permission of Prentice-Hall, Inc., Englewood Cliffs, N.J.

claims that an instructional course improves IQ. For example, in reviewing the report from the viewpoint of an experimental psychologist, Hayes was forced to conclude: "I simply do not believe the result" (1980, p. 144). The reason he did not believe the result is that there is increasing evidence that good problem solving requires plenty of domain-specific knowledge, as will be discussed in the next section.

Schoenfeld (1979) has reported a better controlled study in which students are taught "heuristics," or problem solving strategies, that are directly related to mathematical problem solving. All subjects took a five-problem pretest and five-problem posttest, consisting of proofs, complex algebra story problems, series sum problems, and the like. All subjects received written and tape-recorded instructions on how to solve 20 problems, during several sessions over two weeks. The experimental group was given a list and description of five useful strategies, as summarized in Box 13-10. For experimental subjects, all problems in a session were solved by the same strategy, and subjects were explicitly told that a given problem should be solved by a particular strategy. The control group was given the same set of 20 problems and the same written and recorded instruction, except that there was no list of heuristics, no explicit mention of which strategy was involved for a given problem, and the problems in a given session were not all of the same strategy type.

Even though Schoenfeld used only seven subjects, he did find some interesting results. The experimental group increased from an average of 20 percent correct on the pretest to an average of 65 percent correct on the posttest, while the control group averaged 25 percent correct on both tests. Analysis of subjects' comments during the posttest indicated that the experimental group was able to make effective use of several types of heuristics while the control group did not. These preliminary results suggest that it might be effective to teach heuristics within the context of a specific problem-solving domain, such as mathematics.

Can heuristics be explicitly taught in primary school mathematics as well as

BOX 13–10   Five Problem-Solving Strategies Taught by Schoenfeld

1. Draw a diagram if at all possible.
   Even if you finally solve the problem by algebraic or other means, a diagram can help give you a "feel" for the problem. It may suggest ideas or plausible answers. You may even solve a problem graphically.

2. If there is an integer parameter, look for an inductive argument.
   Is there an "n" or other parameter in the problem which takes on integer values? If you need to find a formula for $f(n)$, you might try one of these:
   A) Calculate $f(1)$, $f(2)$, $f(3)$, $f(4)$, $f(5)$; list them in order, and see if there's a pattern. If there is, you might verify it by induction.
   B) See what happens as you pass from n objects to $n + 1$. If you can tell how to pass from $f(n)$ to $f(n + 1)$, you may build up $f(n)$ inductively.

3. Consider arguing by contradiction or contrapositive
   Contrapositive: Instead of proving the statement "If X is true then Y is true," you can prove the equivalent statement "If Y is false then X must be false."
   Contradiction: Assume, for the sake of argument, that the statement you would like to provide is false. Using this assumption, go on to prove either that one of the given conditions in the problem is false, that something you know to be true is false, or that what you wish to prove is true. If you can do any of these, you have proved what you want.
   Both of these techniques are especially useful when you find it difficult to begin a direct argument because you have little to work with. If negating a statement gives you something solid to manipulate, this may be the technique to use.

4. Consider a similar problem with fewer variables.
   If the problem has a large number of variables and is too confusing to deal with comfortably, construct and solve a similar problem with fewer variables. You may then be able to
   A) Adapt the method of solution to the more complex problem.
   B) Take the result of the simpler problem and build up from there.

5. Try to establish subgoals.
   Can you obtain part of the answer, and perhaps go on from there? Can you decompose the problem so that a number of easier results can be combined to give the total result you want?

From Schoenfeld (1979)

Schoenfeld was able to teach them at higher levels? Carpenter (1980) conducted a longitudinal study of the strategies that children use in the early grades for solving addition and subtraction problems. One strategy used by some inventive students is called "decomposition." As an example of decomposition, consider how a student solved the problem $4 + 7 =$ ____: "Seven and 3 is 10, so I put 1 more on there and got 11." Similarly, another student explained her solution for $6 + 8 =$ ____ as follows: "$6 + 6 = 12$ and 2 more is 14." Another common strategy is "compensation." As an example of compensation, consider how a student solved $4 + 9 =$ ____: "Ten add on 4 is 14 and 1 less than 14 is 13." Another student described the reasoning for $6 + 8 = $ _____ as follows: "I took one from 8 and gave it to 6. $7 + 7 = 14$." Similar techniques were also used by students to solve subtraction problems.

Thornton (1978) conducted a series of experiments in order to determine whether strategies such as these could actually be taught to second- and fourth-graders. Some students (the experimental group) received training in strategies like these for 20 minutes a day, 3 days a week, for 8 weeks. Other students (the control group) learned their arithmetic facts in the traditional way using the same amount of class time. The experimental group performed much better on a posttest and on a delayed retention test that measured students' ability to solve arithmetic problems. In fact, for second-graders, performance for the control group declined on some problems during the training, while it increased noticeably for the experimental group. Such results complement those of Schoenfeld and suggest that young children can learn and make use of problem-solving heuristics for specific kinds of problems.

THE 1980s: SPECIFIC KNOWLEDGE VERSUS GENERAL SKILLS

As the preceding pages reveal, there have been numerous attempts to teach problem solving. The early attempts were motivated by the need for creativity in industry, and later projects were aimed at improving problem solving in school children and college students. The overall assessment of the successful training programs is that they seem to improve people's performance on problems that resemble those in instruction.

The current approach to the creativity-training issue is somewhat different from the listing of good habits and the unrestrained optimism of earlier work. Two major ideas seem to have won wide consensus among cognitive psychologists. To become an expert problem solver in some domain, you have to (1) learn much domain-specific knowledge and (2) acquire some general problem-solving strategies that can be applied to your knowledge base. Let's look at the rationale for each point.

Problem Solving Requires Specific Knowledge

There are several recent sources of evidence for the idea that learning to become an expert problem solver requires a great deal of specific knowledge. For example, consider what you must learn in order to be a grand master chess player. According to estimates by Simon (1980), a grand master must have a repertoire of over 50,000 board positions—that is, configurations of chessmen that mean something. The time needed to become a grand master has traditionally been at least 10 years from the time that a person first begins to play chess, presumably because that is how long it takes to learn the required number of board configurations. Recently, Hayes

(1981) has studied biographies of great composers and found similar support for the 10-year rule—it takes at least 10 years from the time they started playing an instrument to their first great production. Finally, Norman (1980) estimated that expert cooks need approximately 50,000 "kitchen facts" about food preparation and cooking.

Additional evidence exists on computer programs that solve problems. For example, suppose you wanted to become a doctor, known for your excellent ability to diagnose. What problem-solving skills would you need? Recent computer programs called INTERNIST (Pople, 1977) and MYCIN (Shortliffe, 1976) have been developed to make medical diagnoses. In order for these programs to make decisions, they require a massive base of information. In short, they must have a great deal of specific knowledge concerning the probabilities that a certain set of symptoms is related to certain diseases. A few quick and general problem-solving techniques are not enough to make these programs accurate.

Such evidence leads Simon (1980, p. 82) to conclude that "there is no such thing as expertness without knowledge—extensive and accessible knowledge." Similarly, a review by Greeno (1980, p. 21) concludes that "there is no basis in current scientific knowledge for changing our present policy of intensive disciplined training for individuals who aspire to make creative changes in the domains in which they choose to work." In other words, a few hours of training on "general problem skills" is not going to have the same effect as years of acquiring specific knowledge that is related to your particular interest. People are good at figuring out the stock market or making gourmet meals or running an office or designing improved products or solving scientific controversies partly because they possess extensive domain-specific knowledge.

Problem Solving Requires General Skills

In addition to a large and useable base of knowledge, expert problem solvers also need processes for operating on that knowledge. For example, Greeno (1980) suggests that two important skills are "planning" such as using means-ends analysis and "representation" such as understanding the problem. Simon suggests that specific knowledge and general problem-solving skills are like scissors: "The scissors does indeed have two blades and . . . effective professional education calls for attention to both subject-matter knowledge and general skills" (1980, p. 86).

The evidence for the role of general skills comes from several sources. One source of evidence is computer programs that solve problems, such as the medical diagnosis programs mentioned earlier; they also require a set of techniques for setting goals and planning and manipulating information. Similarly, Greeno's (1978) program for solving geometry problems requires an extensive collection of skills that he calls "strategic knowledge."

There is also a growing body of empirical support for the idea that problem-solving heuristics can best be taught within specific domains—such as part of mathematics or science instruction. For example, Schoenfeld's study and Thornton's study in the previous section suggest heuristics can explicitly be taught within the context of mathematics.

Future Research

There is reason to be encouraged by the new interest of experimental psychologists in practical problems, such as whether problem solving can be taught. Recently, Norman called for the establishment of a discipline of "cognitive engineering": "We need to develop the general principles of how to learn, how to remember, how to solve problems, and then to develop applied courses, and then to establish the place of these methods in an academic curriculum" (1980, p. 97). Similarly, Lochhead (1979, p. 1) has called for what he calls "cognitive processes instruction": "We should be teaching students how to think."

These are not new ideas. What is new, however, is the optimisim of psychologists that psychology might actually have matured enough to have something useful to contribute to the design of problem-solving courses. As you can see, there are two extremes in instruction for problem solving—intensive domain-specific learning versus general problem-solving skills. Certainly, most psychologists would opt for a compromise, although there is still no consensus on how much specific and how much general information a problem-solving course should contain.

A typical suggestion comes from Simon (1980). He suggests that problem solving could be taught within the context of a specific subject such as mathematics. In order to gain more experience, students should see many examples worked out and should solve many practice problems. General strategies for setting goals and representing problems could be taught within the context of specific problems, with emphasis on the conditions under which certain operations should or should not be performed. There is also the promising idea that "computer coaches" will someday be a part of problem-solving training (Goldstein and Brown, 1979; Goldstein, 1980). For example, a student can sit down at a terminal and proceed to solve a problem, with the computer giving information about possible strategies and cuing the student about the strategy she is currently using.

EVALUATION

If we took a vote among promoters of creativity-training programs, we would find overwhelming support for the idea that skill in general problem solving can be taught. The following statement from Polya (1960, p. ix) is typical: "Solving problems is a practical art, like swimming, or skiing, or playing the piano; you can learn it only by imitation and practice.'' Yet, a close examination of Polya's strategies (see Chapter 3) suggests that they are closely tied to specific kinds of problems, namely in mathematics.

This chapter follows the course of creativity training from the industrial programs of the 1930s to the curriculum projects of the 1960s to the new field of human cognitive engineering of the 1980s. What have we learned? In spite of strong claims that general creativity can be taught, most objective studies seem to show that students learn specific information and specific strategies that can be used mainly on problems like those they were given during instruction. At the present, after 50 years of experience with creativity-training courses, there is no overwhelming evidence that global skills can be learned independently of specific fields (such as mathematics or engineering or product design). This lesson is important for both the theory and teaching of problem solving. It is related to the evidence in Chapter 12 that differences between experts and novices may be characterized partly by differences in the amount and organization of knowledge for a particular domain. Successful courses in problem solving are courses that emphasize specific knowledge and strategies applicable within a specific domain; successful theories of problem solving might also concentrate on describing the knowledge and processes involved in particular real-world problem domains.

A statement by National Education Association (1961), entitled *The Central Purpose of American Education,* asserts: ''The purpose which runs through and strengthens all other educational purposes—the common thread of education—is the development of the ability to think.'' There is reason to be optimistic, for it appears that during the years to come, psychologists will concentrate in earnest on the issue of how to teach people to think.

Suggested Readings

Bloom, B. S., and Broder, L. J. *Problem-solving processes of college students: An exploratory investigation.* Chicago: University of Chicago Press, 1950. Summarizes a famous study on how to teach problem-solving skills to college students.

Davis, G. A. *Psychology of problem solving.* New York: Basic Books, 1973. Part 3 provides a review of creativity training programs.

Davis, G. A., and Scott, J. A. *Training creative thinking.* Huntington, N.Y.: Krieger, 1978. Contains papers by many well-known practitioners of creativity training.

Lochhead, J., and Clement, J. *Cognitive process instruction: Research on teaching thinking skills.* Philadelphia: Franklin Institute Press, 1979. Contains articles by many well-known cognitive psychologists interested in creativity training.

Tuma, D. T., and Reif, F. *Problem solving and education: Issues in teaching and research.* Hillsdale, N.J.: Erlbaum, 1980. Contains papers by teachers, administrators, and cognitive psychologists concerning the role of instruction for problem solving.

CHAPTER 14

MATHEMATICAL PROBLEM SOLVING: Thinking as Based on Domain-Specific Knowledge

Analysis of Mathematical Problem Solving

Linguistic and Semantic Knowledge

Schematic Knowledge

Procedural Knowledge

Strategic Knowledge

Sex Differences

Which school subject is "loaded" with problem-solving exercises? Did you say math? If you thumb through a mathematics textbook, you are likely to notice that most of the pages are devoted to problems—either by showing you problems worked out or by asking you to solve some "exercises." Thus, the mathematics classroom offers a sort of natural laboratory in which we can study how people acquire and use problem-solving skills.

For example, let's consider some of the problems that students are taught to solve in our nation's schools. Box 14-1 lists some typical math problems for high school students. Go ahead and solve each one, indicating your answer by circling the appropriate letter. (The answers are given at the bottom of the Box.) Suppose we gave these problems to a group of high school seniors, students who have progressed through 12 years in the "educational system." How well do you think they would do on each problem?

――――――――――――――――――――――――――――――――――――――

Fortunately, we do not have to guess how well students are learning to solve problems like these, because many states have instituted formal assessments of students' learning. For example, a test called the "Survey of Basic Skills" is given each year to all seniors in California public schools (California Assessment Program, 1980).* The statistics for the most recent year available reveal the following percent correct for the six problems given in Box 14-1: 47, 44, 35, 56 and 33 percent, respectively. Thus, on these typical problems, twelfth-graders averaged less than 50 percent correct (with 20–25 percent correct expected if students simply guessed). The overall percentage correct on the entire mathematics test was slightly less than 67 percent and had been at about that level for the previous five years. Similarly dismal percentages were obtained on math tests given to third- and sixth-graders, using problems appropriate for those grade levels.

Equally troubling results have been reported by national surveys of mathematical problem solving in the United States. For example, in the latest National Assessment of Educational Progress (reported by Carpenter, Corbitt, Kepner, Lindquist, and Reyes, 1980), 70,000 students were given problems such as the following:

Lemonade costs 95¢ for one 56 ounce bottle.
At the school fair, Bob sold cups holding 8 ounces for 20¢ each.
How much money did the school make on each bottle?

Only 11 percent of the thirteen-year-olds and 29 percent of the seventeen-year-olds were able to find the correct answer.

Why are these problems so hard to solve? Why is it so difficult to teach our children how to solve such problems? In spite of years of training and practice in solving mathematics problems, why do students greet simple story problems with moans, fearful faces, and incorrect answers? If we knew the answers to these questions, we would not only have the basis for a powerful theory of human problem solving, but we could also have a useful impact on education. For example, in reviewing the psychology of learning mathematics, Skemp (1971, p. 13) points out: "Problems of learning and teaching are psychological problems, and before we can

――――――――――――――

*This test includes sections on reading, writing, and mathematics. Similar tests are given to all third- and sixth-graders.

BOX 14–1 Some Story Problems

1. The ratio of men to women at a meeting was 4:5. If there were 20 women at the meeting, how many men were there?

    a. 15   b. 16   c. 25   d. 30

2. An astronaut requires 2.2 pounds of oxygen per day while in space. How many pounds of oxygen are needed for a team of 3 astronauts for 5 days in space?

    a. 13.2   b. 15.2   c. 33   d. 330

3. The number of feet that an object will fall in t seconds (neglecting air resistance) is given by the formula, $s = \frac{1}{2}gt^2$, where s = the number of feet, and g = 32 (the acceleration due to gravity). Assuming there is no air resistance, how far will a parachutist drop in free fall of 10 seconds?

    a. 1600 feet   b. 2440 feet   c. 3220 feet   d. 3400 feet
    e. none of the above

4. A person will pay the lowest price per ounce of rice if she buys:

    a. 12 ounces for 40 cents
    b. 14 ounces for 45 cents
    c. 1 pound, 12 ounces for 85 cents
    d. 2 pounds for 99 cents

5. Three or four students each weighs 60 pounds. What is the weight of the fourth student if the average of the weights of all four students is 70 pounds?

    a. 100 pounds   b. 80 pounds   c. 70 pounds   d. 65 pounds

6. In the figure, the lines AE and CD are perpendicular to AC. What is the distance from A to E?

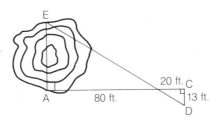

    a. 40 feet   b. 52 feet   c. 60 feet   d. 65 feet   e. none of the above

Answers: b, c, a, c, a, b.

Adapted from California Assessment Program (1980)

make much improvement in the teaching of mathematics, we need to know more about how it is learnt.'' The remainder of this chapter examines what psychologists have learned about how people learn about and solve story problems–what Hinsley, Hayes, and Simon (1977) jokingly refer to as ''those twentieth-century fables.''

BOX 14–2   The Motorboat Problem

A sleek new blue motorboat traveled downstream in 120 minutes with a current of 8 kilometers per hour. The return upstream trip against the same current took 3 hours. Find the speed of the boat in still water.

Solution:

distance = rate × time

distance downstream = distance upstream

(rate of boat + rate of current) × (time downstream) = (rate of boat − rate of current) × (time upstream)

(rate of boat + 8) × (2) = (rate of boat − 8) × 3

2(rate of boat) + 16 = 3(rate of boat) − 24

16 + 24 = 3(rate of boat) − 2(rate of boat)

40 kilometers per hour = rate of boat

ANALYSIS OF MATHEMATICAL PROBLEM SOLVING

Quantitative reasoning occurs when the student is presented with numerical information and must use the rules of mathematics to deduce a numerical answer. Such quantitative reasoning is a form of deductive reasoning; however, in quantitative reasoning the premises and conclusion involve numbers. Mathematical story problems such as those in Box 14-1 require quantitative reasoning.

Let's consider another typical story problem, such as the motorboat problem given in Box 14-2. What does a person need to know in order to be able to solve this problem? Take a moment and try to list all of the things needed. Does your list resemble the one suggested here?

Linguistic knowledge – knowledge of the English language, such as recognizing words, determining that "motorboat" is a noun, or knowing that "sleek new blue motorboat" and "boat" refer to the same object.

Semantic knowledge – knowledge of facts about the world such as "120 minutes equals 2 hours" or that rivers have currents that run upstream and downstream.

Schema knowledge – knowledge of problem types, such as the idea that the motorboat problem is a *current* problem.

Procedural knowledge – knowledge of how to perform a sequence of operations, such as the procedure for long division or the procedure for solving for x.

Strategic knowledge – techniques for how to use the various types of available knowledge in solving a given problem, such as setting subgoals.

BOX 14–3   Analysis of Mathmatical Problem Solving for the Motorboat Problem

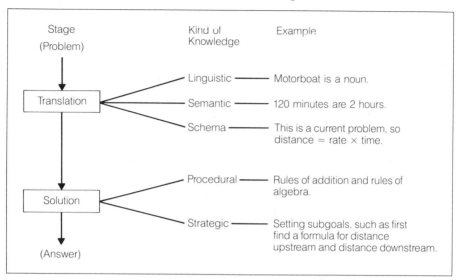

Stage (Problem)	Kind of Knowledge	Example
Translation	Linguistic	Motorboat is a noun.
	Semantic	120 minutes are 2 hours.
	Schema	This is a current problem, so distance = rate × time.
Solution	Procedural	Rules of addition and rules of algebra.
	Strategic	Setting subgoals, such as first find a formula for distance upstream and distance downstream.
(Answer)		

According to most descriptions of mathematical problem solving, the first step is to translate the words of the problem into an internal representation–going from the words of a story problem to an equation, for example. The kinds of knowledge that are important for this translation, or understanding, stage are linguistic, semantic, and schematic. The second major step is to apply the rules of algebra and arithmetic to the internal representation, such as going from the equation to a numerical value for the unknown. For this solution stage, procedural knowledge and strategic knowledge are important. Box 14-3 summarizes the two stages and the kinds of knowledge that might be involved in mathematical problem solving. Let us now examine each of these kinds of needed knowledge, in turn.

LINGUISTIC AND SEMANTIC KNOWLEDGE

Let's suppose that the first stage in solving the motorboat problem is to understand the problem. For example, ''understanding'' the problem might be demonstrated when a person can translate the words into an equation.

Consider the advertisement problem in Box 14-4. Bobrow (1968) developed a computer program, called STUDENT, which solves simple problems such as the advertisement problem. What did STUDENT need to know in order to be able to translate the advertisement problem into an equation? As you may have suspected,

STUDENT needed to know some of the rules of English and some basic facts about the world.

Thus, to solve problems, STUDENT needed to have some basic information in memory. Examples of the information that STUDENT had to be given include the following:

1 foot equals 12 inches

1 yard equals 3 feet

Pounds is the plural of *pound*

People is the plural of *person*

Years younger than MEANS *less than*

Mary is a person

An *uncle* is a person

Squared is an operator

Has is a verb

Distance equals speed times time

Perimeter of a rectangle means twice the sum of the length and width of rectangle

The programs would not run correctly unless such basic information was already in the computer's memory prior to solving the problem. Such work suggests that understanding the problem requires a great deal of specific knowledge.

Box 14-4 summarizes the steps involved in STUDENT's translation of the problem into an equation: (1) Copy the problem word for word, (2) substitute words like "two times" for "twice," (3) locate each word or phrase that describes a variable, such as "the number of customers Tom gets" and note if two or more phrases refer to the same variable, (4) break the problem into simple sentences, (5) translate each simple sentence into equations.

As you can see, STUDENT performs a literal translation of words into equations. To do this, however, requires that STUDENT knows English well enough to distinguish between operators and variables, and some semantic knowledge such as knowing that a dime equals 10 cents. More recently, Hayes and Simon (1974) have developed a program called UNDERSTAND that translates problems into an internal representation.

SCHEMATIC KNOWLEDGE

Let's return for a moment to the motorboat problem. Is there anything else you need to know beyond linguistic and semantic knowledge? You might need to realize that

BOX 14–4   How STUDENT Solves the Advertisement Problem

1. *State the problem.*
   If the number of customers Tom gets is twice the square of 20 percent of the numbers of advertisements he runs, and the number of advertisements he runs is 45, what is the number of customers Tom gets?

2. *Make substitutions.*
   If the number of customers Tom gets is 2 times the square 20 percent of the number of advertisements he runs, and the number of advertisements he runs is 45, what is the number of customers Tom gets?

3. *Tag words and phrases.*
   If the number of (operator) customers Tom gets (verb) is 2 times (operator) the square of (operator) 20 percent (operator) of (operator) the number of (operator) advertisements he (pronoun) runs, and the number of (operator) advertisements he (pronoun) runs is 45, what (question word) is the number of (operation) customers Tom gets (verb)? (question mark)?

4. *Make kernal sentences.*
   The number of customers Tom gets is 2 times the square of 20 percent of the number of advertisements he runs. The number of advertisements he runs is 45. What is the number of customers Tom gets?

5. *Make equations.*
   (Number of customers Tom gets) $= 2(.20)$(Number of advertisements)^2
   (Number of advertisements) $= 45$
   (Number of customers Tom gets) $= (X)$

Adapted from Bobrow (1968). © 1968 MIT Press.

the specific form of the motorboat problem is: (rate of boat + rate of current) × (time downstream) = (rate of boat − rate of current) × (time upstream). This equation represents the structure of the problem and helps the student to know what to look for in the problem. We will refer to the student's knowledge of the form of the problem as "schema knowledge." Thus, if a student notes that the motorboat problem is a problem about currents that can be fit into a general formula, the student has a schema for the problem.

Understanding

You may have noticed that STUDENT does not really "understand" what it is doing and does not "care" whether the variables are related to one another in a logical way. Is this the way humans solve problems? Paige and Simon (1966) gave students problems such as the one in Box 14-5. Some subjects behaved like STUDENT by generating literal translations of the sentences into equations. Other subjects recognized that something was wrong in this problem and corrected it by assuming that the second sentence said, "The value of the quarters exceeds the value of dimes by

BOX 14–5   The Coin Problem

Problem

The number of quarters that a man has is seven times the number of dimes he has. The value of the dimes exceeds the value of quarters by two dollars and fifty cents. How many has he of each coin?

Literal Translation

$$Q = 7 \times D$$
$$D \times (.10) - Q \times (.25) = 2.50$$

Mistranslation

$$Q = 7 \times D$$
$$Q \times (.25) - D \times (.10) = 2.50$$

Recognition of Inconsistency

"This is not possible."
"The dimes cannot be worth more than the quarters if there are less dimes than quarters."

Adapted from Paige and Simon (1966)

$2.50." Finally, some students looked at the problem and said, "This is impossible." Thus, while some students may use literal translation, some students apparently try to "understand" the problem.

How can people be encouraged to successfully understand a story problem? Paige and Simon asked subjects to draw pictures to represent each problem. When subjects drew integrated pictures containing all the information in one diagram, they were much more likely to arrive at the correct answer than when students produced a series of sentence-by-sentence translations, with which they were more easily led astray. Similarly, Mayer and Greeno (1972) asked students to solve "impossible" probability problems such as given in Box 14-6. As described in Chapter 4, if students had learned to solve binomial problems by understanding the underlying concepts, they were more likely to recognize that the problem was impossible; however, if students learned by memorizing the formula, they were more likely to generate a numerical answer. Thus, in addition to linguistic and factual knowledge the student needs knowledge about how to put the variables together in a coherent way.

Recently, Soloway and his colleagues (Clement, Lochhead, and Soloway, 1979; Soloway, Lochhead, and Clement, 1982) have provided some additional information about how to help students avoid errors in translating from words to equations. These researchers presented problems like the "professors and students problem"

BOX 14-6   Some Impossible Probability Problems

When a die is rolled four times, what is the probability of the sequence success, success, failure, failure?

Suppose that two people out of every nine in a certain town like John Wayne movies. If a sample is taken, what is the probability that two people in the sample like John Wayne movies?

Answers: The first problem is not answerable because we cannot tell what the probability of success is. The second problem is unanswerable because we do not know the sample size.

Adapted from Mayer and Greeno (1972)

BOX 14-7   Some Errors in Translating Word Problems

Professors and Students Problem

Write an equation using the variables S and P to represent the following statement: "There are six times as many students as professors at this university." Use S to stand for the number of students and P to stand for the number of professors.

  Correct answer: $S = 6P$
  Percent correct: 63%
  Typical wrong answer: $6S = P$

Cheesecake and Strudel Problem

Write an equation using the variables C and S to represent the following statement: "At Mindy's restaurant, for every four people who order cheesecake, there are five people who order strudel." Let C represent the number of cheesecakes and S represent the number of strudels ordered.

  Correct answer: $5C = 4S$
  Percent correct: 27%
  Typical wrong answer: $4C = 5S$

Adapted from Clement, Lochhead, and Soloway (1979)

---

or the "cheesecake and strudel problem" in Box 14-7 to college students. Their job was simply to translate the story problem into an equation. The subjects—150 engineering students at a major state university—presumably had been selected partially on the basis of their achievement in science and mathematics. As shown in Box 14-7, only 63 percent of the students generated the correct answer, $S = 6P$, for the professors and students problem; the typical wrong answer was $6S = P$. On the cheesecake and strudel problem, the performance was far worse, with only 27 percent giving the correct answer. Note that the engineering students had no difficulty in reading English or in solving algebraic equations. In fact, in a follow-up study using experienced engineers, subjects were able to translate problems like these into simple computer statements. Clement, Lochhead, and Soloway argue that computer language encourages students to represent the problem as an active procedure (for example, telling what to do) while algebraic notation encourages a static view of the problem (telling about a comparison, for example). A student who sees the problem in an active perspective reasons: "If I want to know how many students there are, I must multiply the number of professors by six."

Role of Schemata

A further breakthrough concerning how people understand story problems comes from the work of Hinsley, Hayes, and Simon (1977). Subjects were given a series of algebra problems from standard textbooks and were asked to arrange them into categories. Subjects were quite able to perform this task with high agreement, yielding 18 different categories such as river current (the category for the motorboat problem), DRT, work, triangle, and interest. Box 14-8 lists examples of the 18 categories of problems that subjects created.

Hinsley, Hayes, and Simon (1977) also found that subjects were able to categorize problems almost immediately. After hearing the first few words of a problem such as, "A river steamer travels 36 miles downstream . . . " a student could say, "Hey, that's a river current problem." Hayes, Waterman, and Robinson (1977) and Robinson and Hayes (1978) found that students use their schemata to make judgments concerning what information is relevant in a problem and what is not. For example, in one study the crop duster problem (in Box 14-9) was presented one phrase at a time (Robinson and Hayes, 1978). As each phrase was added to the problem, subjects were asked to judge whether it was necessary for solving the problem (pass one), and then the entire process was repeated (pass two). The bottom of Box 14-9 shows the proportion of relevant judgments for four kinds of information: relevant information is judged important on both passes, space and weight information is judged important on pass one but not on pass two since the subject is aware of the question on pass two, and irrelevant information is judged low in relevance. Apparently, subjects are quite able to make accurate judgments about the relevance of information in a problem as it is being presented.

Many of the difficulties that people have in solving story problems can come from using the wrong schemata. For example, Hinsley, Hayes, and Simon (1977) presented subjects with a problem that could be interpreted as either a triangle problem or a distance-rate-time problem. As you can see in Box 14-10, problem is a sort of distance-rate-time problem with irrelevant information about a triangular

BOX 14–8 Examples of 18 Problem Categories

Category name	Example of Problem
1. Triangle	Jerry walks 1 block east along a vacant lot and then 2 blocks north to a friend's house. Phil starts at the same point and walks diagonally through the vacant lot coming out at the same pount as Jerry. If Jerry walked 217 feet east and 400 feet north, how far did Phil walk?
2. DRT	In sports car race, a Panther starts the course at 9:00 A.M. and averages 75 miles per hour. A Mallotti starts four minutes later and averages 85 miles per hour. If a lap is 15 miles, on which lap will the Panther be overtaken.
3. Averages	Flying east between two cities, a plane's speed is 380 miles per hour. On the return trip, it flies 420 miles per hour. Find the average speed for the round trip.
4. Scale conversion	Two temperature scales are established, one, the R scale where water under fixed conditions freezes at 15 and boils at 405, and the other, the S scale where water freezes at 5 and boils at 70. If the R and S scales are linearly related, find an expression for any temperature R in terms of a temperature S.
5. Ratio	If canned tomatoes come in two sizes, with radius of one 2/3 the radius of the other, find the ratios of the capacities of the two cans.
6. Interest	A certain savings bank pays 3% interest compounded semiannually. How much will $2500 amount to if left on deposit for 20 years?
7. Area	A box containing 180 cubic inches is constructed by cutting from each corner of a cardboard square a small square with side 5 inches, and then turning up the sides. Find the area of the original piece of cardboard.
8. Max-min	A real-estate operator estimates that the monthly profit p in dollars from a building s stories high is given by $p = -2s^{**}2 + 88s$. What height building would he consider most profitable?
9. Mixture	One vegetable oil contains 6% saturated fats and a second contains 26% saturated fats. In making a salad dressing how many ounces of the second may be added to 10 ounces of the first if the percent of saturated fats is not to exceed 16%?

(continued)

relation. Of the six subjects in the study, three attended to the irrelevant triangle information. For example, they drew triangles and tried to determine the lengths of the two legs and the hypotenuse. One subject misread ''4 minutes'' as ''4 miles''

BOX 14–8, *continued*

Category name	Example of Problem
10. River current	A river steamer travels 36 miles downstream in the same time that it travels 24 miles upstream. The steamer's engines drive in still water at a rate which is 12 miles an hour more than the rate of the current. Find the rate of the current.
11. Probability	In an extra-sensory-perception experiment, a blindfolded subject has two rows of blocks before him. Each row has blocks numbered 1 to 10 arranged in random order. The subject is to place one hand on a block in the first row and then try to place his other hand on the block having the same numeral in the second row. If the subject has no ESP, what is the probability of his making a match on the first try?
12. Number	The units digit is 1 more than 3 times the tens digit. The number represented when the digits are interchanged is 8 times the sum of the digits.
13. Work	Mr. Russo takes 3 minutes less than Mr. Lloyd to pack a case when each works alone. One day, after Mr. Russo spent 6 minutes in packing a case, the boss called him away, and Mr. Lloyd finished packing in 4 more minutes. How many minutes would it take Mr. Russo alone to pack a case?
14. Navigation	A pilot leaves an aircraft carrier and flies south at 360 m.p.h., while the carrier proceeds N30W at 30 m.p.h. If the pilot has enough fuel to fly 4 hours, how far south can he fly before returning to his ship?
15. Progressions	From two towns 363 miles apart, Jack and Jill set out to meet each other. If Jill travels 1 mile the first day, 3 the second, 5 the third, and so on, and Jack travels 2 miles the first day, 6 the second, 10 the third, and so on, when will they meet?
16. Progression-2	Find the sum of the first 25 odd positive integers.
17. Physics	The speed of a body falling freely from rest is directly proportional to the length of time that it falls. If a body was falling at 144 ft. per second 4 1/2 seconds after beginning its fall, how fast was it falling 3 3/4 seconds later?
18. Exponentials	The diameter of each successive layer of a wedding cake is 2/3 the previous layer. If the diameter of the first layer of a 5-layer cake is 15 inches, find the sum of the circumferences of all the layers.

Adapted from Hinsley, Hayes, and Simon (1977)

BOX 14–9 Students' Judgments of What Information Is Relevant in the Crop
Duster Problem

Crop Duster Problem

A crop-dusting plane carries 2,000 pounds of Rotenone dusting compound, 250
pounds of high-test fuel, a pilot highly skilled in low-altitude flying, and a duster-
machinery operator, the pilot's younger brother. The plane must dust a rectangular
tobacco field 0.5 miles wide by 0.6 miles long. The dusting compound must be
spread with a density of 200 pounds per 0.001 square mile. Further, the compound
must be spread between 6 AM and 9 AM, when there is sufficient light and before the
morning dew has evaporated, to assure the adherence of the compound to the
plants. The plane can dust a 44 foot wide strip at one time. The plane flies the length
of the field with a 6 mph tailwind and back against the same headwind. With the
wind, the plan uses fuel at a rate of 60 pounds per hour. Against the wind, it uses
fuel at the rate of 80 pounds per hour. The ratio of flying time against the wind to time
with the wind is 9:8. The duster operator must try to spread the compound uniformly
on the ground despite varying speed. (Question is stated next.)

	Proportion of Subjects Rating Each Fact as Relevant	
	Pass 1	Pass 2
1. Problem-relevant items: with a 6 mph tailwind back against the same headwind ratio of speed with wind to speed against wind is 9.8	.84	.89
2. Space items: plan must dust rectangular tobacco field 0.5 miles wide 0.6 miles long per 0.001 sq. mile 44 ft. wide strip plane flies length of field	.93	.45
3. Weight items: 2000 lbs. 60 lbs. per hour 250 lbs. 80 lbs. per hour with a density of 200 lbs.	.93	.48
4. Irrelevant/other items: a crop-dusting plane of Rotenone dusting compound of high test fuel a pilot highly skilled in low-altitude flying a duster-machinery operator the pilot's younger brother the compound must be spread between 6 AM and 9 AM when there is sufficient light and before dew has evaporated to assure adherence of component.	.35	.11

Adapted, with permission of V. H. Winston & Sons,
from Revlin and Leirer (1978) in Revlin and Mayer (1978)

BOX 14–10 The Smalltown Problem

Because of their quiet ways, the inhabitants of Smalltown were especially upset by the terrible New Year's Eve auto accident which claimed the life of one Smalltown resident. The facts were these. Both Smith and Jones were New Year's Eve babies and each had planned a surprise visit to the other on their mutual birthday. Jones had started out for Smith's house traveling due east on Route 210 just two minutes after Smith had left for Jone's house. Smith was traveling directly south on Route 140. Jones was traveling 30 miles per hour faster than Smith even though their houses were only five miles apart as the crow flies. Their cars crashed at the right angle intersection of the two highways. Officer Franklin, who observed the crash, determined that Jones was traveling half again as fast as Smith at the time of the crash. Smith had been driving for just four minutes at the time of the crash. The crash occurred nearer to the house of the dead man than to the house of the survivor. What was the name of the dead man?

Adapted from Hinsley, Hayes, and Simon (1979)

and assumed this was the length of one of the legs; another subject assumed that "5 miles apart" referred to the length of the hypotenuse. The other three subjects ignored the triangle information and focused on the aspects of distance, rate, and time in the problem. For example, one subject stated: "It looks like a distance problem. So Jones is going east two minutes after Smith is going west. So it might be an overtake problem." All three of these subjects initially assumed that one driver was going east and one was going west. Hinsley, Hayes, and Simon concluded that subjects use either a triangle schema or a distance-rate-time schema as a "template" in understanding the problem. These schemata influence what the subject looks for and even encourage mistakes in interpreting the information.

As you might recall from Chapter 3, Luchins (1942) demonstrated that shifting from problems that require one solution approach to problems that require another can cause "einstellung" or "problem-solving set." For example, Loftus and Suppes (1972) found that a word problem is much more difficult to solve if it was a different type of problem from the ones preceding it.

Greeno (1980) and his colleagues have located schemata for children's word problems. For example, Box 14-11 illustrates examples of "cause/change," "combine," and "compare" problems. Although all three problems require the same arithmetic operations, the compare problems are much harder for young children to solve than cause/change problems. Similarly, there is some evidence of a developmental trend; for example, kindergarteners and first-graders perform well on the cause/change problem given in the top of Box 14-11, but do very poorly on the compare problem, while second- and third-graders perform well on both types. When asked to repeat the compare problem, one-third of the children said, "Joe has

BOX 14–11 Three Types of Word Problems

Name	Example	Percent Correct Grades K and 1	Percent Correct Grades 2 and 3
Cause/Change	Joe had 3 marbles. Then Tom gave him 5 more marbles. How many marbles does Joe have now?	94	100
Combine	Joe has 3 marbles. Tom has 5 marbles. How many marbles do they have altogether?	100	100
Compare	Joe has 3 marbles. Tom has 5 more marbles than Joe. How many marbles does Tom have?	15	90
Cause/Change	Joe had 8 marbles. Then he gave 5 marbles to Tom. How many marbles does Joe have now?	100	100
Combine	Joe and Tom have 8 marbles altogether. Joe has some marbles. Tom has five marbles. How many marbles does Joe have?	17	90
Compare	Joe has 8 marbles. He has 5 more marbles than Tom. How many marbles does Tom have?	14	70

Adapted from Riley and Greeno (1978)

3 marbles. Tom has 5 marbles. How many does Tom have?'' Failure to solve word problems may thus be due to lack of an appropriate schema rather than poor arithmetic or logical skills.

In order to gain a broader perspective on the nature of schemata for algebra story problems, Mayer (1981) surveyed the exercise problems from 12 major algebra textbooks approved for use in California secondary schools. Of the approximately 2000 story problems selected, there were about 20 general categories, as shown in Box 14-12. Some of these categories shared the same underlying formula; for example, distance-rate-time, current, and work problems are all based on a formula:

BOX 14–12   Some Problem Categories from Algebra Textbooks

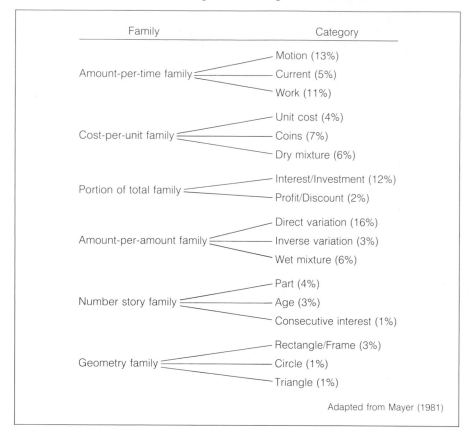

Family	Category
Amount-per-time family	Motion (13%)
	Current (5%)
	Work (11%)
Cost-per-unit family	Unit cost (4%)
	Coins (7%)
	Dry mixture (6%)
Portion of total family	Interest/Investment (12%)
	Profit/Discount (2%)
Amount-per-amount family	Direct variation (16%)
	Inverse variation (3%)
	Wet mixture (6%)
Number story family	Part (4%)
	Age (3%)
	Consecutive interest (1%)
Geometry family	Rectangle/Frame (3%)
	Circle (1%)
	Triangle (1%)

Adapted from Mayer (1981)

amount = rate × time. Also, for any major category, there were many distinct versions of solutions, which are called "templates." Motion problems, for example, had 13 different templates, including simple distance-rate-time, vehicles approaching from opposite directions, vehicles starting from the same point and departing in opposite directions, one vehicle overtaking another, one vehicle making a round trip, speed changing during a trip, and so on. Box 14-13 lists some of the templates for current problems. Can you see where the motorboat problem fits in? In all, there were about 100 different templates among all of the problems in algebra textbooks. This survey suggests that proficiency in solving standard textbook problems might simply involve learning to recognize the various categories and templates for the major problems.

BOX 14–13 Some Templates for Current Problems

Name	Description	Example
Total time	A boat or plane travels a certain distance with the current and a certain distance against the current in a total time.	The current in a stream moves at 4 kilometers per hour. A boat travels 4 kilometers upstream and 12 kilometers downstream in a total of 2 hours. What is the speed of the boat in still water?
Round trip	A boat travels with the current in a certain time and returns against the current in a certain amount of time.	A boat travels 3.15 hours downstream, where the current is 5.82 kilometers per hour. It returns in 9.97 hours. Find the speed of the boat in still water.
Equal time	A boat travels a certain distance with a current in the same time it can travel a certain distance against the current.	A boat travels at a rate of 15 kilometers per hour in still water. It travels 60 kilometers upstream in the same time that it travels 90 kilometers downstream. What is the rate of the current?
Part	The boat travels at a certain rate with the current and a certain rate against the current.	Fairfield's rowing team can row downstream at a rate of 7 miles per hour. They can row back to the starting point at a rate of 3 miles per hour. Find their rowing rate in still water and the rate of the current.
Relative	The time to travel with the current is compared to the time to travel the same distance against the current.	The air speed of an airplane is 225 miles per hour. Flying from city A to city B, it has a tailwind of 25 miles per hour. It takes 3 hours longer to fly from B to A than from A to B. How far apart are the two cities?

PROCEDURAL KNOWLEDGE

Let's return to the motorboat problem. So far, we have seen that in order to solve this problem you need linguistic and factual knowledge, as well as schematic knowledge. Such knowledge is useful in understanding and representing the problem. To solve the problem, once you understand it, you must have some additional knowledge. For example, you must know the procedures used in mathematics for making computations and for solving equations. This type of knowledge is discussed in this section.

BOX 14–14   A Process Model for Simple Addition

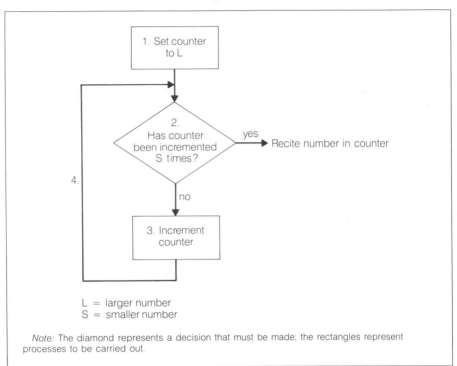

L = larger number
S = smaller number

Note: The diamond represents a decision that must be made; the rectangles represent processes to be carried out.

Role of Arithmetic Algorithms

To solve problems like the motorboat problem, you have to be able to perform computations such as $2 \times 8 = $ _____ or $16 + 24 = $ _____ or $3 - 2 = $ _____. In order to compute answers to arithmetic problems, a learner needs to know the algorithm for generating the correct answer. An *algorithm* is an exact procedure for accomplishing some task, such as adding numbers. Thus, a person's procedural knowledge includes arithmetic algorithms.

Groen and Parkman (1972) suggested five different process models to represent children's addition algorithms for problems of the form, $m + n = $ _____. A process model is simply a listing of the decisions and processes that are involved in a certain algorithm. For example, one of the most popular process models for adding single-digit numbers is given as a flowchart in Box 14-14. The steps may be summarized as follows:

1. Set a counter to the value of the larger of *m* and *n*.

2. Decide whether the counter has been incremented as many times as the value of the smaller of m and n. If yes, stop and recite the value in the counter as the answer; if no, continue to step 3.

3. Increase counter by 1.

4. Go to step 2.

This procedure is called the "min model" because you set the counter to the maximum of m and n and increase it by the minimum of m and n.

Suppose you had a problem such as $2 + 5 = $ ____. Using the procedure just listed, your first step is to set the counter to the larger number, 5. The second step is to decide whether you have incremented the counter two times; since you have not yet incremented it at all, you go on to step 3. At step 3, you increment the counter so that it now contains 6. Returning to step 2, you decide whether you have incremented the counter twice yet; since you have only incremented it once, you go on to step 3. At step 3, you increment the counter to 7. Returning to step 2, you have now incremented the counter two times so you may stop and rewrite the answer, 7.

Based on this model, can you predict which problems will take the longest amounts of time to solve? Suppose we gave these problems: $2 + 3 = $ ____, $3 + 2 = $ ____, $2 + 5 = $ ____, $2 + 7 = $ ____. According to the min model, all problems should take equal time to solve because each one requires you to set a counter and increment it two times. However, what about these problems: $5 + 0 = $ ____, $5 + 1 = $ ____, $5 + 2 = $ ____, $5 + 3 = $ ____, $5 + 4 = $ ____? In this case the first problem requires no extra cycle through step 3 (incrementing), the second problem requires one, the third requires two, the fourth requires three, and the fifth requires four. Thus, computation time should be longest for $5 + 4 = $ ____, and so on; in other words, the min model predicts that response times should increase as the size of the smaller number (the minimum of n and m) increases. These predictions are summarized in Box 14-15.

To test these predictions, as well as those of the other four addition process models, Groen and Parkman (1972) presented simple one-digit addition problems to 37 first-graders and recorded the time to answer each one. Box 14-16 shows the average time needed to answer each problem. As you can see, response time seems to increase as predicted by the min model. The min model was best able to predict the performance of the children. Similarly, when this experiment was conducted with adults, the min model was best at predicting their response times; however, adults were much faster than children—each additional cycle through step 3 took about 20 milliseconds compared to about 400 milliseconds in children.

Similar models have been developed by Resnick and her colleagues (Resnick, 1976) to describe what children know about how to subtract. This work suggests a developmental trend in which simple but inefficient models are used by younger

BOX 14–15 Some Predictions of the Min Model

Problems	Number of times counter is increased	List of steps	Description
0 + 5 = _____ or 5 + 0 = _____	0	1,2	Set counter and don't increment
1 + 5 = _____ or 5 + 1 = _____	1	1,2,3,4,2	Set counter and increment once
2 + 5 = _____ or 5 + 2 = _____	2	1,2,3,4,2,3,4,2	Set counter and increment twice
3 + 5 = _____ or 5 + 3 = _____	3	1,2,3,4,2,3,4,2,3,4,2	Set counter and increment 3 times
4 + 5 = _____ or 5 + 4 = _____	4	1,2,3,4,2,3,4,2,3,4,2,3,4,2	Set counter and increment 4 times

BOX 14–16 Average Time to Solve Simple Addition Problems

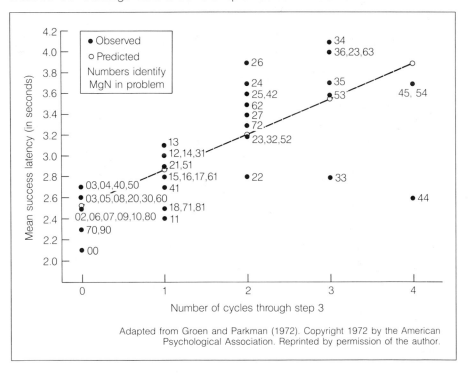

Adapted from Groen and Parkman (1972). Copyright 1972 by the American Psychological Association. Reprinted by permission of the author.

BOX 14–17   Some Subtraction Bugs

Number of occurrences in 1325 students	Name	Example	Description
57	Borrow from zero	$\begin{array}{r}103\\-\ 45\\\hline 158\end{array}$ $\begin{array}{r}803\\-508\\\hline 395\end{array}$	When borrowing from a column whose top digit is 0, the student writes 9, but does not continue borrowing from the column to the left of zero.
54	Smaller from larger	$\begin{array}{r}253\\-118\\\hline 145\end{array}$	The student subtracts the smaller digit in each column from the larger, regardless of which one is on top.
10	Zero minus a number equals the number	$\begin{array}{r}140\\-\ 21\\\hline 121\end{array}$	Whenever the top digit in a column is 0, the student writes the bottom digit as the answer.
10	Move over zero, borrow	$\begin{array}{r}304\\-\ 75\\\hline 139\end{array}$	When the student needs to borrow from a column whose top digit is 0, he skips that column and borrows from the next one.
34	Zero minus a number equals the number *and* move over zero, borrow	$\begin{array}{r}304\\-\ 75\\\hline 179\end{array}$	Whenever the top digit in a column is 0, the student writes the bottom digit as the answer. When the student needs to borrow from a column whose top digit is zero, he skips that column and borrows from the next one.

children but more complex and efficient ones are used by older children. Models for addition and subtraction procedures are important because they describe in a precise way, what people have in their memories.

As any teacher knows, students may use arithmetic algorithms that are slightly flawed. For example, a student may know the procedure for three-digit subtraction except that it contains one small "bug"—that is, one small procedural step that is wrong. A student who uses an algorithm with one or more bugs may get the correct answer sometimes and may make errors other times. Rather than stating that a particular student performs at a certain level on a test, it is more useful to describe what procedural knowledge the student has, bugs and all. For example, Brown and Burton (1978) have been able to specify some of the procedural bugs in children's algorithms for three-digit subtraction. Examples are given in Box 14-17. Note that some students may be making only one wrong move (as for the first five examples) or may be committing several errors (as for the last example).

Brown and Burton gave a set of 15 subtraction problems to 1325 primary school students. They used a computer program called BUGGY to analyze each student's procedural knowledge of three-digit subtraction. If a student's answers were all correct, BUGGY would categorize that student as using the correct algorithm. If there were many errors, BUGGY would attempt to find one bug that could account for most or all of the errors. If no single bug seemed to account for the errors, then all possible combinations were tried, until BUGGY found the combination that best accounted for the errors. As you can see in Box 14-17, 57 subjects out of 1325 seemed to have the "Borrow from zero" bug, while 34 seemed to have both the "Diff $0 - n = n$" bug and the "Move over zero, borrow" bug at the same time, and so on. The "Borrow from zero" bug was the most common, occurring alone or in combination with other bugs in 153 of the 1325 students.

The BUGGY program was based on hundreds of bugs or bug combinations, but it still was not completely successful in diagnosing students' subtraction algorithms. The program was able to find algorithms (including bugs) that either completely or partially produced the answers given by 43 percent of the students. The other students seemed to be making random errors or they were inconsistent in their procedural mistakes. Brown and Burton's BUGGY program is an advance over previous methods of evaluating performance because BUGGY provides a clear description of the procedural knowledge of each student.

Role of Algebraic Algorithms

Algebraic algorithms are another kind of procedural knowledge that you must have to solve the motorboat problem. For example, suppose you had to solve the following equation:

$$2(R + 8) = 3(R - 8)$$

where R is the rate of the boat. Mayer (1982) has described that you would need the following algebraic skills as necessary to solve it:

Clear Parentheses (CP)—for example, how to go from the given equation to $2R + 16 = 3R - 24$

Move Variable (MV)—how to go from the equation to $16 - 3R = 2R - 24$

Move Number (MN)—how to go from the equation to $16 + 24 = 3R - 2R$

Combine Variable (CV)—how to go from the equation to $16 + 24 = R$

Combine Number (CN)—how to go from the equation to $40 = R$

As with arithmetic algorithms, there are many possible bugs involved in using algebraic procedures. For example, Carry, Lewis, and Bernard (1980) have listed over 100 bugs that students committed in solving equations. Box 14-18 gives some

BOX 14–18   Some Bugs in Solving Equations

Operator Errors

deletion

$$\frac{x - 10}{x + 5} \longrightarrow -2$$

transposition

$$28x - 11 = 12x - 3 \longrightarrow 40x = -14$$

recombination

$$x + x \longrightarrow x^2$$

combining fractions

$$\frac{x}{1} + \frac{x + 1}{2} \longrightarrow \frac{x + x + 1}{2}$$

cross-multiplication

$$\frac{1}{2} = \frac{x - 10}{x + 5} \longrightarrow \frac{x + 5}{2(x - 10)}$$

splitting equations

$$\frac{5}{10} - \frac{x - 10}{x + 5} \longrightarrow 5 = x - 10 \text{ and } 10 = x + 5$$

reciprocal operations

$$\frac{1}{x} + \frac{1}{2}x \longrightarrow \frac{1}{x + 2x}$$

Application Errors

application

$$x + 2(x - 1) \longrightarrow x^2 + 3x + 2$$

Execution Errors

partial execution

$$2(x + 1) \longrightarrow 2x + 1$$

replacement

$$-\frac{x + 3}{x} = -2 \longrightarrow -x + 3 = -2$$

Adapted from Carry, Lewis, and Bernard (1980)

---

examples of them. Similar error analyses have been performed by Matz (1980) and by Davis and McKnight (1979).

Simon (1980) has recently pointed out that algebra textbooks tend to emphasize algebraic procedures (such as adding equal quantities to both sides of an equation) but fail to emphasize the conditions under which an algorithm should be applied. In other words, procedures are taught, but strategies for when to use them are often not taught.

STRATEGIC KNOWLEDGE

So far we have listed the types of knowledge needed to translate the motorboat problem (linguistic, semantic, and schema) and to solve it (arithmetic and algebraic algorithms). This section explores one final type of knowledge that is needed to control the use of these kinds of information—strategic knowledge. A *strategy* is a general problem-solving technique; strategies do not guarantee that you find an answer, but they help guide you in solving problems. For example, Polya's (1968) suggestion to "break the problem into smaller problems" is an example of a strategy.

In the equations for the riverboat problem, the initial state is $2(R + 8) = 3(R - 8)$ and the goal state is $R =$ _____ . Strategic knowledge is needed to help you move from the initial to the goal state.

Bundy (1976) has proposed a framework for describing strategies involved in solving equations. He suggests three basic techniques or strategies:

> *Attraction* —rearranging the two instances of the unknown so that they can be changed to one instance of the unknown by carrying out a simple arithmetic operation, such as moving from $2R + 16 = 2R - 24$ to $16 = 3R - 2R - 24$.
>
> *Collection* —carrying out a simple arithmetic operation so that two instances of an unknown can be changed to one, such as moving from $16 = 3R - 2R - 24$ to $16 = R - 24$.
>
> *Isolation* —remove any numbers that are on the same side of the equation as the unknown such as moving from $16 = R - 24$ to $16 + 24 = R$.

In solving a linear equation such as $2(R + 8) = 3(R - 8)$, a student might use a strategy of first trying to attract, then trying to collect, and then trying to isolate. For example, if this version of the Bundy system is correct, we would predict that the first step would be: $0 = 3(R - 8) = 2(R + 8)$. This move is an example of attraction because it tries to get the unknowns on the same side of the equation.

Although Bundy's system was intended mainly as a framework for a computer program that solves equations, you might wonder whether it is also a good psychological theory. To answer that question Lewis (1981) compared how college students solved equations to how Bundy's system might solve equations. For example, consider the equation $9(X + 40) = 5(X + 40)$. According to Lewis, Bundy's system would attempt to use attraction, then collection, then isolation. However, as shown in Box 14-19, most college students began by multiplying out the parentheses, with some students using a canceling strategy. Thus, for many problems, including those like our motorboat equation, there are several different strategies.

In a recent series of studies, Mayer, Larkin, and Kadane (1983) investigated strategies used by students to solve equations similar to those involved in the motorboat problem. In particular, two major strategies were investigated:

> *Reduce strategy* —trying to make the equation less complex by carrying out all indicated arithmetic operations.

BOX 14–19 Strategies for Solving $9(x + 40) = 5(x + 40)$

Name	Number of students	Example of first step
Attraction	3	$9(x + 40) - 5(x + 40) = 0$
Multiply out	25	$9x + 360 = 5x + 200$
Cancel	6	$9 = 5$

Adapted from Carry, Lewis, and Bernard (1980)

Isolate strategy—trying to get all the *x* terms on the left side of the equals and the numbers on the right side.

Mayer, Larkin, and Kadane were able to locate some situations in which the isolate or reduce strategy was used. In addition, intensive study of a few subjects revealed considerable individual differences; some subjects consistently used one strategy and some subjects employed the other.

SEX DIFFERENCES

The issue of sex differences in mathematical problem solving has been raised often, especially in the popular press. For example, in 1980 *Newsweek* ran a story entitled, "Do Males Have a Math Gene?" and the same week *Time* devoted a page to "The Gender Factor in Math." In spite of the occasionally intense public attention and strong opinions sometimes given in popular publications, it is possible to examine the sex differences issue from a scientific point of view. In particular, let us examine two related questions: (1) Are there sex differences in children's scores on tests of mathematical ability and achievement? (2) If so, why are there differences?

Are There Differences?

In their book, *The Psychology of Sex Differences*, Maccoby and Jacklin (1974) devote a section to sex differences in mathematical ability. In particular, they summarize the findings of 27 different studies or sets of studies. In a typical study, a standard test of mathematical ability (such as the SAT math or ACT math) is given to a large sample of school children. Maccoby and Jacklin suggest looking at the results separately for three age groups, ranging from 3 to 21.

For the youngest children (ages 3 to 8), there were either no differences between the average score for boys and the average score for girls, or in cases where there

BOX 14–20   Large-Scale Studies of Sex Differences in Mathematical Ability

Study

Study	Age	Sample size Boys	Sample size Girls	Mean scores Boys	Mean scores Girls	Size of mean difference*	Sex scoring higher
SRI (1972)	5	1,799	1,724	25.46	27.40	−.12	F
	7	1,596	1,488	38.44	40.58	−.16	F
Svensson (1971) (Sweden):							
School I–1961	13	2,950	2,878	41.53	39.85	.17	M
School II–1961	13	1,499	1,578	41.72	40.02	.17	M
School I–1966	13	731	769	35.14	34.09	.08	M
School II–1966	13	3,097	3,047	37.26	35.02	.16	M
Droege (1967); GATB (numerical subscore)	14	3,398	3,680	97.70	100.19	.18	F
	15	3,348	3,491	99.37	101.74	.16	F
	16	3,229	3,395	102.76	103.08	.02	F
	17	3,028	3,139	106.54	105.70	.05	M
Project Talent; Flanagan et al. (1961)	14	1,152	990	7.14	5.81	.36	M
	17	1,153	1,250	11.58	7.86	.64	M
ACT 1966 norm manual (math subscore); Monday et al. (1966–67)	18	133,882	104,263	21.10	18.0	.47	M

*The difference between the means has been divided by the weighted mean of the standard deviations of the two sex distributions; that is, the difference is expressed as a standard score.

Adapted from Maccoby and Jacklyn (1974)

were differences, girls averaged better than boys. For children 9- to 12-years old, some studies found no difference; those that did find differences showed boys scoring higher than girls. In the 13 to 21 age group, boys tended to score higher on the average than girls in most of the studies. Maccoby and Jacklin (1974) listed five studies that involved very large samples involving thousands of students. Box 14-20 lists the results of these large-scale studies. Of the four studies involving children above age 12, three find that boys score higher and one finds essentially no difference.

BOX 14–21   Math Test Results by Sex and by Age

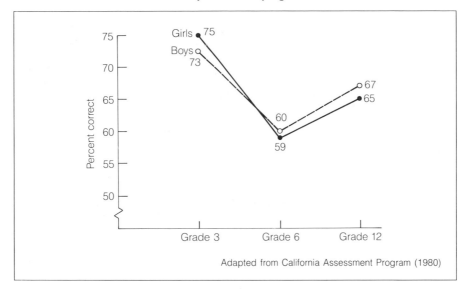

Adapted from California Assessment Program (1980)

More recently, Marshall (1980) has analyzed the data from standardized mathematics achievement tests given to all third-, sixth-, and twelfth-graders in California public schools for the past five years. These data, from the California Assessment Program (1980), give consistent evidence that at grade 3, girls have a slightly higher average score; at grade 6, boys have a slightly higher average score; and by grade 12, boys have a substantially higher score. This pattern is summarized in Box 14-21. Such a pattern is consistent with most studies (Fennema, 1974; Hilton and Berglund, 1974; Maccoby and Jacklin, 1974). Thus, there is an apparent trend in which sex differences in mathematical performance depend on age.

Sex differences also seem to depend on the type of problem that is given. For example, Backman (1972) found that high school boys averaged better than girls on tests that involved mathematical problem solving other than computation, but there were no differences for tests of computation. A similar pattern was observed in the data of Fennema and Sherman (1978); sixth-grade girls were more successful than boys on tests of computation and less successful on tests of application and problem solving. Although the sex differences are not statistically significant in several cases, the trend is an interesting one that suggests further study is needed. In an analysis of California Assessment Program data, Marshall (1980) has found evidence that girls score significantly higher than boys on some computation problems while boys tend to score higher on some applications problems.

Why Are There Differences?

Now comes the hard part. Let's assume for the moment that we believe the data that boys tend to average higher than girls on mathematical problem-solving tests, as summarized in the previous passage. The tough theoretical question is why such results are obtained. In this section, we will explore some possible explanations.

First, let's examine the "different experience" argument. Boys' superiority in math during high school years may be due to their greater interest in math. For example, in primary grades students generally have no choice about which courses they will take—everyone must study arithmetic. In high school students have options concerning whether or not they will take math, and there is evidence that boys elect to take more math courses than girls in high school. Thus, performance on math ability tests may be due to the fact that boys have taken more courses rather than any difference in underlying aptitude.

In order to test this idea, Fennema and Sherman (1977) tested approximately 1200 high school students on a battery of tests including math achievement, attitudes, experience in math, parents' attitude, and so on. As expected, boys scored higher than girls on math achievement tests. However, when the statistical analysis took the number of math-related courses taken into account, the differences were reduced or disappeared. We could stop at this, happy to have solved the "sex-differences" problem, if it were not for several troublesome facts. One problem is that Fennema and Sherman seem to have analyzed the data for each school separately; this yields a smaller sample size and could influence whether differences are significant. A second problem is that other researchers have not been able to substantiate this finding.

More recently, Benbow and Stanley (1980) published a paper titled "Sex Differences in Mathematical Ability: Fact or Artifact?" It is based on a study of 9927 "intellectually gifted" junior high school students selected from five states and the District of Columbia for Project Talent. The goal of Project Talent is to locate the most talented students early in their lives so they can be prepared for appropriate careers. The study covers six years (1972 to 1979) and involves students in the upper 2–5 percent of their classes in mathematical ability. Box 14-22 summarizes the SAT math scores for the most talented boys and girls in the seventh and eighth grades. Benbow and Stanley argue that if Fennema and Sherman (1974, 1977) are right concerning the importance of the number of math courses taken, then there should be no differences between boys and girls in junior high (see Box 14-22). Junior high students have not yet been able to choose whether to take additional math courses. As Box 14-22 shows, boys in the sample tended to score higher than girls on SAT math; in addition, the brightest boys tend to score higher than the brightest girls, and the percentage of students scoring over 600 (out of 800) is higher for boys. Based

BOX 14–22 Sex Differences in SAT Math Scores for Project Talent Students

Test date	Grade	Number		SAT-V Score*		SAT-M Scores†		Highest Score		Percentage Scoring Above 600 on SAT-M	
		Boys	Girls	Boys	Girls	Boys	Girls	Boys	Girls	Boys	Girls
March 1972	7	90	77			460	423	740	590	7.8	0
	8+	133	96			528	458	790	600	27.1	0
January 1973	7	135	88	385	374	495	440	800	620	8.1	1.1
	8+	286	158	431	442	551	511	800	650	22.7	8.2
January 1974	7	372	222			473	440	760	630	6.5	1.8
	8+	556	369			540	503	750	700	21.6	7.9
December 1976	7	495	356	370	368	455	421	780	610	5.5	0.6
	8‡	12	10	487	390	598	482	750	600	58.3	0
January 1978	7 and 8‡	1549	1249	375	372	448	413	790	760	5.3	0.8
January 1979	7 and 8‡	2046	1628	370	370	436	404	790	760	3.2	0.9

*Mean score for a random sample of high school juniors and seniors was 368 for males and females (8).
†Mean for juniors and seniors: males, 416; females, 390 (8).
‡These rare 8th graders were accelerated at least 1 year in school grade placement.

Adapted from Benbow and Stanley (1980). Copyright 1980 by the American Association for the Advancement of Science.

on these findings, Benbow and Stanley state (1980, p. 1263): "The sex difference in mathematical reasoning ability we found was observed before girls and boys started to differ significantly in the number and type of mathematics courses taken."

Although the results of Benbow and Stanley cast doubts on the theory that sex differences are due to differences in the number of math courses taken, the study does not provide definitive evidence in support of an alternative theory. Furthermore, the Benbow and Stanley study has been criticized on the grounds that the search process for locating talented boys may have been more effective than the search process for locating talented girls. In addition, there was no emphasis given to possible differences on students' attitudes, parents' expectations, and so on. It seems likely that by the seventh and eighth grades students have acquired attitudes, expectations, and different levels of math-related experience. Thus, at present, there is a need for more large-scale studies using normal populations before we accept or reject the idea that differences in scores are due to different experiences.

Another explanation for sex differences in the raw scores is the "socialization" argument. There is growing evidence (Maccoby and Jacklin, 1974; Fennema, 1974; Fennema and Sherman, 1977, 1978) that children are taught that math is for boys, that girls are given less experience relevant to arithmetic in early years, and that girls tend to have lower confidence and expectations for themselves in mathematics. In a recent study, Fennema and Sherman note that girls' attitudes concerning math seem to sour as they get older: "At younger ages, girls did not see mathematics as any less useful than did boys, nor did they perceive any less positive attitudes toward them as students of mathematics from parents or teachers. However, as early as sixth grade, girls expressed less confidence than boys in their ability to do mathematics, and the subject was clearly sex-typed male, especially by boys. In the high school years these differential attitudinal influences continued and were joined by a host of other negative attitudinal influences" (1978, p. 202). For example, Fennema and Sherman (1974) found that when statistical analyses took students' attitudes and math-socialization experiences into account, sex differences in math achievement scores were reduced or disappeared. Unfortunately, such statistical adjustments are not as convincing as a "real-life experiment" would be. If social attitudes changed so that math was no longer perceived as a "male domain," we would expect to see a reduction or elimination of sex differences in math achievement. Until such attitude change is complete in our society or until we have much more statistical data, we cannot definitely accept or reject the socialization argument.

Another explanation is that sex differences in mathematical ability are due, at least in part, to genetic differences between boys and girls. For example, Benbow and Stanley (1980, p. 1264) suggest: "We favor the hypothesis that sex differences in achievement and attitude toward mathematics result from superior male mathematical ability, which may in turn be related to greater male ability on spatial tasks.

This male superiority is probably an expression of a combination of both endogenous and exogenous variables . . . Putting one's faith in the boy-versus-girl socialization processes as the only permissible explanation of the sex differences in mathematics is premature.'' These may strike you as strong words; yet, Benbow and Stanley are unable to offer any positive evidence to support a genetic theory of sex differences in mathematical ability. Although magazines may stir their readers with headlines about ''math genes'' in males, there is at present no hard evidence to support such a hypothesis. In addition, it is unclear how a genetic theory can explain why sex-differences change with age. However, in spite of how distasteful or just plain silly the genetic theory is to many people, we must remember that the test of a theory lies in careful study and empirical data rather than our own biases.

In summary, to the question, ''Why do we sometimes observe sex differences in math scores?'', the answer is, ''We're not sure, but a good hypothesis is that there are differences in socialization.'' There is a sense in which the question of sex differences in mathematical problem solving is really a minor one. If we are interested in major factors that influence mathematical problem solving, there is evidence that we should focus on the educational and economic level of the parents or even the number of hours per day that a student watches televisions. For example, Box 14-23 shows math achievement scores for twelfth graders in California public schools (California Assessment Program, 1980); the first figure shows that students who have well-educated parents score an average of 18 percentage points higher than those who have parents with less education. The second figure shows that students whose parents have professional occupations score an average of 20 percentage points higher than students who have parents in unskilled occupations; the third figure shows that students who watch little or no television score an average of 16 points higher than those who watch 6 or more hours of television daily. Compare these differences to the sex difference of only 2 points. The sex of the student is actually a minor factor.

EVALUATION

Research on mathematical problem solving has blossomed in the past decade. There is increasing evidence that people who are able to solve mathematics problems possess appropriate knowledge. This work has implications both for psychological theories of problem solving and for practical teaching in schools. Although this work is really just in its infancy, we someday may be able to specify the semantic, schematic, procedural, and strategic knowledge involved in various problems. In addition, we may be able to better assess what is learned, diagnose errors or gaps in that knowledge, and focus instruction accordingly. The ability of psychology to

BOX 14–23 Math Scores by Parents' Educational Level,
by Parents' Occupational Level,
and by Number of Hours of Television Watching

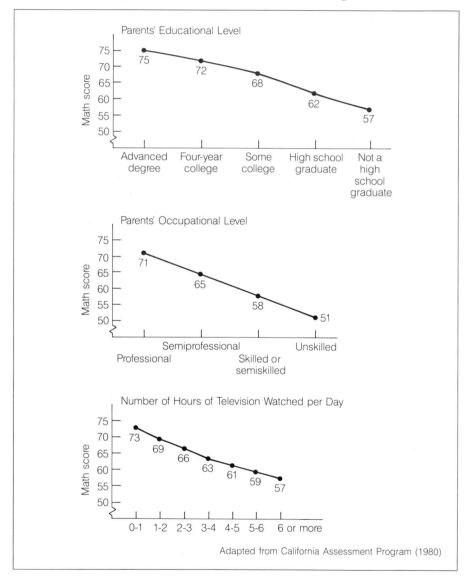

Adapted from California Assessment Program (1980)

study complex, actual problems suggests a growing maturity of the field. In addition, by looking to the real world for problems to study, psychology is pushed forward and is challenged to develop new and better theories.

Suggested Reading

Resnick, L. B., and Ford, W. *The psychology of mathematics for instruction.* Hillsdale, N.J.: Erlbaum, 1981. Provides an introduction to research and theory on the psychology of mathematical problem solving.

REFERENCES

Ach, N. Determining tendencies. In J. M. Mandler and G. Mandler (Eds.), *Thinking: From association to Gestalt*. New York: Wiley, 1964. (Originally published in German in 1905.)

Adams, J. *Learning and memory: An introduction*. Homewood, Ill.: Dorsey, 1976.

Adams, J. L. *Conceptual blockbusting*. San Francisco: W. H. Freeman and Company, 1974.

Adamson, R. E. Functional fixedness as related to problem solving: A repetition of three experiments. *Journal of Experimental Psychology*, 1952, *44*, 288–291.

Adamson, R. E., and Taylor, D. W. Functional fixedness as related to elapsed time and set. *Journal of Experimental Psychology*, 1954, *47*, 122–216.

Anastasi, A., and Schaefer, C. E. Note on concepts of creativity and intelligence. *Journal of Creative Behavior*, 1971, *3*, 113–116.

Anderson, J. R. *Language, memory, and thought*. Hillsdale, N.J.: Erlbaum, 1976.

Anderson, J. R. *Cognitive psychology and its implications*. San Francisco: W. H. Freeman and Company, 1980.

Anderson, R. C., Reynolds, R.E., Schallert, D. L., and Goetz, E. T. Frameworks for comprehending discourse. *American Educational Research Journal*, 1977, *14*, 367–382.

Atwood, M. E., and Polson, P. G. A process model for water jug problems. *Cognitive Psychology*, 1976, *8*, 191–216.

Ausubel, D. P. *Educational psychology: A cognitive view*. New York: Holt, Rinehart and Winston, 1968.

Backman, M. E. Patterns of mental abilities: Ethnic, socioeconomic, and sex differences. *American Educational Research Journal*, 1972, *9*, 1–12.

Bakan, P. Hypnotizability, laterality of eye movements, and functional brain asymmetry. *Perceptual and Motor Skills,* 1969, *28,* 927–932.

Bartlett, F. C. *Remembering: A study in experimental and social psychology.* London: Cambridge University Press, 1932.

Bartlett, F. C. *Thinking.* London: Allen & Unwin, 1958.

Battersby, W. S., Teuber, H. L., and Bender, M. B. Problem solving behavior in men with frontal or occipital brain injuries. *Journal of Psychology,* 1953, *35,* 329–351.

Battig, W. F., and Bourne, L. E., Jr. Concept identification as a function of intra- and inter-dimension variability. *Journal of Experimental Psychology,* 1961, *61,* 329–333.

Baum, M. H. Single concept learning as a function of intralist generalization. *Journal of Experimental Psychology,* 1954, *47,* 89–94.

Begg, I., and Denny, P. Empirical reconciliation of atmosphere and conversion inter-pretations of syllogistic reasoning errors. *Journal of Experimental Psychology,* 1969, *81,* 351–354.

Begg, I., and Paivio, A. Concreteness and imagery in sentence meaning. *Journal of Verbal Learning and Verbal Behavior,* 1969, *8,* 821–827.

Beilin, H. Developmental determinants of word and nonsense anagram solution. *Journal of Verbal Learning and Verbal Behavior,* 1967, *6,* 523–527.

Beilin, H. The training and acquisition of logical operations. In M. F. Rosskopf, L. P. Steffe, and S. Tabach (Eds.), *Piagetian cognitive-developmental research and mathematical education.* Washington, D.C.: National Council of Teachers of Mathematics, 1971.

Beilin, H., and Horn, R. Transition probability effects in anagram problem solving. *Journal of Experimental Psychology,* 1962, *63,* 514–518.

Benbow, C., and Stanley, J. Sex differences in mathematics ability: Fact or artifact? *Science,* 1980, *210,* 1262–1264.

Benton, A. L. *Right-left discrimination and finger localization: Development and pathology.* New York: Hoeber, 1959.

Berlin, B., and Kay, P. *Basic color terms: Their universality and evolution.* University of California Press, 1969.

Berlyne, D. E. *Structure and direction in thinking.* New York: Wiley, 1965.

Birch, H. G. The relation of previous experience to insightful problem solving. *Journal of Comparative Psychology,* 1945, *38,* 367–383.

Birch, H. G., and Rabinowitz, H. S. The negative effect of previous experience on productive thinking. *Journal of Experimental Psychology,* 1951, *41,* 121–125.

Bjork, R. A. All-or-none subprocesses in learning a complex sequence. *Journal of Mathematical Psychology,* 1968, *5,* 182–195.

Bloom, B. S., and Broder, L. J. *Problem-solving processes of college students. An explora-tory investigation.* Chicago: University of Chicago Press, 1950.

Bobrow, D. G. Natural language input for a computer problem-solving system. In M. Minsky (Ed.), *Semantic information processing.* Cambridge, Mass.: M.I.T. Press, 1968.

Boring, E. G. Intelligence as the tests test it. *New Republic,* 1923, *35,* 35–37.

Bouchard, T. J. What ever happened to brainstorming? *Journal of Creative Behavior,* 1971, *3,* 182–189.

Bourne, L. E., Jr. *Human conceptual behavior*. Boston: Allyn & Bacon, 1966.

Bourne, L. E., Jr. Knowing and using concepts. *Psychological Review*, 1970, *77*, 546–556.

Bourne, L. E., Jr., Ekstrand, B. R., and Dominowski, R. L. *The psychology of thinking*. Englewood Cliffs, N.J.: Prentice-Hall, 1971.

Bower, G. H., and Trabasso, T. R. Reversals prior to solution in concept identification. *Journal of Experimental Psychology*, 1963, *66*, 409–418.

Bower, G. H., and Trabasso, T. R. Concept identification. In R. C. Atkinson (Ed.), *Studies in mathematical psychology*. Stanford, Calif.: Stanford University Press, 1964.

Brainerd, C. J. Neo-Piagetian training experiments revisted: Is there any support for the cognitive-developmental stage hypothesis? *Cognition*, 1974, *2*, 349–370.

Bransford, J. D. *Human cognition: Learning, understanding and remembering*. Belmont, Calif.: Wadsworth, 1979.

Bransford, J. D., and Franks, J. J. The abstraction of linguistic ideas. *Cognitive Psychology*, 1971, *2*, 331–350.

Bransford, J. D., and Johnson, M. K. Contextual prerequisites for understanding: Some investigations of comprehension and recall. *Journal of Verbal Learning and Verbal Behavior*, 1972, *61*, 717–726.

Braun, H. W., and Geiselhart, R. Age differences in the acquisition and extinction of the conditioned eyelid response. *Journal of Experimental Psychology*, 1959, *57*, 386–388.

Brown, A. L., and DeLoache, J. S. Skills, plans, and self-regulation. In R. S. Siegler (Ed.), *Children's thinking: What develops?* Hillsdale, N.J.: Erlbaum, 1978.

Brown, F. G. *Principles of educational and psychological testing*. (3rd ed.) New York: Holt, Rinehart and Winston, 1983.

Brown, J. S., and Burton, R. Diagnostic models for procedural bugs in basic mathematical skills. *Cognitive Science*, 1978, *2*, 155–192.

Brown, R. W., and Berko, J. Word association and the acquisition of grammar. *Child Development*, 1960, *31*, 1–14.

Brown, R. W., and Lenneberg, E. H. A study of language and cognition. *Journal of Abnormal and Social Psychology*, 1954, *49*, 454–462.

Brown, R. W., and McNeil, D. The "tip-of-the-tongue" phenomena. *Journal of Verbal Learning and Verbal Behavior*, 1966, *5*, 325–337.

Brownell, W. A. Psychological considerations in the learning and teaching of arithmetic. In *The teaching of arithmetic: Tenth yearbook of the National Council of Teachers of Mathematics*. New York: Columbia University Press, 1935.

Brownell, W. A., and Moser, H. E. Meaningful *vs.* mechanical learning: A study in grade III subtraction. In *Duke University research studies in education, No. 8*. Durham, N.C.: Duke University Press, 1949.

Bruner, J. S. The act of discovery. *Harvard Educational Review*, 1961, *31*, 21–32.

Bruner, J. S. The course of cognitive growth. *American Psychologist*, 1964, *19*, 1–15.

Bruner, J. S. Some elements of discovery. In L. S. Shulman and E. R. Keisler (Eds.), *Learning by discovery*. Chicago: Rand McNally, 1966.

Bruner, J. S. *Toward a theory of instruction*. New York: Norton, 1968.

Bruner, J. S. *Beyond the information given: Studies in the psychology of knowing.* New York: Norton, 1973.

Bruner, J. S., Goodnow, J. J., and Austin, G. A. *A study of thinking.* New York: Wiley, 1956.

Bruner, J. S., and Kenney, H. J. Representation and mathematics learning. In L. N. Morrisett and J. Vinsonhaler (Eds.), *Mathematical learning. Monographs of the Society for Research in Child Development,* 1965 (Ser. no. 99), 30.

Bruner, J. S., and Kenney, H. Multiple ordering. In J. S. Bruner, R. R. Olver, and P. M. Greenfield (Eds.), *Studies in cognitive growth.* New York: Wiley, 1966.

Bruner, J. S., Olver, R. R., and Greenfield, P. M. (Eds.), *Studies in cognitive growth.* New York: Wiley, 1966.

Bryant, P. E., and Trabasso, T. Transitive inferences and memory in young children. *Nature,* 1971, *232,* 456–458.

Buchanan, B., Sutherland, G., and Feiganbaum, E. A. Heuristic DENTRAL: A program for generating explanatory hypotheses in organic chemistry. In *Machine Intelligence 4.* New York: Elsevier, 1969.

Bundy, A. Analyzing mathematical proofs. Research report No. 2. Edinburgh: Department of Artificial Intelligence, University of Edinburgh, 1975.

Buros, O. K. *Mental measurements yearbook.* Highland Park, N.J.: Gryphon Press, 1978.

Burrows, D., and Okada, R. Serial position effects in high-speed memory search. *Perception and Psychophysics,* 1971, *10,* 305–308.

California Assessment Program. *Student achievement in California schools: 1979–80 annual report.* Sacramento: California State Department of Education, 1980.

Campione, J. C., and Brown, A. L. *Toward a theory of intelligence: Contributions from research with retarded children.* Norwood, N.J.: Ablex, 1979.

Carmichael, L. L., Hogan, H. P., and Walter, A. A. An experimental study of the effect of language on the reproduction of visually perceived form. *Journal of Experimental Psychology,* 1932, *15,* 73–86.

Carpenter, P. A., and Just, M. A. Sentence comprehension: A psycholinguistic processing model of verification. *Psychological Review,* 1975, *82,* 45–73.

Carpenter, T. P. Hueristic strategies used to solve addition and subtraction problems. In R. Karplus (Ed.), *Proceedings of the fourth international conference for the psychology of mathematics education.* Berkeley: University of California, 1980.

Carpenter, T. P., Corbitt, M. K., Kepner, H. S., and Lindquist, M. M. National assessment: A perspective of mathematics achievement in the United States. In R. Karplus (Ed.), *Proceedings of the fourth international conference for the psychology of mathematics instruction.* Berkeley: University of California, 1980.

Carroll, J. B. Psychometric tests as cognitive tasks: A new structure of intellect. In L. B. Resnick (Ed.), *The nature of intelligence.* Hillsdale, N.J.: Erlbaum, 1976.

Carry, L. R., Lewis, C., and Bernard, J. E. *Psychology of equation solving: An information processing study.* Department of Curriculum and Instruction, University of Texas at Austin, 1980.

Case, R. Intellectual development from birth to adulthood: A neo-Piagetian interpretation. In R. S. Siegler (Ed.), *Children's Thinking: What develops?* Hillsdale, N.J.: Erlbaum, 1978a.

Case, R. Implications of developmental psychology for the design of effective instruction. In A. M. Lesgold, J. W. Pelligrino, S. D. Fokkema, and R. Glaser (Eds.), *Cognitive psychology and instruction.* New York: Plenum, 1978b.

Cavanagh, J. P. Relation between the immediate memory span and the memory search rate. *Psychological Review,* 1972, *79,* 525–530.

Ceraso, J., and Provitera, A. Sources of error in syllogistic reasoning. *Cognitive Psychology,* 1971, *2,* 400–410.

Chapman, L. J., and Chapman, J. P. Atmosphere effect reexamined. *Journal of Experimental Psychology,* 1959, *58,* 220–226.

Chapman, L. J., and Chapman, J. P. Genesis of popular but erroneous psychodiagnostic observations. *Journal of Abnormal Psychology,* 1967, *73,* 193–204.

Chapman, L. J., and Chapman, J. P. Illusory correlation as an obstacle to the use of valid psychodiagnostic signs. *Journal of Abnormal Psychology,* 1969, *74,* 271–280.

Chapman, R. M. Evoked potentials of the brain related to thinking. In F. J. McGuigan and R. A. Schoonover (Eds.), *The psychophysiology of thinking.* New York: Academic Press, 1973.

Chase, W. G., and Clark, H. H. Mental operations in the comparison of sentences and pictures. In L. Gregg (Ed.), *Cognition in learning and memory.* New York: Wiley, 1972.

Chase, W. G., and Simon, H. A. Perception in chess. *Cognitive Psychology,* 1973, *4,* 55–81.

Chi, M. T. H. Short-term memory limitations in children: Capacity or processing deficits. *Memory and Cognition,* 1976, *4,* 559–572.

Chi, M. T. H. Knowledge structures and memory development. In R. S. Siegler (Ed.), *Children's thinking: What develops?* Hillsdale, N.J.: Erlbaum, 1978.

Chomsky, N. *Syntactic structures.* The Hague: Mouton, 1957.

Chomsky, N. Verbal behavior (a review). *Language,* 1959, *35,* 26–58.

Chomsky, N. *Aspects of the theory of syntax.* Cambridge: M.I.T. Press, 1965.

Chomsky, N. *Language and mind.* New York: Harcourt, Brace Jovanovich, 1968.

Clark, H. H. Linguistic processes in deductive reasoning. *Psychological Review,* 1969, *76,* 387–404.

Clark, H. H., and Chase, W. G. On the process of comparing sentences against pictures. *Cognitive Psychology,* 1972, *3,* 472–517.

Clement, J., Lochhead, J., and Soloway, E. Translation between symbol systems: Isolating a common difficulty in solving algebra word problems. COINS technical report No. 79–19. Amherst: Department of Computer and Information Sciences, University of Massachusetts, March 1979.

Clifton, C., and Birenbaum, S. Effects of serial position and delay of probe in a memory scan task. *Journal of Experimental Psychology,* 1970, *86,* 69–76.

Coler, C. N. Verbal behavior in relation to reasoning and values. In H. Guetzkow (Ed.), *Group leadership and men*. Pittsburgh: Carnegie Press, 1951.

Cohen, L. J. On the psychology of prediction: Whose is the fallacy? *Cognition*, 1979, *7*, 385–407.

Cohen, L. J. Whose is the fallacy? A rejoinder to Daniel Kahneman and Amos Tversky. *Cognition*, 1980, *8*, 89–92.

Colby, K. M. Computer simulation of neurotic processes. In R. W. Stacey and B. D. Waxman (Eds.), *Computers in biomedical research*. New York: Academic Press, 1965.

Colby, K. M., Watt, J., and Gilbert, J. P. A computer model of psychotherapy. *Journal of Nervous and Mental Diseases*, 1966, *142*, 148–152.

Collins, A. M., and Loftus, E. F. A spreading activation theory of semantic processing. *Psychological Review*, 1975, *82*, 407–428.

Collins, A. M., and Quillian, M. R. Retrieval time from semantic memory. *Journal of Verbal Learning and Verbal Behavior*, 1969, *8*, 240–247.

Collins, A. M., and Quillian, M. R. How to make a language user. In E. Tulving and W. Donaldson (Eds.), *Organization of memory*. New York: Wiley, 1972.

Conrad, C. Cognitive economy in semantic memory. *Journal of Experimental Psychology*, 1972, *92*, 149–154.

Cooper, L. A. Mental rotation of random two-dimensional forms. *Cognitive Psychology*, 1975, *7*, 20–43.

Cooper, L. A. Duration of a mental analog of an external rotation. *Perception & Psychophysics*, 1976, *19*, 296–302.

Cooper, L. A., and Shepard, R. N. Chronometric studies of the rotation of mental images. In W. G. Chase (Ed.), *Visual information processing*. New York: Academic Press, 1973a.

Cooper, L. A., and Shepard, R. N. The time required to prepare for a rotated stimulus. *Memory & Cognition*, 1973b, *1*, 246–250.

Corman, B. R. The effect of varying amounts and kinds of information as guidance in problem solving. *Psychological Monographs*, 1957, *71*, Whole No. 431.

Covington, M. V., Crutchfield, R. S., and Davies, L. B. *The productive thinking program*. Berkeley, Calif.: Brazelton, 1966.

Covington, M. V., Crutchfield, R. S., Davies, L. B., and Olton, R. M. *The productive thinking program*. Columbus, Ohio: Merrill, 1974.

Crawford, R. P. *The techniques of creative thinking*. New York: Hawthorn, 1954.

Cronbach, L. J. The two disciplines of scientific psychology. *American Psychologist*, 1957, *12*, 671–684.

Dattman, P. E., and Israel, H. The order of dominance among conceptual capacities: An experimental test of Heidbreder's hypothesis. *Journal of Psychology*, 1951, *31*, 147–160.

Davis, G. A. *Psychology of problem solving: Theory and practice*. New York: Basic Books, 1973.

Davis, G. A., and Houtman, S. E. *Thinking creatively: A guide to training imagination*. Madison: Wisconsin Research and Development Center, 1968.

Davis, G. A., and Scott, J. A. *Training creative thinking.* Huntington, N.Y.: Krieger, 1978.

Davis, R. B., and McKnight, C. C. Modeling the processes of mathematical thinking. *Journal of Children's Mathematical Behavior,* 1979, *2,* 91–113.

Delgado, J. M. R. *Physical control of the mind.* New York: Harper & Row, 1969.

DeSoto, C. B., Learning and social structure. *Journal of Abnormal and Social Psychology,* 1960, *60,* 417–421.

DeSoto, C. B., London, M., and Handel, S. Social reasoning and spatial paralogic. *Journal of Personality and Social Psychology,* 1965, *2,* 513–521.

Devnich, G. E. Words as "Gestalten." *Journal of Experimental Psychology,* 1937, *20,* 297–300.

Dominowski, R. L., and Duncan, C. P. Anagram solving as a function of bigram frequency. *Journal of Verbal Learning and Verbal Behavior,* 1964, *3,* 321–325.

Donchin, E., and Israel, J. B. Event-related potentials: Approaches to cognitive psychology. In R. E. Snow, P. Federico, and W. E. Montague (Eds.), *Aptitude, learning, and instruction.* Vol. 2. Hillsdale, N.J.: Erlbaum, 1980.

Donders, F. C. Over de snelheid van psychische processen. *Ondersoekingen gedaan in het Physiologisch Laboratium der Utrechtsche Hoogeschool,* 1868–1869, *2,* 92–120. W. G. Koster (Trans.), *Acta Psychologica,* 1969, *30,* 412–431.

Doob, L. W. Eidetic images among the Ibo. *Ethnology,* 1964, *3,* 357–363.

Dooling, D. J., and Lachman, R. Effects of comprehension on the retention of prose. *Journal of Experimental Psychology,* 1971, *88,* 216–222.

Dooling, D. J., and Mullet, R. L. Locus of thematic effects in retention of prose. *Journal of Experimental Psychology,* 1973, *97,* 404–406.

Duncker, K. On problem solving. *Psychological Monographs,* 1945, *58*:5, Whole No. 270.

Dunnette, M. D., Campbell, J., and Jaastad, K. Effect of group participation on brain-storming effectiveness for two industrial samples. *Journal of Applied Psychology,* 1963, *47,* 30–37.

Edwards, M. W. A survey of problem solving courses. *Journal of Creative Behavior,* 1968, *2,* 33–51.

Egan, D. E., and Greeno, J. G. Theory of rule induction: Knowledge acquired in concept learning, serial pattern learning, and problem solving. In L. W. Gregg, (Ed.), *Knowledge and Cognition.* Hillsdale, N.J.: Erlbaum, 1974.

Ehrlichman, H., Weiner, S., and Baker, A. Effects of verbal and spatial questions on initial gaze shifts. *Neuropsychologia,* 1974, *12,* 265–277.

Ekstrom, R. B., French, J. W., and Harman, H. H. *Manual for Kit of Factor-Referenced Cognitive Tests.* Princeton, N.J.: Educational Testing Service, 1976.

Elkind, D. Introduction. In J. Piaget, *Six psychological studies.* New York: Random House, 1967.

Erickson, J. R. A set analysis theory of behavior in formal syllogistic reasoning tasks. In R. L. Solso (Ed.), *Theories of cognitive psychology: The Loyola symposium.* Hillsdale, N.J.: Erlbaum, 1974.

Erickson, J. R. Research on syllogistic reasoning. In R. Revlin and R. E. Mayer (Eds.), *Human Reasoning.* New York: Wiley/Winston, 1978.

Ernst, G. W., and Newell, A. *GPS: A case study in generality and problem solving.* New York: Academic Press, 1969.

Ervin, S. M. Changes with age in the verbal determinants of word-association. *American Journal of Psychology,* 1961, *74,* 361–372.

Evans, J. Current issues in the psychology of reasoning. *British Journal of Psychology,* 1980, *71,* 227–239.

Evans, T. G. A program for the solution of a class of geometry-analogy intelligence test questions. In M. L. Minsky (Ed.), *Semantic information processing,* Cambridge, Mass.: M.I.T. Press, 1968.

Ewert, P. H., and Lambert, J. F. Part II: The effect of verbal instructions upon the formation of a concept. *Journal of General Psychology,* 1932, *6,* 400–411.

Feigenbaum, E. A. Information processing and memory. In D. A. Norman (Ed.), *Models of human memory.* New York: Academic Press, 1970, 451–469.

Feldhusen, J. F., Treffinger, D. J., and Bahlke, S. J. Developing creative thinking: The Purdue creativity program. *Journal of Creative Behavior,* 1970, *4,* 85–90.

Fennema, E. L. Mathematics learning and the sexes: A review. *Journal for Research in Mathematics Education,* 1974, *5,* 126–139.

Fennema, E. L., and Sherman, J. A. Sex-related differences in mathematics achievement, spatial visualization and affective factors. *American Educational Research Journal,* 1977, *14,* 51–71.

Fennema, E. L., and Sherman, J. A. Sex-related differences in mathematics achievement and related factors: A further study. *Journal for Research in Mathematics Education,* 1978, *9,* 189–203.

Flavell, J. H., and Wellman, H. M. Metamemory. In R. V. Kail and J. W. Hagen (Eds.), *Perspectives on the development of memory and cognition.* Hillsdale, N.J.: Erlbaum, 1977.

Frank, F. Perception and language in conservation. In J. S. Bruner, R. R. Olver, and P. M. Greenfield (Eds.), *Studies in cognitive growth.* New York: Wiley, 1966.

Franks, J. J., and Bransford, J. D. Abstraction of visual patterns. *Journal of Experimental Psychology,* 1971, *90,* 65–74.

Frase, L. T. Structural analysis of the knowledge that results from learning about text. *Journal of Educational Psychology,* 1969, *60,* Monograph Supplement 6.

Frase, L. T. Influence of sentence order and amount of higher level text processing upon reproductive and productive memory. *American Educational Research Journal,* 1970, *7,* 307–319.

Frase, L. T. Maintenance and control in the acquisition of knowledge from written materials. In R. O. Freedle and J. B. Carroll (Eds.), *Language comprehension and the acquisition of knowledge.* Washington, D.C.: Winston, 1972.

Friebergs, V., and Tulving, E. The effect of practice on utilization of information from positive and negative instances in concept identification. *Canadian Journal of Psychology,* 1961, *15,* 101–106.

Gagné, R. M. Learning hierarchies. *Educational Psychology,* 1968, *6,* 1–9.

Gagné, R. M., and Brown, L. T. Some factors in the programming of conceptual learning. *Journal of Experimental Psychology,* 1961, *62,* 313–321.

Gagné, R. M., and Smith, E. C. A study of the effects of verbalization on problem solving. *Journal of Experimental Psychology*, 1962, *63*, 12–18.

Galton, F. *Hereditary genius.* London: Macmillan, 1869.

Galton, F. *Inquiries into human faculty and its development.* London: Macmillan, 1883.

Gelernter, H. Realization of a geometry theorem proving machine. In *Proceedings of 1959 international conference on information processing.* Paris: UNESCO, 1960.

Gelman, R. Conservation acquisition: A problem of learning to attend to the relevant attributes. *Journal of Experimental Child Psychology*, 1969, *7*, 67–87.

Gelman, R., and Gallistel, C. R. *The child's understanding of number.* Cambridge, Mass.: Harvard University Press, 1978.

Getzels, J. W., and Jackson, P. W. The highly intelligent and the highly creative adolescent: A summary of some research findings. In C. W. Taylor and F. Barron (Eds.), *Scientific Creativity: Its Recognition and Development.* New York: Wiley, 1963.

Glaser, R., and Resnick, L. B. Instructional psychology. *Annual Review of Psychology*, 1972, *23*, 207–276.

Glucksberg, S., and Danks, J. Effects of discriminative labels and of nonsense labels upon availability of novel function. *Journal of Verbal Learning and Verbal Behavior*, 1968, *7*, 72–76.

Glucksberg, S., and Weisberg, R. W. Verbal behavior and problem solving: Some effects of labeling in a functional fixedness problem. *Journal of Experimental Psychology*, 1966, *71*, 659–664.

Goldberg, R. A., Schwartz, S., and Stewart, M. Individual differences in cognitive processes. *Journal of Educational Psychology*, 1977, *69*, 9–14.

Goldschmidt, M. The role of experience in the rate and sequence of cognitive development. In D. R. Green, M. Ford, and G. Flammer (Eds.), *Measurement and Piaget.* New York: McGraw-Hill, 1971.

Goldstein, I. Developing a computational representation for problem-solving skills. In D. T. Tuma and F. Reif (Eds.), *Problem solving and education: Issues in teaching and learning.* Hillsdale, N.J.: Erlbaum, 1980.

Goldstein, I., and Brown, J. S. The computer as a personal assistant for learning. In J. Lochhead and J. Clement (Eds.), *Cognitive process instruction.* Philadelphia: Franklin Institute Press, 1979.

Gordon, W. J. J. *Synectics.* New York: Harper & Row, 1961.

Greenblatt, R. B., Eastlake, D. E., and Crocker, S. D. The Greenblat chess program. *Proceedings of the 1967 joint computer conference*, 1967, *30*, 801–810.

Greeno, J. G. The structure of memory and the process of solving problems. In R. L. Solso (Ed.), *Contemporary issues in cognitive psychology: The Loyola symposium.* Washington, D.C.: Winston, 1973.

Greeno, J. G. Hobbits and orcs: Acquisition of a sequential concept. *Cognitive Psychology*, 1974, *6*, 270–292.

Greeno, J. G. Cognitive objectives of instruction: Theory of knowledge for solving problems and answering questions. In D. Klahr (Ed.), *Cognition and instruction.* Hillsdale, N.J.: Erlbaum, 1976.

Greeno, J. G. Natures of problem solving abilities. In W. K. Estes (Ed.), *Handbook of learning and cognitive processes*. Vol. 5. Hillsdale, N.J.: Erlbaum, 1978a.

Greeno, J. G. A study of problem solving. In R. Glaser (Ed.), *Advances in Instructional Psychology*. Vol. 1. Hillsdale, N.J.: Erlbaum, 1978b.

Greeno, J. G. Some examples of cognitive task analysis with instructional implications. In R. E. Snow, P. Federico, and W. E. Montague (Eds.), *Aptitude, learning, and instruction*. Vol. 2. Hillsdale, N.J.: Erlbaum, 1980.

Greeno, J. G. Trends in the theory of knowledge for problem solving. In D. T. Tuma and F. Reif (Eds.), *Problem solving and education: Issues in teaching and learning*. Hillsdale, N.J.: Erlbaum, 1980.

Gregg, L. W., and Simon, H. A. Process models and stochastic theories of simple concept formation. *Journal of Mathematical Psychology*, 1967, *4*, 246–276.

Griggs, R. A. Logical errors in comprehending set inclusion relations in meaningful text. No. 74-7. Bloomington: Indiana University Mathematical Psychology Program, 1974.

Groen, G. J., and Parkman, J. M. A chronometric analysis of simple addition. *Psychological Review*, 1972, *79*, 329–343.

Guilford, J. P. The three faces of intellect. *American Psychologist*, 1959, *14*, 469–479.

Guilford, J. P. *The nature of human intelligence*. New York: McGraw-Hill, 1967.

Gur, R. E., Gur, R. C., and Harris, L. Cerebral activation as measured by subjects' lateral eye movements is influenced by experimenter location. *Neuropsychologia*, 1975, *15*, 35–44.

Guthrie, E. R., and Horton, G. P. *Cats in a puzzle box*. New York: Holt, Rinehart and Winston, 1946.

Haber, R. Eidetic images. *Scientific American*, April 1969, 36–44. Offprint 522.

Harlow, H. F. The formation of learning sets. *Psychological Review*, 1949, *56*, 51–56.

Harlow, H. F., and Harlow, M. K. Learning to think. *Scientific American*, August 1949, 36–39. Offprint 415.

Hayes, J. R. Problem topology and the solution process. *Journal of Verbal Learning and Verbal Behavior*, 1965, *4*, 371–379.

Hayes, J. R. Memory, goals, and problem solving. In B. Kleinmuntz (Ed.), *Problem solving: Research, method, and theory*. New York: Wiley, 1966.

Hayes, J. R. *Cognitive psychology*. Homewood, Ill.: Dorsey, 1978.

Hayes, J. R. Teaching problem-solving mechanisms. In D. T. Tuma and F. Reif (Eds.), *Problem solving and education: Issues in teaching and learning*. Hillsdale, N.J.: Erlbaum, 1980.

Hayes, J. R. *The complete problem solver*. Philadelphia: Franklin Institute Press, 1981.

Hayes, J. R., and Simon, H. A. Understanding written instructions. In L. W. Gregg (Ed.), *Knowledge and cognition*. Hillsdale, N.J.: Erlbaum, 1974.

Hayes, J. R., and Simon, H. A. Psychological differences among problem isomorphs. In N. J. Castellan, D. B. Pisoni, and G. R. Potts (Eds.), *Cognitive theory*. Vol. 2. Hillsdale, N.J.: Erlbaum, 1977.

Hayes, J. R., Waterman, D. A., and Robinson, C. S. Identifying relevant aspects of a problem text. *Cognitive Science*, 1977, *1*, 297–313.

Haygood, R. C., and Bourne, L. E., Jr. Attribute and rule learning aspects of conceptual behavior. *Psychological Review*, 1965, *72*, 175–195.

Haygood, R. C., Harbert, T. L., and Omlor, J. A. Intradimensional variability and concept learning. *Journal of Experimental Psychology*, 1970, *83*, 216–219.

Haygood, R. C., and Stevenson, M. Effects of number of irrelevant dimensions in non-conjunctive concept learning. *Journal of Experimental Psychology*, 1967, *74*, 302–304.

Heffley, E., Wickens, C., and Donchin, E. Intramodality selective attention and P300: Reexamination in a visual monitoring task. *Psychophysiology*, 1978, *15*, 269–270.

Heidbreder, E. The attainment of concepts: I. Terminology and methodology. *Journal of General Psychology*, 1946, *35*, 173–189.

Heidbreder, E. The attainment of concepts: III. The process. *Journal of Psychology*, 1947, *24*, 93–108.

Heider, E. R. *The Dugum Dani: A Papuan culture in the highlands of West New Guinea.* Chicago: Aldine, 1970.

Heider, E. R. Universals in color naming and memory. *Journal of Experimental Psychology*, 1972, *93*, 10–20.

Heider, E. R., and Oliver, D. C. The structure of the color space in naming and memory for two languages. *Cognitive Psychology*, 1972, *3*, 337–354.

Hilgard, E. R., Ergren, R. D., and Irvine, R. P. Errors in transfer following learning by understanding: Further studies with Katona's card trick experiments. *Journal of Experimental Psychology*, 1954, *47*, 457–464.

Hilgard, E. R., Irvine, R. P., and Whipple, J. E. Rote memorization, understanding, and transfer: An extension of Katona's card trick experiment. *Journal of Experimental Psychology*, 1953, *46*, 288–292.

Hilton, T. L., and Berglund, G. W. Sex differences in mathematics achievement: A longitudinal study. *Journal of Educational Research*, 1974, *67*, 231–237.

Hinsley, D., Hayes, J. R., and Simon, H. A. From words to equations. In P. Carpenter and M. Just (Eds.), *Cognitive processes in comprehension.* Hillsdale, N.J: Erlbaum, 1977.

Hofstadter, D. R. *Godel, Escher, Bach: An eternal golden braid.* New York: Vintage Books, 1980.

Hogaboam, T. W., and Pellegrino, J. W. Hunting for individual differences in cognitive processes: Verbal ability and semantic processing of pictures and words. *Memory & Cognition*, 1978, *6*, 189–193.

Holtzman, T. G., Glaser, R., and Pellegrino, J. W. Process training derived from a computer simulation theory. *Memory and Cognition*, 1976, *4*, 349–356.

Hull, C. L. Quantitative aspects of the evolution of concepts. *Psychological Monographs*, 1920, *28*, No. 123.

Hull, C. L. *Principles of behavior.* New York: Appleton-Century-Crofts, 1943.

Hulse, S., Deese, J., and Egeth, H. *The psychology of learning.* New York: McGraw-Hill, 1975.

Humphrey, G. *Thinking: An introduction to its experimental psychology.* New York: Wiley, 1963.

Hunt, E. The mechanisms of verbal ability. *Psychological Review*, 1978, *85*, 109–130.

Hunt, E. G., Frost, N., and Lunneborg, C. L. Individual differences in cognition: A new approach to intelligence. In G. Bower (Ed.), *Advances in learning and motivation*. Vol. 7. New York: Academic Press, 1973.

Hunt, E., Lunneborg, C., and Lewis, J. What does it mean to be high verbal? *Cognitive Psychology*, 1975, *7*, 194–227.

Hunt, E., and MacLeod, C. M. The sentence-picture verification paradigm: A case study of two conflicting approaches to individual differences. In R. J. Sternberg and D. K. Determan (Eds.), *Human intelligence*. Norwood, N.J.: Albex, 1979.

Hunt, E. B., Martin, J., and Stone, P. I. *Experiments in induction*. New York: Academic Press, 1966.

Huttenlocher, J. Constructing spatial images: A strategy in reasoning. *Psychological Review*, 1968, *75*, 550–560.

Hyman, R., and Frost, N. Gradients and schema in pattern recognition. In P. M. A. Rabbitt (Ed.), *Attention and performance*. Vol. 5. New York: Academic Press, 1974.

Inhelder, B., and Piaget, J. *The growth of logical thinking from childhood to adolescence*. New York: Basic Books, 1958. (A. Parson and S. Milgram, Trans.; original French edition, 1955.)

Jacobson, E. Electrophysiology of mental activity. *American Journal of Psychology*, 1932, *44*, 677–694.

James, W. *The principles of psychology*. New York: Holt, Rinehart and Winston, 1890.

Janis, I. L., and Frick, F. The relationship between attitudes toward conclusions and errors in judging logical validity of syllogisms. *Journal of Experimental Psychology*, 1943, *33*, 73–77.

Jeffries, R., Polson, P. G., Razran, L., and Atwood, M. E. A process model for missionaries-cannibals and other river-crossing problems. *Cognitive Psychology*, 1977, *9*, 412–440.

Jenkins, J. J. Remember that old theory of memory? Well, forget it! *American Psychologist*, 1974, *29*, 785–795.

John, E. R., and Schwartz, E. L. The neurophysiology of information processing and cognition. In M. R. Rosenweig and L. W. Porter (Eds.), *Annual Review of Psychology*. Vol. 29. Palo Alto, Calif.: Annual Reviews, 1978.

Johnson, D. M. *A systematic introduction to the psychology of thinking*. New York: Harper & Row, 1972.

Johnson, R. E. Recall of prose as a function of the structural importance of linguistic units. *Journal of Verbal Learning and Verbal Behavior*, 1970, *9*, 12–20.

Johnson-Laird, P. N., Legrenzi, P., and Legrenzi, M. Reasoning and a sense of reality. *British Journal of Psychology*, 1972, *63*, 395–400.

Johnson-Laird, P. N., and Steedman, M. The psychology of syllogisms. *Cognitive Psychology*, 1978, *10*, 64–99.

Johnson-Laird, P. N., and Wason, P. C. A theoretical analysis of insight into a reasoning task. In P. N. Johnson-Laird and P. C. Wason (Ed.), *Thinking: Readings in Cognitive Science*. Cambridge, England: Cambridge University Press, 1977.

Judson, A. I., and Cofer, C. N. Reasoning as an associative process: I. "Direction" in a simple verbal problem. *Psychological Reports*, 1956, *2*, 469–476.

Just, M. A., and Carpenter, P. A. Comprehension of negation with quantification. *Journal of Verbal Learning and Verbal Behavior*, 1971, *10*, 244–253.

Just, M. A., and Carpenter, P. A. Eye fixations and cognitive processes. *Cognitive Psychology*, 1976, *8*, 441–480.

Kahneman, D., and Tversky, A. On the psychology of prediction. *Psychological Review*, 1973, *80*, 237–251.

Kahneman, D., and Tversky, A. On the interpretation of intuitive probability: A reply to Jonathan Cohen. *Cognition*, 1979, *7*, 409–411.

Kail, R. *The development of memory in children*. San Francisco: W. H. Freeman and Company, 1979.

Katona, G. Organizing and memorizing: A reply to Dr. Melton. *American Journal of Psychology*, 1942, *55*, 273–275.

Kendler, H. H., and D'Amato, M. F. A comparison of reversal and nonreversal shifts in human concept information. *Journal of Experimental Psychology*, 1955, *49*, 165–174.

Kendler, H. H., and Kendler, T. S. Inferential behavior in preschool children. *Journal of Experimental Psychology*, 1956, *51*, 311–314.

Kendler, H. H., and Kendler, T. S. Vertical and horizontal processes in problem solving. *Psychological Review*, 1962a, *69*, 1–16.

Kendler, H. H., and Kendler, T. S. From discrimination learning to cognitive development: A neobehavioristic odyssey. In W. K. Estes (Ed.), *Handbook of learning and cognitive processes*. Vol. 1. Hillsdale, N.J.: Erlbaum, 1975.

Kendler, T. S., and Kendler, H. H. Reversal and nonreversal shifts in kindergarten children. *Journal of Experimental Psychology*, 1959, *58*, 56–60.

Kendler, T. S., and Kendler, H. H. Inferential behavior as a function of subgoal constancy and age. *Journal of Experimental Psychology*, 1962b, *64*, 460–466.

Kinsbourne, M. Eye and head turning indicates cerebral lateralization. *Science*, 1972, *176*, 539–541.

Kinsbourne, M. Direction of gaze and distribution of cerebral thought processes. *Neuropsychologia*, 1974, *12*, 279–281.

Kintsch, W. Notes on the structure of semantic memory. In E. Tulving and W. Donaldson (Eds.), *Organization of memory*. New York: 1972.

Kintsch, W. *The representation of meaning in memory*. Hillsdale, N.J.: Erlbaum, 1974.

Kintsch, W. Memory for prose. In C. N. Cofer (Ed.), *The structure of human memory*. San Francisco: W. H. Freeman and Company, 1976.

Klahr, D. Goal formation, planning, and learning by pre-school problem solvers or "My Socks are in the Dryer." In R. S. Siegler (Ed.), *Children's thinking: What develops?* Hillsdale, N.J.: Erlbaum, 1978.

Klahr, D., and Wallace, J. G. *Cognitive development: An information processing view*. Hillsdale, N.J.: Erlbaum, 1976.

Klatzky, R. *Human memory*. (2nd ed.) San Francisco: W. H. Freeman and Company, 1980.

Kocel, K., Galin, D., Ornstein, R., and Merrin, R. Lateral eye movement and cognitive mode. *Psychonomic Science*, 1972, *27*, 223–224.

Kohler, W. *The mentality of apes.* New York: Harcourt Brace Jovanovich, 1925.

Kohler, W. *Gestalt psychology.* New York: Liveright, 1929.

Kohler, W. *The task of Gestalt psychology.* Princeton, N.J.: Princeton University Press, 1969.

Kotovsky, K., and Simon, H. A. Empirical tests of a theory of human acquisition of concepts for sequential patterns. *Cognitive Psychology,* 1973, *4,* 399–424.

Kuhn, D. Inducing development experimentally: Components on a research paradigm. *Developmental Psychology,* 1974, *10,* 590–600.

Kulpe, O. The modern psychology of thinking. In J. M. Mandler and G. Mandler (Eds.), *Thinking: From association to Gestalt.* New York: Wiley, 1964. (Originally published in German in 1912.)

Landauer, T. K., and Meyer, D. E. Category size and semantic-memory retrieval. *Journal of Verbal Learning and Verbal Behavior,* 1972, *11,* 539–549.

Larkin, J. H. Information processing models and science instruction. In J. Lochhead and J. Clement (Eds.), *Cognitive process instruction.* Philadelphia: Franklin Institute Press, 1979.

Larkin, J. H. Teaching problem solving in physics: The psychological laboratory and the practical classroom. In D. T. Tuma and F. Reif (Eds.), *Problem solving and education: Issues in teaching and research.* Hillsdale, N.J.: Erlbaum, 1980.

Larkin, J. H., McDermott, J., Simon, D. P., and Simon, H. A. Expert and novice performance in solving physics problems. *Science,* 1980, *208,* 1335–1342.

Lefford, A. The influence of emotional subject matter on logical reasoning. *Journal of General Psychology,* 1946, *34,* 127–151.

Lenneburg, E. H. A probabilistic approach to language learning. *Behavioral Science,* 1957, *2,* 1–12.

Levine, M. Hypothesis behavior by humans during discrimination learning. *Journal of Experimental Psychology,* 1966, *71,* 331–338.

Levine, M. *A cognitive theory of learning.* Hillsdale, N.J.: Erlbaum, 1975.

Lewis, C. Skill in algebra. In J. R. Anderson (Ed.), *Cognitive skills and their acquisition.* Hillsdale, N.J.: Erlbaum, 1981.

Lindsay, P. H., and Norman, D. A. *Human information processing: An introduction to psychology.* New York: Academic Press, 1972.

Lochhead, J. An introduction to cognitive process instruction. In J. Lochhead and J. Clement (Eds.), *Cognitive process instruction.* Philadelphia: Franklin Institute Press, 1979.

Loftus, E. F., and Suppes, P. Structural variables that determine problem-solving difficulty in computer-assisted instruction. *Journal of Educational Psychology,* 1972, *63,* 531–542.

Luchins, A. S. Mechanization in problem solving. *Psychological Monographs,* 1942, *54:6,* Whole No. 248.

Luchins, A. S., and Luchins, E. H. New experimental attempts at preventing mechanization in problem solving. *Journal of General Psychology,* 1950, *42,* 279–297.

Luchins, A. S., and Luchins, E. H. *Wertheimer's seminars revisited: Problem solving and thinking.* Albany: State University of New York, 1970.

Maccoby, E., and Jacklin, C. *Psychology of sex differences*. Stanford, Calif.: Stanford University Press, 1974.

MacLeod, C. M., Hunt, E. B., and Mathews, N. N. Individual differences in the verification of sentence-picture relationships. *Journal of Verbal Learning and Verbal Behavior*, 1978, *17*, 493–508.

Maier, N. R. F. Reasoning in Humans I: On direction. *Journal of Comparative Psychology*, 1930, *10*, 115–143.

Maier, N. R. F. Reasoning in humans II: The solution of a problem and its appearance in consciousness. *Journal of Comparative Psychology*, 1931, *12*, 181–194.

Maier, N. R. F. An aspect of human reasoning. *British Journal of Psychology*, 1933, *14*, 144–155.

Maier, N. R. F. Reasoning in humans III: The mechanisms of equivalent stimuli of reasoning. *Journal of Experimental Psychology*, 1945, *35*, 349–360.

Maier, N. R. F., and Burke, R. J. Response availability as a factor in the problem-solving performance of males and females. *Journal of Personality and Social Psychology*, 1967, *5*, 304–310.

Maltzman, I. Thinking: From a behavioristic point of view. *Psychological Review*, 1955, *62*, 275–286.

Maltzman, I., and Morrisett, L. Different strengths of set in solution of anagrams. *Journal of Experimental Psychology*, 1952, *44*, 242–246.

Maltzman, I., and Morrisett, L. Effects of task instructions on solution of different classes of anagrams. *Journal of Experimental Psychology*, 1953, *45*, 351–354.

Mandler, J. M., and Mandler, G. *Thinking: From association to Gestalt*. New York: Wiley, 1964.

Mansfield, R. S., Busse, T. V., and Krepelka, E. J. The effectiveness of creativity training. *Review of Educational Research*, 1978, *48*, 517–536.

Marbe, K. The psychology of judgments. In J. M. Mandler and G. Mandler (Eds.), *Thinking: From association to Gestalt*. New York: Wiley, 1964. (Originally published in German in 1901.)

Marshall, S. *Sex differences in children's mathematical achievement*. Santa Barbara, Calif.: University of California, Department of Psychology, 1980.

Martin, E., and Roberts, K. H. Sentence length and sentence retention in the free-learning situation. *Psychonomic Science*, 1967, *8*, 535–536.

Matz, M. Towards a computational theory of algebraic competence. *Journal of Children's Mathematical Behavior*, 1980, *3*, 531–542.

Max, L. W. Experimental study of the motor theory of consciousness: III. Action-current responses in deaf-mutes during sleep, sensory stimulation, and dreams. *Journal of Comparative Psychology*, 1953, *19*, 469–486.

Max, L. W. Experimental study of the motor theory of consciousness: IV. Action-current responses in the deaf during awakening, kinesthetic imagery and abstract thinking. *Journal of Comparative Psychology*, 1937, *24*, 301–344.

Mayer, A., and Orth, J. The qualitative investigation of association. In J. M. Mandler and G. Mandler (Eds.), *Thinking: From association to Gestalt*. New York: Wiley, 1964. (Originally published in German in 1901.)

Mayer, R. E. Different problem-solving competencies established in learning computer programming with and without meaningful models. *Journal of Educational Psychology,* 1975, *67,* 725–734.

Mayer, R. E. Qualitatively different encoding strategies for linear reasoning premises: Evidence for single association and distance theories. *Journal of Experimental Psychology: Human Learning and Memory,* 1979, *5,* 1–10.

Mayer, R. E. Frequency norms and structural analysis of algebra story problems into families, categories, and templates. *Instructional Science,* 1981, *10,* 135–175.

Mayer, R. E. Different problem-solving strategies for algebra word and equation problems. *Journal of Experimental Psychology: Learning, Memory, and Cognition,* 1982, *8,* 448–462.

Mayer, R. E., and Greeno, J. G. Structural differences between learning outcomes produced by different instructional methods. *Journal of Educational Psychology,* 1972, *63,* 165–173.

Mayer, R. E., Larkin, J. H., and Kadane, J. A cognitive analysis of mathematical problem solving ability. In R. Sternberg (Ed.), *Advances in the psychology of human intelligence.* Vol. 2. Hillsdale, N.J.: Erlbaum, 1983.

Mayzner, M. S., and Tresselt, M. E. Anagram solution times: A function of letter-order and word frequency. *Journal of Experimental Psychology,* 1958, *56,* 350–376.

Mayzner, M. S., and Tresselt, M. E. Anagram solution times: A function of transition probabilities. *Journal of Psychology,* 1959, *47,* 117–125.

Mayzner, M. S., and Tresselt, M. E. Anagram solution times: A function of word transition probabilities. *Journal of Experimental Psychology,* 1962, *63,* 510–513.

Mayzner, M. S., and Tresselt, M. E. Anagram solution times: A function of word length and letter position variables. *Journals of Psychology,* 1963, *55,* 469–475.

Mayzner, M. S., and Tresselt, M. E. Anagram solution times: A function of multiple-solution anagrams. *Journal of Experimental Psychology,* 1966, *71,* 66–73.

McGuigan, F. J. *Thinking: Studies of convert language processes.* New York: Appleton-Century-Crofts, 1966.

McGuigan, F. J. Electrical measurement of covert processes as an explication of "higher mental events." In F. J. McGuigan and R. A. Schoonover (Eds.), *The psychobiology of thinking.* New York: Academic Press, 1973.

McGuigan, F. J., Keller, B., and Stanton, E. Covert language responses during silent reading. *Journal of Educational Psychology,* 1964, *55,* 339–343.

McGuire, W. J. A syllogistic analysis of cognitive relationships. In M. J. Rosenberg and C. I. Hovland (Eds.), *Attitude organization and change.* New Haven, Conn.: Yale University Press, 1960.

McKeachie, W. J., and Doyle, C. L. *Psychology.* Reading, Mass.: Addison-Wesley, 1970.

Mehler, J. Some effects of grammar transformations on the recall of English sentences. *Journal of Verbal Learning and Verbal Behavior,* 1963, *2,* 346–351.

Melton, A. W. Review of Katona's *Organizing and memorizing. American Journal of Psychology,* 1941, *54,* 455–457.

Metzler, J., and Shepard, R. N. Transformational studies of the internal representation of three-dimensional objects. In R. L. Solso (Ed.), *Theories in cognitive psychology: The Loyola Symposium.* Hillsdale, N.J.: Erlbaum, 1974.

Messer, A. Experimental-Psychological investigations on thinking. In J. M. Mandler and G. Mandler (Eds.), *Thinking: From association to Gestalt.* New York: Wiley, 1964. (Originally published in German in 1906.)

Meyer, B. J. F. *The organization of prose and its effects on memory.* Amsterdam: North-Holland, 1975.

Meyer, B. J. F. The structure of prose: Effects on learning and memory and implications for educational practice. In R. C. Anderson, R. J. Spiro, and W. E. Montague (Eds.), *Schooling and the acquisition of knowledge.* Hillsdale, N.J.: Erlbaum, 1977.

Meyer, B. J. F., and McConkie, G. W. What is recalled after hearing a passage? *Journal of Educational Psychology,* 1973, *65,* 109–117.

Meyer, D. E. On the representation and retrieval of stored semantic information. *Cognitive Psychology,* 1970, *1,* 242–300.

Miller, G. A. Some psychological studies of grammar. *American Psychologist,* 1962, *17,* 748–762.

Miller, G. A., Galanter, E., and Pribram, K. H. *Plans and the structure of behavior.* New York: Holt, Rinehart and Winston, 1960.

Miller, G. A., and Selfridge, J. A. Verbal context and the recall of meaningful material. *American Journal of Psychology,* 1950, *63,* 176–185.

Minsky, M. A framework for representing knowledge. In P. H. Winston (Ed.), *The psychology of computer vision.* New York: McGraw-Hill, 1975.

Moeser, S. D., and Tarrant, B. L. Learning a network of comparisons. *Journal of Experimental Psychology: Human Learning and Memory,* 1977, 643–659.

Morgan, J. J. B., and Morton, J. T. The distortion of syllogistic reasoning produced by personal convictions. *Journal of Social Psychology,* 1944, *20,* 39–59.

Murray, F. B. Teaching strategies and conservation training. In A. M. Lesgold, J. W. Pellegrino, S. D. Fokkema, and R. Glaser (Eds.), *Cognitive psychology and instruction.* New York: Plenum Press, 1978.

Myers, R. E., and Torrance, E. P. *Invitations to thinking and doing.* Boston: Ginn, 1964.

Nair, P. *An experiment in conservation.* Cambridge, Mass.: Harvard University Center for Cognitive Studies, Annual Report, 1963.

National Educational Association. *The Central Purpose of American Education.* Washington, D.C.: National Educational Association, 1961. (Also reprinted in A. E. Lawson. *The psychology of thinking for thinking and creativity.* Columbus, Ohio: ERIC Clearinghouse for Science, Mathematics, and Environmental Education, 1979.)

Neimark, E. D., and Santa, J. L. Thinking and concept attainment. In M. R. Rosenzweig and L. W. Porter (Eds.), *Annual Review of Psychology.* Vol. 26. Palo Alto, Calif.: Annual Reviews, 1975.

Neisser, U. *Cognitive Psychology.* New York: Appleton-Century-Crofts, 1967.

Neisser, U., and Lazar, R. Searching for novel targets. *Perceptual Motor Skills,* 1964, *19,* 427–432.

Neisser, U., Novick, R., and Lazar, R. Searching for ten targets simultaneously. *Perceptual Motor Skills*, 1963, *17*, 955–961.

Neumann, P. G. Visual prototype formation with discontinuous representation of dimensions of variability. *Memory and Cognition*. 1977, *5*, 187–197.

Newell, A., Shaw, J. C., and Simon, H. A. Empirical exploration of the logic theory machine: A case study in heuristics. *Proceedings of the joint computer conference*, 1957, 218–230.

Newell, A., Shaw, J. C., and Simon, H. A. Chess-playing programs and the problem of complexity. *IBM Journal of Research and Development*, 1958, *2*, 320–335.

Newell, A., and Simon, H. A. *Human problem solving*. Englewood Cliffs, N.J.: Prentice-Hall, 1972.

Newport, E. L., and Bellugi, U. Linguistic expression of category levels in a visual-gestural language: A flower is a flower is a flower. In E. Rosch and B. B. Lloyd (Eds.), *Cognition and categorization*. Hillsdale, N.J.: Erlbaum, 1978.

Norman, D. A. Cognitive engineering and education. In D. T. Tuma and F. Reif (Eds.), *Problem solving and education: Issues in teaching and learning*. Hillsdale, N.J.: Erlbaum, 1980.

Olton, R. M., and Crutchfield, R. S. Developing the skills of productive thinking. In P. Mussen, J. Langer, and M. V. Covington (Eds.), *New directions in developmental psychology*. New York: Holt, Rinehart and Winston, 1969.

Olver, R. R., and Hornsby, J. R. On equivalence. In J. S. Bruner, R. R. Olver, and P. M. Greenfield (Eds.), *Studies in cognitive growth*. New York: Wiley, 1966.

Osborn, A. F. *Applied imagination*. New York: Scribner's, 1963.

Osgood, C. E. A behavioral analysis of perception and language as cognitive phenomena. In J. S. Bruner (Ed.), *Contemporary approaches to cognition*. Cambridge, Mass.: Harvard University Press, 1957.

Osgood, C. E. Meaning cannot be an r_m? *Journal of Verbal Learning and Verbal Behavior*, 1966, *5*, 402–407.

Osler, S. F., and Fivel, M. W. Concept attainment: I. The role of age and intelligence in concept attainment by induction. *Journal of Experimental Psychology*, 1961, *62*, 1–8.

Pachella, R. G., and Miller, J. O. Stimulus probability and same-different classification. *Perception and Psychophysics*, 1976, *19*, 29–34.

Paige, J. M., and Simon, H. A. Cognitive processes in solving algebra word problems. In B. Kleinmuntz (Ed.), *Problem solving: Research, method and theory*. New York: Wiley, 1966.

Paivio, A. *Imagery and verbal processes*. New York: Holt, Rinehart and Winston, 1971.

Palermo, D. S. Word associations and children's verbal behavior. In L. P. Lipsitt and C. C. Spiker (Eds.), *Advances in child development and behavior*. Vol. 1. New York: Academic Press, 1963.

Palermo, D. S., and Jenkins, J. J. *Word association norms: Grade school through college*. Minneapolis: University of Minnesota Press, 1963.

Papert, S., and Solomon, C. *Twenty things to do with a computer*. Cambridge, Mass.: AI Laboratory Report AI-M-248, 1971.

Parnes, S. J. *Creative behavior guidebook*. New York: Scribner's, 1967.

Parrott, G. L. The effects of instructions, transfer, and content on reasoning time. Unpublished Ph.D. thesis, Michigan State University, 1969.

Pascaul-Leone, J. A mathematical model for the transition rule in Piaget's developmental stages. *Acta Psychologica*, 1970, *32*, 301–345.

Pellegrino, J. W., and Glaser, R. Cognitive correlates and components in the analysis of individual differences. In R. J. Sternberg and D. K. Determan (Eds.), *Human intelligence*. Norwood, N.J.: Ablex, 1979.

Pellegrino, J. W., and Lyon, D. R. The components of a componential analysis. *Intelligence*, 1979, *3*, 169–186.

Penfield, W. *The excitable cortex in conscious man*. Springfield, Ill.: Thomas, 1958.

Penfield, W. Consciousness, memory, and man's conditioned reflexes. In K. H. Pribram (Ed.), *On the biology of learning*. New York: Harcourt Brace Jovanovich, 1969.

Peterson, L. R., and Peterson, M. J. Short-term retention of individual verbal items. *Journal of Experimental Psychology*, 1959, *58*, 193–198.

Phillips, J. L. *The origins of intellect: Piaget's theory*. San Francisco: W. H. Freeman and Company, 1969.

Piaget, J. *Judgment and reasoning in the child*. New York: Harcourt Brace Jovanovich, 1926. (M. Worden, Trans.; original French edition, 1924.)

Piaget, J. *The moral judgment of the child*. New York: Harcourt Brace Jovanovich, 1932. (M. Gabain, Trans.)

Piaget, J. *Play, dreams and imitation in childhood*. New York: Norton, 1951. (C. Gattegno and F. M. Hodgson, Trans., original French edition, 1945.)

Piaget, J. *The child's conception of number*. London: Routledge & Kegan Paul, 1952. (C. Gattegno and F. M. Hodgson, Trans.; original French edition, 1941.)

Piaget, J. *The origins of intelligence in children*. New York: International Universities Press, 1952. (M. Cook, Trans.; original French edition, 1936.)

Piaget, J. *The construction of reality in the child*. New York: Basic Books, 1954. (M. Cook, Trans.; original French edition, 1937.)

Piaget, J., and Inhelder, B. *The child's conception of space*. London: Routledge & Kegan Paul, 1956. (F. J. Langdon and J. L. Lunzer, Trans.; original French edition, 1948.)

Pichert, J., and Anderson, R. C. Taking different perspectives on a story. *Journal of Educational Psychology*, 1977, *69*, 309–315.

Poincaré, H. Mathematical creation. In *The foundations of science*. (G. H. Halstead, Trans.) New York: Science Press, 1913.

Pollio, H. R., and Reinhart, D. Rules and counting behavior. *Cognitive Psychology*, 1970, *1*, 388–402.

Polya, G. *How to solve it*. Garden City, N.Y.: Doubleday Anchor, 1957.

Polya, G. Mathematical discovery. Vol. II: *On understanding, learning and teaching problem solving*. New York: Wiley, 1968.

Pople, H. Problem solving: An exercise in synthetic reasoning. *Proceedings of the fifth international joint conference on artificial intelligence*. Pittsburgh: Carnegie-Mellon University, 1977.

Popper, K. R. *The logic of scientific discovery.* New York: Harper & Row, 1959.

Posner, M. I. Abstraction and the process of recognition. In G. H. Bower and J. T. Spence (Eds.), *The psychology of learning and motivation.* Vol. 3. New York: Academic Press, 1969.

Posner, M. I. *Cognition: An introduction.* Glenview, Ill.: Scott, Foresman, 1973.

Posner, M. I. *Chronometric explorations of mind.* Hillsdale, N.J.: Erlbaum, 1978.

Posner, M. I., Boies, S. J., Eichelman, W. H., and Taylor, R. L. Retention of visual and name codes of single letters. *Journal of Experimental Psychology,* 1969, *79,* 1–16.

Posner, M. I., and Keele, S. W. On the genesis of abstract ideas. *Journal of Experimental Psychology,* 1968, *77,* 353–363.

Posner, M. I., and Keele, S. W. Retention of abstract ideas. *Journal of Experimental Psychology,* 1970, *83,* 304–308.

Posner, M. I., Lewis, J., and Conrad, C. Component processes in reading: A performance analysis. In J. Kavanaugh and I. Mattingly (Eds.), *Language by ear and by eye.* Cambridge, Mass.: M.I.T. Press, 1972.

Posner, M. I., and Mitchell, R. F. Chronometric analysis of classification. *Psychological Review,* 1967, *74*, 392–409.

Potts, G. R. Information processing strategies used in the encoding of linear orderings. *Journal of Verbal Learning and Verbal Behavior,* 1972, *11,* 727–740.

Potts, G. R. Storing and retrieving information about ordered relationships. *Journal of Experimental Psychology,* 1974, *103,* 431–439.

Potts, G. R. The role of inference in memory for real and artificial information. In R. Revlin and R. E. Mayer (Eds.), *Human Reasoning.* Washington, D.C.: Winston/Wiley, 1978.

Preston, M. S., Guthrie, J. T., and Childs, B. Visual evoked responses in normal and disabled readers. *Psychophysiology,* 1974, *11,* 452–457.

Raaheim, K. Problem solving and past experience. In P. H. Mussen (Ed.), European research in cognitive development. *Monograph Supplement of the Society for Research on Child Development,* 1965, *30,* No. 2.

Raeburn, V. P. Priorities in item recognition. *Memory and Cognition,* 1974, *2,* 663–669.

Razran, G. H. S. Conditioned responses in children: A behavioral and quantitative critical review of experimental studies. *Archives of Psychology,* 1933, No. 14.

Reed, S. K. Pattern recognition and categorization. *Cognitive Psychology,* 1972, *3,* 382–407.

Reed, S. K., Ernsrt, G. W., and Banerjii, R. The role of analogy in transfer between similar problem states. *Cognitive Psychology,* 1974, *6,* 436–450.

Rees, H. J., and Israel, H. E. An investigation of the establishment and operation of mental sets. *Psychological Monographs,* 1935, *46,* No. 210.

Reese, H. W. Verbal mediation as a function of age level. *Psychological Bulletin,* 1962, *59,* 502–509.

Reif, F. Theoretical and educational concerns with problem solving: Bridging the gaps with human cognitive engineering. In D. T. Tuma and F. Reif (Eds.), *Problem solving and education: Issues in teaching and research.* Hillsdale, N.J.: Erlbaum, 1980.

Reitman, W. R. *Cognition and thought: An information processing approach.* New York: Wiley, 1965.

Reitman, W. R., Grove, R. B., and Shoup, R. G. Argus: An information processing model of thinking. *Behavioral Science,* 1964, *9,* 270–281.

Resnick, L. B. Task analysis in instructional design: Some cases from mathematics. In D. Klahr (Ed.), *Cognition and instruction.* Hillsdale, N.J.: Erlbaum, 1976.

Restle, F. A metric and an ordering on sets. *Psychometrika,* 1959, *57,* 9–14.

Restle, F. The selection of strategies in cue learning. *Psychological Review.* 1962, *69,* 329–343.

Restle, F. Theory of serial pattern learning: Structural trees. *Psychological Review,* 1970, *77,* 481–495.

Restle, F., and Davis, J. H. Success and speed of problem solving by individuals and groups. *Psychological Review,* 1962, *69,* 520–536.

Restle, F., and Greeno, J. G. *Introduction to mathematical psychology.* Reading, Mass.: Addison-Wesley, 1970.

Revlin, R., and Leirer, V. O. The effect of personal biases on syllogistic reasoning: Rational decisions from personalized representations. In R. Revlin and R. E. Mayer (Eds.), *Human reasoning.* Washington, D.C.: Winston/Wiley, 1978.

Revlin, R., and Leirer, V. O. Understanding quantified categorical expressions. *Memory and Cognition,* 1980, *8,* 447–458.

Revlis, R. Two models of syllogistic reasoning: Feature selection and conversion. *Journal of Verbal Learning and Verbal Behavior,* 1975, *14,* 180–195.

Riley, C. A. The representation of comparative relations and the transitive inference task. *Journal of Experimental Child Psychology,* 1976, *22,* 1–22.

Riley, C. A., and Trabasso, T. Comparatives, logical structures and encoding in a transitive inference task. *Journal of Experimental Child Psychology,* 1974, *17,* 187–203.

Riley, M. S., and Greeno, J. G. Importance of semantic structure in the difficulty of arithmetic word problems. Paper presented at the Midwestern Psychological Association, Chicago, May 1978.

Rips, L. J., and Marcus, S. L. Suppositions and the analysis of conditional sentences. In M. A. Just and P. A. Carpenter (Eds.), *Cognitive processes in comprehension.* Hillsdale, N.J.: Erlbaum, 1977.

Rips, L. J., Shoben, E. J., and Smith, E. E. Semantic distance and the verification of semantic relations. *Journal of Verbal Learning and Verbal Behavior,* 1973, *12,* 1–20.

Robinson, C. S., and Hayes, J. R. Making inferences about relevance in understanding problems. In R. Revlin and R. E. Mayer (Eds.), *Human reasoning.* Washington: Winston/Wiley, 1978.

Rogers, C. R. *On becoming a person: A therapist's view of psychotherapy.* Boston: Houghton Mifflin, 1961.

Rosch, E. H. Natural categories. *Cognitive Psychology,* 1973, *4,* 328–350.

Rosch, E. Cognitive representations of semantic categories. *Journal of Experimental Psychology: General,* 1975, *104,* 192–233.

Rosch, E. Principles of categorization. In E. Rosch and B. B. Lloyd (Eds.), *Cognition and categorization*. Hillsdale, N.J.: Erlbaum, 1978.

Rosch, E., and Mervis, C. B. Family resemblances: Studies in the internal structure of categories. *Cognitive Psychology*, 1975, *7*, 573–605.

Rosch, E. H., Mervis, C. B., Gray, W. D., Johnson, D. M., and Boyes-Braem, P. Basic objects in natural categories. *Cognitive Psychology*, 1976, *8*, 382–439.

Rosenthal, R., and Jacobson, L. *Pygmalion in the classroom*. New York: Holt Rinehart and Winston, 1968.

Roughead, W. G., and Scandura, J. M. What is learned in mathematical discovery. *Journal of Educational Psychology*, 1968, *59*, 283–289.

Rubinstein, M. F. *Patterns of problem-solving*. Englewood Cliffs, N.J.: Prentice-Hall, 1975.

Rubinstein, M. F. A decade of experience in teaching an interdisciplinary problem-solving course. In D. T. Tuma and F. Reif (Eds.), *Problem solving and education: Issues in teaching and research*. Hillsdale, N.J.: Erlbaum, 1980.

Ruger, H. The psychology of efficiency. *Archives of Psychology*, 1910, No. 15.

Rumelhart, D. E. Notes on a schema for stories. In D. G. Brown and A. Collins (Eds.), *Representation and understanding: Studies in cognitive science*. New York: Academic Press, 1975.

Rumelhart, D. E., and Abrahamson, A. A. A model for analogical reasoning. *Cognitive Psychology*, 1973, *5*, 1–28.

Rumelhart, D. E., Lindsay, P. H., and Norman, D. A. A process model for long-term memory. In E. Tulving and W. Donaldson (Eds.), *Organization of memory*. New York: Academic Press, 1972.

Sachs, J. D. S. Recognition memory for syntactic and semantic aspects of connected discourse. *Perception and Psychophysics*, 1967, *2*, 437–442.

Safren, M. A. Associations, set, and the solution of word problems. *Journal of Experimental Psychology*, 1962, *64*, 40–45.

Samuel, A. L. Some studies in machine learning using the game of checkers. In E. A. Feigenbaum and J. Feldman (Eds.), *Computers and thought*. New York: McGraw-Hill, 1963.

Sapir, E. *Culture, language, and personality*. Berkeley: University of California Press, 1960.

Saugstad, P., and Raaheim, K. Problem solving, past experience and availability of functions, *British Journal of Psychology*, 1960, *51*, 97–104.

Schallert, D. L. Improving memory for prose: The relationship between depth of processing and context. *Journal of Verbal Learning and Verbal Behavior*, 1976, *15*, 621–632.

Schank, R. C., and Abelson, R. P. *Scripts, plans, goals, and understanding*. Hillsdale, N.J.: Erlbaum, 1977.

Schoenfeld, H. H. Explicit heuristic training as a variable in problem solving performance. *Journal for Research in Mathematics Education*, 1979, *10*, 173–187.

Scholz, K. W., and Potts, G. R. Cognitive processing of linear orderings. *Journal of Experimental Psychology*, 1974, *102*, 323–326.

Scriven, M. Comments. In R. C. Anderson, R. Spiro, and W. E. Montague (Eds.), *Schooling and the acquisition of knowledge*. Hillsdale, N.J.: Erlbaum, 1977.

Sells, S. B. The atmosphere effect: An experimental study of reasoning. *Archives of Psychology*, 1936, No. 200.

Selz, O. The revision of the fundamental conceptions of intellectual processes. In J. M. Mandler and G. Mandler (Eds.), *Thinking· From association to Gestalt*. New York: Wiley, 1964. (Originally published in German in 1913.)

Shepard, R. Form, formation, and transformation of internal representations. In R. L. Solso (Ed.), *Information processing and cognition: The Loyola Symposium*. Hillsdale, N.J.: Erlbaum, 1975.

Shepard, R. N., and Metzler, J. Mental rotation of three-dimensional objects. *Science,* 1971, *171,* 701–703.

Shields, D. T. Brain responses to stimuli in disorders of information processing. *Journal of Learning Disabilities,* 1973, *6,* 501–505.

Shortliffe, E. *Computer-based medical consultations: MYCIN*. New York: Elsevier, 1976.

Shulman, L. S. Psychological controversies in the teaching of science and mathematics. *Science Teacher,* 1968, *35,* 34–38, 89–90.

Shulman, L. S., and Keisler, E. R. (Eds.), *Learning by discovery*. Chicago: Rand McNally, 1966.

Siegler, R. S. The origins of scientific reasoning. In R. S. Siegler (Ed.), *Children's thinking: What develops?* Hillsdale, N.J.: Erlbaum, 1978.

Siegler, R. S. Three aspects of cognitive development. *Cognitive Psychology,* 1976, *4,* 481–520.

Simon, D. P., and Simon, H. A. Individual differences in solving physics problems. In R. S. Siegler (Ed.), *Children's thinking: What develops?* Hillsdale, N.J.: Erlbaum, 1978.

Simon, D. P., and Simon, H. A. A tale of two protocols. In J. Lochhead and J. Clement (Eds.), *Cognitive process instruction*. Philadelphia: Franklin Institute Press, 1979.

Simon, H. A. An information processing theory of intellectual development. In W. Kessen and C. Kohlman (Eds.), *Thought in the young child. Society for Research in Child Development Monographs,* 1962, *27*(2), 150–155.

Simon, H. A. The architecture of complexity. In H. A. Simon, *The Sciences of the Artificial*. Cambridge, Mass.: M.I.T. Press, 1969.

Simon, H. A. Information processing theory of human problem solving. In W. K. Estes (Ed.), *Handbook of learning and cognitive processes*. Hillsdale, N.J.: Erlbaum, 1978.

Simon, H. A. *Models of thought*. New Haven, Conn.: Yale University Press, 1979.

Simon, H. A. Problem solving and education. In D. T. Tuma and F. Reif (Eds.), *Problem solving and education: Issues in teaching and learning*. Hillsdale, N.J.: Erlbaum, 1980.

Simon, H. A., and Hayes, J. R. The understanding process: Problem isomorphs. *Cognitive Psychology,* 1976, *8,* 165–190.

Simon, H. A., and Kotovsky, K. Human acquisition of concepts for sequential patterns. *Psychological Review,* 1963, *70,* 534–546.

Simon, H. A., and Reed, S. K. Modeling strategy shifts in a problem solving task. *Cognitive Psychology,* 1976, *8,* 86–97.

Skemp, R. R. *The psychology of learning mathematics*. Harmondsworth, England: Penguin Books, 1971.

Skinner, B. F. *Verbal behavior*. New York: Appleton-Century-Crofts, 1957.

Smith, E. E., Shoben, E. J., and Rips, L. J. Structure and process in semantic memory: A feature model of semantic decisions. *Psychological Review*, 1974, *81*, 214–241.

Soloway, E., Lochhead, J., and Clement, J. Does computer programming enhance problem-solving ability? Some positive evidence on algebra word problems. In R. J. Seidel, R. E. Anderson, and B. Hunter (Eds.), *Computer literacy*. New York: Academic Press, 1982.

Spearman, C. General intelligence objectively determined and measured. *American Journal of Psychology*, 1904, *15*, 201–293.

Spearman, C. *The abilities of man*. New York: Macmillan, 1927.

Staudenmayer, H. Understanding conditional reasoning with meaningful propositions. In R. J. Falmagne (Ed.), *Reasoning: Representation and process in children and adults*. Hillsdale, N. J.: Erlbaum, 1975.

Staudenmayer, H., and Bourne, L. E. The nature of denied propositions in the conditional sentence reasoning task: Interpretation and learning. In R. Revlin and R. E. Mayer (Eds.), *Human reasoning*. New York: Wiley/Winston, 1978.

Sternberg, R. J. *Intelligence, information processing, and analogical reasoning*. Hillsdale, N.J.: Erlbaum, 1977.

Sternberg, R. J. The nature of mental abilities. *American Psychologist*, 1979, *34*, 214–230.

Sternberg, R. J. Componentman as vice-president: A reply to Pellegrino and Lyon's analysis of "The components of a componential analysis." *Intelligence*, 1980, *4*, 83–95.

Sternberg, R. J., Guyote, M. J., and Turner, M. E. Deductive reasoning. In R. E. Snow, P. Federico, and W. E. Montague (Eds.), *Aptitude, learning, and instruction*. Hillsdale, N.J.: Erlbaum, 1980.

Sternberg, S. High speed scanning in human memory. *Science*, 1966, *153*, 652–654.

Sternberg, S. The discovery of processing stages: Extensions of Donders' method. *Acta Psychologica*, 1969, *30*, 276–315.

Sternberg, S. Memory scanning: New findings and current controversies. *Quarterly Journal of Experimental Psychology*, 1975, *27*, 1–32.

Stevens, A. L., and Collins, A. Multiple conceptual models of a complex system. In R. E. Snow, P. Federico, and W. E. Montague (Eds.), *Aptitude, learning and instruction*. Vol. 2. Hillsdale, N.J.: Erlbaum, 1980.

Stratton, R. P. Atmosphere and conversion errors in syllogistic reasoning with contextual material and the effect of differential training. Unpublished M. A. thesis, Michigan State University, 1967.

Strauss, S. Inducing cognitive development and learning: A review of short-term training experiments. *Cognition*, 1972, *1*, 329–357.

Suchman, J. R. Inquiry training in the elementary school. *Science Teacher*, 1960, *27*, 42–47.

Suchman, J. R. *Inquiry development program in physical science*. Chicago: Science Research Associates, 1966.

Suchman, J. R. *Evaluating inquiry in physical science*. Chicago: Science Research Associates, 1969.

Suppes, P., Loftus, E. F., and Jerman, M. Problem-solving on a computer-based teletype. *Educational Studies in Mathematics*, 1969, *2*, 1–15.

Sussman, G. J., and Stallman, R. M. Heuristic techniques in computer aided circuit analysis. *IEEE Transactions on Circuits and Systems*, 1975, *22*, No. 11.

Sutton, S., Braren, M., Zubin, J., and John, E. R. Evoked potential correlates of stimulus uncertainty. *Science*, 1965, *150*, 1187–1188.

Taplin, J. E., and Staudenmayer, H. Interpretation of abstract conditional sentences in deductive reasoning. *Journal of Verbal Learning and Verbal Behavior*, 1973, *12*, 530–542.

Taylor, D. T., Berry, P. C., and Block, C. H. Does group participation when using brainstorming facilitate or inhibit creative thinking? *Administrator's Science Quarterly*, 1958, *3*, 23–47.

Thomas, J. C., Jr. An analysis of behavior in the hobbits-orcs problem. *Cognitive Psychology*, 1974, *6*, 257–269.

Thorndike, E. L. Animal intelligence: An experimental study of the associative processes in animals. *Psychological Monographs*, 1898, *2*, No. 8.

Thorndike, E. L. *Animal intelligence*. New York: Macmillan, 1911.

Thorndike, E. L., and Lorge, I. *A teacher's word book of 30,000 words*. New York: Columbia University Press, 1944.

Thorndyke, P. W. Cognitive structures in comprehension and memory of narrative discourse. *Cognitive Psychology*, 1977, *9*, 77–110.

Thornton, C. A. Emphasizing thinking strategies in basic fact instruction. *Journal for Research in Mathematics Education*, 1978, *9*, 214–227.

Thurstone, L. L. *Primary mental abilities*. Chicago: University of Chicago Press, 1938.

Torrance, E. P. *Torrance tests of creative thinking*. Princeton, N.J.: Personnel Press, 1966.

Torrance, E. P. Can we teach children to think creatively? *Journal of Creative Behavior*, 1972, *6*, 114–143.

Trabasso, T. R. Stimulus emphasis and all-or-none learning in concept identification. *Journal of Experimental Psychology*, 1963, *65*, 398–406.

Trabasso, T. R., and Bower, G. H. Presolution reversal and dimensional shifts in concept identification. *Journal of Experimental Psychology*, 1964, *67*, 398–399.

Trabasso, T. R., and Bower, G. H. *Attention in learning*. New York: Wiley, 1968.

Trabasso, T., Isen, A. M., Dolecki, P., McLanahan, A. G., Riley, C. A., and Tucker, T. How do children solve class-inclusion problems? In R. S. Siegler (Ed.), *Children's thinking: What develops?* Hillsdale, N.J.: Erlbaum, 1978.

Trabasso, T. R., Rollins, H., and Shaughnessy, E. Storage and verification stages in processing concepts. *Cognitive Psychology*, 1971, *2*, 239–289.

Treffinger, D. J., and Gowan, J. C. An updated representative list of methods and educational programs for stimulating creativity. *Journal of Creative Behavior*, 1971, *5*, 127–139.

Tresselt, M. E., and Mayzner, M. S. Normative solution times for a sample of 134 solution words and 378 associated anagrams. *Psychonomic Monograph Supplement No. 15*, 1966, *1*, 293–298.

Turing, A. M. Computing machinery and intelligence. *Mind,* 1950, *59,* 433–450.

Tversky, A., and Kahneman, D. Availability: A heuristic for judging frequency and probability. *Cognitive Psychology,* 1973, *5,* 207–232.

Tversky, A., and Kahneman, D. Judgment under uncertainty: heuristics and biases. *Science,* 1974, *125,* 1124–1131.

Underwood, B. J. False recognition produced by implicit verbal responses. *Journal of Experimental Psychology,* 1965, *70,* 122–129.

Underwood, B. J., and Richardson, J. Some verbal materials for the study of concept formation. *Psychological Bulletin,* 1956, *53,* 84–95.

Vervalin, C. H. Just what is creativity? In G. A. Davis and J. A. Scott (Eds.), *Training Creative Thinking.* Huntington, N.Y.: Krieger, 1978.

Walker, C. M., and Bourne, L. E., Jr. The identifications of concepts as a function of amount of relevant and irrelevant information. *American Journal of Psychology,* 1961, *74,* 410–417.

Wallas, G. *The art of thought.* New York: Harcourt Brace Jovanovich, 1926.

Wason, P. C. Reasoning. In B. M. Foss (Ed.), *New Horizons in Psychology.* Harmondsworth, England: Penguin, 1966.

Wason, P. C. Reasoning about a rule. *Quarterly Journal of Experimental Psychology,* 1968, *20,* 273–281.

Wason, P. C., and Johnson-Laird, P. N. *Psychology of reasoning: Structure and content.* Cambridge, Mass.: Harvard University Press, 1972.

Watson, J. B. *Behaviorism.* New York: Norton, 1930.

Watt, H. J. Experimental contribution to a theory of thinking. In J. M. Mandler and G. Mandler (Eds.), *Thinking: From association to Gestalt.* New York: Wiley, 1964. (Originally published in *Journal of Anatomical Physiology,* 1905, *40,* 257–266.)

Weiner, N. *Cybernetics.* New York: Wiley, 1948.

Weir, M. W., and Stevenson, H. W. The effect of verbalization in children's learning as a function of chronological age. *Child Development.* 1959, *30,* 143–149.

Weisberg, R., and Suls, J. An information processing model of Duncker's candle problem. *Cognitive Psychology,* 1973, *4,* 255–276.

Weisskopf-Joelson, E., and Eliseo, T. S. An experimental study of the study of the effectiveness of brainstorming. *Journal of Applied Psychology,* 1961, *45,* 45–49.

Weitzman, B. Behavior therapy and psychotherapy. *Psychological Review,* 1967, *74,* 300–317.

Weizenbaum, J. Contextual understanding by computers. In P. A. Kolers and M. Eden (Eds.), *Recognizing patterns.* Cambridge: M.I.T. Press, 1968.

Werner, H., and Kaplan, E. The acquisition of word meanings: A developmental study. *Monographs of the Society for Research in Child Development,* 1952, *15,* No. 51, vii.

Wertheimer, M. *Productive thinking.* New York: Harper & Row, 1959.

White, S. H. Learning. In H. W. Stevenson (Ed.), *Child psychology, 62nd yearbook of the National Society of Social Studies Educators, Part 1.* Chicago: University of Chicago Press, 1963.

White, S. H. Evidence for a hierarchical arrangement of learning processes. In L. P. Lipsitt and C. C. Spiker (Eds.), *Advances in child development and behavior*. Vol. 2. New York: Academic Press, 1965.

Whorf, B. *Language, thought, and reality*. Cambridge, Mass.: M.I.T. Press, 1956.

Wickelgren, W. A. How to solve problems: *Elements of a theory of problems and problem solving*. San Francisco: W. H. Freeman and Company, 1974.

Wickens, T. D., and Millward, R. B. Attribute elimination strategies for concept identification with practiced subjects. *Journal of Mathematical Psychology*, 1971, *8*, 453–480.

Wilkins, M. C. The effect of changed material on ability to do formal syllogistic reasoning. *Archives of Psychology*, 1928, No. 102.

Winograd, T. A program for understanding natural language. *Cognitive Psychology*, 1972, *3*, 1–192.

Winston, P. H. *The psychology of computer vision*. New York: McGraw-Hill, 1975.

Winston, P. H. *Artificial intelligence*. Reading, Mass.: Addison-Wesley, 1977.

Wittrock, M. C. The learning by discovery hypothesis. In L. S. Shulman and E. R. Keisler (Eds.), *Learning by discovery*. Chicago: Rand McNally, 1966.

Wittrock, M. C. *The brain and psychology*. New York: Academic Press, 1980.

Wittrock, M. C., Marks, C., and Doctorow, M. Reading as a generative process. *Journal of Educational Psychology*, 1975, *67*, 484–489.

Woodrow, H., and Lowell, F. Children's association frequency tables. *Psychological Monographs*, 1916, *22*, No. 5 (Whole No. 97)

Woodworth, R. S., and Sells, S. B. An atmosphere effect in formal syllogistic reasoning. *Journal of Experimental Psychology*, 1935, *18*, 451–460.

Worden, P. E. The development of the category-recall function under three retrieval conditions. *Child Development*, 1974, *45*, 1054–1059.

Wundt, W. *An introduction to psychology*. New York: Arno Press, 1973. (Originally published in German in 1911.)

Zangwill, O. L. Remembering revisited. *Quarterly Journal of Experimental Psychology*, 1972, *24*, 123–138.

Zobrist, A. L., and Carlson, F. R. An advice-taking chess computer. *Scientific American*, June 1973, 92–105.

AUTHOR INDEX

SUBJECT INDEX